WINDOWS TO LINUX BUSINESS DESKTOP MIGRATION

WINDOWS TO LINUX BUSINESS DESKTOP MIGRATION

MARK HINKLE

CHARLES RIVER MEDIA, INC.
Hingham, Massachusetts

...be reproduced in any way, stored in a retrieval system of any ...or media, electronic or mechanical, including, but not limited ...ning, *without prior permission* in writing from the publisher.

Contents

Preface

Chances are that if you are a desktop computer user you are familiar with and probably use one of the Microsoft® Windows® operating systems, as the operating systems by Microsoft are the most popular. Windows became the most widely utilized desktop operating system by getting to the PC market early and becoming dominant on the x86 processing platform made popular by Intel®. Over time, Intel was challenged by AMD with competing products, which, along with other market factors, increased competition and led to a consequent reduction in prices for desktop hardware. The emergence of open source applications is driving competition in much the same way in the software market. Open source software and the popular Linux operating system are emerging as a cost-effective alternative to Microsoft Windows and the Apple® Mac OS® on the desktop. The worldwide trend in open source adoption is showing up not only in business, but also in education and government. open source software offers flexibility and value, enabling organizations to provide top notch information technology systems that maximize the value they obtain from their IT budgets.

This book will provide you with information about the benefits of Open Source operating systems for desktop computing and supporting infrastructure. Linux has been successful in server deployments. HP reached the milestone of shipping one million Linux servers in the spring of 2005, though the same level of success on the desktop is yet to be seen. Capitalizing on the yet unrealized values of Open Source could potentially yield huge returns to IT consumers, but being prepared starts with doing due diligence on this promising technology. This book does not advocate Linux on the desktop; rather, it provides the tools and background for IT decision makers to evaluate Linux as desktop platform and make decisions on how it could be implemented in their own enterprises. Experimenting with a Linux desktop can give you leverage with vendors by giving you alternatives and flexibility and reducing your dependence on solutions that continually sap your resources with expensive upgrades and support costs.

Linux is in a transitional stage, moving from the data center to the desktop. As hardware vendors start to support Linux and more applications become available, PC users will have more choices for their business productivity desktop. However, this transition may follow a slow and steady adoption curve, in contrast to the extremely fast acceptance of the Web by companies in the mid-1990s as an important medium for sales and communication. This trend deserves close scrutiny and research such as that presented in the chapters of this book.

Microsoft also contends that alternative operating systems may pose a threat to its market share. It noted in its 2003 Annual Report that it was seeing significant competitive pressures from the likes of HP, IBM, and Sun Microsystems, especially with regard to open source software, and especially with regard Linux.

The city of Largo, Florida, announces on its Web site that it runs its desktop infrastructure on Linux and boasts about the hundreds of thousands of taxpayer dollars that it has saved over traditional alternatives (City of Largo). The choice is a legitimate one as many organizations have realized. The issue at hand is how to make the leap with as little disruption as possible and in the end realize tangible benefits. The aim of this book is to accomplish three goals:

- Provide an understanding what justifies a Windows to Linux desktop migration
- Demonstrate how to form a basic Linux strategy with consideration given to both the benefits and drawbacks of a Linux desktop migration
- Provide tactics for successfully moving to the Linux desktop from Windows

Note that title of the book includes the word "migration," which implies a journey from one place to another. This book will demonstrate how to safely accomplish that journey.

WHO WILL BENEFIT MOST FROM THIS BOOK?

The computer users who will most benefit from this book will be IT professionals who are Windows end-users, and strategists (IT Directors, CIOs, and other decision makers) who want to maximize their desktop computing productivity and reduce their overall IT costs. These readers will have a good understanding of their Windows operating systems but want to make comparisons between the Linux and Windows. This book should be an invaluable resource for readers who want to understand how to migrate data and applications to Linux and remain aware of the potential advantages and pitfalls when migrating from one platform to another. This book is a guide for users who are looking for a pragmatic way to take advantage of Linux with minimal sacrifice. Minimizing disruption factors weighs heavily in a successful Windows-to-Linux strategy. The loss of initial productivity could be a deciding short-term factor for your cost justification analysis. The references and information contained in this book are directed at technology users, but not necessarily at highly skilled or Linux-savvy users who, on their own, have the skills to successfully implement a Linux desktop.

STRATEGY AND TACTICS

This book offers both strategies to increase your success when implementing a Linux desktop and the tactical advice to enact that strategy, including the best ways to provide equivalent or better desktop environments to your current Windows users. This book will focus on the situations that offer the biggest advantages from the viewpoints of the end-user and the administrator who is responsible for overall IT costs. The key for a successful implementation of Linux is a sound overall strategy that minimizes disruption and yields an equivalent or improved level of usefulness for desktop computing. There will be cases where Linux may not be the best solution. For example, organizations that have end users who are less technically adept, highly mobile, and who use notebook computers or a large number of peripherals (specifically Windows CE-based peripherals), will probably have a lower rate of success than those with task-based workers who utilize highly repetitive, limited scope applications. This book is not a sales pitch on the virtue of Linux desktop operating systems, but rather it is a guide to finding the most advantageous situations for alternative desktop migration to Linux.

POINT OF VIEW

Subjects are discussed in this book from the point of view of the Windows user or Windows desktop administrator. Regardless of the desktop operating platform, the tasks that PC users want to complete are fairly common. The focus of this book is to help those users continue to maintain their ability to accomplish those tasks on the Linux platform using both Open Source and commercial software. Many of the examples provided here will be considered from the perspective of how the task is accomplished in Windows versus how the task can be completed in a Linux environment or by drawing comparisons between the two systems.

A LINUX OPERATING SYSTEM TO BOOT

Because many PC users are looking to evaluate their chances of success with Linux this book includes a copy of the popular bootable Linux CD-ROM, Knoppix. The Knoppix CD-ROM is designed to run on most any PC with a bootable CD drive. The Knoppix CD-ROM will allow you to evaluate the merits of Linux by enabling you to boot from the CD drive and then run Linux without interfering with your Windows installation. Because it runs directly from the CD-ROM file system and doesn't overwrite the Windows hard drive, you can evaluate the Linux environment without disruption. This is advantageous because you can utilize many of the features of Linux, work along with the examples in the book, and take a test run with little risk to your current desktop. Additionally, if you decide to take your evaluation to the next level, the Knoppix CD-ROM can be used to install Linux side by side with the existing Windows installation. The CD falls under the GNU Public License (GPL) license and can be copied and redistributed without licensing costs so that many users in the enterprise can benefit from one Linux for just the cost of duplication of the media .

Part

I

Developing a Linux Desktop Strategy

Desktop computing plays such a large role in the daily operations of so many businesses that developing a successful strategy for adoption of Linux in the enterprise requires serious thought and research. The first part of this book will discuss the strategies and elements that may influence the decision for Linux desktop adoption. We will be specifically looking at the cost benefit of particular situations throughout the enterprise where Linux can make the biggest positive impact. Strategies for desktop Linux adoption will vary by enterprise. While anecdotal stories and TCO studies are usually good sources of information, you should acknowledge that rarely do the conditions in one organization exactly mimic those in another.

As you are reading about desktop strategy, take note where in your enterprise certain advantageous situations arise, and conversely look for potential pitfalls for adoption as noted in the examples. Keeping a few themes in mind as you move forward will give you the best perspective on desktop Linux.

Desktop Linux is an evolving operating system. As each day passes, more applications become available and significant improvements occur in application quality and operating system enhancements. This is due in large part to a global community comprised of individuals and companies that are contributing improvements and fixing flaws. At the same time, new users are adopting the operating system and providing demand for these products. This evolution is happening faster in some areas than others, and your research today may indicate that an immediate change in operating system is not warranted, though it will become obvious that it has potential as a future solution. Linux is a moving target and understanding how it may become the ideal solution and watching for that point on the horizon will allow you to capitalize on these events.

Second, future desktop deployments may look different then they do today. Advancement of pervasive network access vis-à-vis wireless connectivity is unfettering desktop computing from a hard-wired connection. Thin client computing and other hosted application solutions will allow the enterprise to combine the flexibility of mobile computing with powerful Intel- and AMD-based servers that can provide a great deal of horsepower at minimal cost. By watching trends and rethinking the way you compute, you may find that a PC with local storage and processing running a proprietary operating system no longer makes sense. You may come to the realization that to continue to be competitive in business, IT costs must be brought in check and value solutions become the norm rather than leading-edge technologies that offer little return on investment.

The following chapters offer a state of the union for Linux combined with forward-looking statements on how desktop Linux adoption is progressing. Using Microsoft Windows as a reference, the following strategic look at desktop Linux should offer an understanding of forces affecting Linux on the desktop and provide foreshadowing of the tactics to be discussed later on.

1 Why Migrate to the Linux Desktop from Windows

In This Chapter

- Understanding the Costs of the Desktop
- Open Source
- Single Vendor Dependence
- Length of Product Usable Life
- Up Time/Productivity
- Stability
- Security
- Open Source Development Model
- Linux Design
- Momentum
- Summary
- Other Resources
- References

Linux migration should be undertaken for one simple reason: to provide greater value to your current enterprise. A "holy war" fired by anti-Microsoft sentiment can cloud judgment on what truly constitutes a good reason for Linux migration. Understanding the foundations of a good business decision is crucial when you begin to investigate an alternative operating system like Linux. This list summarizes good reasons for considering Linux desktop migration.

Software licensing costs: Software costs may be lower with Linux due to lack of royalties and more competitive options for product support. In the open source community this is sometimes called free software and often accompanied by the saying, "free as in beer," meaning it doesn't cost anything, and not to be confused with "free as in freedom," which refers to the freedom to use the software as you like.

Breaking single vendor dependency: Current Windows software may have locked you into single vendor dependencies (e.g., Microsoft Office); lack of competition for software products forces prices higher, and results in feature sets that address the widest constituency rather than being tailored to your enterprise needs.

Length of usable product life: Some software products may push end-users into an unnecessary upgrade schedule. Existing hardware may not be adequate to run new operating systems that exceed the needs of the PC user.

Reliability: Downtime and system failures erode user productivity.

Security: All enterprises are concerned about data security, the propagation of viruses and spyware, as well as other vulnerabilities that affect the performance of popular desktop computing environments.

An important element in determining the merits of a Linux migration is understanding the impact of various operating systems in addressing these factors. When making comparisons strive to look for tangible, quantifiable factors that can be used in for later cost justifications.

UNDERSTANDING THE COSTS OF THE DESKTOP

Obtaining a clear picture of the costs of your desktop computing environment is of critical importance, especially in the context of how it affects your bottom line.

Computing Total Cost of Ownership (TCO)

The costs of your desktop solution are compromised of a number of factors in addition to the acquisition costs (royalties and media for example). You must also consider the cost of maintaining the environment, the cost of downtime, and the cost of vendor lock-in (product schedules that entail consistent upgrades to maintain compatibility). It's easy to understand the differences between products when evaluating software acquisition costs because, at the end of the transaction, you know how much money you paid for a product. However, this is far from the actual cost of desktop computing which also includes those expenses that result from the performance and use of your software. For example, when you install the system there is the cost of the IT professional who installs the software at your office and configures the computer. You will need to consider whether that time is more or less for one operating system over another. Other costs may be less tangible but are often more expensive. For example, if a PC is out of service for a worker who makes sales inquiries, is the time that the worker is not utilizing his PC costing you or your company money? Are you paying him a salary while his primary tool is not in working order? Consider this example of how downtime affected productivity in an inbound call center.

Scenario: Opportunity Cost of the Unavailable PC

Sales agents accept calls into an inbound 800 number at the rate of about 12 per hour. Those calls are closed at a rate of about 30 percent. The average sale is for a monthly service subscription that costs $20 a month with the average customer life being 9 months. Each sale generates an average of $180 of revenue. So the agent, in the course of an hour, averages 4 sales for a total of about $720 of revenue. At times people waiting on hold hang up and the opportunity is lost, and hold times are increased when some sales agents are unavailable to take calls. These missed opportunities costs even more lost revenue. All of the sales agents in this call center rely on their Windows PCs for data entry and account creation. Without their PCs they are unable to do their jobs and they miss their opportunity to sell, which is their one and only job function. These agents are often victims of viruses or other PC problems that have a typical time to resolution for the help desk personnel of about 4 hours. In addition, the time for the help desk personnel, at $40 an hour, costs the company an additional $160 per incident. When you start factoring in the loss of sales, the costs of lost opportunities, and the price of repair personnel, the purchase price of a $700 PC, even adding in $1000 worth of software, is less and less relevant.

This example demonstrates that the consequences of PC downtime directly impact your bottom line. This fictitious example may relate to your enterprise. You may want to fill in your own numbers to get an idea of how similar outages would affect you. The cost of downtime is seldom quantified and could be a silent cost sapping your profits more than you realize. You should determine whether you suffer these types of outages and, if so, do they result from weaknesses in your current desktop technology.

Licensing and Royalties

Sometimes the words licensing and royalties are incorrectly used as synonyms. There is an important distinction. Licensing refers to the terms of use of a software package, while royalties are compensation paid for the use of a software package. Royalties may be a condition of the product licensing. One of the most innovative ideas for many people considering Linux and the supporting cast of open source software is the idea that software is "free." That is true, but it is important to understand that there is free as in "no purchase price," (also expressed in the lingo of open source advocates as "free as in beer") and then there is free as in "freedom," which implies the ability to modify, change, and improve as well as redistribute your changes. In the Linux world there are a number of licenses that commercial software vendors consider to be novel. The best known and probably the most popular is the GNU Public License (GPL) (see a sample GNU Public License in Appendix A), which in its essence says that you are receiving the software with express permission to change, modify, and redistribute the software as long as you maintain the GPL in your derivative works. For example, Red Hat, a leading Linux distributor, sells its software, but it does so by preserving the GPL. Red Hat simply charges a fee for the distribution service and media, which is perfectly legal. So with Linux, you may still need to purchase your software, but the price may remain more in line with actual costs of production, in contrast to a price set by a single vendor/supplier. There are a number of licenses that grant freedoms to the end user that are not consistent with traditional commercial software licenses.

OPEN SOURCE

With many commercial applications, the idea of sharing the programming code with the end user is foreign. The companies that manufacture these programs (for instance, Microsoft Windows and the Microsoft Office Suite) protect their work by taking the programming code and compiling it into binaries. All end users see is the end result of this work. This is a valid practice that helps companies protect their investment in their software. In open source applications, there are no secrets about how the software works. The code is available for end user and peer review. The argument for this type of model is that users can customize software to their needs and contribute to a project if they desire to help improve it. This is advantageous because you can easily collaborate to improve upon or tailor these packages to your needs. Some companies distribute their source code but require that you to purchase a license to use it. It is important to understand going forward that each piece of software, whether it is Open Source and free or Open Source but restricted in its use, should be evaluated carefully before you deploy it.

You may ask, "Would average users really edit code in their applications?" *Probably not.* In a big enterprise, though, would it be nice to have the option to fix bugs that effect hundreds or thousands of users without having to wait until the next product release? *Absolutely.* An industry may also benefit from specialization. For example, perhaps the medical industry could benefit from the inclusion of medical billing codes in the styles list of an office product used for typing medical reports. Being able to repackage a "medical industry version" of a commonly available open source product could make sense.

Free Open Source Software Applications (FOSS)

Free Open Source Software (FOSS) is attractive to the enterprise for reasons that reach beyond the initial acquisition costs. Because there are few restrictions on re-distribution, tracking and procuring software licenses for the software is not necessary. For example, IT staff needn't worry about per seat licensing restrictions and procurement of licensed copies once they have established that an application is qualified as FOSS. The obvious advantage is that this eliminates one of the most time-consuming and counterproductive parts of the support person's job. There are thousands of useful FOSS applications available today, and the breadth of these applications is so wide that they could replace many, if not all, of the commercial applications you are using. Community groups often work on products that have similar functionality, and there is often more than one choice for task-based packages like word processors, Web browsers, and email clients.

Imagine a world where you didn't have to track software for compliance to licensing terms. In a large enterprise you may find that you have someone dedicated to making sure that you are always in compliance. If you make a mistake and are subject to audit, you may be accessed fines relating to incorrectly licensed software. If you are using FOSS applications you could alleviate the need to track, at least for licensing purposes, their use. Needless to say, if you are familiar with proprietary software, understanding free software is a big change in direction. Understanding the spirit of free software may help clarify the objectives of the licensing model.

The Free Software Movement

The hype about Linux and open source software merits a small history lesson on the subject of the Free Software Movement. This is probably the most eye-catching and misunderstood benefit of Linux, especially for organizations that are used to a completely proprietary and closed source software model. The free software movement can be traced to Richard M. Stallman, known simply as RMS, who founded two of the community groups whose goals were to further the idea and implementation of sharing of software and help the community provide better products. Free software, for the purpose of this discussion, applies to software with source code that programmers can read, modify, and redistribute. Through this process the software can evolve to a better quality than might a piece of software tightly controlled by a single group or vendor. This methodology lends itself to contributions at many levels, from developers to end users, who can adapt it or to fix bugs without the oversight and approval of one entity. RMS champions this philosophy as the founder of the Free Software Foundation.

The other project, which is more focused on an actual product or collection of software that adheres to the free software philosophy, is the GNU project. The GNU project was the real beginning of the GNU/Linux operating system, and started with an announcement by Richard Stallman in the later half of 1983. The GNU project is an ambitious attempt to create a free operating system unencumbered by the restrictions that were being placed on copyrighted and "closed source" operating systems, but this project was started before Linux actually came into being. The name Linux really refers to the kernel of the operating system, which provides access to the machine's hardware and processes. This was the missing component of the GNU operating system that Linux eventually provided. The combination of the GNU project and the Linux kernel collectively became what we call Linux. The Linux kernel was a product of the efforts of Linus Torvalds, a Finnish college student at the time, who started to share his Linux kernel in September 1991 while studying at the University of Helsinki. To this day Torvalds owns the Linux registered trademark which, unlike many other trademarks, can be used under a very liberal license. Many times you will see the operating system referred to as GNU/Linux which is the most correct reference. Most times, though, when people use the term Linux, they are indicating the operating system and supporting programs as a whole. One thing to consider is that there is free software and there is open source software. As was addressed earlier, there are two types of free when it comes to open source software. There is "free as in freedom" and "free as in beer."

Free as in Freedom

Many people interpret "free software" as referring to price. In the Linux world this causes much confusion because the reference to free means that you have "freedom." These freedoms are outlined in the following list:

- The freedom to use the program for any reason.
- The freedom to adapt the program to suit your needs, which implies that you have access to the source code so that you can make these changes.
- The freedom to redistribute copies, either without a charge or for a fee.
- Freedom to distribute modified versions of the program, so that the community can benefit from your improvements.

This freedom is what allows companies like Red Hat and Novell to charge fees and build businesses around their products. Often times you will hear the phrases "free as in freedom" and "free as in beer." The previous list defines what is meant by "free as in freedom." However, "free as in beer" refers to the price. Many programs are available for free through download without paying any fees to any person or organization. You may run into these terms as you investigate the costs of migrating to a Linux desktop. Understanding the difference may help your decision-making process, because one does not necessarily indicate the other.

The Copyleft Method

The *copyleft* method for making software and other works free is contrary to the general practice of copyright. Copyright exists to protect the creator of a work so that they have the exclusive right to publish a given work. Copyleft is a method for making a work free from encumbrances other than the requirement that all modifications and extensions of the program remain free. The way copyleft works is by first stating that a work, for our purposes this would be a program, is copyrighted. Once the copyright is stated, the terms for distribution are added. This is a legal instrument that grants everyone the right to modify and redistribute the program's code or any derivative works but requires that, upon redistribution, the distribution terms originally granted to the person who received that work must be maintained. In essence, this allows code to be shared but prevents it from being taken behind closed doors then redistributed with modifications. This prevents hijacking of community efforts, and mandates that improvements are returned to the public domain. Figure 1.1 shows the relationship between free and open source software.

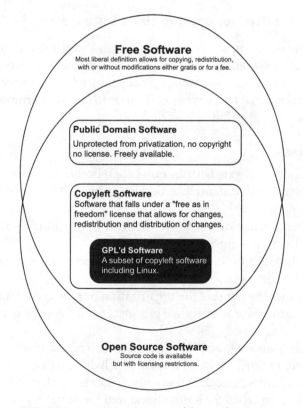

FIGURE 1.1 Open source and free software are not always mutually inclusive.

The Open Source Definition

The open source definition was drafted by Bruce Perens in 1997 as it applied to an early and still popular Linux distribution called Debian. The open source definition embodies the spirit and intent of most developers of open source software and as more commercial entities enter this space they may technically be Open Source by sharing their source code but they may not provide the same level of openness desired by the "community" of open source developers. Why is this important to you as a business user? The issue is that companies that can exist in a symbiotic relationship with open source developers may have a greater chance of success as they can leverage community works and develop products with reduced R&D expense. Companies that only dabble in Open Source may alienate these developers and lose this competitive edge. The generally recognized authority on Open Source is the Open Source Initiative (OSI). The Open Source Initiative is a nonprofit corporation that tracks and certifies licenses dedicated to managing and promoting the Open Source Definition.

Common Licenses Used for Desktop Linux Software

Software licensing is much too important and complex a topic to cover fully in this book. Understanding the terms of each piece of software as it applies to your enterprise is a grave responsibility that you need to take ownership of. The following list is a reference to the types of licenses that cover commonly used Linux software that may be part of the Linux desktop.

BSD License

The Berkley Software Distribution (BSD) license is a result of software released from the University of California at Berkley. Initially it included three general conditions:

- Maintenance of the copyright with redistribution of source code and a disclaimer limiting liability.
- Redistribution of binary forms of the software where required to maintain a copyright.
- Neither the name of the organization nor the contributors to the project can be used to endorse derivative products from the code without their prior consent.

This license allowed software authors to take software that was in the public domain and redistribute only binaries, which did not insure that derivative works would be Open Source. The BSD license has since been changed since its inception, but in general, the spirit of the license has stayed the same. An example of software that falls under a BSD license includes the Mac OS X operating system which is based on the BSD Unix code. The BSD license does not follow the copyleft mentality.

GNU Public License (GPL)

Linux falls under the GPL which is a true copyleft-type license. The GPL is designed to guarantee fundamental rights of free software. The GPL is a fairly straightforward license though it draws a lot of criticisms. The most prominent three rights are as follows:

- The right to copyright your software.
- The right to copy, modify, use, and distribute that software. (The ability to modify indicates that source code for the software must be available.)
- These same rights are transferable to anyone who receives the software.

An example of use of the GPL is in the licensing of the Linux kernel.

Lesser GNU Public License (LGPL)

The LGPL is very similar to the GPL but with one fundamental difference. It became apparent that certain nonfree software libraries may help facilitate the use of free software. Also, in Section 3 of the LGPL, there is a provision for converting any piece of LGPL software into a GPL piece of software. The reason for doing this would be to create a version of the software that can't be used in nonfree software products. An example of a desktop software package that falls under the LGPL is the OpenOffice.org suite. The LGPL does place a copyleft restriction on individual source code but not on certain shared libraries. Shared libraries may be closed source but called by the open source program to accomplish certain tasks.

Mozilla Public Licenses (MPL)

The MPL is relatively new in comparison to the GPL. It was created by Netscape to enable them to release the Netscape source code to the community. The MPL has a few distinctions, including the ability for MPL software to be combined with proprietary code to create a "larger work." The differentiation is made at the source file level so there are some boundaries. MPL code and GPL code cannot be combined, but MPL and LGPL code can be combined into a larger work. The rudimentary difference between MPL code and others is that it can be combined with proprietary software if the source files are different. The MPL is not completely simpatico with copyleft methods but it shares much of the same spirit. An example of software that falls under the MPL is the Firefox browser.

X11 License

The X11 license, which is sometimes referred to as the MIT license, is a very simple license that is almost without restriction other than a requirement that the text of the license be included in all copies. Typically, a valid use of the X11 license is when you want to show authorship or ownership of your software without placing any restrictions on it This license applied to older versions of XFree86 which provides the graphical interface for Linux PCs. Newer versions of XFree86 are licensed under the XFree86 1.1 license which is not compatible with the GPL.

SUN Industry Standards Source License

The Sun Industry Standards Source was authored by Sun and applied to the OpenOffice.org XML document format before OpenOffice.org 2.0. As the name of the license implies, it is in place to make sure that the XML document formats are never encumbered by royalties or other restrictions. Sun also uses this license for the Sun Grid Engine, an open source software solution used in distributed computing applications.

Licensing is an important thing to understand when using or redistributing open source software. It is worth your time to investigate the terms of licenses that you use in your enterprise, but with open source licenses you will likely find that you benefit from a great degree of freedom. Sun has since retired this license.

SINGLE VENDOR DEPENDENCE

Wouldn't it be nice to be the only lemonade vendor in the middle of the desert? With lack of competition and heavy need you could charge prices well above the cost of the goods. Some Microsoft users might feel like they are shopping for lemonade in the desert, because they are at the mercy of the vendor that most every business would expect you to interact with. Most desktop PC users are using Windows as their operating system, and changing operating systems results in an expensive and disruptive migration path. Interoperability between systems is an often overlooked and critical part of your IT strategy. Single vendor dependence could be not only a factor of licensing, but the formats used to store data and communicate between systems. Using protocols that are publicly documented, such as those that adhere to a standard, makes it easier to interoperate between systems supplied by multiple vendors. For example, OpenOffice.org using the XML open file formats.

Understanding the dependence on file formats and interoperability issues between spreadsheet packages for example, could affect the way you invoice or take orders. However, the ability to read legacy documents is not an unmovable barrier, it just requires research, planning, and understanding what steps to take in migration. Moving from a package that's supplied only by one vendor to a software package serviced by a multitude of vendors is a liberating move. You will be able to take advantage of a multivendor platform, and, in the event you become displeased with one vendor's pricing or product decisions, you can easily migrate to a new Linux distribution vendor. In the corporate Linux arena, both Novell and Red Hat offer competing products, and there are many other vendors that all build products upon the same core technology. All of these companies leverage common work and add their own innovation so there is no need to "reinvent the wheel." Companies that share common programs can spend their development resources in areas that truly add value, tweaking performance and adding innovative features and applications, rather than competing on parts of the operating system and applications that offer little returned value no matter what the improvement. For example, basic text editors and device drivers in most cases wouldn't create a competitive edge or provide incrementally more value across Linux vendors. The value may be realized in service offerings or tools that are used to update these packages. For instance, Red Hat offers an update service that provides security patches, newer program versions, and systems enhancements to a core batch of free and open source software.

The Windows operating system is the antithesis of this thinking. Windows is the world's most widely deployed operating system and it does work well. Hardware vendors realize this and supply drivers for Windows and insure their products run well with this operating system. However, when you have such a widely deployed operating system you provide products that appeal to the lowest common denominator. So the same system that is used in a doctor's office is being used on oil rigs and steel mills. Is there really a lot of similarity in how these companies use their computers? Does it make sense for them to have the exact same system to accomplish the tasks to make them successful? With Microsoft, developer resources are spread thin to address all of these users' needs. The amount of innovation that benefits each constituency is limited.

While it's hard to quantify the exact cost of single vendor dependence, it may be the factor which most affects your bottom-line IT costs. Also, the cost of what you aren't getting out your desktop investment may be even greater than you can honestly quantify. The bottom line is single vendor dependence is bad economics because it limits competition and locks you into an upgrade cycle that is beyond your control.

LENGTH OF PRODUCT USABLE LIFE

The jobs of many task-based workers change very slowly, and their needs for computing are pretty static. Microsoft Windows operating systems in many cases change faster than end user needs do. Also, in an effort to provide the widest scope of features to the widest demographic of PC end users, Microsoft operating systems have increased their feature sets and, consequently, the minimum hardware requirements for the operating system have increased as well. The result has been operating systems for the lowest common denominator. Now this is not in itself a bad thing because by developing a wide user base there is a great deal of ease in interoperability for Windows PC users. The downfall is that to join this club you pay a premium in software licensing and other costs involved with keeping your hardware current. Take a look at a sampling of hardware requirements for Microsoft desktop operating systems over the last ten years' products. Take note of the frequency of releases for operating systems (not counting NT Workstation and ME) and the increasing hardware requirements. Maybe the changes aren't drastic, but the requirements continue to increase. In fact, many users may have been perfectly capable of using Windows 95 from release until today, but reliance on "support" from Microsoft has pushed the upgrade of the operating system as well as the hardware on which it runs.

Windows 95 released August 1995—Minimum Hardware Requirements

- Personal computer with a 386DX or higher processor (486 recommended).
- 4 megabytes (MB) of memory (8 MB recommended).
- Typical hard disk space required to upgrade to Windows 95: 35–40 MB The actual requirement varies depending on the features you choose to install.

Windows 98 released June 1998—Minimum Hardware Requirements

- A personal computer with a 486DX 66 megahertz (MHz) or faster processor (Pentium central processing unit recommended)
- 16 MB of memory (24 MB recommended)
- 120 MB minimum of free hard disk space
- CD-ROM or DVD-ROM drive
- VGA or higher resolution monitor (16-bit or 24-bit color SVGA recommended)

Windows 2000 released February 2000—Minimum Hardware Requirements

- A personal computer with a 133 MHz or higher Pentium-compatible CPU
- At least 64 MB of memory
- 2 GB hard drive with a minimum of 650 MB free space
- Single- and dual-CPU systems are supported by Windows 2000 Professional
- CD-ROM or DVD-ROM drive
- VGA or higher resolution monitor

Windows XP released October 2001—Minimum Hardware Requirements

- A personal computer with a 300 MHz or higher processor clock speed recommended; 233 MHz minimum required (single or dual processor system); Intel Pentium/Celeron family, or AMD K6/Athlon/Duron family, or compatible processor
- 128 MB of memory or more recommended (64 MB minimum supported; may limit performance and some features)
- 1.5 gigabytes (GB) of available hard disk space
- CD-ROM or DVD-ROM drive
- Super VGA (800 x 600) or higher resolution video adapter and monitor

Now consider that today's Linux distributions can be run on hardware that predates the Pentium but also on today's fastest hardware, and that it is not limited to the x86 processor. As a result of the modularity of the system you just take what best suits your needs. Even companies that are using proprietary hardware such as Sun SPARC or Macintosh can standardize their operating systems to a great degree using Linux. Also, because the Windows operating system is utilized among corporate and home users alike, there are many features, like rich multimedia capabilities, that might be desirable to the home user who uses the PC for entertainment but that would detract from the productivity of a business user. The bottom line is that Linux software doesn't necessarily have to drive any type of upgrade cycle, whether it is by way of the core operating system or hardware.

UP TIME/PRODUCTIVITY

In many cases the true cost of desktop computing lies in the productivity of the end user of the system. The cost of an individual PC outage is not just a factor of the system administrator's time but also includes that of the worker who utilizes that computer. In a large enterprise, not only does administrative overhead add up, so does the unproductive time users spend while they are unable to do their prescribed work.

Scenario: PC Fails for Filing Clerk

Take the example of a filing clerk in a large company who processes insurance claims. That clerk files an average of 20 claims per hour and makes an hourly wage of $12. During the course of the day, the clerk's PC becomes infected by a computer virus and the overhead on the PC slows its productivity, allowing the clerk to file

only 15 claims an hour. Then the PC locks up and becomes unresponsive, requir-
ing a reboot. During that reboot, which takes about two minutes, the employee goes
to the proverbial water cooler and complains to a coworker about how his PC isn't
working. This walk and conversation take about 10 minutes. During hour two the
clerk only processes 10 claims. Finally, after the process repeats itself twice more, the
employee calls the help desk and a technician arrives on the scene to diagnose and
repair the problem. The cost to the company for that employee's time is about $30
per hour. During the hour and a half it takes the technician to fix the problem (di-
agnose, remove the virus, and update virus definitions as a preventative measure)
the claims clerk is totally unproductive. When all is said and done, the clerk
processes 55 fewer claims that day, which costs the company $33. You must also
calculate the added expense of the $45 for the technician's time spent fixing the
problem. This comes to an individual incident cost of $78. Now consider that this
company has one thousand clerks, each of whom has this problem once a quarter.
That cost is now $78,000 per quarter or $312,000 annually. When you start look-
ing at how the small things add up, the cost of using systems that suffer from these
types of problems quickly adds up.

The questions here are, "Are those problems avoidable?" and "Does this happen in your enterprise?" Linux has characteristics that can reduce these problems, like tremendous uptime capabilities and the ability to "harden" PCs to prevent changes from causing system instability. The acquisition costs of a PC start to pale in comparison to problems related to viruses, operating system crashes, or the overhead involved with maintaining them. In later chapters we will talk about how Linux is very well suited as a high-availability operating system and can be secured to be less susceptible to adverse changes.

STABILITY

If you can't use your PC then you are probably costing the organization money by not providing the service that you are being paid to provide. Linux and its phenomenal uptime can help maximize productivity of knowledge workers especially because they rely heavily on their computers. Take, for example, the number of times a worker reboots in a given day. If a system requires frequent updates that require reboots, this can be time consuming. Windows has many systems that are tied to the core operating system and kernel, and updates often result in a reboot. That monolithic architecture in earlier Windows operating systems required frequent reboots. Over time there has been significantly less need to reboot Windows due to various architectural improvements, but because Microsoft's roots are firmly grounded in a single-user operating system, it was not a critical design requirement to avoid a reboot because it only affected one user. However, Linux, with its multi-user influences vis-à-vis UNIX, was designed knowing full well that reboots might affect multiple users, and so the methods for updating and restarting services were clearly independent in almost every case from the need to reboot. Linux lineage is derived from a multiuser high-availability operating system which results in uptime advantages in both the server and the desktop.

Viruses

Computer viruses and worms that affected Windows increased by a factor of four or greater in the first half of 2004 as compared to the same period in 2003, according to Windows virus software manufacturer Symantec® (Symantec, 2004). In its biannual Internet security report Symantec offered a number of key findings:

- During the first half of 2004, the time between disclosure of a vulnerability and the release of an exploit for that vulnerability was 5.8 days.
- From the period spanning January 1 through June 30, 2004, the Symantec Vulnerability Database listed 1,237 new vulnerabilities. Of those vulnerabilities 96 percent were described as being moderately or highly severe, while 70 percent were noted to be easy to exploit.
- 4,496 new Windows-specific viruses and worms were recorded during a six-month period, more than 4.5 times the number in the same period in 2003.

Symantec also noted that there could be a trend developing in Linux and mobile computing viruses. This is mainly because there are a growing number of mobile and Linux users attaching their devices to the Internet daily. This news may seem like it bodes badly for Linux, but does it? Of course, it's very hard to make "perfectly" secure software, and most any security expert will tell you that when you attach your PC to a network, you open it up to some vulnerability. The thing you need to consider is who will be there to provide you support in fixing these vulnerabilities. One company or a community of companies and developers can apply a greater number of resources to these problems. What is your recourse if a single vendor refuses or can't react quickly? Do you sacrifice the use of a product that you invested in until the problem is fixed, or do you have the freedom to get help from other suppliers?

SECURITY

When discussing Linux security, it bears pointing out that as a desktop platform, Linux has a considerably lower market share than Windows on the PC desktop, and as such, it is a much smaller target for those hackers that may want to cause mischief. That being said, it also offers a great advantage in security circles. The idea that there are no secrets to how something works has inherent advantages because it allows more people to scrutinize the code behind the software. A community of developers can ferret out problems and bugs, and patches can be submitted by any number of developers. In proprietary software packages, the vendor that makes the software institutes those fixes. In an open source model, many users can band together to supply fixes collaboratively. Also, the very strict adherence to user and group policies in Linux make it very difficult for a nonprivileged user to do any damage beyond the access that is granted to that user. Many system administrators can very effectively "lock down" a Linux system to prevent end users from making changes that will bring the PC down. This is counter to the policies of some closed source companies whose preference is to receive security flaw reports directly and then take the actions which they think are appropriate. This sounds reasonable doesn't it? What if that flaw only affects one out of a hundred users of their product? What if the company deems it unprofitable to fix the problem and it moves it to a low priority? What if an unscrupulous hacker discovers the flaw and compromises your network and steals your company's secrets or your customer's credit card numbers? It's analogous to a member of your cleaning staff leaving your back door open when he leaves, remembering it when he gets home, and then not telling you, hoping to lock it before you realize the door is open. If nothing happens, no problem. But what happens if you get robbed blind?

OPEN SOURCE DEVELOPMENT MODEL

Have you ever bought a software package that conflicts with another or tried to get cooperation between independent software vendors (ISVs) and been flustered by their unwillingness or inability to cooperate due to worries about trade secrets and proprietary code bases? The open source development model offers a huge advantage because it inspires a feeling of *esprit de corps*—the spirit of a group that makes the members want the group to succeed. This is a very interesting paradigm to the software vendors most of us buy software from today. The main advantage here is that because there are no secrets, there is accountability; programmers submitting code to their products are mostly doing so on a world stage and collaboration is much easier. Also, because there are a number of vendors who redistribute open source software such as the Linux kernel, there are many eyes watching the product and testing and improving upon the core product and rarely do improvements spearheaded by one company not make it into the products of other companies. Sharing the load of the core operating system among a number of companies, non-profits, and community developers brings a broader, more democratic element to the software development process. The focus of software vendors can be on adding value rather than maintaining those parts of the software that offer little distinguishable value.

LINUX DESIGN

There are fundamental differences between the Windows and Linux operating systems that make them both desirable in different circumstances. Often Windows is touted as being completely integrated because the desktop operating system is developed by the same company that delivers back office solutions. They have the ability to dovetail features between the two groups of products. Linux, on the other hand, offers a wide degree of customization through adherence to open standards and the possiblity for innovations to reflect the efforts of many companies, groups, and individuals.

To understand the advantages of Linux, observe the history of the two operating systems. Microsoft initially started building operating systems for single-user applications on the up-and-coming IBM PC. Their initial product was a desktop operating system, which at the time was thought to have limitations including 640KB of memory; a limitation caused by needing the video memory in the available address space. Eventually Microsoft overcame all these limitations as hardware architecture progressed. As the popularity of Microsoft Windows operating systems grew, Microsoft had considerations of previous designs and backwards compatibility during a pivotal point in the emergence of the PC. Linux, by coming late to the PC market, had some advantages, including the opportunity to study other operating systems and learn from their successes and failures. Additionally, Linux benefits from its similarity to UNIX and includes many of the features that made UNIX an obvious enterprise choice for reliable computing. UNIX, a multiuser system, had different considerations in its design than did Microsoft Windows and its predecessor MS-DOS.

Windows started out as a desktop OS and expanded to encompass the needs of the server OS market. Linux, on the other hand, followed the example of UNIX by becoming a multiuser, multiprocessing operating system from very early on. These very robust features make Linux a powerful and efficient operating system designed to offer maximum uptime, which was critical in server-based computing and exceptionally useful in desktop computing.

Windows was initially aimed at the desktop user whose needs included a graphical interface; the Windows OS tightly integrates the graphical interface and the kernel, which is the engine that drives the operating system. Since graphics are very resource intensive and in Windows the graphics system is tied to the kernel, video and operating system performance intersect; failures or problems with one can affect the other. The Linux operating system can use sophisticated graphical interfaces that can be turned on and off by the user. Granted, today's desktop user probably will prefer a graphical display system, but Linux is not married to one system or another.

This modular design also prevents failures of the graphics system from causing the whole system to fail. In other words, subsystems within Linux that fail do not necessarily compromise the whole machine. Also, because of the Linux kernel design and robust scheduler, priority can be given to critical tasks ahead of secondary tasks. Whether it's graphical displays or sound systems or other parts of the operating system is irrelevant. The fact that there are multiple groups providing critical parts enables technology to be modular and provides the benefit of more design ideas. Working in an open source model also allows for collaboration and sharing of information rather than making each party redesign everything from the ground up.

Another example of Linux design that benefits the end user is the differences between the Windows registry and Linux configuration settings. In Windows 98 the registry is comprised of two files, *User.dat* and *System.dat*, which contain the majority of the settings utilized by Windows and the programs installed under Windows. As time passes, the addition of new programs and hardware, along with operating system updates, causes the registry to grow—in some cases to monstrous size. Oftentimes the registry contains data that becomes extraneous and is peppered with settings used by necessary programs right beside those of malicious programs like spyware. In fact, a cottage industry has developed to provide utilities for "cleaning" and maintaining this huge file. Because it's a critical file for Windows operation, a corrupt registry can prevent Windows from booting properly if at all. Because the registry has such impact on the operating system, an error in one seemingly insignificant application can cause the whole operating system to fail if it incorrectly writes to the registry. Now the registry does have one advantage. Because it was intended to be a standard place to hold settings and system information, adding and removing software through a control panel is facilitated by this master database, though not managed completely. Linux, on the other hand, is more modular, and program settings and configuration files are specific to the application and not the operating system. The only similarity to the registry would be in the package manager. Under Linux the two most common are RPM (RPM Package Manager) and APT (Advanced Package Tool, used for Debian-based distributions). These databases include lists of all packages installed throughout a system. They also give software developers a standard to distribute software under. However, a corrupt RPM database doesn't prevent the system from booting. This system works well but has its own set of warts. In comparison though, the Windows system for package installation and configurations is far more comprehensive and centralized, which from a design standpoint can be considered a potentially larger point of failure.

Server Evolution versus Desktop Evolution

Operating systems evolve most directly from the needs of the users but are shepherded by the software vendor. In the case of Windows, the need for a desktop operating system was the first step; over time the need for file and print services evolved. As soon as networks and the Internet evolved, the need for servers that could be used to serve data and provide communication and messaging, particularly email and Web servers, became a critical component of the enterprise network. At the same time as the need for stable, reliable, cost-effective servers evolved not only in the enterprise but also in the small and medium business, Linux was coming of age. Linux's early success as a server operating system was fueled by its reputation for stability and security. These factors were of the utmost importance because the services provided by these servers affected many users. Linux was a natural choice for many applications because of its low acquisition cost and its ability to utilize the x86 platform, which was much cheaper than the proprietary hardware that was specific to the many flavors of UNIX. While Windows gained market share first on the desktop and then the server, Linux's rise to prominence is taking the opposite path to becoming one of the most widely deployed operating systems.

Linux on the desktop is still very much in its infancy, but it is a very viable alternative for a large number of desktop PC users. It also benefits from its server legacy. The fact that most changes can be made to live systems without reboots is as advantageous to a desktop user as it is to a server administrator. Also, because the Linux OS was designed as a multiuser system, its ability to service multiple desktop users from the same PC has distinct advantages. Most all Linux distributions adhere to a very strict users and groups schema that is intended to isolate users of the same PC and keep their settings and data separate from one another. Programs can be made available to but unalterable by all nonprivileged users. This practice allows the Linux desktop to be as rigid as the administrator deems necessary for preventing unauthorized changes to a system either by the end user or by a malicious piece of software like a worm or a virus.

MOMENTUM

It's hard to explain the intangibles behind the potential of Linux as a desktop operating system other than to say it's got momentum. Linux is the great Cinderella story: initially the product of a Finnish college student, it soon developed a legion of loyal fans dedicated to improving and sharing their improvements. Before IT giants IBM and Novell threw their support behind the operating system, it was powering servers all over the Internet. Consider that Apple has been working on operating systems since the late 1970s and Linus Torvalds started working on Linux in 1991, not as a commercial venture but as an individual project, and that in the next 10 years Linux shipped on computers manufactured by the likes of Dell, Sun, and IBM. Even more interesting is that there is no clear profit motive for the people contributing to the efforts. Nonprofit foundations like Mozilla.org offer a browser alternative to Internet Explorer which is growing in popularity and which could eventually become the most widely used browser despite the fact that it is not distributed with the dominant desktop operating system. Linux is being promoted by industry consortiums and private citizens alike, who share improvements and add functionality that can be integrated into "distributions" of Linux, often without the burden of royalties. The sheer number of developers for open source operating systems are many times that of any one company. Due to private and corporate collaborative efforts, it's likely that Linux will be a serious and comparable desktop operating system for all classes of user in the very near future.

SUMMARY

Overall, you shouldn't be taking your decision to move to the Linux desktop lightly. It's not an easy decision to make. There may be some disruption to your day-to-day operations, but it's a long-term strategic choice to migrate. It's important to understand the consequences both positive and negative in undertaking any new OS, whether it is Linux, UNIX, or even Mac OS. The decision should simply rest on how such a move will affect your bottom line. The contention of this book is that with a well-thought-out plan the adoption of the Linux OS as a desktop operating system will enhance your enterprise and provide you choices. These choices in vendor and applications will offer you more flexibility to negotiate software and maintenance terms. Improved uptime and fewer security breaches will improve knowledge worker productivity. Also, by creating a competitive marketplace for desktop computing, economics dictate that increased competition will reduce the price of the products offered. Ironically, this intense pressure in operating systems will most likely benefit not only Linux users but Windows users as well, who will profit from Microsoft's reactions perhaps in more competitive pricing in reaction to this new threat.

OTHER RESOURCES

- XFree86 – *www.xfree86.org*
- Mozilla Project – *www.mozilla.org*
- Debian Linux – *www.debian.org*
- Open Source Initiative – *www.opensource.org*
- GNU Operating System – *www.gnu.org*
- Free Software Foundation – *www.fsf.org*
- Richard Stallman's Home Page – *www.stallman.org*

REFERENCES

Dvorak, John C. "Magic Number: 30 Billion," *PC Magazine*, (August 4th, 2003). Available online at *http://www.pcmag.com/article2/0,4149,1210067,00.asp*.

Microsoft Corporation, "Windows 95 Installation Requirements," Article ID 138349. Available online at *http://support.microsoft.com/kb/138349*.

Microsoft Corporation, "Minimum Hardware Requirements for a Windows 98 Installation," Article ID 182571. Available online at *http://support.microsoft.com/kb/182751*.

Microsoft Corporation, "Windows 2000 System Requirements." Available online at *http://www.microsoft.com/windows2000/professional/evaluation/sysreqs/default.asp*.

Microsoft Corporation, "Windows XP Professional System Requirements." Available online at *http://www.microsoft.com/windowsxp/pro/evaluation/sysreqs.mspx*.

Symantec, "Symantec Internet Security Report." Available online at *http://www.symantec.com/press/2004/n040315b.html*.

2   Desktop Computing Needs Analysis

In This Chapter

- Needs Analysis
- Hardware Interoperability
- Taking an Application Inventory and Determining Usage Patterns
- Rewriting Applications
- Acquiring Expertise
- Summary
- Other Resources
- References

Have you ever visited the grocery store without a list? Do you know what happens when you do? The tendency is to buy things you don't need and to forget those things that you do need. The same idea applies when you look at an IT solution; if you don't evaluate in detail what you need and plan ahead for what you might need, you may be left without the things you and your enterprise need to successfully run your business. That's why it's important to do a *needs analysis*. A good Linux desktop needs analysis will encompass the following factors.

Analyze Usage Patterns: You can't successfully do this completely from your desk. Successful needs analysis will be conducted through your discussions and observations with end users. This will also set the stage for getting their buy-in for the actual migration later. At the very least it will likely uncover deficiencies in your legacy-computing environment.

Application Needs Analysis: Application inventory may be the number one inhibitor to migrating to desktop Linux. Companies that have a legacy application that is specific to their enterprise which will only run on Windows. Taking an inventory of what applications are being used today and, ideally, what applications are needed or unutilized will help you put together a migration plan that doesn't leave a functional gap in desktop environments.

Hardware Analysis: Current IT vendors, especially the largest ones (HP, Dell, Gateway), do not offer Linux support on all of their PCs. If you have a hardware standard and relationship with a vendor you need to discern whether its hardware going forward will cooperate with your objectives. You may find that community support for hardware is adequate or even that Linux vendor support will fulfill your needs.

Data Migration: You may have large amounts of data in email, or office documents that may be stored in proprietary formats like Microsoft Word and Excel. Linux native office suites can handle these formats but with some caveats. Some other proprietary formats may not have a Linux application equivalent. When given an option, choosing open standards for file storage formats will make future migrations easier and prevent vendor lock-in.

Network Interoperability: File and print sharing will be your biggest concern in the area of network interoperability. Providing the same services without replacing your existing infrastructure would be the ideal situation. Deciding if your existing infrastructure can accommodate new operating systems will weigh heavily in your investigation.

Acquiring Expertise: While your IT staff and end users today may be very skilled with Windows environments, Linux will be somewhat foreign to them. Both systems administrators and end users alike will need to be retrained to handle their new desktop operating systems. You may find that you are over or under supplying end users in your current OS configuration. The best exercise you can undertake is to interview workers on the applications they currently use, and find out what applications they would like but don't have access to. You should realize the reasons why they don't have access to these applications commonly include software licensing costs and security. Linux alternatives may overcome both barriers.

NEEDS ANALYSIS

Creating a needs analysis should be as valuable to an accountant as it is to an IT director. Understanding the impact of a Linux desktop migration can help justify the move from one platform to another to non-IT personnel.

Financial Considerations: Financial considerations are the bottom line as they apply to your company. Acquisition costs are one of the more easily quantifiable parts of the equation because money changes hands during this part of the process, though increased productivity and decreased overhead in systems management may be the real savings.

User Productivity: User productivity could be the most important deciding factor in a Linux desktop migration. It's also the hardest to compute. Deriving a set of metrics before moving forward into a new installation may not influence your decision as much as it will help you measure success.

Systems Management: Because of Linux's rise in the data center, management tools have been developed for large multisystem installations: to change configurations, monitor status, and update and install software. These tools can be translated to the desktop because the architectures are the same.

As you do your needs analysis, these three areas will be important plot lines in your Linux desktop migration story.

Profiles of the Desktop Users

Not every PC user is identical, but in the large enterprise you will find pockets of users with common needs. By grouping these workers you can create a profile of the type of computing needed for each class of worker. Also, you can decide if there are candidates within the organization that may be better served by a Linux desktop or thin-client computing model as opposed to users with complex needs who may be the most demanding because they require high mobility or processing power. The key concept to understand is that the more complex the end user's needs, the higher the likelihood of computing failures independent of the operating system. In the case of the Linux desktop, the most likely candidates for near-term success with Linux are those with the least amount of risk and less complex needs, or those that do have complex needs but also have a high aptitude for troubleshooting and maintaining their own PCs. Figure 2.1 shows a model where the outer rings demonstrate a favorable risk/return for Linux use by desktop user profiles, while the inner rings show the most complex and, accordingly, the most risky desktop Linux cases.

In fact, on the server side of the risk/return model in Figure 2.1, the risk/return is more a historical statement than it is a state of being; increased development efforts and commercial support have made every case noted on the right side of Linux server computing mode viable, and the desktop computing side of Linux is following closely behind. The evolution of Linux on the server was very rapid and you can find many examples of successful implementations at every level, from the small business to the large enterprise, though its humble beginnings were on the edge of

Linux Computing Risk Reward Analysis

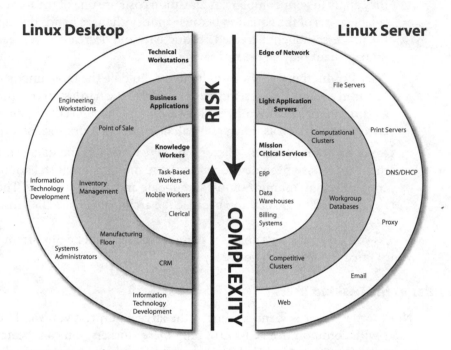

Linux Desktop

Linux Server

Technical Workstations

Engineering Workstations

Business Applications

Point of Sale

Knowledge Workers

Information Technology Development

Inventory Management

Task-Based Workers

Mobile Workers

Clerical

Manufacturing Floor

Systems Administrators

CRM

Information Technology Development

RISK

COMPLEXITY

Edge of Network

File Servers

Light Application Servers

Print Servers

Computational Clusters

Mission Critical Services

ERP

DNS/DHCP

Data Warehouses

Workgroup Databases

Billing Systems

Proxy

Competitive Clusters

Email

Web

FIGURE 2.1 The Linux risk/return computing analysis indicates that, as the complexity of the desktop requirements increase, so does the likelihood of failure.

the network. From there it slowly crept toward the more mission-critical applications. It is a common belief among Linux experts that desktop Linux is evolving in much the same way. Low-risk trials lead the way for the more complex users to implement a Linux desktop. Also, the management capabilities developed for the server deployment and management are translating to the desktop; proven system management tools used in the data center can just as easily be applied to desktop computing. As increased application availability and hardware support improve, the same software that is managing Linux server installations will be available for desktop management. There is little difference in the mechanisms for configuration and software management between the Linux desktop and the server. So rather than waiting for the support infrastructure to evolve for desktop users, once that market arrives there should be a very robust set of tools to manage these installations.

Technical Workstations

The technical workstation user is the most likely early-adopter of the Linux desktop. They are usually of a high technical aptitude and use their desktops for a variety of applications that involve application development or computations. They also may be systems administrators or researchers who use computation software that has high processing needs. One common example of a technical workstation user that benefits from Linux is the one who has access to a very powerful set of tools including those used for programming and application development or those used for highly processor-intensive applications.

Example: Technical Workstation Users: Movie Animators

In the days of Walt Disney® and Mickey Mouse®, animation was the result of teams of artists drawing sequence after sequence of movements, giving still pictures life when they where played in rapid succession. That task today is being greatly supplemented with computers. Dreamworks®, the immensely successful movie company, was using IRIX workstations manufactured by Silicon Graphics Incorporated (SGI) before making the movie Shrek. *They investigated Linux workstations on HP hardware to complete* Shrek. *Soon after they made* Spirit: Stallion of the Cimmarron, *Linux had become the desktop standard because it could handle the complex math that was used in "ray tracing," the method animators use to create, or render, animation. The result of this cost-efficient powerhouse use allowed for an additional element in realism. For example, in the movie* Toy Story *the backgrounds were static, but in* Shrek *the background moved as plants blew in the breeze. Linux on commodity hardware offered a better value than a commercial solution on commercial hardware. In this case, the commercial OS wasn't Windows but the logic remains the same: open systems on commodity hardware can and will reduce costs [Turner04].*

Other examples of technical workstation users include systems administrators and programmers. For many users the sticking point isn't the functionality of the underlying Linux operating system but application availability. In the technical workstation market this is not usually the case. The tools that this class of user needs are usually available for Linux workstations, especially when it comes to compilers like the GNU Compiler Collection (GCC), which currently contains front ends for C, C++, Objective-C, Fortran, Java, and Ada. The collection is a very comprehensive tool set free of royalties so they aren't costing development labs on a per seat licensing basis. If that isn't enough, there are plenty of programming IDEs (Integrated Development Environments) that are available for Linux, including emacs, Eclipse, and Netbeans for Java. Besides the programming tools there are a number of network and administrative tools that are available for free. For network administrators you can find a virtually unlimited supply of tools to troubleshoot and manage networks, including the following:

SSH: Secure Shell is a secure connectivity protocol that allows the user to connect to servers with an encrypted connection, which replaces less secure protocols like telnet.

Ethereal: A network protocol analyzer to troubleshoot and analyze network traffic.

AMANDA: The Advanced Maryland Automatic Network Archiver is a backup server that system administrators can use to back up multiple hosts. It can be used to back up all the PCs on a LAN, but also serves well for most any PC or server.

OpenNMS: OpenNMS is a network management system that fills three functional areas: service polling, which monitors service levels of services on a network; performance, where data is collected via SNMP and from remote systems; and event management, which includes a notification system for network events.

Many of these tools offer equivalent or better alternatives or meet minimum needs at much lower prices then their expensive commercial equivalents. Overall, today's technical workstation user may be just as well or better served by the Linux desktop than by Windows.

Single-Application Kiosks or Fixed-Use PCs

Kiosks, or single-task PCs, are used throughout a variety of businesses. The kiosk is probably one of the most attractive uses for a Linux PC. Take the example of the Point of Sale (POS) terminal, where users have a very limited application set or even a single application. The terminal is used by multiple users, such as in a cash register type of setup; downtime has a direct effect on sales and customer service. A Linux terminal makes perfect sense for this application because its high availability means it is likely that updates can be processed without interrupting operations. Also, since the Linux has a multiuser heritage, it lends itself to multiple cashiers logging into the same PC as happens in retail outlets. Point of Sale applications can then reside on a network and personnel can connect to them over the network.

NOTE

Burlington Coat Factory Warehouse Corporation recognized the value of using Linux desktops for their retail business in 1998 when they made the decision to investigate Linux as the operating system to host their Point of Sale applications. By 2002 they had migrated an average of 15 cash registers in 350 stores to PCs running Linux [Silwa03].

Knowledge Workers

Knowledge workers are those users who use their desktop computer as a primary part of their job. They likely use a group of core applications including a full office suite that at least includes a word processor and spreadsheet. They access the World Wide Web through a Web browser and they send email. In addition to this group of core applications, these knowledge workers most likely use applications that are specific to their enterprise or industry. These knowledge workers are the hardest to pigeonhole because of their diversity. They are also the most complex and risky candidates for Windows-to-Linux migration. Despite the fact that knowledge workers can be the most complex implementations, knowledge workers can and do successfully implement Linux desktops.

Task-Based Workers

Narrow task-oriented workers, sometimes referred to as *transactional workers,* use their PCs to do very repetitive tasks. Because the vast majority of their work relies on doing the same thing over and over again, it also stands to reason that they use one or two applications very heavily and others less frequently. Any computer users that do the same thing on few applications, such as telemarketers and medical records transcription staff, would be good cases for Linux migration. Also, since these limited task-oriented users have modest needs, consider whether their hardware will need to change significantly over the upcoming years. Given that their tasks change very little, if at all, evaluate whether improvements in hardware may have little affect on their productivity. Operating system upgrades may not be a function of the users' needs, but of the vendor's need to attract new buyers by adding new features that may not add any value to those already using their products. In this case, consumers may be coerced into an operating system upgrades cycle as support for past operating systems is dropped. Linux, on the other hand, could offer the freedom of numerous software vendors who compete to support your needs.

The German import company Heinz Tröber chose to run its ERP software on Linux rather than Microsoft Windows, citing frequent crashes and wasted time by employees waiting for recovery as reasons for exploring alternatives. Its solution was to move to a thin client computing solution of Linux hosted on IBM servers and redisplayed via X Windows to "dumb terminals" running Linux. Feedback was very positive regarding the reduction in crashes in comparison to the previous Windows solution[Marson05].

"Average" Needs Users

The average needs user is the user that uses the core applications and a limited number of additional applications that may or may not have native Linux-equivalent applications. They use very few, if any, peripheral devices like PDAs or scanners. They are permanently connected to a network and have good aptitude at using their Windows desktops but have little to medium ability to self-administer their workstation. These users can realize the benefits of Windows-to-Linux migration tools where a native Linux environment supplies the core of their desktop environment, but a hosted Windows session serves their legacy Windows applications on Linux applications. These Windows-on-Linux applications will be discussed later, but include technologies to bridge Windows applications to Linux such as WINE, Win4Lin', VMWare®, and Citrix®. Average needs users compromise the bulk of computer users today and are ripe for Linux migration, even though it is slightly more complex than migrating task-based workers.

> *Giesendorfer Grundschule Public Elementary in Berlin, Germany, had a student body of approximately 430 students ranging from preschool through 6th grade. Faced with the problem of maintaining and upgrading computing resources, both hardware and software, their need exceeded their financial means to keep pace with Windows upgrades. Individual workstations were retrofitted to use Linux as a thick client, and others where converted to Linux thin clients. All used Open Office.org, Evolution mail client, and GIMP, a graphics program. Lacking a Linux alternative to certain Windows programs, they used Win4Lin to repurpose their Windows operating systems and applications and continue to provide the same level of service to their students. Back-office systems where also served by open source software where Samba provided file and print sharing, SQUID provided a proxy server, and Apache, an open source Web server, ran their Web site. Overall, students continued to use a wide variety of applications but were no longer completely dependent on a Microsoft Windows environment.*

Power Desktop PC Users

Power users are those who push the capabilities of their PCs regardless of the operating system. Besides the core applications common with average needs knowledge workers, they probably use a very diverse number of applications that may be only available for the Windows user. These applications, being a critical part of their work lives, will need a migration path. Also, these users may have specialized needs in the form of peripherals, such as the draftsman's specialized printers, or the medical personnel's computer interfaces to equipment like x-ray machines. These will be the hardest area for Linux to address, mainly because these users don't have a critical mass of Linux users driving development to meet their needs yet.

Mobile PC Users

Mobile users are those users whose primary desktop system is a notebook or laptop computer. They may also fall into one of the other categories. They most likely use a variety of network connections that may include Ethernet, modem, and wireless. They typically have some sort of peripheral devices that include mobile phones (possibly with Bluetooth® integration) and PDAs. These users can be the most demanding of all the desktop users mainly because they have the most complex needs, and in relation to the Linux adoption bull's-eye referenced in Figure 2.1, they would be dead center as the most risky and complex user profile. Despite the fact that mobile users have such a high level of need, they can be supported under Linux and, in some cases, you will find that they receive just as great a benefit as the low risk user.

No matter what your enterprise desktop computing makeup is, there is probably a way to maintain or improve the status quo for most desktop computing situations while reducing costs.

HARDWARE INTEROPERABILITY

When purchasing new hardware on which to deploy Linux, you will need to do some advance work. Windows PCs are well supported by hardware vendors and Dell, HP, and Gateway sell PCs with Windows driver support. Linux users, on the other hand, are faced with other challenges including driver support and recognition and the prospect that there may be no way to make PCs designed for Windows fully functional under Linux. This is not a hopeless situation though; areas that are not being addressed by the big vendors have left a hole that is being ably filled by smaller white box builders. Many of these builders specialize in Linux-capable hardware or provide value-added services to insure that your PC functions as expected under Linux.

White Box Manufacturers

When mainstream vendors cannot or chose not to address the needs of smaller contingents of PC users, *white box* vendors step up, building solutions for these special needs users. In Linux today there are no vendors the size of a Dell, HP, or even Gateway that offer Linux on all their hardware, but there are many emerging vendors that are focused on offering competitively priced options that compete with these PCs.

Desktop PCs

CPUBuilders by Stratitec: CPUBuilders, a brand established by Midwestern PC manufacturer Stratitec, focuses on low- and mid-range PCs that are sold both directly and through Sam's Club, a Wal-Mart owned retailer.

Microtel: Microtel is another white box manufacturer that sells Linux-equipped PCs through Wal-Mart. These PCs are equipped with Linux distributions from Xandros and Linspire.

Pogo Linux: Pogo Linux is a Linux hardware vendor that focuses on Intel and AMD processor-based Linux hardware. They sell higher end technical workstations used by system administrators who are often administering servers from the same manufacturer.

These are only a few examples of Linux white box manufacturers. It's likely that whatever your need, there is someone somewhere willing to provide you hardware. They may not be of the same profile as your current desktop PC vendor, though that is not necessarily an indication of their quality.

Mobile Computers

The mobile laptop is most susceptible to the problems that users face in regard to hardware support, but there are a few companies that have done an excellent job addressing the needs of mobile PC users.

LinuxCertified: LinuxCertified is a company that originally focused on Linux training, and as an add-on to the training they provided refurbished Linux laptops. Past customers returned to LinuxCertified for not only training but also for laptops that ran Linux with no additional configuration. It has since started to sell LinuxCertified laptops directly.

EmperorLinux: EmperorLinux is a value-added reseller that focuses on taking popular laptop models from manufacturers and then configuring them to run with a number of Linux distributions. They specialize in filling the gaps that are left by the original equipment manufacturers with regards to Linux.

Just because your current vendor doesn't support desktop Linux doesn't mean you can't benefit from its hardware under Linux. These resellers are all focused on providing as good or even better results than you have with Windows PCs.

The Linux Hardware Databases

Most of the popular Linux manufacturers maintain databases populated mainly by user submissions on successes with getting certain hardware to work properly under Linux. Whether you are making a purchase decision or looking to redeploy your existing Windows hardware under Linux, these databases are an excellent place to start doing your homework.

SuSE Linux Hardware Database (now part of Novell): The SuSE has extended search capabilities and the ability to search by hardware type and architecture.

Red Hat: Red Hat maintains a certified hardware list that offers advanced search capabilities. Its certification program helps the company provide support for hardware that it knows has been tested to work on Red Hat Linux.

Mandriva: Mandriva maintains a comprehensive list of compatible hardware that is sortable by all sorts of criteria, including architecture and product version numbers. Because Mandrake is a popular desktop Linux distribution it is often a good source for desktop and mobile hardware reports.

LinuxHardware.Net: Allows users to submit their details about success or failures installing Linux on given hardware. The Web site accepts verbatim user submissions, so anecdotal information about hardware and other information is not always complete here, but the site is usually helpful in determining your likelihood for success with a particular Linux distribution.

Google: Because of the changing landscape of desktop Linux, one of the best sources for current information is doing a search via Google's search engine on the hardware you would like to use. First-hand user accounts may lend the most insight into what hardware works well and what steps might need to be taken to get hardware to work under Linux.

Usenet Newsgroups: Usenet is a haven for old school Linux users; it's often one of the most comprehensive and diverse places to look for information on obscure questions. Google also indexes Usenet groups (*http://groups-beta. google.com/*), so you can search them from a Web browser. Usenet groups are interactive, so questions can be posted there. One particular Usenet group, *comp.os.linux.hardware,* is specifically aimed at Linux hardware compatibility. You can post questions and look for anecdotal evidence that your proposed hardware solution will work here.

Linux Compatible: Linux Compatible is another Linux-user-supported site that serves as a watchdog for updates from manufacturers as well as other Linux installation-related news. The comprehensive Linux list includes not only information on whether a device or even application works well on Linux, but also allows users to comment and support or contradict previous user posts.

TuxMobile: TuxMobile is a comprehensive resource for finding anecdotal information on mobile Linux for portable computers, PDAs, and even mobile phones.

The best way to confirm compatibility for hardware is to simply try to install Linux on a pilot machine. However, by and large, most hardware is supported under Linux and works well. The hardware that is less likely to be supported is the newest technology, such as the 802.11g wireless cards and peripherals. The open source community spends a good bit of time providing drivers for hardware, but because individuals lack relationships with hardware manufacturers they must acquire their test equipment on their own accord. Over time, as Linux takes a larger share of the desktop market it is likely that more hardware vendors will consider providing native Linux drivers for their hardware.

Desktop Hardware and Notebook Hardware

It might be best to evaluate desktop users and notebook users separately when considering a Linux migration. Laptop hardware users are often harder to accommodate with full hardware compatibility because Linux is often not supported by all of the hardware manufacturers.

Wireless Cards

Wireless cards under Linux offer a precarious situation, because wireless card manufacturers typically don't provide Linux drivers for their hardware. It falls to the Linux community and Linux vendors to develop methods for configuring these cards. Typically the result is limited at best, and the interfaces are somewhat more complicated or at least less obvious than the wireless monitoring software that resides in the Windows toolbar.

NOTE

There are two notable ways to get Windows WiFi drivers to load in the event there is no native equipment. One is a open source program called ndiswrapper which provides a way to load the driver supplied by your Windows manufacturer under Linux. The other is a commercial program by Linuxant. Linuxant produces a product called DriverLoader, which can be used like ndiswrapper to load the Windows drivers and allow them to interact with the Linux operating system.

Power Management

Linuxs' ability to manage ACPI and APM (two of the most common power management technologies used in mobile computing) is getting better as time passes, but often the implementation is not perfect. The ability to suspend, resume, and regulate operation of fans for PCs are features that may not work as expected under Linux.

Advanced Power Management (APM) is supported by the system BIOS ROM. For APM to work with Linux it must support version 1.0 or later of the APM standard. APM requires that the kernel include the correct modules. Advanced Configuration and Power Interface (ACPI) is a specification developed in partnership between Toshiba, Intel, and Microsoft which, among other things, includes specifications for power management. Just as APM requires kernel integration, so does ACPI.

Intel® Centrino™ Drivers

Intel has a number of initiatives for supporting Linux but many of them are filtered through open source projects. The PRO/Wireless 2100 Network Connection mini PCI adapter is supported through a community project, and the Intel® PRO/Wireless 2100 Driver for Linux through a development community, as is the Intel PRO/Wireless 2200BG Network Connection mini PCI adapter. However, Intel has not shared its source code for the drivers that optimize these devices including both wireless cards and chip power management. Centrino is solely used on mobile hardware like notebooks, so Centrino support may be a problem for mobile Linux users rather than workstation users.

Docking Stations

Linux and docking stations don't always work together as seamlessly as they do on Windows, but starting with the 2.4 version of the Linux kernel *hotplugging* became a standard feature. Hotplugging involves the use of a kernel thread that monitors the status of a docking station and watches for changes. The combination of an older PC and a Linux distribution that doesn't include hotplug support in its kernel may not provide satisfactory levels of performance for mobile users.

Network Compatibility

Linux network compatibility issues are usually limited, especially with standard TCP/IP networks over Ethernet. The problems are more often with integration to existing file and print services that are served by either Novell or Microsoft Windows. Novell network support is fast becoming an nonissue because in 2003 Novell acquired German Linux developer SuSE and has quickly adopted a very Linux-friendly approach for its portfolio of products. The community-driven Samba project, on the other hand, is ably handling Microsoft interoperability. Samba is a free open source software suite that provides seamless file and print service to SMB/CIFS implementations and facilitates interoperability between Linux/Unix servers and Windows-based clients. Samba can also be used as a primary domain controller (PDC) for Windows clients without the need for licensing. Additionally, the latest versions of Samba now provide the ability to join Microsoft Active Directory domains.

Linux Application Planning

At this point in the Linux desktop market there are two main inhibitors for Linux adoption. They are application availability and vendor hardware support. Of the two, application availability is probably the easier to overcome with existing hardware. As for hardware, you should research the level of Linux support for your hardware by searching the Internet or checking with Linux distribution vendors and then try to procure hardware that has been proven to work with Linux. Many Free and Open Source (FOSS) applications are adequate substitutes for your existing core applications. Identifying these key applications and making the move piecemeal rather than replacing a whole user environment can level out the disruption caused by the introduction of a new operating system. Identifying core Linux applications that can replace your current applications on Windows is a good first step. In later chapters there will be discussions of methods to make your Windows applications portable across platforms until native applications are offered.

Being in position for other largely disruptive events like planned hardware refreshes and end of support life for software products can present opportunities for Linux migration. By keeping Linux in mind as a potential solution when these types of events occur, you can capitalize on those opportunities with a well-planned Linux desktop strategy. A wholesale replacement of your IT infrastructure makes very little sense unless coupled with these critical events, but strategic changes could start to yield cost savings. Also, when reviewing Total Cost of Ownership (TCO) studies for Linux, keep in mind that many of these studies often assume that the costs will be associated with complete replacement of your infrastructure and that's why they often include assumptions that migration will be expensive. However, when looking at TCO from a position of Linux migration coupled with logical infrastructure upgrades, the picture gets rosier. The key for any new system is that it offers the same or better performance. If costs for one solution are higher than other solutions, then the expensive option must offer some benefit like increased productivity. If costs of the new system are lower, it should meet the needs of the enterprise with no reduction in productivity.

TAKING AN APPLICATION INVENTORY AND DETERMINING USAGE PATTERNS

Earlier, the discussion of roles or profiles of desktop users was discussed and certain high-benefit/low-risk cases were identified—specifically task-based workers who accomplished primarily a small number of specific tasks. All users use their computers to accomplish tasks, and some users have a larger breadth of tasks they accomplish with their PCs. The important first step is to identify the applications you need to accomplish those tasks. The real state of the Linux desktop is that the underlying operating system is very robust. The complications that will be the most difficult for you to overcome will be the migration of applications and hardware support. In the low-risk/high-reward categories you will most likely find that these two obstacles are most easily overcome. The center of the Linux desktop adoption "bulls-eye," which involves the highest risk due to complexity, will be the last cases to have functionality equivalent to what they had on Windows. The ideal situation is one where all Windows applications can be migrated to equivalent open source applications despite the platform. Finding the proverbial low-hanging fruit for migration will be relatively easy once you do an enterprise inventory. Table 2.1 is a very simple worksheet showing an application inventory for a small to medium business.

TABLE 2.1   Application Acquisition Worksheet

PC User Name or Classification of Users	Windows Applications Used	Replacement Open Source Applications on Linux
Administrative Staff	*Microsoft Office*	OpenOffice.org
	Microsoft Outlook accessing a Microsoft Exchange Server	Novell Evolution with Ximian Connector
Clerical Workers	*Microsoft Office*	OpenOffice.org
	Internet Explorer	Firefox
	Company CRM application built with VB GUI interface	No native Linux substitute Windows applications on Linux solution needed
	Microsoft Outlook accessing a Microsoft Exchange Server	Novell Evolution with Ximian Connector
Salespeople	*Microsoft Office*	OpenOffice.org
	Internet Explorer	Firefox
	Microsoft Outlook accessing a Microsoft Exchange Server	Novell Evolution with Ximian Connector
	ACT! Or Goldmine! Sales Contact Manager	No native Linux substitute Windows applications on Linux solution needed or move to a Web-based solution, e.g., Salesforce.com, SugarCRM

Linux Migration via Web-Based Applications

Consider what applications you have today that run via a browser; perhaps you have Customer Resource Management (CRM) database front ends or other applications that have moved to the network. This paradigm shift in desktop computing can help lessen the pains of migrating Windows' users to Linux. Once applications are in the network the end user device can be more flexible, especially if those applications are served via an open standard like HTML or Java. Before procuring new applications it may be worthwhile to consider network-ready applications well before a desktop change. Regardless of the platform, Web-based applications normally benefit from centralized deployment and administration. They have also suffered in the past from a less robust feature set than native applications. That's changing as more robust applications are being built using Java and other technologies. Many enterprises that won't be moving to Linux will be implementing Web services replacements for natively written client server applications. Even without specifying a desktop choice there are many arguments for this shift to the server. Nevertheless a Web services strategy can be advantageous in helping remove application availability barriers for Linux desktop adoption.

REWRITING APPLICATIONS

Here's where Linux migrations fail most often. Most every business has at least one critical application; it may be a billing database or manufacturing application, it may be something that you have invested considerable time writing yourself or having written for you. Representatives from the city of Paris, France, stated that their plans stalled for Linux adoption due to two reasons: the expense of having to rewrite programs and the cost of training thousands of employees on new software. That's why in the early stages of Linux desktop deployments, it's worth looking at Windows on Linux migration solutions. There are two categories that you could consider. The first is to run Windows applications on the actual desktop using a virtual machine or emulator. This option will discussed in detail in later chapters, but what's important to know at this point is that through the use of a virtual machine such as VMware or Win4Lin you can move your Windows installations onto Linux. If you have only a few applications, you may be interested in trying to run them using the emulator WINE. The other solution is to use technologies that redisplay a core set of applications running on Windows Terminal Server on a Linux desktop. This method is popular because the applications run on the operating system that they were intended to but can be easily decommissioned when native Linux applications become available. Redisplay of applications also has the advantage of making applications portable outside the enterprise. In case of problems with facilities, inclement weather, or travel, desktop users can benefit from the ability to access applications securely over a network connection.

ACQUIRING EXPERTISE

Some IT projects evolve rather than are implemented. Backroom experiments can become production systems very quickly, often with little formal training other than that gained on the job. When you make as radical a change as Windows to Linux migration your chances of success are much greater if you start planning early, and part of that planning involves gathering expertise and training before you implement the new system.

Look for Local Expertise: Linux Users Groups (LUGs)

In any good technology implementation plan, acquisition of technical skills to support a new technology is a grave concern. One of the most valuable sources of Linux expertise is available for free from your local Linux Users Group, or LUG. LUGs can be the most comprehensive and cost-effective sources of information for the company migrating to Linux. LUGs are usually nonprofit organizations that may be sponsored by corporate donations to cover the cost of minor expenses such as Web hosting for their Web site. IT professionals who use Linux in their personal and professional lives usually attend these organizations in bookstores, churches, and schools whenever possible. A typical LUG meeting usually includes an educational program followed by some socializing and swapping of stories among members who can trade technical expertise and show off their latest Linux or other "techie" creations. There are many lists of where to find LUGs. Probably the most comprehensive is at Linux.org where they list LUGs in all 50 states and others all over the world.

Another common service LUGs provide is the "Linux Installfest" where anyone can bring a PC or server to a common location where members of the LUG aid users in the installation and configuration of Linux. Many times you get the benefit of a few hours of a highly skilled system administrator's time to help you successfully install and get up and running. LUGs cost you little more than your time and an optional donation of a few dollars for pizza.

In addition to education and installation services, the LUG can serve as a source of support information, usually by virtue of a discussion group or mailing list. Members can pose questions and usually receive a high level of expertise from practitioners who have run into similar problems. LUGs are also a logical place for you to recruit expertise for your organization as they provide a peer group that often can verify any member's level of expertise.

Training and Certification

Teenagers who can ably ride a bike are not permitted to drive a car without some instruction. Their likelihood of success is not as good as it will be if they are provided some training. The same logic should apply to the training of your staff before switching their desktop environments. When the topic of training comes up the subject of IT certification is likely to soon follow. IT certification is often met with a skeptical eye and in the Linux world this is no different. The idea of a certification is most useful to help insure a minimum level of skill for systems administrators, not a complete level of competence. Certification and training is not a prerequisite for Linux migration but could help increase your level of success. The following programs are aimed at general certification. Some offer desktop-oriented certifications and provide a good background for Windows administration staff to evaluate and implement Linux as an alternative desktop.

Linux Professional Institute

The Linux Professional Institute is a nonprofit organization headquartered in Toronto, Canada, and is one of the most widely recognized Linux training organizations in the world. The LPI came into being after some vendors like Red Hat had already started training programs. However, the LPI boasts an advisory board that is represented by vendors and community members trying to develop a standard for Linux training. The testing is very distribution neutral unless otherwise stated. LPI certification can be used to measure the base level of expertise but does not require the same level of analysis and troubleshooting as provided by Red Hat.

Red Hat Global Training–*http://www.redhat.com/training/*

Red Hat is one of the largest and most well-known "pure" Linux companies in the world and they offer a very well-respected training program. The differentiator with the Red Hat program is that it focuses more on hands-on problem solving and less on the multiple-choice testing that is common among other certifications. All Red Hat certifications require students to pass a certification lab exam. However, the Red Hat certification is very specific to the Red Hat products. There are two Red Hat certifications that are often recognized with distinction across the IT industry, the RHCT and the RHCE.

Red Hat Certified Technician (RHCT)

The RHCT certification is the entry-level certification for Red Hat Certification which focuses on a core set of system administration skills mainly related to configuration and installation of a Linux system. The Red Hat Certified Technician designation focuses on tools and troubleshooting of Linux systems in a lab setting. Testing is comprehensive and practical.

Red Hat Certified Engineer (RHCE)

The RHCE is additive to the RHCT certification. The RHCE is also a hands-on learning and testing situation. The training in itself will be helpful to any Linux user, but it's important to note that all Linux distributions are not exactly the same. While this certification is by all accounts very good, not all skills will translate directly to other companies or community products. However, if you choose Red Hat as your software vendor you will most assuredly benefit from its training program.

Novell Linux Certifications

Novell is relatively new to the Linux certification arena; until 2003 it really had very little to do with the Linux industry. However, it has a world-class training organization that has for years certified its partners and industry professionals through such designations as the Certified Novell Engineer (CNE) and Certified Novell Administrator (CNA). Since acquiring SuSE Linux Novell has worked on a new set of training courses including the Novell Certified Linux Engineer (CLE) and Novell Certified Linux Professional (CLP).

Novell Certified Linux Engineer

The Novell CLE is advanced certification for system administrators that are running Novell Nterprise Linux Services. The focus is on installing and managing installations in heterogeneous environments. As with Red Hat certification, students need to pass a lab test to achieve certification.

Novell Certified Linux Professional

The Novell CLP is not as advanced as the Novell Certified Linux Engineer. The Novell CLP is a good starting point for Linux certification. It focuses on the fundamentals of Linux system administration, including installation and managing an installation, compiling the Linux kernel, and troubleshooting network processes. The CLP requires the candidate to pass a Novell Practicum to achieve the certification.

Whatever your decision on Linux training and certification, these programs aren't the end all solution to IT knowledge. You will find that actual use and support of the Linux desktop will build the skills of the IT staff and users faster than any other method. Training can be a valuable supplement to this work experience.

End User Training

End user training can be the factor that makes adoption successful for migrating workers. Immersing them unprepared into a new desktop operating system, especially one that is complex, can yield disastrous results. However, you may want to temper your fears. A Linux usability study by Relevantive, a German consulting company, noted that 80% of the participants believed they would reach the same level of competence within one week (Relevantive, A.G., 2003). You may find that giving end users an introduction to the new technologies beforehand through both independent study and formalized classes will yield beneficial results.

Bootable Linux Homework

Often people are curious about the future. Providing them with a Linux kit they can play with before forcing a transition on them can be helpful. Developing an education packet that they can use at work or at home may provide them an opportunity to gain new skills and give them the tools to pose intelligent questions before moving to a Linux desktop. This ability to practice might help educate the IT staff on potential problems before they are under pressure to solve them in a work environment. Giving them a copy of the CD-ROM included with this book could provide them an inexpensive way to experiment. Besides the business productivity applications on the Knoppix disk, there are a few games that employees and their families alike might enjoy. If the right amount of salesmanship is applied, employees might choose to do this homework of their own volition and off the clock in the interest of entertainment and learning.

ON THE CD

Linux Labs

In future chapters there will be discussion about how to temporarily repurpose Windows PC labs into Linux labs for training. Providing a training program along with preselecting applications that can be used under Windows and then travel to Linux as native applications (e.g., Firefox Web browser, OpenOffice.org Office Suite) can provide economic solutions to employee education.

Support Infrastructure

A factor that may influence your decision to move to a Linux desktop in part of your enterprise will be the staff that supports your IT infrastructure. Without their confidence that the Linux desktop is better for the organization, your migration will more than likely fail. Some employees may resent the retiring of skills they may have already gained, such as Microsoft certifications, but others will embrace the opportunity to learn something new.

Do-IT-Yourself (DIY) with In-House IT Staff

If you currently run a Windows shop your transition to Linux will include some learning curve. Your IT administrative staff may be extremely skilled but their expertise in Linux may be limited. One of the best ways to make sure they are equipped to support your users migrating to Linux is for them to be the first adopters of Linux in your enterprise. The only way to truly get the nuances of the Linux desktop is to immerse yourself in the environment. Solving the problems firsthand will also speed the Linux curve for IT staffers.

Outsourced Support

Maybe you don't keep in-house IT expertise to administer your IT infrastructure and you rely on a systems integrator or other vendor for Linux. Your IT services vendor may already have the skills needed to migrate. If it doesn't you should probably start shopping for someone with proven Linux expertise. Your local LUG is a good place to start looking. Consultants often participate in these groups and may provide you a chance to screen and find new expertise. Understanding industry certifications and which, if any, of these are held by potential contractors is also a good way to screen the minimum level of expertise.

SUMMARY

There could be volumes dedicated to how to conduct a needs analysis for a Linux desktop migration. However, these volumes can be boiled down to four concepts discussed so far in this book.

1. Understand where current costs in desktop computing lie.
2. Understand what functions need to be accomplished by desktop computing users.
3. Take an application inventory to understand what applications are used to accomplish desktop computing tasks.
4. Evaluate the risks associated with disruption to current users and evaluate if savings for all these factors are justified.

This understanding marks the first step in making an informed decision on Linux adoption. Relying on anecdotal evidence from other Total Cost of Ownership studies more than anything else will give you information on how Linux desktops have influenced the bottom line of other companies, not *yours*. Understanding your needs and doing your own research is a better way to meet your needs and insure success, whether it's for a network assessment or desktop migration. To quote Henry Ford, "Before everything else, getting ready is the secret to success." That's why adequate planning and preparation cannot be stressed enough when undertaking a cross-platform migration. There can be no more emphatic cry to make sure you get the most out of your desktop computing infrastructure then this, "Do your research." Making good decisions starts with understanding what's going on in your enterprise, then gathering the resources to make sure new solutions best address your business conditions.

OTHER RESOURCES

- OpenSSH—*www.openssh.com*
- Ethereal—*www.ethereal.com*
- CPUBuilders by Stratitec—*www.cpubuilders.com*
- Microtel—*www.microtelinc.com*
- Emperor Linux—*www.emperorlinux.com*
- Pogo Linux—*www.pogolinux.com*
- Linux Certified—*www.linuxcertified.com*
- Index of Linux User Groups (LUGS)—*www.linux.org/groups/index.html*
- Linux Professional Institute—*www.lpi.org*
- Red Hat Training—*www.redhat.com/training/*
- GNU Emacs—*www.gnu.org/software/emacs/emacs.html*
- GNU Compiler Collection—*http://gcc.gnu.org/*
- Amanda—*www.amanda.org*
- OpenNMS—*www.opennms.org*
- SuSE Linux Hardware Database—*http://hardwaredb.suse.de/?LANG=en_UK*
- Red Hat Hardware Compatibility List—*http://hardware.redhat.com/hcl/*
- Red Hat Certification Program—*http://hardware.redhat.com/hcl/?pagename =redhatready*
- MandrakeLinux—*www.linux-mandrake.com/en/hardware.php3*
- LinuxHardware.Net—*www.linuxhardware.net*
- Linux Compatible—*www.linuxcompatible.org*
- Linuxant—*www.linuxant.com*
- Ndiswrapper—*http://ndiswrapper.sourceforge.com*

- Samba—*www.samba.org*
- Eclipse—*www.eclipse.org*
- Netbeans—*www.netbeans.org*
- Emacs—*www.gnu.org/software/emacs/*

REFERENCES

[Mason05] Mason, Ingrid, "Desktop Linux Wins Plaudits for Stability," *ZDNet UK* (March 10, 2005). Available online at *http://news.zdnet.co.uk/software/linuxunix/0,39020390,39190950,00.htm.*

[Muehlig03] Muehlig, Hortsmann Brucherseifer, and Ackerman, Relevantive, *Linux Usability Study* (August 13, 2003).

[Silwa03] Silwa, Carol, "Sidebar: Early Adopter Stands Firm on Linux Desktop," *ComputerWorld* (December 15, 2003). Available online at *http://www.computerworld.com/softwaretopics/os/linux/story/0,10801,88191,00.html.*

[Turner03] Turner, James, "On Location in the Render Farm," *LinuxWorld Magazine* (November/December 2003): p. 37.

3 Preparing for Your Linux Migration

In This Chapter

- Inflection Points Provide Logical Opportunities for Migration
- Utility in Desktop Computing
- Staging Open Source Applications on Windows
- File- and Print-Sharing Conversions or Accommodations
- Hardware Redeploy or Buy Decisions
- End User Acceptance
- Summary
- Other Resources
- References

P reparation for Linux migration can and should start long before the act of moving to Linux. The combination of research and training Linux skills within an enterprise are important. But there are other preparatory steps you can take once you have committed to the migration from one platform to another. These steps include the following:

Planning to capitalize on events that lend themselves to Linux desktop migration: Certain events lend themselves to migration to Linux, including hardware refreshes and software upgrades. Looking at the horizon for these logical events can make your migration easier.

Staging strategies: Staging the migration from Windows to Linux is important. Staging applications on Windows for native Linux adoption later can ease disruption.

Hardware replacement or redeployment decisions: Evaluating the compatibility of existing hardware along with projected usable hardware life will help you decide on the potential.

Pilot program: Conducting a pilot of the new desktop environment is a good step. Planning will improve your chance of success, but it's very difficult to anticipate every scenario.

Garner end user buy in: If there is any way to gain user acceptance of new technologies before the fact, do it. If end users of new technologies perceive that the new solution will benefit them, chances are they will be more successful.

Replacing Windows will probably have the most profound effect you could imagine on your enterprise IT infrastructure. You will most likely find that the experience will cause mixed results as some users will resist change, and others will welcome a new environment that gives them a more stable work environment. Systems administration staff and help desk personnel will quickly recognize the value and inherent advantages of a Linux environment.

INFLECTION POINTS PROVIDE LOGICAL OPPORTUNITIES FOR MIGRATION

Andy Grove, Intel Chairman and renowned business strategist, refers to *inflection points* as the times in a business's life where fundamentals are about to change. The change in fundamentals in the case of this discussion is migration of Windows operating system to Linux. In Mr. Grove's conversations he speaks in general terms, not necessarily regarding IT infrastructure, but his comments are no less relevant. A well-executed Linux migration in an enterprise where IT costs are a significant part of capital and operating expenses can be the inflection point that springs your business to new heights of productivity through better use of capital and improved productivity. Certain opportunities such as logical desktop hardware upgrade cycles and end of Windows operating system life are excellent opportunities to investigate Linux desktop migration. The key to taking advantage of these opportunities is to plan ahead. Staging and planning for these events should happen well in advance. Even if your enterprise isn't ready for a full-fledged Linux migration you can start to move from one platform to another, and at the very least you could benefit from open source software in your Windows enterprise and move gradually toward a Linux desktop migration. This concept is illustrated in Figure 3.1.

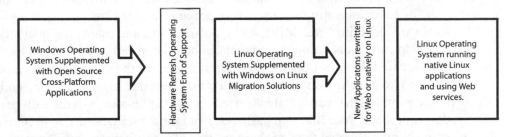

Linux Desktop Migration Capitilizing on Disruptive Events

Windows Operating System Supplemented with Open Source Cross-Platform Applications

Hardware Refresh Operating System End of Support

Linux Operating System Supplemented with Windows on Linux Migration Solutions

New Applicatons rewritten for Web or natively on Linux

Linux Operating System running native Linux applications and using Web services.

FIGURE 3.1   Certain events are logical catalysts for Linux adoption, including hardware refreshes and end of support life for incumbent operating systems.

UTILITY IN DESKTOP COMPUTING

The majority of desktop users are Windows users. As such we are familiar with a group of applications that is common to all Windows users; these are sometimes referred to as core applications. This core set of applications are often complimented with media players, image viewers, and games. These ancillary applications are often a convenience or diversion rather than a requirement for the desktop users to adequately complete their jobs. *Does a waitress who uses an ordering system in a restaurant need to browse the Web or check her email? Does a paper mill worker who checks production statistics need to view jpeg images or play solitaire?*

In many manufacturing plants, software may be twenty years old and run on dumb terminals serviced by a central server. The problem that many enterprises face is that they are reliant on terminals and systems that are proprietary. The dumb terminals may have terminal emulation protocols running on them to allow them to communicate with servers. Manufacturers may no longer make replacement terminals and parts, new computers may be overkill for very basic needs, and specialized equipment doesn't benefit from the costs of a commodity PC. So IT decision makers are saddled with the decision to update to overpowered and expensive equipment or to buy scarcely available equipment replacements.

Some companies may have basic desktop computing needs that entail email and word processing only. Several may just require a desktop browser. These companies may find that computers with fast processors and loads of disk space may offer substantially more than a typical user will ever need. That's why the idea of utility in desktop computing is very important, especially in the large enterprise or government installation where an extra couple of hundred dollars per seat translates into millions of dollars in the form of thousands of underutilized computers.

The Linux operating system is very portable, and it runs on a wide variety of hardware including Intel, MIPS, ARM, Solaris, PPC, and many, many others. The ability to run an operating system that can be customized to a variety of hardware and be pared down or beefed up to meet the needs of the end user offers a powerful one-two punch for supplying solutions that best match the needs of an end user. Understanding that you dictate the needs of your enterprise, not the software vendor, is probably your first step in success of a Linux installation. You need to make your shopping list and then go about the task of identifying the vendor most suited to your needs. If you feel that you have the skills needed to do so, you can go to the software bazaar available on the Internet and download the parts you need to make a successful Linux installation. Otherwise the highly competitive Linux distribution market may have a solution that can be best matched to your needs.

STAGING OPEN SOURCE APPLICATIONS ON WINDOWS

Before you even consider your move to Linux you should consider what open source applications could be used in place of costly commercial Windows applications. There are a number of applications that you could be using today that will allow desktop users to maintain their productivity and save your IT budget substantial licensing fees. It can also set the stage for further adoption by minimizing the learning curve for users migrating operating systems, as the native Linux applications and those that are cross platform will perform almost identically, as Figure 3.2 illustrates.

Office Suites

For clerical and administrative workers, office suites are probably the most frequently used tool. There are a number of cross-platform alternatives to the pervasive Microsoft Office Suite. The open source alternative that seems to be the best equivalent is the OpenOffice.org suite (a commercial version of this package is Sun's StarOffice), which includes the same type of applications you would expect to find in your current office suite: word processor, spreadsheet, database, and presentation software. Many alternative office suites can read other formats; for example, OpenOffice.org can read both the Microsoft Document and Excel Spreadsheet formats, with the exception of macros. Migration of documents from one format to another is as easy as opening a document in one format and saving in the new format. To avoid confusion, a good practice is to define a set of document standards across the enterprise before migration or introduction of an alter-

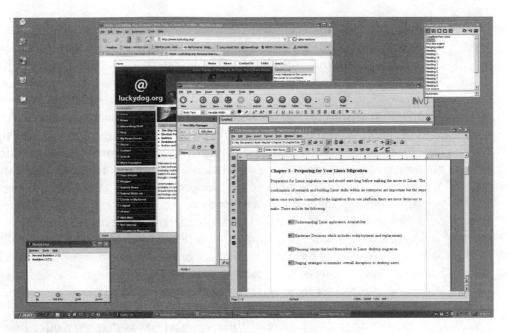

FIGURE 3.2 Open source applications Firefox, OpenOffice.org, GIMP, and Nvu running on Windows XP are also available for Linux.

native office suite. Where OpenOffice.org shines is that it is stable and can open legacy Microsoft Office document formats, so moving from one Office suite to another is very manageable. Documents that don't translate well can be exported into Portable Document Format (PDF) to maintain their formatting.

Proceed with caution. Overall interoperability between Microsoft Office and OpenOffice.org is good. The one feature that does not translate when migrating from Microsoft Office to OpenOffice.org is macros. Macros included in Microsoft Office files are usually written in Visual Basic which doesn't run natively on Linux. There are no open source equivalents that let you run these macros even though OpenOffice.org does have its own macro capabilities. Your best course of action if you have legacy documents that rely on these macros is to rewrite the macros under the OpenOffice.org applications and run Microsoft native applications using one of the Windows to Linux migration products discussed in Chapter 10. Another area that may have problems is formatting of embedded OLE objects such as tables of contents and indices.

Web Browsers

Internet Explorer (IE) has played a dominant role in desktop Web surfing, largely due to its tight integration with the Windows operating system. However, it hasn't always ruled the roost with respect to Internet browsers. Netscape at one point dominated the Web as the most popular Web browsers, but the progression by Microsoft to assimilate Internet Explorer as a core component of the Windows operating system has led to IE dominance. The tables once again are starting to turn. Developers have been working on improving the functionality of non-Microsoft browsers for years, and the latest browsers are not only available on a variety of platforms but offer a number of innovations including tab-based browsing and pop-up blocking under the Mozilla project. Additionally, there are a number of other browsers that would make good substitutes for Internet Explorer.

A reason to consider switching is due to IE's tight integration with the Windows operating system and file manager. Failure or rampant resource usage with IE can have wide system effects. Also, using an alternative browser such as Mozilla allows Windows' users to get accustomed to the package on Windows and gives them one less thing to learn as they adopt Linux.

Another attractive feature of these applications is that they offer innovative features that make it into their products much more quickly than new features appear in IE. For example, well before IE included pop-up blocking, Mozilla was knocking down pesky pop-up advertisements. Also, Mozilla features tab-based browsing that makes it a simple click to switch browser windows without having to maximize and minimize individual windows. The most progressive browser of the Mozilla clan is the Firefox browser version 1.0 (shown in Figure 3.3) that was released on November 9, 2004.

The Firefox browser is a fast and highly feature-rich browser that puts most other browsers to shame. It integrates the best features of many Web browsers and makes the browser independent of the host operating system. In November 2004, OneStat.com, the number one provider of real-time Web analytics, reported that Mozilla's browsers have a total global usage share of 7.35 percent (Brinkman).

NOTE

The one area where Mozilla-based browsers do have some problems is when they run into ActiveX-dependent Web pages. ActiveX is a group of Microsoft technologies used to build interactive Web pages that tend to utilize rich multimedia. The ActiveX technology that is used commonly in Web pages doesn't always work in Mozilla and when it does, it is only by virtue of an ActiveX plug-in. This can be viewed as a mixed blessing. There is much debate about the security of ActiveX; in the past it has been used in exploits of the Windows operating system and applications. Testing critical Web pages for compatibility should be a part of your premigration checklist. This issue also illustrates the problems of using proprietary technologies that don't adhere to open standards.

FIGURE 3.3   Firefox Web browser running on Windows XP with tab-based browsing.

OpenOffice.org and Mozilla are just two examples of applications that can be staged on Windows and then utilized on Linux. Because they will have the same format for settings and documents on either operating system, implementing them on Windows makes sense from a training standpoint, once again offering small disruptions that can be part of a whole OS migration. It already starts the process of ensuring that settings can be migrated across platforms.

The OpenCD Project

The OpenCD project is an excellent way to start evaluating open source applications that may someday replace those proprietary applications that you use today. The OpenCD project (Figure 3.4) aims to introduce Microsoft Windows users to free and open source software by providing high-quality programs that would appeal to a broad audience. The thing that makes the OpenCD project interesting is that users can be educated on a variety of applications through a multimedia presentation that launches when the CD is inserted into a Windows CD-ROM drive. The applications are varied and come with a full description, screenshots, and a folder of extras that may not fall into any of the other categories.

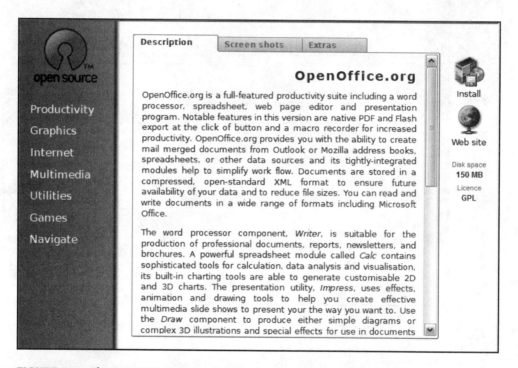

FIGURE 3.4 The OpenCD project is an ideal way to demonstrate open source applications because not only does it include the applications but it also provides tutorials and screenshots.

The OpenCD project is one of many resources that can help provide education and resources to end users well before they are asked to make the move to the Linux desktop. It also gives them an alternative to commercial Windows applications that may be costly or may pose security risks.

FILE- AND PRINT-SHARING CONVERSIONS OR ACCOMMODATIONS

Probably the first place Linux makes sense in your desktop computing infrastructure is not as a desktop operating system but as a file and print server. The Linux OS complimented by the popular SAMBA project allows computers running Linux to appear to Windows desktop servers in a way almost identical to Windows file and print servers. The advantage for Linux is that, unlike Windows server products, SAMBA doesn't include the requirements of Client Access Licenses (CALs) that are now part of Microsoft Server licensing. You can connect to Windows file and print services with Linux, but it would be wise to consult your server licensing agreement to see what the terms are. You might find that the terms of use require an access license to connect to these servers. For example, if you owned a copy of Windows XP before April 24, 2003, you may be eligible for a complimentary CAL, but after that date it may no longer be true. The only way to know for sure is to consult your licenses. Once again managing licenses is an added expense not only from the perspective of acquisition costs but also in terms of the time of the person who does the counting. In a large enterprise this might be someone's full-time job; in a small one, it may be one more time-sapping task for an overworked IT staffer.

If you switch to Linux and use SAMBA you won't need to worry about CALs. SAMBA is licensed under the GPL. This may make a significant impact on your internal licensing costs if you have to buy commercial server software and CALs today. Also, the SAMBA file and print server is not limited to run one platform. It runs on Microsoft Windows, UNIX, Linux IBM System 390, OpenVMS, and others. Samba can be deployed as a single standalone server or in more complex configurations with multiple offices and a variety of interconnected LANs.

Documentation for assembling file and print services using SAMBA is very good and there are numerous Web resources to help you understand the best practices for installing a SAMBA server or set of SAMBA servers. Just because SAMBA can be obtained with little cost doesn't mean it is inferior. On the contrary, there are many cases where Samba has been reported to outperform Windows 2000 server for file serving throughput and response time [Howorth, 2004]. Obviously there are also reports to the contrary, but it is a safe bet that you could replace Windows file and print services with Linux and have a good experience. Linux using SAMBA as an alternative to Windows server is an example of a very low-risk/high-reward situation.

HARDWARE REDEPLOY OR BUY DECISIONS

As mentioned earlier, the second of the two main Linux desktop opportunities is the decision to buy new hardware or repurpose old. A good first step is to review your current hardware inventory and determine its compatibility. By and large most pointing devices, network cards, monitors, printers, and even scanners work fine with the majority of Linux desktop distributions. The places that you run into the most problems are with the more exotic hardware like non-Palm-OS PDAs and specialty items like Bluetooth printers. You will find in many cases that there is an open source alternative that is able to connect these devices, though sometimes to a lesser extent than the manufacturer-supported software and drivers. Any time you install an operating system from scratch it requires human interaction. New PCs offer the advantage of coming imaged with the operating system.

Redeployment

Redeployment of existing hardware under Linux is one of two potential paths to take. If you are using Windows without incident today it may not be the best time to deploy Linux. However, if you are at a point where you are considering upgrades of desktop hardware, the opportunity for using Linux may have arrived. In many cases the reason for redeploying existing hardware may be that you are at the end of a support cycle for a Microsoft operating system. If you are faced with upgrading to Windows XP from Windows 98, you may be at a logical point to deploy a Linux desktop. If your computing needs haven't changed and you have relatively modest needs on the Windows operating system, you may want to consider moving at the end of your support life. To accomplish this it may be time to consider a new paradigm of computing, such as thin clients served by a Linux server, or an Linux operating system that is pared down to just the required components to extend the usable life of desktop hardware. There are also tools that could be used to automate the installation of Linux and keep labor expenses low during a redeployment.

Kickstart is a utility included in Red Hat Enterprise Linux that automates the installation. To use Kickstart administrators create a single file that answers all the questions that are asked in the installation process. The Kickstart file can be kept on a server so that multiple installs can be kicked off over the network. RHEL also includes graphical tools to create these Kickstart files through its Kickstart Configurator. Tools that automate the installation are critical for large-scale reinstallations.

Reinstallation

If you choose to deploy Linux by installing the Linux operating system on existing Windows systems, you should consider how you would preserve data and settings during this installation. The ideal solution is to provide storage on the server, then move the settings and files from the Windows desktop to the server. After you have removed all valuable files from your desktop PCs, you can then install Linux on the same hard drive. Most Linux distributions today include disk utilities to clean the drive and repartition it for Linux use. If you choose to wipe the drive clean you will lose all data and applications, so be sure you have removed all necessary information first.

There are other alternatives for installing Linux as well. During the Linux installation, you can choose to resize the Windows partition to make room for the Linux installation. Keep in mind, you may need as much as 2GB for a full-blown Linux installation with applications. If you do install Linux alongside with Windows you will be able to *dual-boot*, or choose which operating system you want to start when you power up your PC. This preserves the old installation and provides rollback so that Windows installations are left intact. Additionally, the Linux system can be configured to read or read and write to the old filesystem so documents and other data can be accessed by open source programs running under Windows. While this tactic does provide a fallback, it's really not the ideal solution, as users may not take the steps to migrate and start using the new systems as desired.

Windows and Linux use different filesystems. Windows operating systems use the FAT16, FAT32, or NTFS filesystems. Linux typically uses the ext2, ext3, ReiserFS, or a number of others. Windows doesn't have the capabilities to read the Linux filesystems, but Linux can read and write to a number of Windows filesystems. The benefit of this is that Linux installations can mount a filesystem and access the files that lie on the Windows partition. Linux can read and write to FAT filesystems reliably. Linux has experimental support for writing to NTFS, but it may not be considered to be totally reliable.

Conversion to Thin Client Setup

One way to move your desktop infrastructure to Linux may involve a paradigm shift. This shift in paradigm is from fat client computing to thin client computing. Fat client computing refers to a model like your home computer that executes programs locally on the local processor and has a hard drive where data and programs are stored. Thin client computing involves stateless PCs or thin client terminals at the workers' desks. Because processing and data is done on the server, the desktop terminal is used simply for redisplay and user input. This option is particularly attractive because you can stage the Linux installations on a central server well before the actual replacement of the Windows desktop PCs. Reducing the number of moving parts at the desktop makes the client a limited point of failure and transfers the computing and storage to a central server or bank of servers. In later chapters we will discuss the benefits of thin client computing in detail. The advantages to consider for thin client in terms of hardware redeployment can involve extending your usable hardware life and leveraging your existing IT investment, as well as letting you stage for a migration, limiting downtime as you redeploy your new infrastructure.

Repurposing Fat Clients to Thin Clients

You can buy new thin client terminals rather cheaply. Because there is no need for local storage or cutting-edge processors, they are generally cheaper than buying a new desktop PC. Though it's not necessary to do this, you can use the existing hardware to convert a system to thin client PCs. Even pre-Pentium class Intel PCs can be repurposed as Linux thin client terminals. The key components are a keyboard, mouse, processor, RAM, network card, and screen. Since the requirements for data input and redisplay are relatively modest, PCs that may otherwise have been taken out of service can now have an extended useful life as thin client or "dumb" terminals.

The Linux Terminal Server Project (LTSP) is one of the most popular Linux thin client projects. The LTSP is an ideal project for any enterprise that faces a desktop hardware and/or software refresh. As the numbers of users increases, the prospect of centralized desktop computing becomes more attractive. The general formula is to invest in servers that can serve many thin client terminals. With the price of hardware dropping to new lows, modest PCs with a fairly substantial amount of cheap RAM and plenty of storage could serve many desktop users over a network. The same money invested in a server that would yield many more desktops served than would be possible with the same expenditures on individual PCs. The way that many people take advantage of the LTSP is by running a special bootable CD locally on the PC. This converts the PC into a dumb terminal that connects back to the Linux Terminal Server where the processing takes place. The methods for accomplishing this will be discussed in later chapters. The important thing to note right now is that there is no mandate to reinstall the operating system when you repurpose your desktop computers. Also, some computers that may have had failing parts, such as disk drives, can still be useful as terminals.

END USER ACCEPTANCE

A well-implemented technology plan on its own is not a complete recipe for success. Communicating and getting stakeholder buy-in is equally important for a new implementation to go well. One notable 2003 study by Releventive AG provided data on Linux desktop usability for the city of Berlin, Germany. Their findings where that the participants enjoyed using the Linux desktop and found that productivity didn't decrease. They also found that some applications were more usable than their Windows XP equivalents and that the look and feel was accepted with little or no resistance [Muehlig03].

Environment Familiarity

There are two schools of thought on the Linux desktop. One common approach is to mimic the same core basics that computer users are familiar with under Microsoft Windows, supplanting recognizable features of the Windows desktop with Linux replacements including the Start menu, My Computer folder, and Recycle Bin. The verdict is out on whether it is a benefit to continue to adhere to a somewhat familiar standard or whether it's better to capitalize on the opportunity an open system brings to completely reinvent the desktop. Some innovations on Linux may bring about changes more drastic than any other operating system.

Technology Acceptance Model

The Technology Acceptance Model (TAM) was developed by Bagozzi, Davis, and Warshaw, who believed that technology acceptance was influenced by two significant measures: usefulness and ease-of-use. They said that technologies such as the PC are complicated and that an element of doubt exists among those strategists trying to implement a successful adoption. They noted that users of these technologies form preconceived notions and develop expectations before learning the technology. Their attitudes may be negative or they may not have the conviction that they would with older established solutions, and their actual usage of these technologies may be influenced by these preconceived notions [Bagozzi92]. Bagozzi and company also went on to describe the idea of *perceived usefulness* (PU) and *perceived ease of use* (EOU). Perceived usefulness is the degree to which a person believes that a new system or solution will add value to his job or improve his ability to perform, and perceived ease-of-use is the level of belief that a system will be free from effort. If Davis is right about perception influencing outcomes, it's only natural for the IT staff to offer some salesmanship on the subject. Making end users aware of the potential benefits can help influence the outcome. When you train your staff or present the new operating system, do it in a very positive light. Inform users of the lower risk of crashes, give them examples of the uptime of Linux, and maybe even explain to them how you can push out critical updates to their operating systems without the need to reboot them every time. Give them lots of evidence that this switch to Linux can improve their overall productivity, and you will probably find it will.

SUMMARY

A successful Linux migration starts with planning. Staging cross-platform open source applications on Windows before migrating will shorten the learning curve when switching to Linux. The most successful Linux installations will most likely coincide with the procurement of new hardware or operating system refreshes. Looking at alternatives like thin client computing can leverage existing PCs and extend their usable life. Combining Linux migration and other disruptive events will likely provide the best options for a successful enterprise migration.

OTHER RESOURCES

- OpenOffice.org—*www.openoffice.org*
- Sun's StarOffice—*http://wwws.sun.com/software/star/staroffice/index.html*
- Firefox—*www.mozilla.org/products/firefox/*
- The Mozilla Project—*www.mozilla.org*
- WINE—*www.winehq.com*
- VMware—*www.vmware.com*
- Win4Lin—*www.win4lin.com*
- Microsoft Active X Controls Home Page—*www.microsoft.com/com/default.mspx*
- SAMBA—*www.samba.org*
- Windows Terminal Server—*www.microsoft.com/windowsserver2003/technologies/terminalservices/default.mspx*
- Windows Client Access Licensing—*www.microsoft.com/windowsserver2003/howtobuy/licensing/caloverview.mspx*
- Linux Terminal Server Project—*www.ltsp.org*
- Red Hat Linux—*www.redhat.com*
- ACPI4Linux—*www.acpi4linux.com*

REFERENCES

[Bagozzi92] Bagozzi, R. P., Davis, F. D., & Warshaw, P. R. "Development and Test of a Theory of Technological Learning and Usage." *Human Relations* (1992) pp. 660-686.

[Brinkman] Brinkman, Neils, OneStat, *http://www.onestat.com/html/aboutus_pressbox34.html.*

[Howorth03] Howorth, Roger, "Samba Extends Lead Over Win 2003," *ITWeek* (October 14, 2003). Available online at *http://www.itweek.co.uk/itweek/news/2085218/samba-extends-lead-win-2003.*

Intel, Intel Centrino Support Website, *http://support.intel.com/support/notebook/ centrino/*.

[Muehllig03] Muehllig, Jan, Brucherseifer, Eva, & Ackerman, Ralf, "Linux Usability Study," relevanceAG (August 13, 2003). Available online at *http://www. linux-usability.de/download/linux_usability_report_en.pdf*.

Part
II
Linux Desktop
Deployment Tactics

Deploying a Linux distribution can be both trying and rewarding as it pushes IT staff to learn new technologies and feel the frustration of using unfamiliar technology. Understanding the benefits of a new installation at both the IT staffer level and the end user desktop and clearly articulating those benefits will increase the chances of success. A desktop operating system refresh is perhaps the most unique type of software installation because its effects are immediately felt throughout the organization. A well-executed strategy can improve desktop computing productivity through both perceived and actual improvements in the work environment.

Over the course of the next few chapters the discussion will cover both limited commitment installations and complete fat client operating system replacements. First we will examine limited commitment installations through Linux live filesystem CD-ROMs that offer opportunities for both low-risk desktop Linux piloting and experimentation. Other strategies for replacements will offer comparisons between operating systems and applications, outlining both benefits and disadvantages of the various options.

This book will talk about methods of deployment, but it is no substitute for the documentation that accompanies your Linux system. It should be used in conjunction with the "how-to" documentation to maximize desktop Linux success. Overall this section is meant as a guide to where to look for information or what areas merit additional research. You will also find that applications as they appear in this book will be rapidly updated by a community of developers dedicated to making improvements every day.

4 Live Linux CD-ROMs

In This Chapter

- Live Linux Filesystem CD-ROM Distributions
- How Live Linux CD-ROMs Work
- Linux Test Drive
- IT Tool Kit with Linux
- Repurposing Windows PCs
- Building your own Linux Live Filesystem CD-ROM Distribution
- Summary
- Other Resources
- References

You have read to this point about the many things that make Linux an attractive operating system, including its flexibility and almost infinite number of configurations. However nothing drives the point home more than experimenting with the software. With this chapter we begin the technical content of this book, geared to the practitioner who wants to begin taking advantage of the capabilities of Linux. As someone who is new to Linux you may find that having a system that can be brought online quickly would be of great value for your research. Live Linux CD-ROMs like the one included with this book can help you start to familiarize yourself with Linux and the complimentary open source applications. The Live Linux CD-ROM executes from the CD-ROM and loads into random access memory (RAM). It doesn't install on your hard drive unless you specify that it do so. Many of

ON THE CD

the popular Linux distributions, such as Novell and Mandriva, have Live Linux CD-ROM demos of their products. You can use these to make a "try before you buy" CD. A live Linux CD can serve many functions that would be helpful to an IT manager including any one or all of the following:

Linux Test Drive: Knoppix can be used to open office documents on your hard drive, try applications, and help familiarize you with the Linux operating system without a full Linux commitment.

Portable Toolkit: Sometimes due to operating system failures, it is no longer possible to boot from your operating system. Booting with a live filesystem CD-ROM can allow you to boot the computer and make repairs to the permanently installed operating system.

Repurposing PCs: PCs with failing hard drives can still be used by booting them from a CD-ROM. Damaged PCs can be used as workstations for the user with modest needs even without replacing the flawed hardware.

These are only a few of many uses for bootable Linux CD-ROM distributions. These CD-ROMs can provide tools to accomplish a number of tasks. In the case of the enterprise looking to migrate to Linux, it will be invaluable for your pre-migration planning.

LIVE LINUX FILESYSTEM CD-ROM DISTRIBUTIONS

ON THE CD

This book includes the popular Knoppix Live Linux CD-ROM, which is one of the most widely-used bootable Linux distributions. However there are many types of live Linux CD-ROM distributions. Each one is bootable from a CD-ROM drive but each one addresses different, specific goals. There is a growing number of special-purpose distributions that may be better suited for one purpose over another. Morphix, as shown in Figure 4.1, is designed to be customized, or *morphed*, to the format that best serves the end user.

Gnoppix is very similar to Knoppix, but rather than using the KDE desktop environment, Gnoppix uses the GNOME desktop environment. If you are contemplating using the GNOME desktop included with most Linux distributions, you may want to evaluate the Gnoppix distribution for an adequate test drive of the GNOME desktop. As shown in Figure 4.2, the GNOME desktop is very similar to the Windows or Apple Macintosh environments.

Knoppix-STD is a security-oriented version of Knoppix; STD actually stands for *security tools distribution*. Figure 4.3 offers a different presentation than Morphix because it is not designed for desktop productivity but for security auditing.

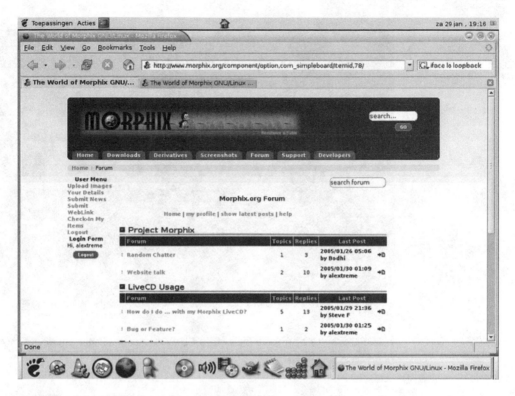

FIGURE 4.1   Morphix bootable CD-ROM is designed for customization because it can be easily morphed into new configurations.

MEPIS is designed both as a Live Linux CD-ROM and as an installation CD-ROM. MEPIS is focused on ease of use for migrating small business Linux users. MEPIS comes in two versions: SimplyMEPIS for the novice and ProMEPIS for the business professional. SimplyMEPIS, shown in Figure 4.4, offers a very clean interface and documentation at your fingertips.

The Linux Bootable Business Card (LNX-BBC) is a 50 MB distribution designed to fit on a business card–sized CD-ROM. The aim is to provide a portable rescue disk that can easily be carried in a wallet and used whenever trouble arises. The LNX-BBC is the smallest of the Linux distributions mentioned here and, while it can run in graphical mode, the majority of practical applications for this distribution happen on the command line.

Pointing out the different distributions available for your free download and use illustrates not only the flexibility of the operating system but also the resources you can acquire with little more investment than your time.

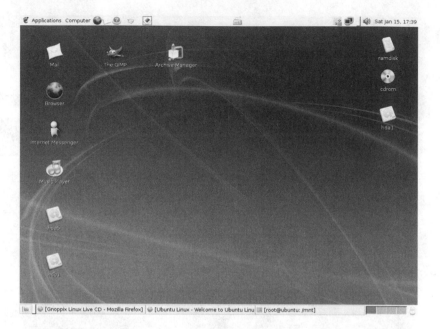

FIGURE 4.2   Gnoppix live filesystem CD-ROM has a similar environment to Windows or Mac OS.

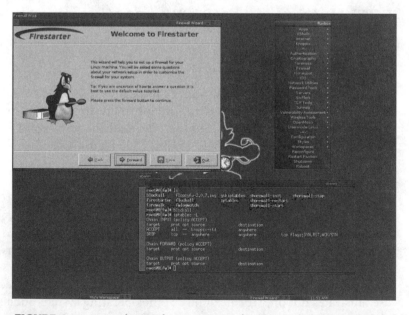

FIGURE 4.3   Knoppix-STD is a remastered version of Knoppix outfitted with computer forensics and security tools.

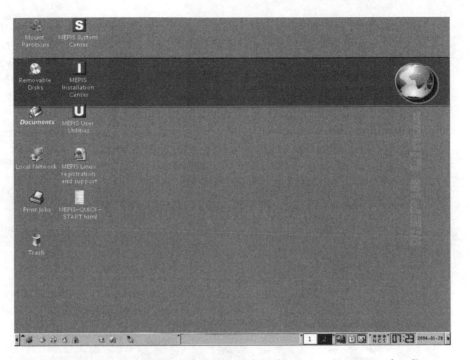

FIGURE 4.4 SimplyMEPIS includes a similar desktop experience to other live filesystem CDs as well as documentation.

HOW LIVE LINUX CD-ROMS WORK

Live Linux CD-ROMs work by reading a compressed filesystem from the CD-ROM into random access memory. Combined with the ability to use on-the-fly decompression and automatic hardware detection, the bootable Linux CD-ROM reads the operating system into memory then autodetects hardware to offer a very functional operating system that doesn't need to write to a permanent hard disk. Instead it saves temporarily (for the length of the session) the settings and files it needs in a RAM disk. The minimum requirements to run Knoppix are an Intel-compatible CPU (i486 or later) and twenty megabytes of RAM, though the more RAM the better. This is especially the case if you want to run business productivity programs like OpenOffice.org, which has a recommended minimum of at least 128MB of RAM. You'll also need a bootable CD-ROM drive, a standard SVGA-compatible graphics card, and a PS/2 or USB mouse. Once booted, the Knoppix CD-ROM allows the PC to function the same way that a traditional PC does with the operating system installed on a hard drive. Ideally Knoppix will recognize the hardware on the PC, but in some cases the Knoppix CD-ROM doesn't recognize every piece of equipment. That's not a terminal problem; the Knoppix boot procedure allows you to pass "cheat codes" that tell Knoppix and other live filesystem CD-ROM distributions how to behave with respect to certain hardware. More information is available on this option in Appendix D. However, the best thing about Knoppix is its portability and noninvasive nature. As Figure 4.5 points out, any system information that is needed is kept in RAM and is destroyed upon reboot.

How A Live Linux CD ROM Works

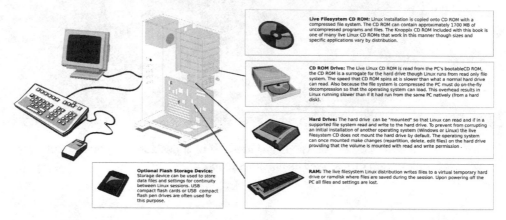

FIGURE 4.5   Illustration of how a Live Linux CD-ROM operates.

In addition to cheat codes, Appendix D of this book includes a quick-start guide to help you understand the basics of using Knoppix. This guide will cover how to start Knoppix and navigate within the operating system. It may be useful to read the guide before using the CD-ROM to accomplish any of the following tasks.

LINUX TEST DRIVE

Wouldn't it be nice to test every new IT system in detail before you buy it? That way you could address any user concerns and incompatibilities before switching over production systems. In many cases when you make enterprise changes you can't be sure that everything will work until it's rolled out. Sometimes you can bring up a system in tandem with a legacy system, but many times it's not practical to do so. Now consider what kind of effect a new operating system will have on your enterprise desktop users. Lost productivity and other failures could cripple operations. The ability to test and evaluate desktop applications without a commitment to desktop OS replacement is an attractive tool to those evaluating a move to Linux.

Evaluating Applications and Document Compatibility

One of the early steps recommended for your desktop migration is to identify applications that can be substituted for the native Linux applications. The bootable Live Linux CD-ROM is a great indicator of what is available for the Linux operating system. It requires very little investment of time, and setup is virtually flawless. To actually see the Linux desktop in action you simply pop the CD-ROM in the drive and reboot (providing the PC is set to boot from the CD-ROM drive before the hard drive). The system will boot into a functional Linux desktop, as shown in Figure 4.6.

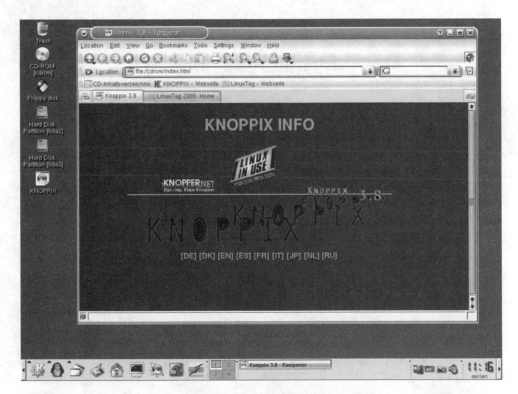

FIGURE 4.6   The Knoppix desktop is very similar to Windows XP with a Start button and applications that can be launched from the toolbar or "kicker."

Testing Office Document Compatibility with Linux

Testing the OpenOffice.org suite as a replacement for Microsoft Office is likely one of the first places you will want to investigate for compatibility. If you store your office documents locally you can use OpenOffice.org to open Microsoft Office documents and make sure that they are readable and editable. To do this you simple navigate to where your documents are stored by looking on the Knoppix desktop at the hard drive icons. If you have one partition, clicking on it will allow you to open the hard drive and see the partition that houses your Windows installation. Once open, you can navigate to your My Documents folder using Konqueror. You can then launch OpenOffice.org as shown in Figure 4.7 to see if the document is readable in OpenOffice.org Writer.

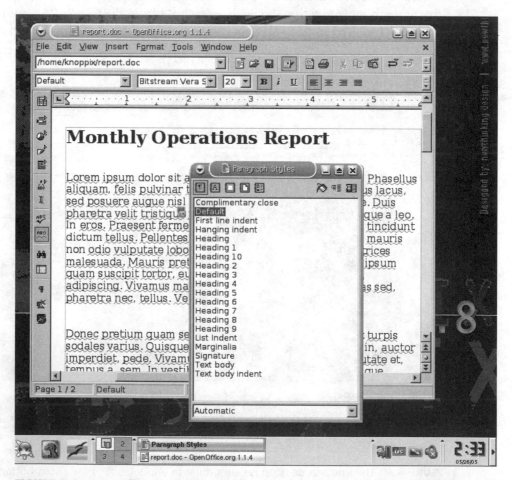

FIGURE 4.7   OpenOffice.org's Writer can be used to open a Word document that was created in Microsoft Office and resides on the hard drive.

Training Labs

Bootable Linux distributions solve one of the problems many organizations have with regards to training. If you are lucky enough to have facilities complete with dedicated training computers it's very likely that these computers run some variety of Windows. Setting up a Linux training lab could be very time consuming, but it doesn't have to be so. You can burn copies of a bootable Linux CD-ROM and convert your current machines to temporary Linux workstations. Also, this doesn't commit the PCs to full-time Linux duty, so you get multiple uses out of the PCs. Figure 4.8 shows a lab using the Knoppix CD-ROMs to convert each PC into a Linux thick client. You can also connect the PCs to a terminal server in thin client mode, as we will demonstrate later in this chapter.

Converting a Windows Training Lab with Live Linux CD-ROMs

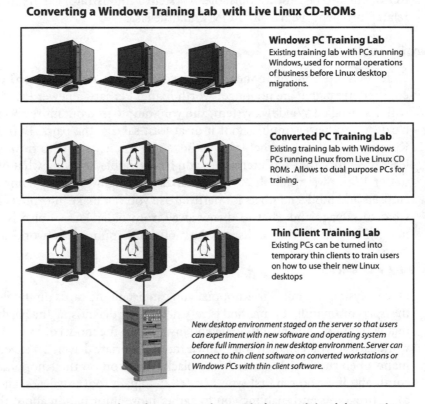

Windows PC Training Lab
Existing training lab with PCs running Windows, used for normal operations of business before Linux desktop migrations.

Converted PC Training Lab
Existing training lab with Windows PCs running Linux from Live Linux CD ROMs . Allows to dual purpose PCs for training.

Thin Client Training Lab
Existing PCs can be turned into temporary thin clients to train users on how to use their new Linux desktops

New desktop environment staged on the server so that users can experiment with new software and operating system before full immersion in new desktop environment. Server can connect to thin client software on converted workstations or Windows PCs with thin client software.

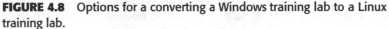

FIGURE 4.8 Options for a converting a Windows training lab to a Linux training lab.

Getting stakeholder buy in, as we mentioned earlier, is very important for the success of a migration. Providing training and at least a test drive before moving to Linux can give you at least a chance to sell the perceived value of a solution in a non-confrontational environment such as a training lab. Also, this is a good time to start listening to end user objections and planning how to overcome those objections.

IT TOOL KIT WITH LINUX

The Knoppix CD-ROM comes with productivity applications as well as a robust set of tools. When a Linux system fails, the bootable Linux CD-ROM can be used to repair the operating system or at least rescue data from the system. This invaluable tool is useful not only because of the variety of applications included on the CD-ROM, but also because it's portable. A system administrator can fix many software-related problems with a CD-ROM and little else.

Diagnostic Tools

Older PCs often end up in the back of a storage room after they stop booting or encounter errors that are no longer worth fixing. Perhaps a newer PC stops working with its installed Windows system, and you want to find out more about the system hardware to better troubleshoot it or at least salvage the parts. Booting from the Knoppix CD-ROM can help you gather some forensics data to troubleshoot or at least inventory the PC. Often times you have trouble knowing what driver to load under Windows; using the tools under Linux might give you some insight into chipsets and model numbers for hardware so you can make informed choices about what to salvage and what to throw away from older PCs. It also is helpful with newer PCs when trying to discern the model of a sound or network card.

Identifying PCI Cards

Once a system is booted in Knoppix, you can list all the cards on the PCI bus using the *lspci* command. This method is very helpful for diagnosing the hardware in a PC that won't boot, potentially giving you insight into the model of a video card or network card so you can then track down the appropriate driver. To execute the command open the Linux terminal (the black CRT icon on the Knoppix bar). At the command line you can first type *su <enter>* to gain root privileges, allowing access to all programs and enabling you to gather more information about the PC. Once you have root access, go to the command line interface by clicking the black screen terminal on the Knoppix toolbar. Then type *lspci –v*. The *ls* is short for list, *pci* means the application should look at the PCI bus, and *–v* sets the verbose switch so that you get more information. Listing 4.1 shows the listing for a laptop computer.

LISTING 4.1   Code Listing in Title Case

```
knoppix@1[knoppix]$ lspci -v
0000:00:00.0 Host bridge: Intel Corp.
82845G/GL[Brookdale-G]/GE/PE DRAM Control ler/Host-Hub Interface (rev
03)
        Flags: bus master, fast devsel, latency 0
        Memory at e0000000 (32-bit, prefetchable) [size=256M]
        Capabilities: <available only to root>

0000:00:01.0 PCI bridge: Intel Corp.
82845G/GL[Brookdale-G]/GE/PE Host-to-AGP B ridge (rev 03) (prog-if 00
[Normal decode])
        Flags: bus master, 66MHz, fast devsel, latency 96
        Bus: primary=00, secondary=01, subordinate=01,
sec-latency=32
        I/O behind bridge: 00003000-00003fff
        Memory behind bridge: d0100000-d01fffff
        Prefetchable memory behind bridge:
d8000000-dfffffff

0000:00:1d.0 USB Controller: Intel Corp. 82801DB/DBL/DBM
(ICH4/ICH4-L/ICH4-M) U
SB UHCI Controller #1 (rev 02) (prog-if 00 [UHCI])
        Subsystem: COMPAL Electronics Inc: Unknown device
0012
        Flags: bus master, medium devsel, latency 0, IRQ 16
        I/O ports at 1800 [size=32]

0000:00:1d.1 USB Controller: Intel Corp. 82801DB/DBL/DBM
(ICH4/ICH4-L/ICH4-M) U
SB UHCI Controller #2 (rev 02) (prog-if 00 [UHCI])
        Subsystem: COMPAL Electronics Inc: Unknown device
0012
        Flags: bus master, medium devsel, latency 0, IRQ 19
        I/O ports at 1820 [size=32]

0000:00:1d.2 USB Controller: Intel Corp. 82801DB/DBL/DBM
(ICH4/ICH4-L/ICH4-M) U
SB UHCI Controller #3 (rev 02) (prog-if 00 [UHCI])
        Subsystem: COMPAL Electronics Inc: Unknown device
0012
        Flags: bus master, medium devsel, latency 0, IRQ 18
        I/O ports at 1840 [size=32]
```

```
0000:00:1d.7 USB Controller: Intel Corp. 82801DB/DBM
(ICH4/ICH4-M) USB 2.0 EHCI
 Controller (rev 02) (prog-if 20 [EHCI])
        Subsystem: COMPAL Electronics Inc: Unknown device
0012
        Flags: bus master, medium devsel, latency 0, IRQ 23
        Memory at d0000000 (32-bit, non-prefetchable) [size=1K]
        Capabilities: <available only to root>

0000:00:1e.0 PCI bridge: Intel Corp. 82801 PCI Bridge (rev
82) (prog-if 00 [Nor
mal decode])
        Flags: bus master, fast devsel, latency 0
        Bus: primary=00, secondary=02, subordinate=02,
sec-latency=32
        I/O behind bridge: 00004000-00004fff
        Memory behind bridge: d0200000-d02fffff
        Prefetchable memory behind bridge:
f0000000-f00fffff

0000:00:1f.0 ISA bridge: Intel Corp. 82801DB/DBL
(ICH4/ICH4-L) LPC Bridge (rev
02)
        Flags: bus master, medium devsel, latency 0

0000:00:1f.1 IDE interface: Intel Corp. 82801DB/DBL
(ICH4/ICH4-L) UltraATA-100
IDE Controller (rev 02) (prog-if 8a [Master SecP PriP])
        Subsystem: COMPAL Electronics Inc: Unknown device
0012
        Flags: bus master, medium devsel, latency 0, IRQ 18
        I/O ports at <unassigned>
        I/O ports at <unassigned>
        I/O ports at <unassigned>
        I/O ports at <unassigned>
        I/O ports at 1860 [size=16]
        Memory at 20000000 (32-bit, non-prefetchable) [size=1K]

0000:00:1f.3 SMBus: Intel Corp. 82801DB/DBL/DBM
(ICH4/ICH4-L/ICH4-M) SMBus Cont
roller (rev 02)
        Subsystem: COMPAL Electronics Inc: Unknown device
0012
```

```
        Flags: medium devsel, IRQ 9
        I/O ports at 1880 [size=32]

0000:00:1f.5 Multimedia audio controller: Intel Corp.
82801DB/DBL/DBM (ICH4/ICH
4-L/ICH4-M) AC'97 Audio Controller (rev 02)
        Subsystem: COMPAL Electronics Inc: Unknown device
0017
        Flags: bus master, medium devsel, latency 0, IRQ 17
        I/O ports at 1c00 [size=256]
        I/O ports at 18c0 [size=64]
        Memory at d0000c00 (32-bit, non-prefetchable) [size=512]
        Memory at d0000800 (32-bit, non-prefetchable) [size=256]
        Capabilities: <available only to root>

0000:00:1f.6 Modem: Intel Corp. 82801DB/DBL/DBM
(ICH4/ICH4-L/ICH4-M) AC'97 Mode
m Controller (rev 02) (prog-if 00 [Generic])
        Subsystem: COMPAL Electronics Inc: Unknown device
0012
        Flags: bus master, medium devsel, latency 0, IRQ 17
        I/O ports at 2400 [size=256]
        I/O ports at 2000 [size=128]
        Capabilities: <available only to root>

0000:01:00.0 VGA compatible controller: ATI Technologies Inc Radeon
R250 Lf [Ra deon Mobility 9000 M9] (rev 01) (prog-if 00 [VGA])
        Subsystem: COMPAL Electronics Inc: Unknown device
0012
      Flags: bus master, stepping, fast Back2Back, 66MHz, medium
devsel, late ncy 66, IRQ 16
        Memory at d8000000 (32-bit, prefetchable) [size=128M]
        I/O ports at 3000 [size=256]
        Memory at d0100000 (32-bit, non-prefetchable) [size=64K]
        Capabilities: <available only to root>

0000:02:00.0 FireWire (IEEE 1394): VIA Technologies, Inc.
IEEE 1394 Host Contro
ller (rev 80) (prog-if 10 [OHCI])
        Subsystem: Texas Instruments: Unknown device 0012
        Flags: bus master, medium devsel, latency 32, IRQ
```

```
16
        Memory at d0200000 (32-bit, non-prefetchable) [size=2K]
        I/O ports at 4400 [size=128]
        Capabilities: <available only to root>


0000:02:01.0 Ethernet controller: Realtek Semiconductor Co., Ltd. RTL-
8139/8139 C/8139C+ (rev 10)
        Subsystem: Texas Instruments: Unknown device 0012
        Flags: bus master, medium devsel, latency 32, IRQ
17
        I/O ports at 4000 [size=256]
        Memory at d0200800 (32-bit, non-prefetchable) [size=256]
        Capabilities: <available only to root>


0000:02:02.0 Network controller: Intersil Corporation Prism
2.5 Wavelan chipset (rev 01)
        Subsystem: Askey Computer Corp.: Unknown device 7000
        Flags: bus master, medium devsel, latency 32, IRQ
18
        Memory at f0000000 (32-bit, prefetchable) [size=4K]
        Capabilities: <available only to root>


0000:02:04.0 CardBus bridge: O2 Micro, Inc. OZ6912 Cardbus Controller
        Subsystem: COMPAL Electronics Inc: Unknown device
0012
        Flags: bus master, stepping, slow devsel, latency 168, IRQ 16
        Memory at 20001000 (32-bit, non-prefetchable) [size=4K]
        Bus: primary=02, secondary=03, subordinate=06,
sec-latency=176
        Memory window 0: 20400000-207ff000 (prefetchable)
        Memory window 1: 20800000-20bff000
        I/O window 0: 00004800-000048ff
        I/O window 1: 00004c00-00004cff
        16-bit legacy interface ports at 0001
```

Listing 4.1 provides a great deal of information about the PC. Each line is a clue to help you track down what hardware is in the PC and where to start looking for drivers. Admittedly, this method is a little more complex than what most of us are familiar with under Windows. In Windows there is very good hardware support because vendors provide drivers for Windows; these same vendors support Linux to a lesser degree if at all. In Windows you would most likely use the *Device Manager* to view hardware information, as illustrated in Figure 4.9.

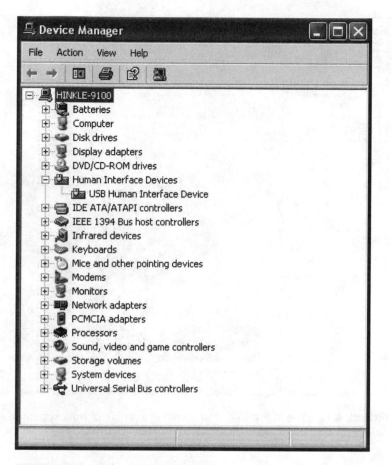

FIGURE 4.9   Device Manager is used to get information about system hardware in Windows, while Linux has a number of methods to derive that information.

In the KDE desktop environment you can also look at a graphical representation of the system hardware in a way very similar to the Windows Device Manager. There are many tools that can show certain operating system attributes including processor type, how memory is being used, PCMCIA, and USB devices. For example, the *KDE Info Center*, included with Knoppix as part of the KDE desktop, can provide much of the same data and more about the Linux desktop as shown in Figure 4.10.

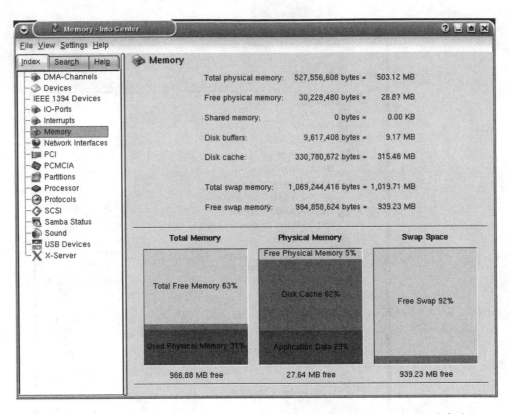

FIGURE 4.10 The KDE Info Center showing a profile of how system memory is being used.

There are many other ways to diagnose your existing PC other than the examples above. A quick search of the Internet is likely to yield tips and tricks for querying other hardware.

Disk Tools

The Knoppix disk can be used to manipulate partitions and delete, alter, or create files. The disk tools included on the Knoppix CD-ROM are so plentiful that you can choose which tool you want to use for the task. However, the graphical tool you may find most familiar is QTParted.

Partitioning

The disk tool that is probably most intuitive to a Windows user is called *QTParted*. It is very similar to the Windows tool PartitionMagic® made by Symantec. The QT-

Parted program is a graphical interface to a Linux disk tool called *parted*. QT refers to the QT graphical tools that are used to build and display the GUI interface. By using QTparted you can look at the disk structure and add, delete, or resize partitions on a hard disk drive. The QTparted program is very handy for wiping and repartitioning an existing disk, though there are reports that this program is not necessarily of equivalent quality to a commercial product, and its developers claim that it is still in developmental stages. QTParted, as illustrated in Figure 4.11, is a graphical tool that is more intuitive and easier to use than partitioning hard drives on the command line.

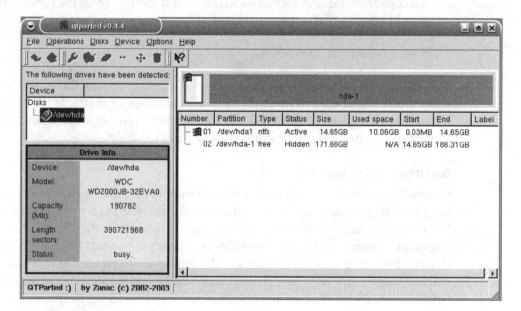

FIGURE 4.11 QTParted recognizes the Windows partition as a filesystem of type NTFS.

Cloning a Hard Drive

Sometimes when you do something in Windows you end up navigating an endless array of menus and Ok buttons. One of the nice features of a Live Linux CD-ROM is that you can simply do something in a straight forward manner from the Linux command line. If you recall, QTParted was described as a graphical tool to resize and partition your hard drive. If you use that tool to look at your disk geometry you can see certain partitions and their sizes. The Linux *dd* command is an excellent way to clone a hard drive partition for backup and QTParted is an easy way to find out what the device names of the partitions are.

For example, imagine that you want to make an exact copy of your hard drive to a USB drive for backup. You open QTParted to discern the drive that you want to clone, then you can directly copy from one partition to the other. You might have a 20 GB hard drive that is */dev/hda* (first device on the IDE controller) and a USB drive */dev/sda* (first SCSI device on the SCSI bus). To make an exact copy, while booted from Knoppix you would go to a prompt and type the following command at the shell prompt:

```
# dd if=/dev/hda of=/dev/sda
```

To copy from the first hard drive to the second hard drive on the IDE controller you would enter the following command:

```
# dd if=/dev/hda of=/dev/hdb
```

The *dd* command is useful because it makes an exact copy of the contents of the drive to the target drive. This is the most rudimentary of methods for creating a backup; you could also do incremental backups and other more sophisticated operations by mastering Linux commands like *rsynch* and *diff*.

Repairing Filesystem Errors

Some of the most commonly used tools in Windows disk management are those related to defragmentation. However, under Linux there isn't an exact equivalent. In DOS-based systems such as Windows 95 and Windows 98 there is no disk usage map kept in memory. Newly created files are written to the next free block and then through the next available free space and the process keeps repeating. This was an inefficient way to write data. With Linux there is more optimization in the way files are written. This added intelligence prevents fragmentation to the degree that you see with Windows. There is no way in Linux to defragment a Windows filesystem with the same level of stability as natively running Windows applications, so the included Knoppix CD-ROM won't be of much use for that task. However, the filesystem under Linux is not without its flaws. Sometimes when a Linux system is shutdown improperly there are problems with the filesystem as a result of an incomplete transaction. Journaling filesystems track these transactions and make decisions as to the what they should check for errors. Other types of filesystems may have to check the whole volume to determine an error, which can take a significant amount of time. In later chapters we will discuss the difference between journaling and other filesystem types. In the mean time, if you run into a case where your Linux filesystem reports errors upon booting, the *fsck* utility can be used to check the integrity of the filesystems. If, upon exiting the fsck program, the code 0 flashes then there were no errors found. If the code is a number 1, then the filesystem was corrected; if the number is 2 then the system should be rebooted; and if the code is 3 then the system had errors that were corrected and it needs rebooted. The exit codes are the sum of codes returned by fsck. If the number is something other than 1, 2, or 3 you can type *man fsck* to find out what those codes mean.

The man command followed by another command starts the man page documentation system included with Linux. Man pages are the documents that are used to give you quick access to help. Admittedly these pages can be confusing to someone used to pointing and clicking, but once you start to understand the format of the pages they often provide a quick reference for the actual syntax needed to accomplish a task.

Rescuing Data from a Workstation

When a PC fails due to operating system problems, the solution for rescuing the data is often very complex. Repairing the operating system is usually very time consuming and sometimes impossible. Also, data could be lost while making repairs. A good analogy is that when a person hurts his neck it's inadvisable to move him because he could become paralyzed by a mistake in the rescue process. With Knoppix you can immobilize the patient (your desktop PC) making no changes to the operating system or data while extracting backups of the files. Booting the PC from CD-ROM and then copying files can insure that critical data is preserved.

Moving Files to a Windows PC or File Server

Perhaps you have a PC running a Microsoft operating system that will no longer boot correctly. Before attempting to repair or reinstall the operating system, you may want to rescue any data. This is a wise idea because the rescue could result in lost data. Using the Knoppix CD-ROM for data rescue, especially in a Windows network, is simple to do and could prevent a later disaster. In the case of a Windows network, you have many Linux tools at your disposal to adequately preserve your data and repair your Windows PC.

The first step is to boot into Knoppix to evaluate the situation and to gain network connectivity. The second is to browse the network for your file server. The *LinNeighborhood* program included with Knoppix is a great way to drag and drop files to another Windows PC or file server, as shown in Figure 4.12.

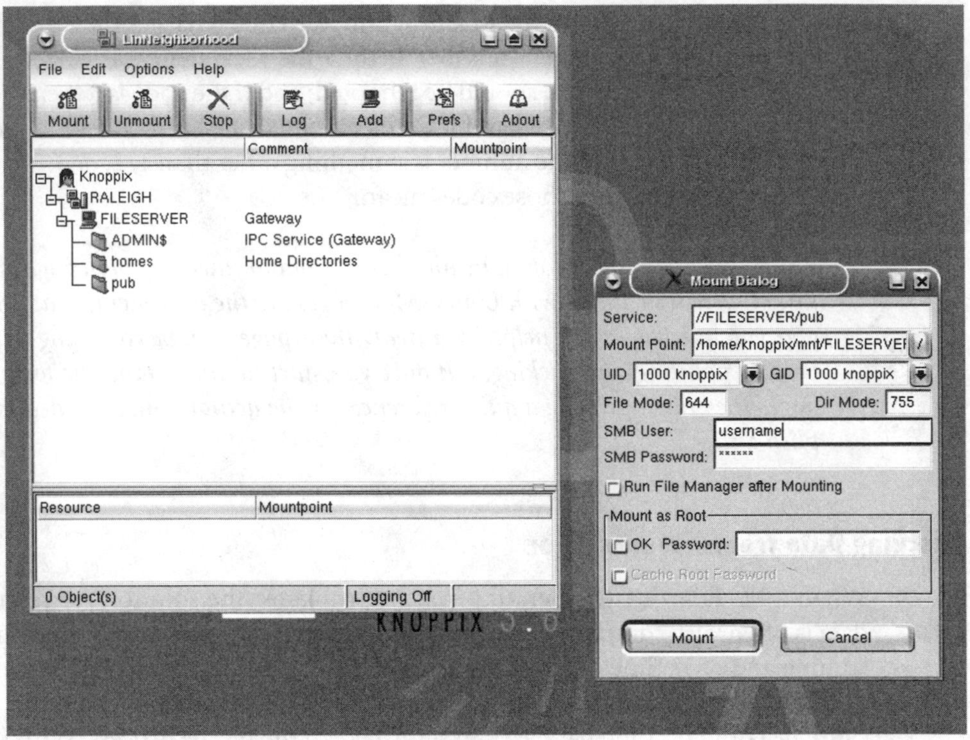

FIGURE 4.12   LinNeighborhood is similar to the Windows 98 Network Neighborhood program.

Burning Files to a CD-ROM

If your PC is equipped with a CD-ROM burner Knoppix can save the day. The Knoppix CD-ROM includes a program called *K3b* that can be used to burn a CD of data from the hard drive to a CD-R or other writeable media. This is extremely handy when there is a lot of data that needs to be moved off the downed PC or you are without a network connection. To run the K3b burning utility go to the K menu in the lower left-hand corner of the Knoppix desktop and navigate to the `K-> Multimedia -> k3b` menu. This will launch the CD/DVD authoring program, which, as you can see from Figure 4.13, looks very similar to Roxio Easy Media Creator® that you might have used under Windows.

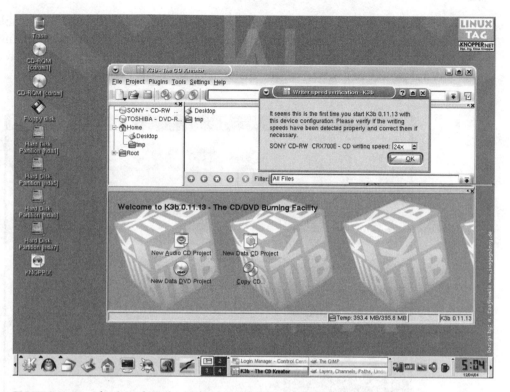

FIGURE 4.13 The interface for K3b CD-ROM-burning software is similar to the popular Windows software Roxio Easy Media Creator.

K3b can create data DVDs and CD-ROMs and supports all common standards for disc burning. The interface is very intuitive and should take little time to understand. Upon running K3b under Knoppix, you may be confronted with a configuration dialogue box asking to run setup because it is the first time you have used it. This is normal, and hardware recognition for CD-R/CD-RW/DVD-R drives is well supported.

Making Data Available to Windows Users with Samba

If you have a mixed enterprise of Windows and Linux desktops you will want to become familiar with Samba, which is software used to provide interoperability between Windows and other operating systems. To start the Samba Server on the Knoppix distribution, you click on `Penguin Menu -> Services -> Start Samba Server`, which will walk you through a set of dialogue boxes, including one that enables you to set a password for accessing the service. Then you simply browse the network for the PC named Knoppix. Figure 4.14 shows the Knoppix server as viewed from a Windows XP *My Network Places* dialogue box.

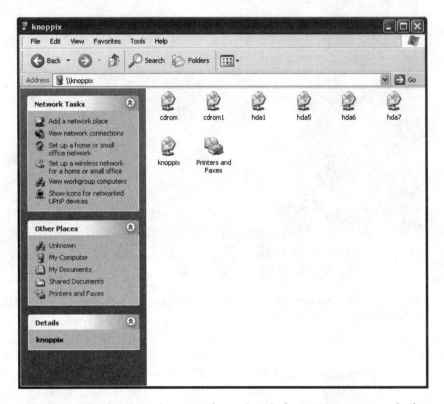

FIGURE 4.14   The Knoppix server shown in Windows XP's My Network Places.

Samba is an important technology for any Linux LAN environment where file and print services are needed. Further discussion on Samba will follow in later chapters. Keep in mind that the tools included with the Samba package can be used on both client PCs and servers.

Secure Dial-up Workstation

Many travelers today rely on their broadband connections to connect to the Internet; these connections are often firewalled to prevent malicious attacks. However, in some cases users may still need to rely on a dialup connection via a POTS line.

When you connect to the Internet without a firewall and other security measures you become vulnerable. Using Knoppix as a way to limit access to your hard drive may protect your Windows installation from damage, by leaving the filesystem of your Windows system readable but not writable. To use Knoppix as a dialer for ISP access just boot the CD-ROM and go to K menu -> Internet -> Modem Dialer to launch a program called *KPPP* which has an interface (shown in Figure 4.15) somewhat similar to *Windows Dial-Up Networking*.

ON THE CD

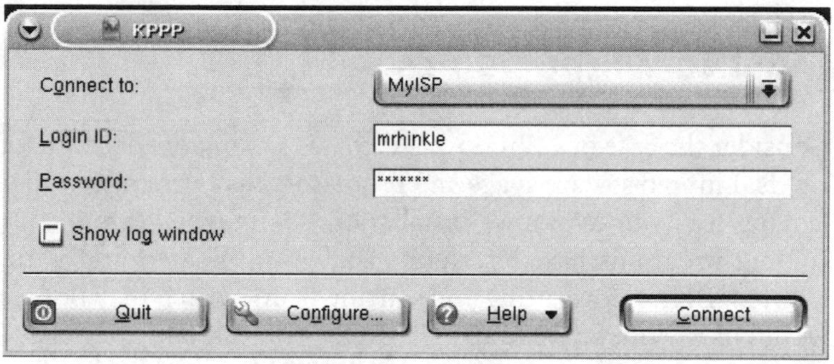

FIGURE 4.15 KPPP Configuration is the central interface for setting up a dial-up connection under Knoppix.

You could even use *iptables* to provide a simple firewall, though with your PC running from a CD-ROM it has a limited risk of being compromised.

NOTE

Iptables is an open source packet filtering program that allows network traffic to travel to and from your Linux PC. The iptables package is somewhat complex in comparison with some of the simpler solutions presented in this book. However, it's a very useful way to convert a Linux PC into a firewall device. Further investigation of iptables for the small enterprise can be conducted by a Web search for iptables and Linux.

Security Tools

One advantage of executing security tasks under Knoppix is that because the filesystem is booted from a read-only medium, a CD-ROM, you start the operating system knowing exactly what state it is in from the beginning. Once booted, you can then audit a PC for security problems and make corrections.

Use Knoppix for Safe Downloading of Security Updates

If your machine becomes compromised by a virus that opens a back door to your network, you may not want to boot into the operating system until the damage is repaired. However, Knoppix runs from a CD-ROM that is unlikely to be compromised because it is a read-only filesystem. In the event that a virus or Trojan horse compromises a PC, you can download updates via Knoppix and save them locally to the hard drive. Then after you remove the network connectivity you can boot back into Windows and safely install the updates.

REPURPOSING WINDOWS PCS

Consider the case of a Windows PC that is no longer adequate for your computing needs. Limited storage space and processors that were once top of the line are now lagging for your Windows installation. Or maybe years of installing and uninstalling programs have left your installation bloated and your hard drive fragmented. Even reformatting and starting from scratch may not yield the results you would like. With a Live Linux CD-ROM you can take the existing PC and convert it to Linux as easily as popping in a CD-ROM and rebooting. However, there are a couple of "gotchas." The first is that by default you will not be able to save files to the disk. This can be made possible by changing the setting for the old hard drives to read-and-write access.

As a safety measure, the Knoppix bootable CD-ROM mounts the hard drives on the host machine in read-only mode. To access the hard drives you must make them readable. You can accomplish this in two ways. The first method is to right-click on the hard drive, choose Properties, and click on the Permissions tab. The other way is to set the permissions using the chmod command from the command line interface. The chmod command can be used to make the hard drive world readable.

You can set the hard drive to readable and writable by clicking on the desktop icon for the hard drive and choosing *Properties* and then the *Permissions* tab as shown in Figure 4.16.

Once the hard drive is set to be readable and writable, users can then edit their documents in the Microsoft Office replacement program, OpenOffice.org. The OpenOffice.org suite offers equivalents to Word (Writer), Excel (Calc), and PowerPoint (Impress). Multiple browser choices and disk tools are available. Using the partition tools included with Knoppix, hard drives can be repartitioned to accommodate a native Linux install or just segregated Linux data storage.

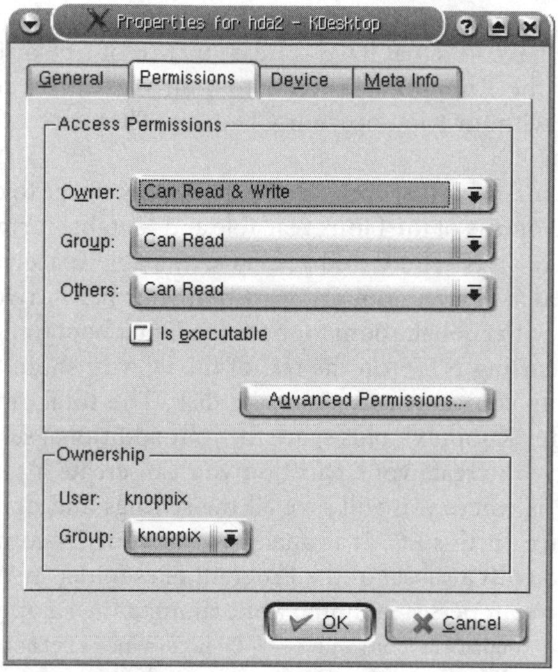

FIGURE 4.16   Changing the properties of the hard drive by right-clicking and choosing Properties

Repurposing or Dual Purposing Windows PCs

Up to this point, discussion of using Knoppix has mostly been in the context of dual-purposing a Windows PC or using it to help cure particular software or operating system failures. The following recipes are designed to provide not only dual-purpose scenarios but also repurposing scenarios allowing the recycling of PCs or creation of projects to help facilitate learning about enterprise scenarios.

Optimizing an Existing PC for Linux

If you are running the Knoppix CD-ROM, you will obviously not have use of that CD drive for other things like browsing data CDs or burning CD-R media. However, Knoppix has a work-around that can allow you to run Knoppix straight from your hard drive without interfering with your existing Windows install. The

Knoppix community has nicknamed this approach "the poor man's install." If you currently have PCs that have at least 700 MB of free disk space, you can copy the image of the Knoppix CD-ROM to your hard drive to provide a way to boot Knoppix without tying up your CD drive. There are a few considerations to this approach.

The hard drive that you install the Knoppix image to cannot be NTFS. It should be FAT32 or one of the Linux readable and writable formats (ext2, ext3, ReiserFS). If you have an NTFS PC and you have available space you can use the previously mentioned QTParted tool to repartition your hard drive and create a compatible partition with enough room for both the Linux boot image and additional settings. If you are using NTFS on the rest of the PC you should add additional space for documents you want to save to the disk. The total amount of space should be 700MB (for Knoppix), plus space for your additional settings and files.

After you create your partition you can create a *persistent home*. This home directory is where you will save all the settings and documents for the user who runs Linux on this PC. It is analogous to your Documents and Settings folders combined with a subset of the Program Files folder in Windows 2000 or XP. You can create your persistent home while running the Knoppix CD-ROM and going to K Menu -> Knoppix > Configure -> Create a persistent KNOPPIX Home directory. Choose the directory to exist on your newly created partition. That partition, as identified in QTParted earlier, will have a name that resembles */dev/hdb1* which is the device (in this case your hard drive partition) Knoppix will use to install its settings.

Now reboot the PC until the Knoppix: prompt is visible. Enter the following cheat code: home = scan tohd=/dev/hdb1 where */dev/hdb1* is the partition you just created for your persistent home and Linux installation. The *tohd*, or "to hard drive" option, will copy the image to the hard drive. This not only frees up the CD drive for other uses, but also improves performance because the hard drive can be accessed faster than the CD drive.

Creating a Portable Desktop with a USB Key

When setting up or repairing a PC it is a pretty standard practice for IT administrators to carry a CD case full of software to be installed and to troubleshoot desktop installations. The Knoppix CD-ROM combined with a USB drive is a great tool that can be used to rescue Linux and Windows PCs as well as to copy a common set of settings and data to individual PCs. The Knoppix CD-ROM in combination with a USB storage device like the very popular USB data storage key makes a powerful tool. To accomplish this you will need a USB key and the bootable Knoppix CD-ROM.

Technically you don't even need a Knoppix CD-ROM after you set up this type of configuration providing you have a significantly large USB key. You can set Knoppix to boot right from a USB device and save files locally. The only caveat is that you may need a USB key with at least one gigabyte of storage to hold the settings and the operating system. Additionally you need to make sure that your PC's BIOS has the ability to boot from a USB device.

To do this properly you will simply insert your Knoppix CD-ROM, attach your USB device, and boot your PC into the Knoppix OS. Once booted into Knoppix you will see the USB key mounted on your desktop. The most likely name for this device will be */dev/sda1*. If you can't find the name, a quick search engine query on Linux USB devices should give you the information you need. To create a persistent home directory on a USB drive you can go to K Menu -> Knoppix > Configure -> Create a persistent KNOPPIX Home directory. You can then browse to the USB drive and create the home directory on your key. The advantages of this are that once you have that persistent home in place you can carry settings and other information to help install or troubleshoot additional systems. You may just use it to document hardware inventories as you move from PC to PC. To recall that persistent home information on the next PC involves a few simple steps. When booting into the Knoppix CD-ROM you can pass parameters at the *boot:* prompt. In the case of a USB key, the most likely location when there are no other USB storage devices is */dev/sda1*. So at the boot prompt you should enter knoppix home=/dev/sda1. If this fails then you can choose to enter boot: Knoppix home-scan, which will search for the persistent home you created, though it may take longer to boot. Now you can take all the files you need with you as you move from PC to PC. This kind of setup is also an alternative to a laptop when you know you will have access to a PC but don't want to interfere with another user's installation. Figure 4.17 shows the persistent home dialogue box.

Access Remote Desktops and Terminal Servers

KDE provides a tool called Remote Desktop Sharing that is also included on the Knoppix companion CD-ROM. Using this software you can connect to other desktops using different remote display protocols. To launch the Remote Desktop connections go to K menu -> Internet -> Remote Desktop Connection. This will launch the Remote Desktop Connection software as shown in Figure 4.18.

Accessing a Windows NT Terminal Server or Windows 2000/2003 Terminal Services

Windows Terminal Services uses a redisplay protocol called Remote Desktop Protocol (RDP). You can use the Remote Desktop Connection software to make a

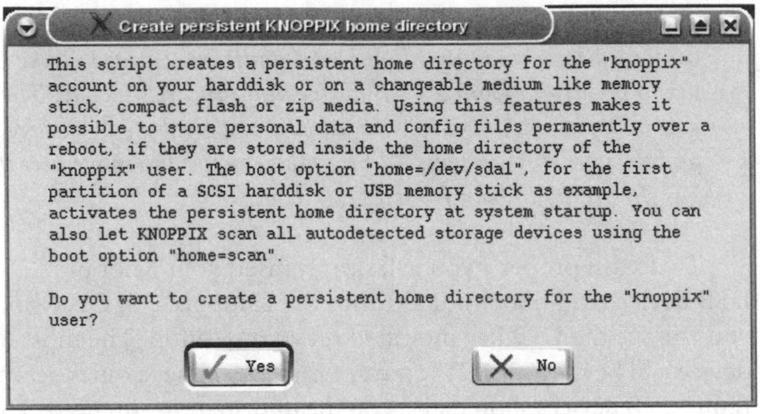

FIGURE 4.17   The Knoppix persistent home dialogue box.

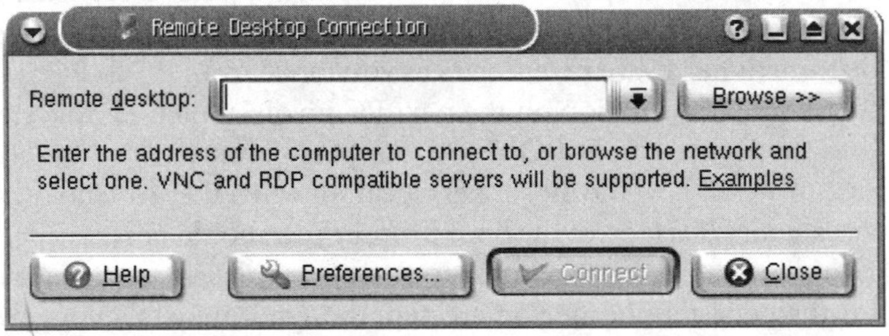

FIGURE 4.18   The KDE Remote Desktop Sharing program.

connection to your Windows Terminal Server from Linux. This can be useful in the event that you already have or are using Windows Terminal Services; you could continue to host your applications on the Windows server while giving your users a safe sandbox to experiment with Linux.

Installing Linux from the Knoppix Live Filesystem CD-ROM

The Knoppix installation script will try to detect a suitable partition to install Linux. It will launch QTParted to try to create those partitions; however, it may not launch the QTParted partitioning tool as the root user so it will not have permissions to create the partitions. If this is the case you can quit the install, go to the terminal window, and type sudo qtparted <enter> to start the installation. For the new install you will have the option to choose beginner, Knoppix, or Debian. You can choose to install beginner for Multi-User System with Hardware Detection.

Building a Thin Client Network with NoMachine and Knoppix

NoMachine is an open source software package that is marketed by NoMachine, a division of Medialogic S.A., an Italian Linux system integrator. NoMachine uses the NX Distributed Computing Architecture to convert Unix or, in this case, Linux computers into *terminal servers*. The NoMachine architecture compresses the X protocol to use less bandwidth by using a combination of three things: it uses an algorithm to compress network traffic; it reduces the time for roundtrip transmissions, and it is adaptive to the amount of bandwidth present at any given time. Not only does NoMachine allow Linux X sessions to be compressed and redisplayed but it can be used as a redisplay client for Windows Terminal Server and Citrix MetaFrame®. NoMachine can be used as a supplemental desktop environment running on your Windows PC.

BUILDING YOUR OWN LINUX LIVE FILESYSTEM CD-ROM DISTRIBUTION

ON THE CD

The solutions in this chapter all focused on using the Knoppix CD-ROM included with this book. This should just start your own creativity flowing, though. It may be advantageous for you to build your own Linux distribution so that you can choose to include only the applications that you need for your users and avoid distractions. Taking the examples above as a jumping-off point, you may choose to make your own tools CD complete with files that are specific to your enterprise. The remastering of a live filesystem CD-ROM is not trivial, but the process and methods for doing so are well documented on the Internet. Also, the Morphix CD-ROM mentioned at the beginning of this chapter was designed to enable end users who want to create distributions to build their own Live Linux CDs.

SUMMARY

As evidenced by the examples in this chapter, the Linux live filesystem distributions offer a lot of tools that have bearing on your Windows environment. They can also be used for a wide variety of projects including resurrecting unusable PCs or diagnosing problems. There are also many different types of bootable Linux distributions that are designed to help solve a certain problem or a group of problems for a specific segment of people. The popular Linux site *Distrowatch* keeps a running list of news about desktop Linux distributions as well as Linux live filesystem CD distributions.

OTHER RESOURCES

- Distrowatch—*www.distrowatch.com*
- Morphix—*www.morphix.org*
- Gnoppix—*www.gnoppix.org*
- KDE—*www.kde.org*
- GNOME—*www.gnome.org*
- Linux Bootable Business Card—*www.lnx-bbc.org*
- Knoppix-STD—*www.knoppix-std.org*
- Knoppix—*www.knoppix.org*
- QTParted—*http://qtparted.sourceforge.net*
- Freesco—*www.freesco.org*
- LinNeighborhood—*www.bnro.de/~schmidjo/*
- Citrix—*www.citrix.com*
- NoMachine—*www.nomachine.com*
- rdesktop—*www.rdesktop.org*
- Distrowatch—*www.distrowatch.com*

REFERENCES

Windows 2000 Terminal Services. Available online at *http://www.microsoft.com/windows2000/technologies/terminal/default.asp*.

Windows 2003 Terminal Services. Available online at *http://www.microsoft.com/windowsserver2003/technologies/terminalservices/default.mspx*.

5 Linux Desktop Deployment

Once you finish evaluating your present desktop environment you need to start to consider your options for desktop configurations. You may want to consider a new paradigm of computing that is server centric rather than desktop centric. You also need to look at the ways that your new desktops will interact with other systems and other desktops that might not be migrating to Linux. The strategic decisions you make early on will be critical to your success in replacing or supplementing your existing IT systems with a Linux desktop. One goal should be to minimize disruption and to supply solutions with better value than you receive from your current legacy systems. You will also need to choose whether you will redeploy systems or acquire new hardware without losing or giving up your legacy systems.

Redeployment: Some enterprises will be best served by installing Linux on the same desktop PCs that once ran Windows. This requires research to make sure that your hardware can support Linux. You can do this by performing searches on the Internet or by inquiring about support from your potential hardware vendors. For the sake of convenience you may choose your desktop distribution based on the ability of that distribution to reliably run on your hardware.

New Hardware Acquisition: The time involved in redeployment of Linux on existing hardware can quickly become expensive. Timing a Linux migration with an already scheduled hardware deployment or upgrade can minimize the impact of a migration because there is already a motivating factor for upgrades. This may factor heavily into your cost justifications for migrating from one platform to another. Wholesale replacement of desktop PCs before their end of lives may negatively affect your IT budgets and increase acquisition costs for a Linux desktop adoption.

Accessing Legacy Systems: When you adopt Linux as your desktop operating system you probably won't stop at the desktop. Evaluate the ability for that desktop to access file and print services that may be served by Linux, Unix, or Windows servers. You may have other systems that are authenticated through directory servers like Microsoft Active Directory. Do not overlook the need to make provisions to accommodate these new or repurposed PCs, especially when it comes to client accessing licenses and the ability to interoperate, e.g., network protocols.

Planning for both hardware and network support is a critical factor, as is how you interconnect that hardware with new systems.

THICK OR THIN DESKTOP DEPLOYMENTS

Most desktop PC users probably think of the "traditional" thick PC when discussing desktop computing, which infers that desktop PCs include a CPU, local storage, and peripherals. With thick clients, processing happens locally on the desktop PC but is connected to, or a *client* of, a local area network that allows users to connect to network resources like file servers and printers. In the thin client computing model, processing happens on the server, which redisplays the data to the client. In these scenarios, the client is simply a vehicle for user input and redisplay. It is usually a pared-down PC with a mouse, keyboard, and display. Very little computing other than input and graphical redisplay happen locally. All processing and storage happen on a server that "powers" the thin client. That's why thin client computing is sometimes referred to as *network computing, client-server,* or *server-centric computing.* These are all rather vague terms, but they all suggest the presence of three elements: a client, a server, and a network. Figure 5.1 is shows a comparision between thick clients and thin client computers.

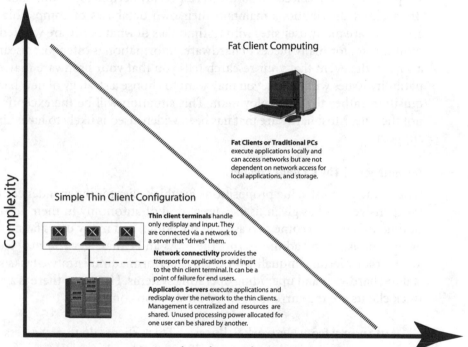

Fat Client Computing

Fat Clients or Traditional PCs
execute applications locally and can access networks but are not dependent on network access for local applications, and storage.

Simple Thin Client Configuration

Thin client terminals handle only redisplay and input. They are connected via a network to a server that "drives" them.

Network connectivity provides the transport for applications and input to the thin client terminal. It can be a point of failure for end users.

Application Servers execute applications and redisplay over the network to the thin clients. Management is centralized and resources are shared. Unused processing power allocated for one user can be shared by another.

Complexity

Network Independence

FIGURE 5.1   Comparison between thick and thin client computing.

Both thick clients and thin clients have advantages and neither one is superior to the other. In later chapters there will be further discussion about how you might go about a deployment and what technologies might compliment that deployment.

Traditional Computing—Thick Client

Traditional desktop computing includes a core PC and accompanying peripherals. It is likely that most of your peripherals, particularly the mouse and keyboard, will be supported under Linux, along with the monitor. More exotic peripherals such as Windows CE-based devices, mobile phones, and scanners may not have that same degree of compatibility. If you recall the example of the Linux adoption bull's-eye, the fewer peripherals and other demands on the desktop, the less the complexity and the accompanying risk. When evaluating your risk and support for certain hardware, you should start by consulting the vendor or searching the Internet for support for various pieces of hardware, especially peripherals. Both SuSE and Mandriva Linux distributions maintain their own databases of compatible hardware and there are many user sites with testimonials of what hardware worked and what didn't. Also, for many pieces of hardware, information is often just a search engine away. In the event that your research tells you that your hardware may have compatibility issues with Linux, you may want to choose a strategy of new hardware acquisition rather than redeployment. This situation will be the exception though, not the rule. Most hardware that has been widely used is likely to have Linux driver support.

Advantages of Thick Client Computing

One of the greatest value propositions for thick client is independence. The rise of inexpensive PCs has given users a great deal of autonomy in their personal computing. PCs have become pervasive in the home, and many users fancy themselves experts in using and administering them. As an IT manager you may feel that you are at risk by letting unqualified PC users perform administrative tasks such as installing hardware and upgrading operating systems. However, there is a reason that thick clients are the current standard for desktop computing.

> **Autonomy from Network Failures:**   Thick clients do their processing locally, so common local computing tasks like authoring documents can occur without the need for a network connection. Email transactions can be queued until connections can be made to a network.

> **Peripheral Support:**   Thick client PCs are usually equipped with a variety of ports including USB, Firewire℠, serial, etc. This is not the case with thin client devices, because the local device is seldom aware of peripherals other than a mouse and keyboard.

> **Distributed Points of Failure:**   In a thick client computing environment, events that occur on a machine that don't require a network do not affect other users. A service outage in the thin client model may affect many users.

> **Diversification of Work Environments:**   PCs can be tailored to the needs of individual users, especially when workstations are not shared among users. Applications can be matched to the end user needs and "one-off configurations" don't affect other users.

All these capabilities make thick client attractive, though as with any solution there are also pitfalls to avoid and limitations that might not make this type of technology right for your situation.

Disadvantages of Thick Client Computing

The thick client PC has become a standard partly because it has become ubiquitous in the home and people who use this technology outside of their jobs will likely have some experience with the environment from personal use. This is both a curse and a blessing. It's a curse because employees likely have different personal needs then they do professional ones. It's a blessing because company resources don't need to be expended in training these users. However, the thick client model does pose certain challenges.

Standardization: Each PC is a distinct element of the overall IT infrastructure that can be altered by the end user configurations. This makes standardization and tracking of resources very difficult. Taking an accounting of each machine throughout the enterprise, especially the large enterprise, can eat up time that could be spent improving the network or PC experience.

Operating System Dependence: If you have standardized an operating system you may have found that you gain advantages from consistency. However, standardization is not without its pitfalls. If you have an operating system–specific problem, then all the computers in the enterprise share that problem. If you are successful in standardizing your desktop platform, you may start to develop applications for that platform. Developing or depending on applications that are only available for a single platform can be dangerous. As you will read many times in this book, one of the most significant obstacles in Linux to Windows migration is application availability. Native Windows or even Linux applications that aren't portable to other platforms can lock you into a decision that may not match future changes in your business.

Maintenance: Because each PC is independent of the others, managing software and configurations is complex. Updating software for a large group of users requires access to each machine, which might include traveling to workstations and performing triage. If the PC is functioning and connected to the network, then PCs might be repaired through the use of remote access software. Ideally you have some tool that enables you to push changes to multiple PCs at once. Of course, in the Windows world these tools all seem to be dependent on some expensive license.

Thick clients are a fine way to offer desktop computing, but it bears having the conversation about whether that is the way you want to continue to provide desktop computing services or if you want to look at the alternatives provided by thin client computing.

Thin Client Computing

Thin client computing occurs when processing of programs is executed on the server and then redisplayed over a network to a thin client device, sometimes called a *dumb terminal*. Typically the device only functions as a way to redisplay graphical information from the server and to provide a means for user input. There is no processing and no awareness of local hardware other than that provided by an embedded operating system. Thin client computing has a lot of promise for companies looking to migrate to Linux but wanting to limit disruption, because user desktops can be staged before they are deployed. Thin client computing applications live in the data center or server room, not at the users' desktop, so staging a thin client deployment can be done without replacing the legacy Windows environment. Once the deployment is staged and tested, desktop PCs can be quickly replaced and thin client devices can be brought online.

Advantages of Thin Client Computing

Thin client computing offers two distinct advantages: utility and desktop mobility. The thin client model allows you to share processing, storage, and other resources among users efficiently. Also, because the desktop computing environment originates from a single point, you can manage the installation centrally without the need to travel to desktops except to plug in the thin client terminal and connect it to the network. The other overwhelming benefit of thin client computing is mobility. By removing desktop computers that are stateful, or maintain most settings and applications locally, and instituting a thin client architecture, desktop environments are no longer tethered to a cubicle. Work environments can be pulled up easily at a desk, a conference room, or even a home office. Just as the productivity worker travels, so can applications and data.

Single Point of Deployment: Applications in the server room can be managed centrally rather than on a one-by-one basis at the end users desktop. Once the install is done for one user on the server, it is likely there are ways to easily clone that installation for other users.

Fewer Moving Parts at the Desktop: Processing and storage are managed in bulk and in a redundant manor (e.g., RAID storage). Desktop terminals have minimal processing requirements and no storage needs which makes them stateless and less likely to fail.

Inexpensive Terminals: Terminals do not require significant local processing or storage which means that hardware is essentially the same as a thick client desktop minus two of the more expensive parts: the processor and the hard drive. Also, many thin clients don't require CD or floppy drives because software is not installed locally.

Disadvantage of Thin Clients

Thin clients are not the perfect solution, though they do lend themselves to being easily managed. If, as a desktop user, you need to connect PDAs and other devices or don't have an always on network connection, then thin client is not for you. If you are looking for improved management capabilities and potential reduction of both desktop hardware and management costs, then thin client is worth investigating.

Network Dependence: Network failures cause the link between the servers that power thin clients and the end user to go down. Thin client users are then left without connectivity to their computing environment. Some technologies compensate for this by caching information locally and synchronizing to the server, though this type of configuration is highly specialized.

Limited Peripheral Support: Because the thin client device usually runs a limited embedded operating system that cannot be altered, there is little ability to attach peripherals such as printers, scanners, or PDAs. If this is a requirement of your users then you should likely consider thick client computing.

Local Printing: Because the thin client device is essentially a dumb terminal, it needs some way to map or redirect printing from the session back to the local printer. This requires a special piece of software that can receive print information back from the server. Some thin client software does include this faculty, though most don't. Instead they rely on the server to map printing functions to networked printers.

This fundamental discussion on fat versus thin clients will be addressed in greater detail in Chapter 11. It merits introducing the notion that your computing environment may be better served by thin computing in some circumstances. However, the discussion from this point on will focus on thick client computing.

So far the discussion has been centered on the premise that thin client computing requires a dedicated device. However, you can use thin client software to display and interact with a Linux desktop. As a Windows user you may already use the popular Windows redisplay software Citrix to access remote systems. Incidentally, Citrix can be used by Linux users to access Microsoft Terminal Services. Conversely, Linux desktops could be served as a compliment to the Windows desktop through the redisplay technologies discussed in Chapter 11. You may even choose to use thin client computing as a way to conduct a Linux desktop pilot where there is no need to repurpose your Windows desktop, but rather simply augment it..

Alternatively, you could use thin client computing as a security device to access remote systems such as CRM databases that may not practically be securely served in a stand-alone network configuration. In a thin client computing model you don't grant access to programs and data locally; instead you use redisplay software so programs and information are accessed remotely and the only thing exchanged between the thin client computer and application server is the user input and graphical data needed to access the system. Data is stored and programs are executed in the safety of the data center. Using thin client computing as a method for accessing customer records or other sensitive data provides an extra layer of security, and the redisplay session can be the gatekeeper to secure systems. Thick client and thin client computing can play a role in your environment where one complements the other.

INSTALLING A THICK CLIENT LINUX DESKTOP

In its history as a desktop operating system, Linux desktop installation has gone from an abysmal and confusing task dotted with questions to an often streamlined process that can be as easy as a few clicks. One advantage of the Linux desktop is that, because there are few hardware vendors that support Linux as compared to Windows, the Linux distribution takes it upon itself to try to supply all the hardware drivers. Most Linux distributions install without third-party drivers, which makes the setup on less exotic hardware fairly painless. In comparison, a Windows installation might require you to locate and find the drivers that are specified by the manufacturer rather than detected by the operating system. Linux distributions have gone to great pains to make the installation self-contained. Take the example of the Knoppix CD included with this book, which can run on a wide array of PCs without additional drivers. Linux also takes into consideration the possibility of other operating systems being present during the install process and can make adjustments to allow you to choose which operating system you want to boot. Most distributions will recognize the presence of a Windows installation and make preparations to coexist as peacefully as possible with the legacy installations by installing and configuring a *bootloader* that lets you chose which operating system you want to boot.

Filesystem

In contrast to a Windows installation, Linux has a wide array of choices with regards to the filesystem you use and the ways it is practical to configure them. During an expert install, almost any of the Linux distributions mentioned in this book may present you with options in these areas. In fact, it is one of the first choices you will be presented when installing Linux.

Windows Filesystems

Windows filesystems have progressed over time from the FAT16 filesystem used in the early days of Microsoft Disk Operating System (MS-DOS) to today's NTFS filesystem, the filesystem of choice for both the home user running Windows XP and enterprise products like Microsoft Windows Server. The evolution of the filesystem was necessary as storage changed and the sheer amount of data a typical user stored grew exponentially. Today's modern filesystems store data more efficiently and with greater reliability. Linux can read all the Windows filesystems and write to most with good reliability. You should understand which ones make good choices for data sharing and interoperability.

FAT16

FAT16 filesystems were first used for the DOS operating system. FAT16 has a volume limit size of 2 gigabytes (GB) and a maximum number of files of approximately 65,000. FAT16 is also limited in the length of filenames by an 8/3 convention, where the name can be a maximum of eight characters long and the extension no more than three characters. The limitations of the 2 GB per volume combined with the maximum number of files per volume for FAT16 forced it to make way for its successor, FAT32. *FAT32* can be read by all versions of Microsoft Windows and was a step forward, enabling Windows operating systems to take advantage of the cheap price of storage. Linux can read and write to FAT16 filesystems reliably.

FAT32

FAT32 filesystems were a default for Windows 98 and have a maximum volume size of 2 terabytes and a nearly unlimited maximum number of files per volume. FAT32 can be read by Windows 9x, Windows ME, Windows 2000, and Windows XP. Linux can read and write reliably to a FAT32 volume, and many of today's flash devices are formatted with that filesystem, enabling them to be read and written to from either Windows or Linux. When choosing a shared storage solution for exchanging files back and forth between Windows and Linux, FAT32 is a good choice.

NTFS

New Technology Filesystem (NTFS) is more robust than earlier filesystems that were used before Windows NT. Just as they were for FAT32, the limits of data storage for this filesystem are 2 terabytes and a nearly unlimited number of files per volume. The length of the filenames can be up to 255 characters. Improvements over the previous FAT filesystems include security, compression, and encryption. NT 3.51 and NT 4 used an earlier version of NTFS, while improvements came in v5.0 of NTFS in conjunction with Windows 2000. Windows XP now uses the latest version of NTFS, version 5.1. Linux can read NTFS but read/write access is still experimental. There are a number of approaches to write to NTFS; right now the most generally accepted way is to load the Windows driver for NTFS and use that in an emulated environment under Linux. This approach works fairly well but does require you to be using an appropriately licensed copy of Windows. In practice you probably won't find a situation where you would be using an NTFS filesystem on a desktop that doesn't already have Windows installed.

NOTE

Because NTFS is a proprietary filesystem the drivers and methods of accessing it are property of Microsoft. Linux can read the NTFS filesystem with no problems but the act of writing to NTFS is a tricky proposition. One way that many desktop users write to local NTFS drives is by using Captive, a piece of software that loads the Microsoft Windows ntsfs.sys driver under the Wine Windows API replacement for Linux. This allows you to write to NTFS safely because you are using the native Windows driver. The only caveat is that you will be restricted to having a licensed copy of Windows because you will need the Windows drivers to accomplish this set up. If you need to have good read/write access to a volume from Linux and Windows, FAT32 is usually the best choice as it is well supported on both operating systems.

Windows has a fairly small set of filesystems you are likely to encounter, and they have basically evolved with Microsoft operating systems. Moving forward, you will find that Linux has a wide variety of filesystems that may be tailored for certain types of use, from data center to desktop.

Linux Filesystems

Linux users have many filesystems that are suited for uses that range from reliable desktop usage to distributed filesystems that are better implemented in distributed storage area networks. For Linux desktop usage you will likely only encounter three filesystems: ext2, ext3, and ReiserFS. As a user migrating to Windows you will likely have to make a choice of which to use during installation with a default or recommended filesystem. You may later find that server installations that write a large amount of data or a large number of small files may benefit from one system over another. Another consideration comes when you need to write to a device from both Windows and Linux, such as when you use a USB flash drive. The filesystem must be supported for both operating systems. FAT32, for example, has good write support under both Linux and Windows, while NTFS can only be reliably read from both but lacks support for writing from Linux.

Ext2

For many years the ext2 filesystem was a standard for Linux systems. It was, at the time, the most practical solution for Linux deployments. However, today it's rare that distributions use ext2 for installation because of the requirement of Linux, upon a system failure, to check system file integrity, with an ext2 filesystem. This happens file by file, which can be very time consuming and varies by the number and size of the files. File checking is accomplished though the *fsck* disk check utility. Besides having to perform what could be a lengthy filesystem check, ext2 also lacked the advanced features to handle very large files and extent-mapped files. If you use ext2 filesystems, it will probably be a default for your /boot partition where data is very rarely written and stability and data integrity will be your overwhelming concern.

Defragmentation is a problem with which most Windows users are familiar. Fragmentation occurs because data is written to the first available block on the disk, and over time, as files are deleted and moved, the bits of data become scattered. The solution is to defragment the data and reorganize it so that it becomes more compact. This defragmentation process for large disk drives can become very time consuming. Linux doesn't, as a rule, require defragmentation as long as there is a little space free on the partition. Linux filesystems defragment themselves automatically without human intervention. Also, many Linux filesystems are journaling filesystems which keep a history or journal of the transactions processed when data is written or deleted from a hard disk. The journal allows information on the status of filesystem writing, this means that, in the event of a crash, all transactions can

be tracked and only files that did not register a success in the journal need to be checked for consistency. In comparison, a Windows system may need to check the whole disk for errors. NTFS is considered by many to be a pseudojournaled filesystem because it logs changes in the filesystem but lacks the ability to reverse them.

Ext3

The ext3 filesystem is an enhanced version of ext2, complete with journaling capabilities which allow you to account for changes before any crash and only checks files that are in question. Ext3 is not only used in desktop installations but frequently in server installations offering the following benefits:

Availability: After a crash from an unexpected system shutdown such as a power failure, ext3 does not require a filesystem check. It relies instead on checking the size of the journal to insure that it is not corrupt.

Journaling Improvements: You can see higher throughput from ext2 to ext3 in many cases because the journaling in ext3 optimizes the motion of the hard drive head.

Data Integrity: There are features in ext3 that will help to guarantee that data is intact. If you were inclined to learn more about how to take advantage of these features, you can choose different levels of reliability, but the default should be adequate for most desktop users. Advanced features like *writeback* and *journal* could be used for database servers.

Speed: Probably the greatest reason for a desktop user to choose ext3, though, is speed. Through optimizations of the hard drive's head motion, you will see higher throughput than with an ext2 filesystem.

Ext3 is most likely the filesystem you will choose or that will be chosen for you in a default Linux install. The next most likely is ReiserFS, especially if you choose a Novell Linux desktop distribution.

ReiserFS

ReiserFS was designed and developed by Hans Reiser; hence the name. ReiserFS is used by many Linux distributions and is an option during most expert installs. The advantage of Reiser over ext2 or ext3 is that is has very fast write speeds for small files under 1K. Also, Reiser can more efficiently store data in contiguous space because it can allocate space in fixed 4K blocks. This is smaller than the incremental size that ext3 uses to store data. If you keep many small files on your hard drive, such as email messages and text files, ReiserFS may be a more effective means of storing your data; otherwise, ext3 is a fine choice.

Understanding Linux's filesystems will allow you to make better decisions during your install. It may be confusing, when you start a desktop install, what filesystems are appropriate for what kind of installation. A potential installation pitfall for Windows users is to choose FAT32 when they install Linux because that is the filesystem they recognize. For native Linux installations you are normally fine to choose the defaults, unless you have special considerations such as needing to access files from Windows and Linux, as in a *dual-boot setup* between the two operating systems.

Disk Partitioning

Windows installations usually occur with a default installation of both a boot partition and a main partition that is formatted for both programs and data storage. This default installation is very simple and usually requires few decisions. In Linux you may want to consider more options for installation including the size of the main, swap, and root partitions, plus the filesystem for each.

Partitions

Partitions are divisions of a single physical drive. A partition is a contiguous set of blocks on a drive. This group of blocks is treated as an independent disk from the standpoint of the Linux operating system. The first sector of the disk holds the *Master Boot Record (MBR)*. The MBR contains a map called a *partition table* of the how the disk is laid out. If you have more than four partitions, additional partitions are nested underneath them.

Tips on Disk Partitioning

Understanding the ways disks are laid out and how that layout relates to the Linux install will help you maximize and best optimize your storage space. The following tips may help you make better decisions when partitioning your disk.

- Hard disks don't need to be completely allocated with partitions. You can choose to leave some space unpartitioned. You can also specify that some partitions be able to grow and not specify an upper limit.
- When using partitioning tools like *QTParted* or *fdisk,* expert options will let you specify the stop and start of each partition. Make sure that the partitions don't overlap or they will corrupt each other.

Many users know relatively little about the geometry of a hard drive. As someone who may be repurposing a PC, you might run into a situation where you want to preserve data. You can use the Knoppix disk and the fdisk program to analyze the geometry of a hard drive before making any decisions on how to install Linux. Most Linux install routines will also recognize existing partitions and prompt you to keep or overwrite them.

Primary Partitions

Primary partitions are the top level divisions of your disk drives. The maximum number of primary partitions that can exist on a disk drive is four. Of these four primary partitions, only one can be specified as active. You can also specify one as an extended DOS partition. The extended DOS partition can then be divided into logical partitions. This means that if you want to boot Linux and Windows alongside each other you would be able to access both operating systems. In the case of Linux you can *mount* the Windows partitions so you can access data in both the Windows and Linux partition, though if the partition is in the NTFS format you would only have experimental support for writing. Be careful in this case; a miscue could damage the Windows installation.

One thing to understand is that if you do have a Windows installation and you install Linux, in most cases the Linux operating system installation is *smart enough* to recognize the existing operating system and add a *bootloader* that lets you choose between the legacy Windows installation and the new Linux installation. Depending on the installation process you will end up with two or more options: one specifying the Linux version (a typical convention is the kernel version like Linux 2.6.11.8 or the name of the Linux distribution) and one for the legacy Windows install (which may be labeled DOS). By default one of the two will be chosen with no user intervention. You can change your configuration to specify one over the other so an unattended reboot will allow the system to start the operating system of choice. You make these changes in the configuration files for your bootloader, which will likely be *GRUB* or *lilo*. In Figure 5.2 you can see that the Linux installation offers you a choice on how to configure GRUB to choose which operating system to boot.

Extended Partitions and Logical Partitions

Extended partitions differ from primary partitions in that they can't be set to boot. The extended partition is a silo that contains all the DOS partitions except for the first one. The extended DOS partition, if it exists, can contain logical partitions, which are additional virtual drives. In Windows you may see them as letter drives

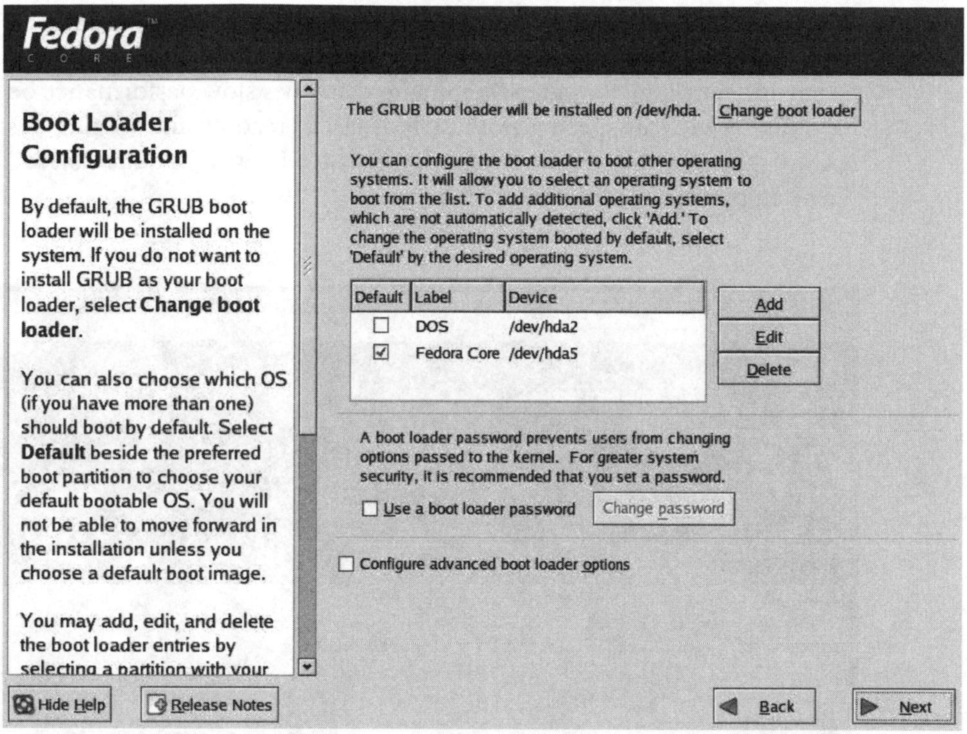

FIGURE 5.2   The Fedora Core installation gives you the option to choose whether you want to boot from Windows, which is labeled as DOS, or Linux, labeled as Fedora Core.

like D, E, or F. In Linux you may see them as part of the filesystem in a /windows directory. Once you have divided the drives you will see no difference from the operating system in each drive's ability to store data, just in their ability to be booted. These logical partitions are simply the subset of the extended partition, and they may have been created to make defragmentation times lower or as a method for organizing certain types of data into separate units.

Swap Partitions

Swapping is the practice of extending RAM by writing information that would normally be held in memory to hard disk. This ability to extend RAM memory allows more programs to use both RAM (physical memory) and virtual memory (swap). Windows has these same capabilities where less critical processes can be swapped to disk. In Windows 98/ME you may have a file called Win386.swp, and in Windows 2000 and later, virtual memory is paged to a file called pagefile.sys. There is a price to pay for swapping though; swapping to disk does slow performance because the hard disk read/write speed is not nearly as fast as reading and writing to solid state RAM. Figure 5.3 shows the a partitions on a 60 GB hard disk; the device /dev/hda8 is a swap partition used for virtual memory.

```
[root@HinkleTop mrhinkle]# /sbin/fdisk

Usage: fdisk [-l] [-b SSZ] [-u] device
E.g.: fdisk /dev/hda  (for the first IDE disk)
  or: fdisk /dev/sdc  (for the third SCSI disk)
  or: fdisk /dev/eda  (for the first PS/2 ESDI drive)
  or: fdisk /dev/rd/c0d0  or: fdisk /dev/ida/c0d0  (for RAID devices)
  ...
[root@HinkleTop mrhinkle]# /sbin/fdisk -l

Disk /dev/hda: 60.0 GB, 60011642880 bytes
255 heads, 63 sectors/track, 7296 cylinders
Units = cylinders of 16065 * 512 = 8225280 bytes

   Device Boot      Start         End      Blocks   Id  System
/dev/hda1   *           1        1912    15358108+   7  HPFS/NTFS
/dev/hda2            1913        7296    43246980    f  W95 Ext'd (LBA)
/dev/hda5            1913        3824    15358108+   c  W95 FAT32 (LBA)
/dev/hda6            3825        3837      104391   83  Linux
/dev/hda7            3838        7166    26740161   83  Linux
/dev/hda8            7167        7296     1044193+  82  Linux swap
[root@HinkleTop mrhinkle]# 
```

FIGURE 5.3 Fdisk being used to list partitions on the first physical hard drive with NTFS, FAT32 and ext3 filesystems. Note that the ID indicates the partition type. ID 82 indicates Linux Swap and 83 indicates a native Linux filesystem.

An option for increasing performance is to use a second hard drive for swapping. This allows data being written for persistent data files to be utilized on one drive while swap can be written on the other. You can use an aging hard drive that no longer has the capacity to be useful this way as an excellent way to boost performance on a Linux PC with a larger primary drive. The general rule for the size of the swap partition is to set aside two times the number of megabytes of RAM used by the PC. However, as memory has become cheaper and PCs have anywhere from 256 to 2 GB of RAM, you may want to keep a one-to-one ratio for any installation with 512 MB of RAM or greater (though it can't hurt to have more if you have the space).

Linux Directory Structure

The Windows filesystem and directory structure is a hierarchical model rather than a volume model. In contrast, everything within the Linux filesystem falls within one tree structure even though there may be many physical drives such as USB storage or network attached storage. Filesystems are attached, or *mounted,* to the hierarchy and appear as subdirectories to the root filesystem. For example, a USB device might appear as a directory under /mnt/flash/, or a CD drive might be accessible from /mnt/cdrom.

Hierarchical vs. Volumes

In Windows, filesystems are recognized as volumes and named as the C, D, E, F, or other lettered drive. In Linux, the filesystem looks more similar to the way you might view your C drive in DOS, where all directories and files fall within one monolithic hierarchy regardless of where they physically reside. With regards to a Windows filesystem, each volume is a discrete logical storage unit that is part of a physical disk, as evidenced by the view of the Windows Explorer interface to My Computer in Figure 5.4.

In Linux, a CD-ROM drive will be represented as a device and when attached, or mounted, to the system, the contents will be available in a directory. There is a saying, "Everything in Linux is a file." The CD drive itself could be represented as a file in the /dev/ directory, but when mounted to the filesystem, the data on the CD-ROM device may be accessed in the /mnt/cdrom directory. Most users will seamlessly access it through a graphical representation on their desktops. For example, on the GNOME desktop the Computer folder holds icons that refer to the filesystems folders and mount points illustrated in a way that will be familiar to some who has used the Windows operating system, as shown in Figure 5.5.

Even though some distributions now include a My Computer-like folder that lists filesystems in the same way that Windows lists volumes, there are differences behind the scenes. The difference is that you can navigate to any attached filesystem in Linux within one directory structure, whereas in Windows, you open the volume that you want to access and navigate to a filesystem within that volume.

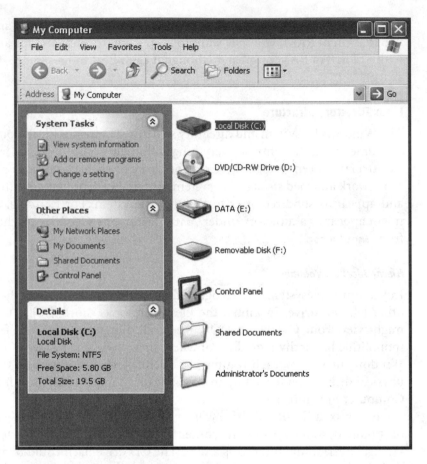

FIGURE 5.4 In Windows, My Computer shows the partitions and devices as volumes.

The Filesystem Hierarchy is a specification of the Linux Standard Base Core Specification, an industry standard for Linux vendors to follow to insure that there is a level of consistency among Linux distributions. The Filesystem Hierarchy Standard specifies the organization of the filesystem. Since many vendors provide Linux distributions and customizations, you should check to see if your preferred vendor adheres to the standard so that, in the event that you choose to move to another Linux distribution, configurations will be similar.

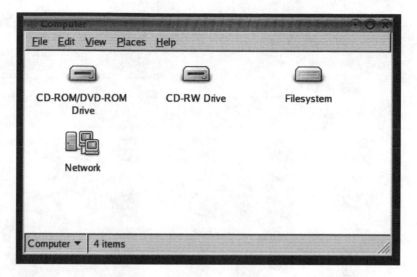

FIGURE 5.5 The GNOME file manager Nautilus represents filesystems in the same way as Windows.

Windows Explorer is a core part of the Windows operating system and does not vary by OEM or distribution point. In contrast, you can find many tools to graphically display the Linux filesystem, depending on the distribution. If you were using the KDE desktop environment, you may use Konqueror, illustrated in Figure 5.6, to browse the filesystem. The Konqueror program is too versatile to be pigeon-holed as a file manager, though; it is also a Web browser and image viewer, and performs many, many more functions.

It is not necessary to include a graphical shell utility at all with Linux because the system is modular; you can accomplish all the same tasks on the Linux console or shell and leave the graphical user interface out of the picture all together. When accessing the filesystem, Microsoft Windows uses the notation `c:\directory\file`. The notation for directories in Linux uses the / to designate the path to a file. For example, the path to where your user information is held under Linux is `/home/username`, where username is the login name you use for the Linux PC. The filesystem is laid out in such a way that groupings of files are logically allocated throughout the system. This is not unlike Windows, where data is normally kept collectively in one place (as in My Documents) and programs are kept in another (as in Program Files). The Linux hierarchy is laid out in the following manner, provided that the Linux distribution adheres to the standard set forth by the Linux Standards Base.

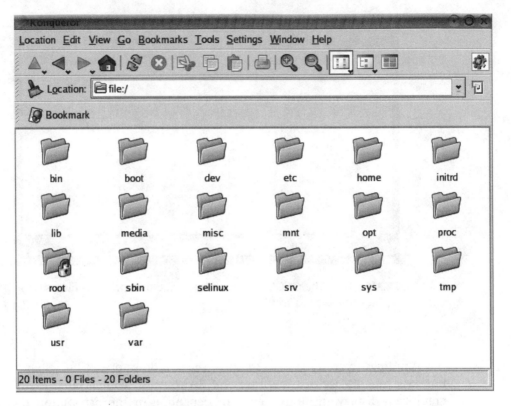

FIGURE 5.6 Konqueror being used to browse a Linux filesystem.

/bin

The bin directory is comparable to your c:\windows folder on a Windows machine because most of the critical programs for using your system are in this directory. *Bin* is short for *binaries,* which is intended to mean programs but really refers to any file that has been compiled. The programs in the bin directory are available to both users and privileged users.

In Linux there is also a hierarchy of users and groups that specifies permissions to read, write, and execute files. Some utilities are specifically designed for the privileged user, so it is a bad practice to allow inexperienced users to execute these commands.

/boot

The boot directory is required for booting your operating system. It is wise to create a separate partition for the /boot so that it is isolated from other, more frequently accessed and altered, directories (the installation program for your distribution will probably do this automatically). As a new Linux user or even a moderately experienced user, it is inadvisable to make any changes in this directory. Incorrect changes to this directory could have terminal effects on your operating system's ability to boot. As a rule, the maximum size needed for your boot partition will be 100 MB.

/dev

Dev is short for devices, and this directory holds files or folders that represent devices. These devices are anything that your computer might use, whether it be a CD drive, hard drive, or printer. There are two types of devices in the /dev directory: *block devices* and *character devices.* Understanding what devices are named in the /dev directory may help you install and configure your desktop later. Table 5.1 shows an overview of common Linux devices.

TABLE 5.1 Naming scheme for /proc devices

Common Name	Device Name	Explanation
IDE Hard Drives	/dev/hda– /dev/hdd	The IDE hard drives in Linux are assigned /dev/hda for the first hard drive, /dev/hdb for the second through, and so on, adding an alphabetical letter for each additional device. These are relative to the first and second drives on the first and second IDE controller. Once the hard drive has been partitioned, the partitions will be appended to the device name with numbers. For example, the second partition on the first hard drive will be /dev/hda2.
SCSI Hard Drives and USB Storage Devices	/dev/sda	SCSI hard drives follow the same naming scheme as IDE hard drives except /dev/hd is replaced with /dev/sd. So the second partition on the second hard drive would be /dev/sdb2. The USB bus presents the USB storage drive as an SCSI drive, so flash drives are often viewed on an IDE-only system as /dev/sda1 and so on.

$\rightarrow$

Common Name	Device Name	Explanation
Floppy Drives	/dev/fd0	The first floppy drive is assigned /dev/fd0.
CD-ROMs	/dev/cdrom	The CD-ROM device is /dev/cdrom; however, you cannot access a device until it's mounted. A common convention is for the device to be mounted or attached on /mnt/cdrom. There are exceptions. SuSE Linux, for example, mounts DVD-RW drives on the /mnt/media directory.
Ethernet Cards	/dev/eth0	Network interfaces are assigned the device name eth followed by a number. In machines that have both a network card and network interface on the motherboard, there may be a eth0 and eth1.
Wireless Cards	/dev/wlan0	802.11 wireless cards are often given the device name /dev/wlan0.

/etc

The /etc directory is sometimes referred to as the etcetera directory because it contains all the system-related files, such as configuration files. The *etc/fstab* and */etc/mtab* files keep track of *mounted* or *attached* filesystems. The */etc/fstab* file tells the system what systems to attach and what physical devices the filesystems reside on, while the */etc/mtab* holds the status information on these filesystems. The fstab includes not only what filesystems to attach, but also in what format and how they should be attached; for example, whether they should be mounted in read-only or read-write mode. Triggers can be set as to what filesystem type to expect when reading that volume (ext2, fat, NTFS, etc.).

Two of the most important files in the operating system are /etc/passwd and /etc/groups, which contain the password and group organization hierarchy on which Linux permissions are based. Each file that is accessed, executed, or written to on the Linux filesystem is subject to the permissions of these gatekeeper files. Traditionally passwords were kept in /etc/passwd in an encrypted format; in a more se-

*cure system the password file will be shadowed so that a password cracking pro-
'gram can't be used to access these passwords. When you use shadow passwords,
only the users' information is included in the /etc/passwd file, not the actual passwords. The passwords are kept in a file called /etc/shadow that is only readable by
root. They are encrypted so that even the root user who can add users to the file
cannot discern the password of individual users. Also because the system must use
the /etc/ passwd file, it must be readable by all programs on the system to identify
who's taking actions on files. When completing a Linux install there may be a field
or checkbox asking if you would like to use shadow password; it is a good practice
to do so to insure the integrity of user accounts.*

To use an analogy, the /etc/ directory is most comparable to the Windows registry because many system-wide configuration files are kept here.

/home

The home directory is where users can save their settings and files and even install
programs. The home directory serves a purpose similar to that of *Documents and
Settings* directory on Windows 2000 or XP. Each user (with the exception of the
root user, who uses /root) has a home directory in the format of /home/username. By
default this directory is only readable and writable by the owner of the directory,
so other users on the system can't interfere with data or programs installed in this
directory.

*In Linux, many files, especially those in the users home directory, start with a ".
which is somewhat similar to the hidden file attribute in Windows. Most methods
for viewing files don't show "." files, just as the default in Windows Explorer is not
to show the hidden files in Windows. In the home directory "." files are often used
to hide configuration files for programs executed as a user. For example, .bash_rc
holds information that can be parsed when you start using your text-based interface or Linux shell. These setting might include customization to the login prompt
or customization of the Linux shell that creates shortcuts for commonly used complex commands.*

/lib

The /lib directory holds libraries, which are files that are used by programs to
accomplish tasks. These libraries provide certain program functions to various
applications. In Windows you may be familiar with files ending in .dll, which stands
for *dynamic link library*. The /lib directory would be comparable to the C:\
Windows\System or C:\Windows\System32 folder that holds Windows .dll files.

/mnt

Mounting is the practice of attaching volumes to a filesystem hierarchy, as when you add a USB flash drive, CD-ROM, or additional hard drives. While the /etc/fstab holds mounting information the /mnt directory is the point at which filesystems are usually attached. In Windows, attached filesystems are represented as a volume in My Computer. You can mount filesystems in places other than the /mnt folder, but this convention is a good way to keep confusion to a minimum.

/opt

Opt is short for optional, and is the place where programs that are not a critical part of the operating system are stored. These may include programs that are available to all users. It's often a place where a system-wide installation of the Mozilla Web browser or OpenOffice.org office suite resides.

/proc

There's a saying that goes "Everything in Linux is a file even when it's not." That's a fairly accurate description of the /proc directory which contains a virtual filesystem that includes run-time information. If you list the files in this directory you will find most of them have a file size of zero. The proc filesystem contains data that many times is used troubleshooting. For example, you could use the command `cat /proc/version` to get the kernel version that the system is currently running.

/root

This is the home directory for the root user. The root user is the administrative user who has the power to change anything on the Linux system. This is not to be confused with the root of the filesystem, which is represented by the "/" symbol.

/sbin

The sbin is where programs used to administer the system are stored. Files that reside in this directory include system utilities like *lspci*, which allows you to list the files attached on the PCI bus, *fdisk*, which is used for reading and manipulating hard drive partitions, and *ifconfig* which is very similar to the Windows networking utility *ipconfig* and which is how you obtain information about networking interfaces.

/usr

The /usr directory, like /opt directory, holds many of the same type of programs that the Program Files directory holds in Windows.

/var

The /var directory holds spool directories for items like local mail and printing. These logs may become very large if there are a large number of services running on the PC, such as a Web or file server. You may want to determine whether logging is necessary for some of these services. Some logs are very helpful when you are troubleshooting Linux. One particularly useful log is the */var/log/messages*, which is the core system log that keeps records of errors with input/output (IO). Services that are running may provide data to this log. You can also see when a user has become a root- or super-user and made changes beyond the scope of his normal permissions. Other services might have individual logs stored here as well.

Nonstandard Directories

One additional piece of information you'll need to put the puzzle together is that some distributions offer some nonstandard directory conventions.

/Windows

SuSE Linux chooses to configure existing Linux Windows installation partitions in the /Windows directory. Windows partitions are then added with their corresponding Windows volume letter. For example, a Windows installation on Volume C under Linux might be mounted as /Windows/C/.

/media

The /media directory is used by SuSE Linux to mount media like CD-ROM drives and floppy drives. The /media directory supplements the /mnt directory as a place to attach filesystems.

/KNOPPIX

The /KNOPPIX directory is a link to the compressed Linux filesystem on the Knoppix CD-ROM. This is specific to Knoppix and would not be part of any other distributions.

/ramdisk

ON THE CD

The Knoppix Linux distribution on this book's companion CD-ROM creates a temporary hard drive in RAM so that files and settings can be temporarily stored. This temporary storage area is /ramdisk. This /ramdisk is particular to Live Linux CD-ROM distributions.

Tools for Disk Partitioning

When it comes to partitioning your drive, the Linux operating system often uses a few Open Source tools. The most common ones are *fdisk*, *Disk Druid*, and *GNU Parted*. A very common tool used to manage disk partitions, fdisk can be accessed from the command line. GNU Parted is a program that can be used to alter disk partitions. It's very commonly used under Linux, and we have already discussed its cousin of sorts, QTParted, a GUI interface coupled with Parted that resembles Partition Magic. Disk Druid is another commonly used disk partitioning tool that is often launched in the beginning of Linux installations for editing disk partitions. Disk Druid has been very popular because of its use by Red Hat and Fedora Core.

GIVE YOUR HARD DRIVE A KICKSTART

You may encounter situations where you will have to reinstall your operating system on your desktop Windows PC, or, in a larger organization, where you have to install the operating system on many machines with identical configurations. You may have to install it on a number of PCs as part of a disaster plan or whenever you experience rapid growth. That's where Red Hat's KickStart can be valuable. It automates installation of several systems. The process is to build one PC that has your preferred configuration; this is called the build machine. Then you use that template to "kick off" additional installs. KickStart then automates the installs and minimizes human interference (and consequently mistakes, providing your master is correct). This is a good measure for fixing failed machines because you basically maintain one master machine and then let it configure your additional PCs painlessly. This tool was designed for use with Red Hat Linux, but many people have *hacked* it for other distributions. A Web search for "kickstart Linux" will yield you a bounty of information on the subject. Also, for more information you can check out the Kickstart mailing list; it is a good place to ask questions and get ideas on how other Linux users are using this tool. SuSE Linux also offers a similar tool called AutoYaST which does pretty much the same thing; it can take a single profile and duplicate that install automatically across many machines.

BOOTLOADERS

Before discussing boot managers, how a PC itself boots merits discussion. Today's computers (that is, x86 PCs with IDE and SCSI hard drives) start by reading the BIOS ROM which is stored on the hard drive. The BIOS either detects or is told by the settings within what devices to look at to boot from. Typical order of devices booting is floppy drive, CD-ROM, and then hard drive. This order can be changed by logging into the PC BIOS. Commonly you hold down the escape or F1 key after powering on the PC to enter the BIOS setup.

After reading the BIOS the PC then looks to the devices. Once it reads a device, for example a hard drive, it reads the Master Boot Record (MBR), then the partition boot sector (specified in the MBR), and then it loads the operating system kernel. Whether you use Windows or Linux the order is the same. DOS, OS/2, and Windows NT all have an optionally installed bootloader called NTLDR that allows you to choose where to boot from. With Linux there are bootloaders as well; the two most common ones are GRUB and LILO.

GRUB—Grand Unified Bootloader

The Grand Unified Bootloader, or GRUB, is one of two of the most commonly used bootloaders in Linux. GRUB executes the boot process in two stages. The first stage is written to the Master Boot Record (MBR) and its only task is to load the program for stage two of the boot process. Stage two is able to access the filesystems and allows users to choose what operating system, or more specifically, from which filesystem, they want to boot. Your Linux distribution of choice should have more information on how GRUB is configured, but in most operating systems the files that hold the configurations for GRUB reside in the /boot/GRUB/ directory. There are three files that are updated with information when using GRUB:

/boot/grub/menu.1st: The menu.1st file holds information about what operating systems can be booted with GRUB.

/boot/grub/devices.map: The devices map tells the operating system what devices are available by translating terminology used by the BIOS to names that the operating system uses.

/etc/grub.conf: This file contains information that is needed for the GRUB shell to correctly install the bootloader. In the example shown in Listing 5.1, you can see that the file has sections that are preceded by the word title. The title is an entry in the menu you will see when you first start this multioperating system PC. The first title entry is booting a Windows 2000 operating system. The second title entry indicates that it will load Red Hat Linux and kernel version 2.4.18-19.8.0.19. The entry underneath the title line that includes (hd0, 0) indicates that the partition to boot Windows 2000 from is on the first physical hard disk and the first partition, while the Red Hat Linux entry indicates the Linux image exists on the eighth partition and the kernel for the operating system lives on the /boot/ directory there.

LISTING 5.1 The grub.conf configuration file

```
# GRUB.conf generated by anaconda
#
# Note that you do not have to rerun grub after making changes to
this file
# NOTICE:  You do not have a /boot partition.  This means that
#          all kernel and initrd paths are relative to /, eg.
#          root (hd0,8)
#          kernel /boot/vmlinuz-version ro root=/dev/hda9
#          initrd /boot/initrd-version.img
#boot=/dev/hda
# By default boot the second entry
default=1
# Fallback to the first entry.
fallback 0
# Boot automatically after 2 minutes
timeout=120
splashimage=(hd0,8)/boot/grub/splash.xpm.gz
title Windows 2000
unhide (hd0,0)
hide (hd0,1)
hide (hd0,2)
rootnoverify (hd0,0)
chainloader +1
makeactive
title Red Hat Linux (2.4.18-19.8.0.19)
     root (hd0,8)
     kernel /boot/bzImage.2.4.18-19.8.0.19 ro root=LABEL=/
hdd=ide-scsi
     initrd /boot/initrd-2.4.18-19.8.0custom.img
title Red Hat Linux (2.4.18-19.8.0custom)
     root (hd0,8)
     kernel /boot/vmlinuz-2.4.18-19.8.0custom ro root=LABEL=/
hdd=ide-scsi
     initrd /boot/initrd-2.4.18-19.8.0custom.img
title Red Hat Linux (2.4.18-14)
     root (hd0,8)
     kernel /boot/vmlinuz-2.4.18-14 ro root=LABEL=/ hdd=ide-scsi
     initrd /boot/initrd-2.4.18-14.img
title MyKernel.26jan03 (Red Hat Linux 2.4.18-14)
     root (hd0,8)
```

```
        kernel /boot/bzImage.myker.26jan03 ro root=LABEL=/ hdd=ide-scsi
        initrd /boot/initrd-2.4.18-19.8.0.img
title Windows 98
hide (hd0,0)
hide (hd0,1)
unhide (hd0,2)
rootnoverify (hd0,2)
chainloader +1
makeactive
title DOS 6.22
hide (hd0,0)
unhide (hd0,1)
hide (hd0,2)
rootnoverify (hd0,1)
chainloader +1
makeactive
title Partition 2 (floppy)
hide (hd0,0)
unhide (hd0,1)
hide (hd0,2)
chainloader (fd0)+1
title Partition 3 (floppy)
hide (hd0,0)
hide (hd0,1)
unhide (hd0,2)
chainloader (fd0)+1
```

LILO

LILO is a very versatile boot loader that can boot Linux and Windows operating systems. When you install LILO, it is installed to the first sector of the MBR. If you choose to reinstall Windows over your Linux installation you will need to make sure that you overwrite the MBR or LILO will still continue to load. You can rewrite the MBR without changing the partition table information by issuing the following command:

```
fdisk /mbr
```

If you want to remove LILO from Linux you can do so by issuing the following command as the root user, assuming that LILO is installed on the first physical hard drive (/dev/had):

dd if=/dev/zero of /dev/had bs =512 count=1

This should overwrite LILO. However, we'll move forward with the assumption that once you have installed Linux, you won't want to go back to Windows. LILO will pull all its configuration data from the file */etc/lilo.conf*. You will need to run LILO from /sbin/lilo as root after making changes. Listing 5.2 gives you an example of the LILO conf file.

LISTING 5.2   The lilo.conf configuration file

```
# Start LILO global section
boot = /dev/hda     # The boot device.  In this case, the first harddrive
delay = 50          # Delay in tenths of seconds between LILO prompt
                    # and loading of default image.
vga = normal        # Force sane state of video. (80x25)
ramdisk = 0         # Paranoia setting (We don't need one so we'll make
sure
                    # one isn't created.  Only if using distrib boot
disks.)
read-only           # All Linux filesystems should be read-only for the
fsck
                    # at boot time.
root = /dev/hdc1    # Every time I boot Linux it will be on the same root
                    # filesystem.
# End LILO global section
```

You may also use other bootloaders to load Linux. Understanding the disk geometry and other information might help you prevent mistakes and at least know where to start to troubleshoot certain problems.

Fixing Boot Errors

At times you may not be able to boot due to corruption of your Master Boot Record. The Master Boot Record is written at the very beginning of your hard drive and is executed by the computer BIOS. The MBR is compromised of a program, such as stage1 of GRUB or NTLDR for Windows, and a partition table that tells the operating system about the geometry of the hard drive. Sometimes this information and program get corrupted. In these cases you need to fix the MBR. You can do this in a number of ways depending on what your goals are for running the operating system.

Removing the Master Boor Record

In case you ever need to remove LILO or GRUB, you will need to overwrite the MBR so you can run Windows again using the Windows bootloader. Or you may just run into errors and want to fix the MBR to continue to choose between booting various operating systems. In all these cases there are relatively easy ways to accomplish the task.

Windows Boot Disk to Fix the MBR

To fix your MBR with your Windows *bootdisk* or Windows recovery CD, navigate to a DOS prompt and, at the prompt, type `fdisk /mbr`. This should overwrite the Master boot. This is an oversimplification of the process and there are variables that affect the way you fix problems with your MBR. You need to research the limitations of fdisk as well as understand what you may have already done to your system. Running commands like this can and will prevent the normal booting of your PC and are normally reserved for extreme problems or when an operating system is being totally reinstalled.

LOGGING IN

When you boot the Knoppix CD-ROM, it does an auto-login, which is a function
ON THE CD that should be reserved for Live Linux CDs only. The auto-login makes sense because the system can't change on CD. Once you are logged in, you can set a password, which is advisable for the normal Linux user, and even keep a persistent home directory. The Knoppix login process does offers pauses to pass parameters during the boot process, including information that can be passed to the operating system which forces decisions that override the auto-configuration. In most desktop installations you will be offered a login prompt, either text or graphical.

Text Login

Linux PCs don't require you to log in graphically or at all. This feature was especially useful back in the days of limited network bandwidth combined with the need for Linux administrators to access systems remotely or for very simple applications which benefited little from complex graphical interfaces. Skilled Linux administrators often prefer to use the simple direct way of accessing the systems because the time to load the environment is minimal. You can choose to load your Linux environment from either, but for a productivity desktop you likely will choose a graphical login method.

Graphical Login

Today's Linux environments by default share a lot of similarities with the Windows operating system. The main difference is the way that these interfaces are presented among Linux vendors. Each one adds its nuances to the final product. However, by and large, they follow a common theme with a bar across the bottom or top of the screen and a *start* button that launches the primary menus. The differences in graphical environments are a result of the underlying software supplying them. In Windows there is one graphical interface. In Linux there are different providers of the X Windows System, which is the foundation for Linux graphical user interfaces. The difference between X and Microsoft Windows is that X is based on the idea of *network transparency*, which provides sovereignty from the hardware or the operating system. If you so desired you could substitute another graphical system and still leave the Linux OS intact, though this is not common.

The Linux desktop environment has a graphical interface that is not married to the local computer on which it runs. This is significant as it will be helpful in grasping the concept of thin client computing in later discussions. The separation of the display from the host allows the desktop environment to become portable. In single user or thick client computers, this is an extra resource, offering systems administrators and help desk personnel the option to remotely provide support services. This model is very popular in Windows but is facilitated through mostly commercial applications like GoToMyPC®, a software package and service provided by Citrix Online, a division of Citrix Systems, Inc. Another benefit of the X windows system is its modularity. In contrast to Windows, where graphical user interfaces can crash the whole system, Linux graphical systems are not likely to require a reboot.

The X Protocol is designed to function between a client and a server. In the desktop environment, the client-server relationship exists on one physical piece of hardware. The X server is the program included with the operating system that actually draws the pictures or pixels on the screen. It handles the input from mice and keyboards and relays it back to an application. It is what allows keyboard strokes, whether from a local keyboard or from the keyboard of a help desk person across the network, to be recognized by the application. The X client is what sends and receives data from the X server. Once again, this is transparent on a thick client PC, but on a thin client it is what allows users to export sessions from a server to the device. The X windows system is started by the command startx; settings are kept in the user's home directory in a file called .xinitrc. If you choose to log in to a PC in text mode, you can then start the X server later.

XDM

XDM is a graphical login screen. In some systems, it's the graphical login that you use for logging in to local hosts or remote computers. XDM is short for X Display

Manager, and it receives and sends requests using the X Display Manager Control Protocol or XDMCP. You have the option to start XDM or another graphical manager when you start your Linux PC, or you can start in text mode. For desktop PCs it is more likely that you will want to start in graphical mode, while servers will probably start in text simply because the graphical console is not used in applications like Web and mail servers, and a graphical interface would unnecessarily use resources that could be dedicated to their core function.

KDM

Another graphical interface that provides the means to log in to the Linux desktop is *kdm*; it is included with the KDE desktop environment. The kdm login manager can be accessed either on the local machine or over the network. Like XDM, it provides you with a graphical username and password field, as shown in Figure 5.7, when you log in to your PC. It also will offer you the choices of session type (GNOME, KDE, and others). To get kdm to start when you boot your machine, you will need to set it at the run level. Though this is usually automated by your Linux installer you can do it manually by editing */etc/inittab*.

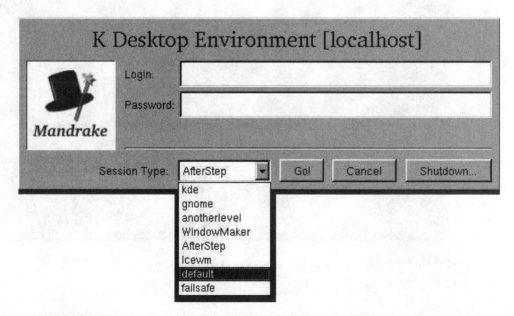

FIGURE 5.7 The figure shows how to log in to the Mandrake KDE desktop environment with a choice of KDE or GNOME, along with a number of other Windows Managers.

GDM

The GNOME display manager is called *gdm*, and it is the graphical presentation for logging in to the GNOME desktop environment. While the presentation to the end user may seem very simple, the actual processes behind the scenes are very complex. As you can see in Figure 5.8, the presentation looks quite a bit different from the kdm illustration in Figure 5.7. This is actually a themed version of the gdm that was part of the Ximian Desktop, a company now owned by Novell. In a situation where you want to present an image to customers, you could theme the login with company-specific information.

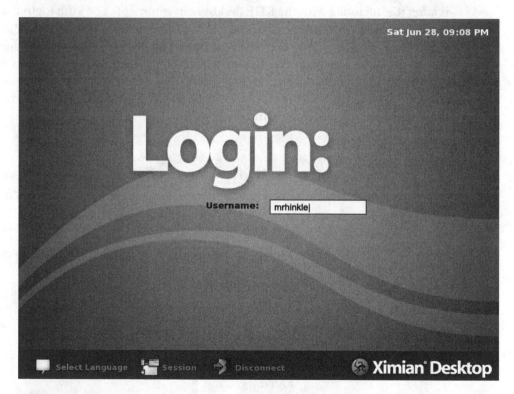

FIGURE 5.8 The gdm login manager with a themed wallpaper.

No matter what your display manager, the point is there are mechanisms that allow you to start your graphical Linux session. To most users this will be seamless, but if you have to troubleshoot login problems, understanding how the system works may give you insight into how to fix a problem.

When you log in via gdm or kdm you can choose to enter your user name and password information, plus you can choose your session type. Once you execute a successful login your session will retain the settings of that use.

The session type may offer you the ability to permanently set your desktop environment to one over another. In Red Hat Linux and Fedora Core, the way to switch desktop environments is to run the *switchdesk* command from the console. This command will launch a graphical utility, as shown in Figure 5.9, that allows you to choose what environment you would like to use by default.

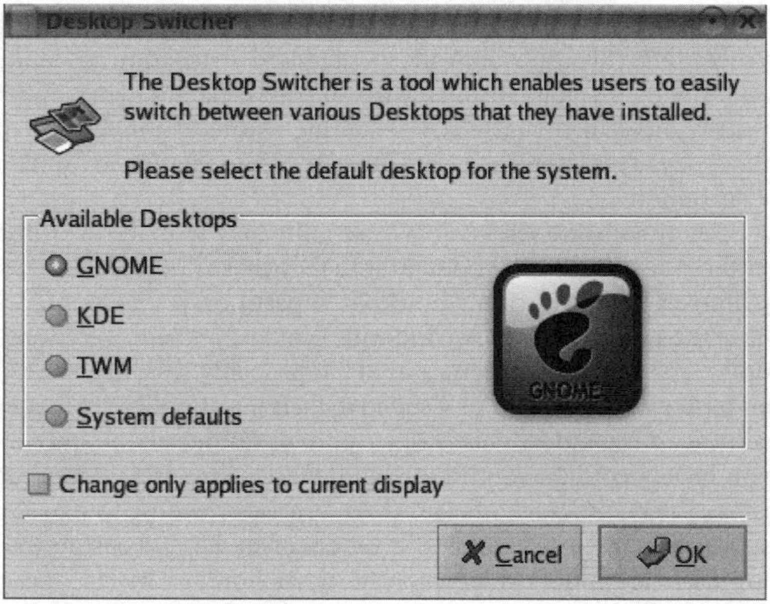

FIGURE 5.9 The switchdesk command will launch a graphical utility that lets you change your default session from one environment to the other.

You can configure any of the login managers mentioned here with relative ease; they are well documented either in the manual provided by your Linux distribution or from a quick search on the Web, which should provide information and tutorials.

SUMMARY

One of the toughest hurdles to overcome when migrating to Linux from Windows is the unfamiliarity with regards to how your new operating system works. The complexity of these systems will likely be masked from the actual user. This is much the way Windows works, making the presentation simple to the user despite the variety of things that are going on in the background. For an administrator or someone who is managing Linux desktops, this overview is designed to provide the tools you need if you should have to troubleshoot a Linux boot process or make decisions on how to install Linux. Linux offers a variety of options for installation. If you have special needs or odd configurations, such as multiple hard drives or multiple operating systems, you should consult your user documentation before proceeding. If you are following the standard installation procedures of your Linux desktop, then you will probably find the information here helpful when presented with choices in the installation routine. None of this information is intended, though, as a replacement for reading the documentation accompanying your Linux distribution.

Many software vendors have taken the time to make their installations unique to their distribution, and often times they make choices for you such as choosing gdm over kdm or deciding how to best partition your system. They probably will have the same success as you did with Windows, where everything works but is not optimized for your particular needs. It probably won't become apparent to most end users what would be best suited to their needs until after they have installed and starting to use Linux. This is why a pilot or test install of Linux is important when you have a configuration that could affect many users. Linux desktop users can tweak their configurations to their enterprise or choose to stay as generic in the install as possible. It's a matter of freedom of choice and customization. Linux desktop users are more like people who buy tailored suits; they get to choose all the features that best fit them. Windows, on the other hand, is like buying off the rack; you must fit into the colors and sizes available for that operating system, rather than finding the operating system that best fits you.

OTHER RESOURCES

- Captive: Free NTFS read/write filesystem for GNU/Linux—*www.jankratochvil.net/project/captive/*
- Mandrake Hardware Database—*www.linux-mandrake.com/en/hardware.php3*
- SuSE Hardware Database—*http://hardwaredb.suse.de/?LANG=en_*
- Filesystem Hierarchy Standard—*www.pathname.com/fhs/*

- Linux Standards Base—*www.linuxbase.org*
- Linux Standards Base Specification—*www.linuxbase.org/spec/*
- Konqueror—*www.konqueror.org*
- GNU Parted—*www.gnu.org/software/parted/*
- Kickstart Mailing List—*https://listman.redhat.com/archives/kickstart-list/*
- YaST Auto Installer AutoYaST—*http://yast.suse.com/autoinstall/*
- XDM and X Terminal mini-HOWTO—*www.tldp.org/HOWTO/XDM-Xterm/*
- The KDM Handbook—*http://docs.kde.org/en/3.3/kdebase/kdm/*
- The Gnome Display Manager Reference Manual—*www.jirka.org/gdm-documentation/t1.html*

6

Using the Linux Desktop

In This Chapter

- Overview of the Linux Environment
- Graphical User Interfaces
- GNOME
- Summary

T he Linux desktop environment is very similar to the Windows or even Mac OS, and many of the elements are presented in a familiar fashion. Generally there is a toolbar with a start button that you can also add program launchers to as well as other items, such as a clock. There is even the equivalent of the Windows *system tray* where commonly used programs like wireless monitors and volume controls can run minimized and be accessed quickly. You may also have a garbage can on your desktop for storing files before finally deleting them. However, you may find distributions of Linux that present a desktop with a completely blank screen. Applications are launched by a menu that appears when you right-click the desktop. You may find unique environments that are like nothing you have used before. If you are using one of the distributions that are mentioned in Appendix C that is probably not the case. Actually, you will probably see something fairly similar to what you saw when you booted the Knoppix Companion CD-ROM. Since there is some commonality among desktop distributions, the focus of this discussion is on how to use the most popular methods for navigating the Linux desktop.

Overview of the Linux Environment: Often times the easiest way to learn something new is by comparing it to something familiar. Most of the examples in this chapter will be presented as comparisons to the way you have done things in the past with Windows. You will find that the presentation of the KDE desktop is very similar to Windows. GNOME may be reminiscent of the Mac OS, because the GNOME toolbar will likely be at the top of the screen with a task manager running as an applet on the bar at the bottom of the screen.

Command Line Interface: Just as Microsoft Windows evolved from a text-based MS-DOS environment, Linux evolved from green screens where all interactions took place via cryptic commands on monochrome terminals. These powerful tools still exist today though many are being replaced by point-and-click alternatives. These powerful underpinnings can offer the knowledgeable Linux user the ability to administer the PC quickly and efficiently.

Graphical Interfaces: There are many ways to configure a Linux graphical user interface; however, the two most common graphical desktop environments are KDE and GNOME. These are the two that are going to be discussed in the greatest detail in this book.

Understanding how to accomplish under Linux the tasks that you once did with Windows will start to build your confidence that this new desktop can provide as good or better functionality as your Windows desktop once did. Also, different is often not better or worse, just different, and you may find that you prefer the way Linux does things in comparison to Windows or you may wish that you could do things as the way you used to. It is likely, though, that with Linux you can configure the desktop in the way that best works for you. The Linux system is very extensible and offers capabilities that are a result of an open system where contributors may have added functions that a core vendor may never have imagined or may have decided was not in the interest of all their users. Single vendor product management is great from a consistency standpoint but can suffer a lowest common denominator mentality, where the end product can't possibly best serve every user. The advantage of the Linux desktop above all others is that it is very adaptable.

OVERVIEW OF THE LINUX ENVIRONMENT

Describing how Linux operates in comparison to Windows is somewhat like comparing a diesel engine to a gasoline-powered one. Overall the end result is the same, but the process for getting the work done is slightly different. Linux often adds a level of complexity that you may not be familiar with as much as you were on Windows. Linux, like Windows, does have a structure of permissions, but it is less transparent to the user than that of Windows. Windows is sometimes accused of taking fewer precautions in a default install than does Linux. It's not uncommon to set up the Windows desktop user with administrator permissions, while Linux provides a highly secure structure with strict permissions to prevent a user from making changes to critical system components. In most Linux distributions the setup will include the provisions for creating not only the root user but at least one additional user for working in the desktop environment (one exception is the Linspire distribution). This practice still makes it easy to use the desktop but more difficult to make system-wide changes. Before we go any further, we should provide a thorough understanding of the hierarchy of the Linux system and the controls that are governed using permissions. These controls provide a means for developing a hardened Linux system because Linux is not only highly functional but secure. Using the tools as intended will help protect your Linux desktop from failures.

Linux is capable of very high security, but sometimes the out-of-the-box configuration is more lax than your enterprise security policies. Part of the hardening, or securing, of Linux involves checking for services that may be running unnecessarily or files that are available for any user on the system to change. In a desktop environment, there are relatively few services that need to be running, especially those related to servers such as Sendmail, Apache Web server, or telnet. All of these services can be exploited by a hacker. If you do need to run any of these services, administrators should carefully watch security warnings posted by CERT which provide information on the latest vulnerabilities, incidents, and fixes for many operating systems. CERT is managed by the Network Systems Survivability Program and funded by the U.S. Department of Defense and the Department of Homeland Security.

Permissions—Users and Groups

Every process on a Linux system is executed by a user. The superuser, or root user, has rights to change anything on the system so, unless necessary, users should have no more access than what they need to complete their tasks. Access to system files and other user data should be avoided. Computer users may login using a username and password that has a subset of permissions or access to the desktop but that doesn't have the ability to make wide, sweeping changes. Some users are not correlated to a person using the computer; they exist only to run a certain type of program or perform a certain task. All users operate with restricted permissions so they can't compromise other parts of the operating system. Every user is part of one or more groups, which makes it easier to share resources and still enforce permissions. Every system at the very least needs a root user; however, logging in as the root user, especially without clear knowledge of what you are doing, can be fatal to your system. Most Linux installation processes prompt you to create at least one nonroot user account. As the diagram in Figure 6.1 shows, every user is a member of a group even if there is only one member per group. Other groups may have multiple members, and files have both individual owners as well as permissions that apply to the groups.

Linux Groups

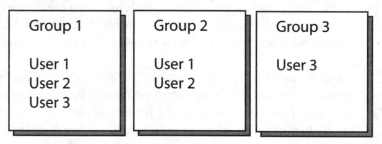

FIGURE 6.1 Every user is a member of one or more groups; users in a group have access to change, execute, and read files governed by the group permissions.

In Windows 95 or 98 you may have had multiple logins to your PC, but they were used to acquire settings held in Profiles. Most often those users could make changes to programs that were shared among the different users who logged into the Windows PC. Linux very seldom gives write access to users in such a way that they can adversely affect other users on the system. This bears similarities to Windows 2000 and XP with the inclusion of the *Limited User* and *Computer Administrator Accounts*. A Computer Administrator has the ability to install programs and hardware, make system wide changes, access and read all nonprivate files, create and delete user accounts, and change other people's accounts, while the Limited user has less access. Figure 6.2 shows the Windows XP dialogue that indicates the presence of an Administrator and limited Guest account.

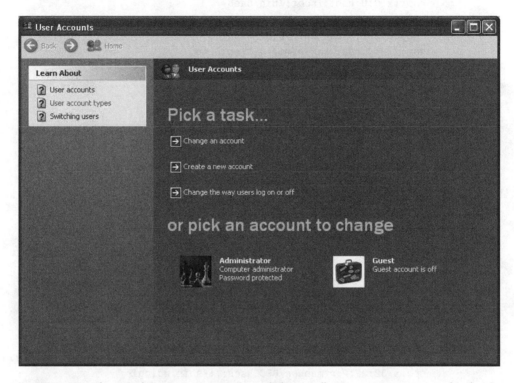

FIGURE 6.2 The Windows XP User Accounts dialogue allows you to create two kinds of user accounts: Computer Administrator and Limited Users.

In Linux, user's and group's information is kept in the files */etc/passwd* and */etc/group*. These are lists of both the users on the system and groups to which those users belong. The file */etc/passwd* may hold information about users, but not all of them are actual PC users. Some are user accounts that are set up to run certain processes, such as Web servers, mail servers, or databases. This allows processes to run as a nonprivileged or partially privileged user, so, for example, if a Web server becomes compromised, it may not compromise the whole operating system if its permissions limit its access. Listing 6.1 shows the listing of a /etc/passwd file. Note that some users who don't log in and use the operating system are denoted by the /sbin/nologin at the end of their entry in the /etc/passwd file.

LISTING 6.1 Code Listing of the /etc/password File.

```
root:x:0:0:root:/root:/bin/bash
bin:x:1:1:bin:/bin:/sbin/nologin
daemon:x:2:2:daemon:/sbin:/sbin/nologin
adm:x:3:4:adm:/var/adm:/sbin/nologin
lp:x:4:7:lp:/var/spool/lpd:/sbin/nologin
sync:x:5:0:sync:/sbin:/bin/sync
shutdown:x:6:0:shutdown:/sbin:/sbin/shutdown
halt:x:7:0:halt:/sbin:/sbin/halt
mail:x:8:12:mail:/var/spool/mail:/sbin/nologin
news:x:9:13:news:/etc/news:
uucp:x:10:14:uucp:/var/spool/uucp:/sbin/nologin
operator:x:11:0:operator:/root:/sbin/nologin
games:x:12:100:games:/usr/games:/sbin/nologin
gopher:x:13:30:gopher:/var/gopher:/sbin/nologin
ftp:x:14:50:FTP User:/var/ftp:/sbin/nologin
nobody:x:99:99:Nobody:/:/sbin/nologin
dbus:x:81:81:System message bus:/:/sbin/nologin
vcsa:x:69:69:virtual console memory owner:/dev:/sbin/nologin
nscd:x:28:28:NSCD Daemon:/:/sbin/nologin
rpm:x:37:37::/var/lib/rpm:/sbin/nologin
haldaemon:x:68:68:HAL daemon:/:/sbin/nologin
netdump:x:34:34:Network Crash Dump user:/var/crash:/bin/bash
sshd:x:74:74:Privilege-separated SSH:/var/empty/sshd:/sbin/nologin
rpc:x:32:32:Portmapper RPC user:/:/sbin/nologin
rpcuser:x:29:29:RPC Service User:/var/lib/nfs:/sbin/nologin
nfsnobody:x:65534:65534:Anonymous NFS User:/var/lib/nfs:/sbin/nologin
mailnull:x:47:47::/var/spool/mqueue:/sbin/nologin
smmsp:x:51:51::/var/spool/mqueue:/sbin/nologin
pcap:x:77:77::/var/arpwatch:/sbin/nologin
apache:x:48:48:Apache:/var/www:/sbin/nologin
squid:x:23:23::/var/spool/squid:/sbin/nologin
webalizer:x:67:67:Webalizer:/var/www/usage:/sbin/nologin
xfs:x:43:43:X Font Server:/etc/X11/fs:/sbin/nologin
ntp:x:38:38::/etc/ntp:/sbin/nologin
gdm:x:42:42::/var/gdm:/sbin/nologin
mrhinkle:x:500:500:Mark R. Hinkle:/home/mrhinkle:/bin/bash
mark:x:501:501:Mark R. Hinkle:/home/mark:/bin/bash
```

The */etc/group* file holds information for groups within a system. In the example shown in Listing 6.2, the group *filesharing* holds users *mrhinkle* and *mark*, which have permissions to access the files belonging to the *filesharing* group. So if a file was group readable, writable, and executable, both users mrhinkle and mark could make changes and execute the file. Note that there is only one user in the root group so that no other users have access to make sweeping system changes. This is equivocal to the administrators group in Windows 2000 or XP. Listing 6.2 shows the contents of an etc/group file.

LISTING 6.2   The contents of an etc/group file

```
root:x:0:root
bin:x:1:root,bin,daemon
daemon:x:2:root,bin,daemon
sys:x:3:root,bin,adm
adm:x:4:root,adm,daemon
tty:x:5:
disk:x:6:root
lp:x:7:daemon,lp
mem:x:8:
kmem:x:9:
wheel:x:10:root
mail:x:12:mail
news:x:13:news
uucp:x:14:uucp
man:x:15:
games:x:20:
gopher:x:30:
dip:x:40:
ftp:x:50:
lock:x:54:
nobody:x:99:
users:x:100:
dbus:x:81:
floppy:x:19:
vcsa:x:69:
nscd:x:28:
rpm:x:37:
haldaemon:x:68:
utmp:x:22:
netdump:x:34:
slocate:x:21:
```

```
sshd:x:74:
rpc:x:32:
rpcuser:x:29:
nfsnobody:x:65534:
mailnull:x:47:
smmsp:x:51:
pcap:x:77:
apache:x:48:
squid:x:23:
webalizer:x:67:
xfs:x:43:
ntp:x:38:
gdm:x:42:
filesharing:x:250:mrhinkle,mark
mrhinkle:x:500:mark: x:501:
```

You can see that all the users listed in the /etc/passwd file have unique names and numbers which are their *userids* (UID). In /etc/group they have one name and number that indicate their *groupid* (GID). In Figure 6.3 you can see that users are added through the graphical YaST tool.

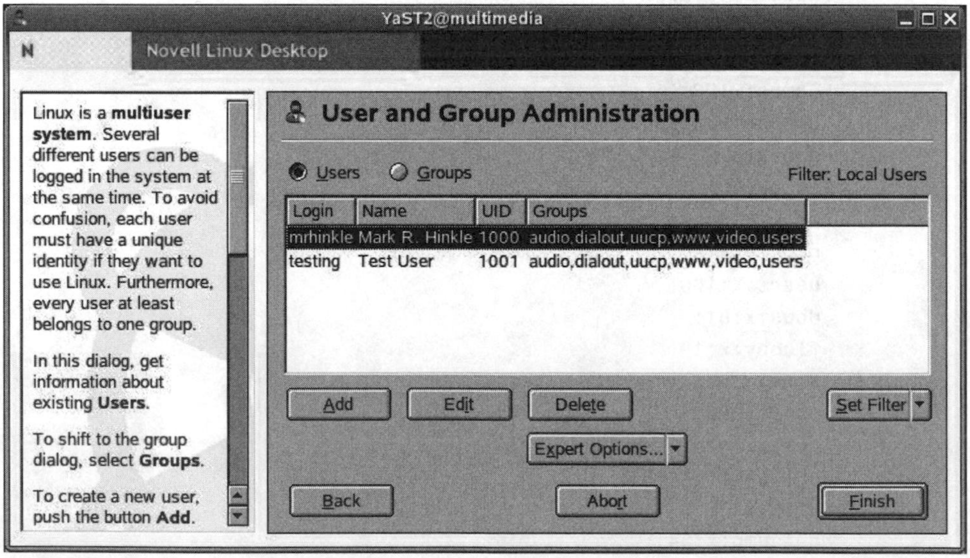

FIGURE 6.3 The Novell Linux Desktop uses YaST to add users and assign them to groups.

Once you understand what users and groups are, you can then look at how they relate to files and directories. You can find out what permissions are placed on files in a directory by using the *ls* command. If you look at Figure 6.4 you will see the listing of all files in a directory. Notice that the files have two columns that include users and groups.

```
[root@www example]# ls
file   file1   file2   file3   file4
[root@www example]# ls -al
total 8
drwxrwxr-x   2 mrhinkle mrhinkle 4096 Aug 18 04:44
drwxr-xr-x   5 mrhinkle mrhinkle 4096 Aug 18 04:05
-rw-rw-r--   1 root     mrhinkle    0 Aug 18 04:44 file
-rw-rw-r--   1 apache   mrhinkle    0 Aug 18 04:04 file1
-rw-rw-r--   1 nobody   mrhinkle    0 Aug 18 04:04 file2
-rw-rw-r--   1 mrhinkle mrhinkle    0 Aug 18 04:05 file3
-rw-r--r--   1 root     root        0 Aug 18 04:44 file4
```

FIGURE 6.4   Listing of files in a Linux directory using the ls command.

The information presented here can be analyzed further, as shown in Figure 6.5 where each line represents a specific file and information about that file. The first column indicates the type of file, either a directory or other type of file. The second column indicates the number of links to the file or directory from within the filesystem. The third and fourth columns indicate the owner and the group. The fifth column indicates the size displayed in bytes, the date stamp indicates when the file was created, and the last column is the filename.

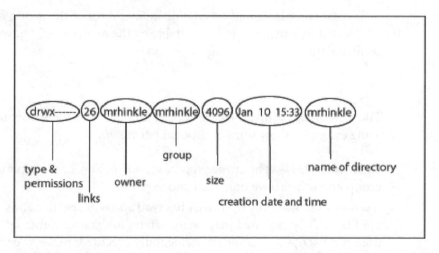

FIGURE 6.5   Each column of the detailed file listing shows different information about the file.

Note that permissions are displayed using the letters r, w, and x. These indicate the three types of permissions a file can have: read (r), write (w), and execute (x). These letters, when written out, are done so in the following notation:

```
-rwxrwxrwx
```

The first set of three indicates what changes can be made by the owner of the file, the second group indicates what can be done by the group that the file belongs to, and the final group (sometimes referred to as the world) indicates what any user can do to the file. This code example indicates that the file is totally unrestricted with full permissions given to the user, group, and world. In the following example we will look at a common setting for Web servers that allow anyone to execute a file or read it but not write to the file (writing also implies deleting).

```
-rwxr-xr-x
```

Notice that dashes have been substituted where permissions were in the previous example. You can also represent permissions numerically. You can do this by using a three-number notation that is the sum of permissions for each of the three domains. For example, the following list shows the numerical values for permissions.

- Read—r – 4
- Write—w – 2
- Execute—x – 1
- None—0

A file that is readable and executable by members of the group and everyone else, but readable, writeable, and executable by the owner would have permissions that look like this:

```
755
```

The numerical permissions are shorter to type than the whole notation. The following examples show some additional permissions:

rwxr-xr-x (755)—The owner has read, write, and execute permissions; the group and others have only read and execute.

-rw------- (600)—Only the owner has read and write permissions. The fact that the file can't be executed may be for safety; for example, this setting might be used for a script that could, if accidentally executed, make sweeping and fatal system changes without proper care.

rw-r--r-- (644)—Only the owner has read and write permissions; the group and others can only read the files.

rwx------ (700)—Only the owner can access the file but then with full permissions.

rwx--x--x (711)—The owner has read, write, and execute permissions; the group and others have only execute.

-rw-rw-rw- (666)—Everyone can read and write to the file. Use caution when applying this permission because it effectively allows anyone to access, alter, or delete the file.

rwxrwxrwx (777)—Everyone can read, write, and execute. This is effectively removes all limitations on a file, so be absolutely sure you want to allow this file to run or be altered by anyone.

Once you understand permissions you can move on to how to make changes to file permissions using the *chmod* command.

Changing Ownership and Permissions

If you have data and you don't write it often, for instance, something like an archived copy of a presentation, you could change the permissions for the files to be read only, that way it is harder, but not impossible, for the file to be overwritten or deleted. You can do this by using the *chmod* command. Chmod sets permissions for a file. The syntax is typically `chmod ### file` where ### are the permissions for owner, group, and all other users. For files that you want to insure won't get overwritten, you can set that number to 444, where the four indicates read only. In the following example, the example file is `example.txt`, creating using the `vi` editor. Once you have created the file, you can use `chmod` to set the files to read only so that you don't overwrite the data there. Notice that if you try to remove the file, you get warned. This isn't a foolproof method and you could answer `y` to the `rm` dialog and the file would be deleted, but the warning should help prompt a user to think twice before editing or deleting the file.

```
mrhinkle@linux:~> vi example.txt
mrhinkle@linux:~> chmod 444 example.txt
mrhinkle@linux:~> rm example.txt
rm: remove write-protected regular file `example.txt'? n
```

As a cautionary step you may want to change the ownership of the files to another user with only read-only attributes. For example, a user that is logged in as `mrhinkle` cannot delete files owned by the mark user if the file is not world writable or group writable. You may want to even create an archive user. Then use the *chown* command to "change owner" to archive. Keep in mind that to do this you must have permissions for that file, so it's easily done as the root user. The syntax for this would be:

```
root@linux:~> chown mark example.txt
```

In the example, the ownership of `example.txt` was changed to user *mark*. If you want to transfer file ownership from one user to another, you may want to log in as root user, then use `chown` to change the ownership of a file from one owner to another. This might be necessary when an employee leaves your company and you want to move and change ownership of his files to another user's /home directory. Make sure you remember to change ownership, because even though you move the files to another directory, they aren't necessarily owned by the owner of the directory in which they reside. The average user will probably never delve into the details of a file's permissions, but a systems administrator or IT help desk person may need to use this practice fairly often. Now that you have a fundamental overview of ownership you can start to look at how processes are executed by users.

Processes

When a program is running it is called a process. This is the same for a Windows PC or a Linux PC. In Windows, a process may be started by clicking on a file called program.exe. In Linux the same thing happens when you run the program by typing its name on the command line or by clicking on a launcher on the desktop. You can look to see what processes are running in Windows by using the Task Manager. In Windows XP, the Task Manager gives information about the program or image name, the user running the process, the CPU usage, and the memory usage. You can run Task Manager by right-clicking on the task bar at the bottom of the Windows desktop as shown in Figure 6.6.

There are other tabs that offer more information, including overall performance of the system and cumulative performance of the PC, users logged in, as well as friendly names of applications (the actual programs as you the user know them, not as illustrator.exe or something less obvious), and networking statistics. The Linux system also offers basically the same functionality using the command line program *top*. The top program shows much of the same information, though it is executed in a text format rather than a graphical format. Figure 6.7 shows a server running top to show what programs are running and how many resources each process is using.

The top command, once executed, is constantly updating as the system changes. In a system where very few programs are running and using system resources, you

Windows Task Manager

File   Options   View   Shut Down   Help

Applications | Processes | Performance | Networking | Users

Image Name	User Name	CPU	Mem Usage
svchost.exe	SYSTEM	00	3,848 K
script-fu.exe	Administrator	00	8,196 K
Illustrator.exe	Administrator	01	76,908 K
WISPTIS.EXE	Administrator	00	3,928 K
gimp-2.0.exe	Administrator	02	24,752 K
realsched.exe	Administrator	00	120 K
firefox.exe	Administrator	00	101,676 K
OUTLOOK.EXE	Administrator	00	44,776 K
iPodService.exe	SYSTEM	00	3,360 K
rundll32.exe	Administrator	00	12,560 K
WINWORD.EXE	Administrator	00	41,320 K
taskmgr.exe	Administrator	01	5,444 K
BCMWLTRY.EXE	SYSTEM	00	10,400 K
WLTRYSVC.EXE	SYSTEM	00	1,152 K
wdfmgr.exe	LOCAL SERVICE	00	1,556 K
alg.exe	LOCAL SERVICE	00	3,324 K
MDM.EXE	SYSTEM	00	2,552 K
LogMeIn.exe	SYSTEM	00	9,616 K

☐ Show processes from all users   End Process

Processes: 61 | CPU Usage: 4% | Commit Charge: 749M / 2463M

FIGURE 6.6   The Windows Task Manager running on Windows XP.

might see top at the "top of the list" as it is busy gathering information about the system. You also may notice that at the top of your screen you will see a summary of system information including its uptime, the number of users (keep in mind some users may be system users that are running services like Web servers), the number of tasks running, and how much CPU and memory is being used. You can also choose to stop a process by using the *xkill* program, which adds a skull and crossbones to your cursor and then you can click on an application that has stopped responding.

*You can also use a program called process from the command line that shows you what programs are running. The process command is executed by typing ps. If you know the name of the process you can also search for it simply by running the ps command and searching the output. The command to do this for a program called program would be **ps –aux | grep program** where the –aux are all switches for show all (a) processes, select by userid (u), and select processes without controlling type (x). You should also note that you can only end processes over which you have permissions.*

```
top - 21:00:06 up  4:00,  7 users,  load average: 0.66, 0.58, 0.47
Tasks: 126 total,   1 running, 125 sleeping,   0 stopped,   0 zombie
Cpu(s): 16.4% us,   2.0% sy,   0.0% ni, 81.2% id,   0.3% wa,   0.0% hi,   0.0% si
Mem:   1030996k total,  1017944k used,     13052k free,     81612k buffers
Swap:  1028120k total,      684k used,   1027436k free,    456612k cached

  PID USER      PR  NI  VIRT  RES  SHR S %CPU %MEM    TIME+  COMMAND
14345 mrhinkle  15   0 22412  12m  19m S 20.3  1.2  0:00.61 screenshot
11858 mrhinkle  16   0 99.2m  65m  40m S  5.7  6.5  4:25.22 firefox-bin
 4741 root      16   0  165m  33m 137m S  3.7  3.4  9:31.73 X
10576 mrhinkle  16   0 29056  15m  24m S  1.0  1.6  0:06.09 kdeinit
14322 mrhinkle  15   0 46360  35m  22m S  1.0  3.5  0:02.34 gimp-2.0
10544 mrhinkle  15   0 10476 6216 9660 S  0.7  0.6  1:30.30 artsd
10881 mrhinkle  15   0  208m 144m 208m S  0.7 14.4 11:45.06 dosexec
10578 mrhinkle  16   0 25564  12m  22m S  0.3  1.2  0:00.57 kdeinit
10582 mrhinkle  15   0 37080  24m  29m S  0.3  2.5  0:08.26 kdeinit
14308 mrhinkle  15   0 31616  16m  27m S  0.3  1.7  0:00.73 kdeinit
14320 mrhinkle  16   0  1976  980 1764 R  0.3  0.1  0:00.14 top
    1 root      16   0   596  236  452 S  0.0  0.0  0:06.29 init
    2 root      RT   0     0    0    0 S  0.0  0.0  0:00.01 migration/0
    3 root      34  19     0    0    0 S  0.0  0.0  0:00.00 ksoftirqd/0
    4 root      RT   0     0    0    0 S  0.0  0.0  0:00.01 migration/1
    5 root      34  19     0    0    0 S  0.0  0.0  0:00.00 ksoftirqd/1
    6 root       5 -10     0    0    0 S  0.0  0.0  0:00.11 events/0
    7 root       5 -10     0    0    0 S  0.0  0.0  0:00.00 events/1
    8 root       8 -10     0    0    0 S  0.0  0.0  0:00.01 khelper
    9 root       5 -10     0    0    0 S  0.0  0.0  0:04.01 kacpid
   10 root       5 -10     0    0    0 S  0.0  0.0  0:01.49 kblockd/0
   11 root       5 -10     0    0    0 S  0.0  0.0  0:00.04 kblockd/1
   45 root      15   0     0    0    0 S  0.0  0.0  0:00.00 kirqd
   46 root      15   0     0    0    0 S  0.0  0.0  0:00.19 pdflush
   47 root      15   0     0    0    0 S  0.0  0.0  0:00.34 pdflush
   48 root      15   0     0    0    0 S  0.0  0.0  0:00.73 kswapd0
   49 root       5 -10     0    0    0 S  0.0  0.0  0:00.00 aio/0
```

FIGURE 6.7 The top command being executed on the command line.

The Command Line Interface

The command line interface (CLI) is the text-based screen that allows you to interact with the Linux operating system in a simple text environment. There are many types of programs that allow you to interact in this format. They are called shell programs or simply shells. The one you will most likely use or be offered when you install your Linux desktop is the bash shell (which stands for Bourne Again SHell). For the purposes of this discussion, the bash shell will be the type of shell referred to. However you may run into three other commonly used shells:

ksh: The Korn shell

tsch: An advanced version of the Berkley Unix C shell

zsh: The Z shell resembles the K or Korn shell but has many additional features

For the desktop PC user, the bash shell should serve you well. If you have programmers who have established a preference in your enterprise, there is no reason why they shouldn't use the shell they are most comfortable with.

Terminal Emulators

Because most of you will use a graphical desktop interface, you will need to find a way to enter your commands on the command line; for this task you will use a terminal emulator. In GNOME, you will be offered options like gnome-terminal, regular xterm, and color xterm on the Utilities menu or, depending how your distribution arranges things, possibly on a System menu. In KDE you will probably find Konsole (identifiable by a seashell icon) or xterm as options from your KMenu.

The Shell

The shell is the text interface to the operating system which lets you communicate via text only. Bash is a UNIX command shell that was written for the GNU project. When bash starts, it processes a number of scripts. The files that it reads first are /etc/profile; then it looks for .bash_profile and .bash_login, which will reside in the user's home directory (/home/username). You can use bash_profile to set shortcuts or scripts that can be used to automate tasks.

Windows users are used to a filename followed by a period and a three letter extension, in the format of program.exe. In Linux this is not the case. The file itself will be parsed and run even without a file extension name; though if you like you can use the same convention for programs you create.

Manipulating Files

The command line interface works much the same way as the DOS interface; you type a series of commands to manipulate files.

Deleting Files: Deleting files on the command line is very simple. You can remove a single file using the *rm* command. For example, to remove the file *olddata* you would issue the following command:

```
rm olddata
```

Moving Files: You can move files using the *mv* file command. To move a file called moveme from */home/mrhinkle/* to */home/mrhinkle/moved/* you would issue the following command:

```
mv /home/mrhinkle/moveme /home/mrhinkle/moved/
```

The result would be that the file *moveme* would be moved to the */home/mrhinkle/moved/* directory.

Renaming Files: To rename a file, you would once again use the move command, but you would use the move command as if you were moving the file to a new name. For example, if you were to rename the */home/mrhinkle/moved/ moveme* file to *renamed* you would issue the following command:

```
mv moveme renamed
```

The result would be that the file is now renamed to a file named *renamed*.

Navigating the Filesystem: To the navigate the filesystem, you change directories using the *cd* command. The cd command works by entering the command followed by the path to the directory you want to enter. For example, to enter the directory */usr/share/* you would issue the following command:

```
cd /usr/share/
```

DOS to Linux Conversions

Many Windows users were once DOS users and may be more comfortable with a DOS to Linux analogy. Table 6.1 lists DOS commands and their Linux counterpart.

TABLE 6.1 Dos to Linux Conversions

DOS Commands	Linux Equivalent	Use
attrib	chmod	Changes the permissions of a file
cd	cd	Changes the directory to a different directory in the filesystem
cls	clear	Clears the text from the terminal screen
copy	cp	Copies files
del	rm	Deletes files
dir	ls	Lists files in a directory
md	mkdir	Creates a directory
more	more/less	More and less both allow you to view the contents of a file
move	mv	Moves a file from within the filesystem
rd	rm -rf	Removes a directory and its contents
ren	mv	When you rename a file in Linux you move the file from one name to another
type	cat	Displays the contents of a file
ver	Cat	Displays the contents of a file; short for concatenate

Searching for Files

Searching for files on the command line is not intuitive; you can use the `find` command, which can search the whole filesystem or a subset of the directories, by specifying a start point. For example, to find out if a user had any MP3 files in his home directory, you could execute the find command using a wildcard and find all files with that search pattern.

```
Find /home —name *mp3
```

The results will be a list of all files in the /home/ directory and subdirectories that match the search pattern `mp3`. This is a handy tool, but if you where looking through the whole system it could be very time consuming. The find command operates in a brute force way, carefully checking every directory. Another option is to use the *slocate* command to find files on your system. The slocate command works by building an index that can be quickly searched to find files on the system. The caveat is that slocate can only find indexed files, so if you have your Linux PC set to run the index at some point and time, and if you create a file after the index was updated, then the program will not return the search result.

Shell Applications

The shell is an extremely powerful tool that can accomplish an almost unlimited number of tasks. It also supports very powerful and robust scripting languages so that a number of very complex operations can be completed via a shell script. However, for the purpose of the average desktop user, these tasks will probably be limited to reading and editing files. That is why our discussion will just briefly touch on these functions, though it may be worth researching the capabilities of the bash shell even more.

Editing and Viewing Files

You can view files using the command *less*. *Less* is a simple file viewer that allows you to move forward and backward through a file. So to enter a file, you simply type the command `less` followed by the filename. For example, for the file *example* you would type `less example.txt` and then navigate forwards and backwards using your arrow keys. If you want to edit a file you would use the VIM editor, which can be launched by typing *vi* or *vim*. You can normally perform these operations in a graphical mode, but when you encounter a problem that does not allow your system to boot, or if you need to access the system remotely via a graphical interface, it can be very useful, just as under Windows you might choose to boot your system into a text-only safe mode.

Midnight Commander: A Robust Text-Based File Manager

Midnight Commander is a directory-browsing and file manipulation program that is very similar to the Norton Commander file manager that is popular for DOS and Windows. You can run Midnight Commander (Figure 6.8) as an alternative to typing the commands to navigate files on the command line (providing the package is installed). Once again this is just a shortcut for users who may need to navigate the filesystem but don't have the time to learn the commands to navigate the filesystem using the bash shell.

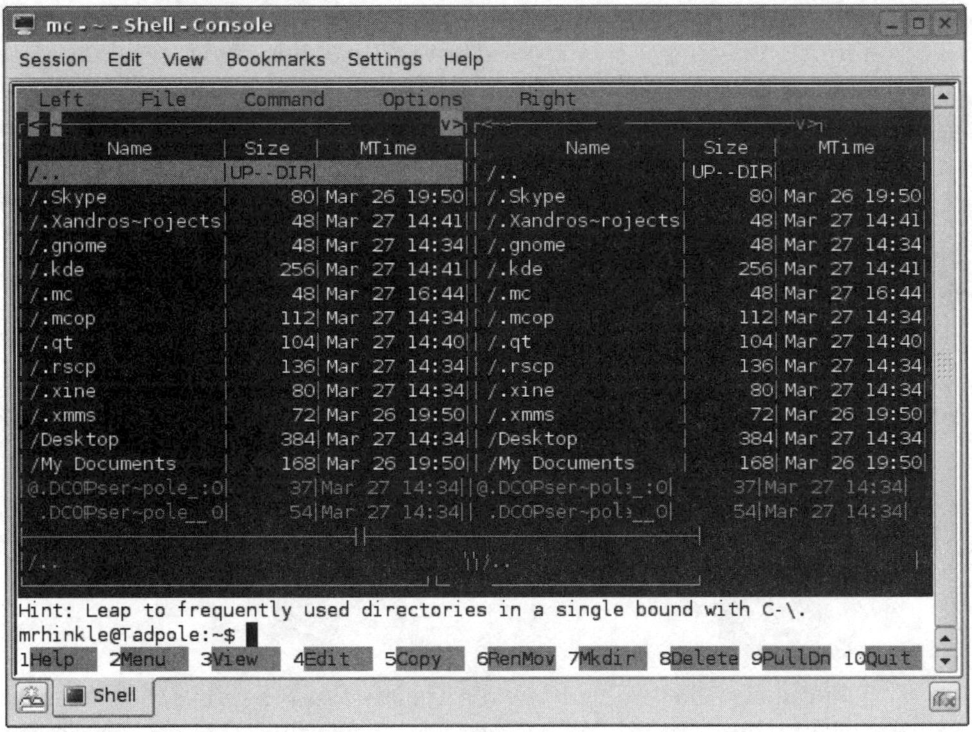

FIGURE 6.8 Midnight Commander is a menu-driven file manager for the terminal.

Midnight Commander would not likely be considered a standard interface to the Linux filesystem, but it's a free and easy way to acquire a program that has similarities to some DOS tools. It is one example of the many free tools that can be used to enhance your Linux desktop installation.

Getting Help

Most often, the provider of your Linux distribution will provide a manual either on the system or on its Web site. If you purchase media and documentation you have access to those resources. There may be a support systems included with your Linux distribution that links to a help system within your desktop. However, beyond that there are help systems built into the Linux operating system. At the command line you can use the *man* and *info* commands to find out more about how to use specific functions of the system. In many applications there are help menus that link to HTML or online help just as there are with other systems.

Man

Man pages are one-page descriptions of Linux programs and a very traditional, though to many a very cryptic, form of help. The format for using man is to use the command *man*. If you want help with the *rm* command, for example, typing man rm will yield the man page, as shown in Figure 6.9. Many of the common Linux commands offer online help through the man page system.

NAME
    rm - remove files or directories

SYNOPSIS
    rm [OPTION]... FILE...

DESCRIPTION
    This manual page documents the GNU version of rm. rm removes each specified file. By default, it does not remove directories.

    If a file is unwritable, the standard input is a tty, and the -f or --force option is not given, rm prompts the user for whether to remove the file. If the response does not begin with â ˜yâ ™ or â ˜Yâ ™, the file is skipped.

OPTIONS
    Remove (unlink) the FILE(s).

    -d, --directory
    unlink FILE, even if it is a non-empty directory (super-user only)

    -f, --force
    ignore nonexistent files, never prompt

    -i, --interactive
    prompt before any removal

    -r, -R, --recursive
    remove the contents of directories recursively

    -v, --verbose
    explain what is being done

    --help display this help and exit

    --version
    output version information and exit

To remove a file whose name starts with a â ˜-â ™, for example â ˜-fooâ ™, use one of these commands:

rm.td/rm -- -foo

rm.td/rm ./-foo

Note that if you use rm to remove a file, it is usually possible to recover the contents of that file. If you want more assurance that the contents are truly unrecoverable, consider using shred.

AUTHOR
    Written by Paul Rubin, David MacKenzie, Richard Stallman, and Jim Meyering.

REPORTING BUGS
    Report bugs to <bug-coreutils@gnu.org>.

COPYRIGHT
    Copyright Â© 2002 Free Software Foundation, Inc.
    This is free software; see the source for copying conditions. There is NO warranty; not even for MERCHANTABILITY or FITNESS FOR A PARTICULAR PURPOSE.

SEE ALSO
    shred(1)

    The full documentation for rm is maintained as a Texinfo manual. If the info and rm programs are properly installed at your site, the command

    info rm

    should give you access to the complete manual.

rm (coreutils) 4.5.3   August 2003   RM(1)

FIGURE 6.9   Man pages are text-based help available from the command line interface.

Info

The GNU project distributes most of its manuals in *info* format. If your system has the info manual for a particular program available you can view the manual in the info reader by typing `info` and the program name at the command line. For each manual there is a header that tells you about the manual. Not every command has an info manual, but many do and it is often a way to quickly get help when navigating the Linux shell. Figure 6.10 shows the info page for the rm command.

File: coreutils.info, Node: rm invocation, Next: shred invocation, Prev: mv invocation, Up: Basic operations

11.5 `rm': Remove files or directories
===

`rm' removes each given FILE. By default, it does not remove directories. Synopsis:

   rm [OPTION]... [FILE]...

   If a file is unwritable, standard input is a terminal, and the `-f'
or `--force' option is not given, or the `-i' or `--interactive' option _is_ given, `rm' prompts the user for whether to remove the file. If the response does not begin with `y' or `Y', the file is skipped.

   Warning: If you use `rm' to remove a file, it is usually possible to recover the contents of that file. If you want more assurance that the contents are truly unrecoverable, consider using `shred'.

   The program accepts the following options. Also see *Note Common options::.

`-d'
`--directory'
   Attempt to remove directories using the `unlink'
function rather
    than the `rmdir' function, and don't require a directory to be
    empty before trying to unlink it. This works only if you have
    appropriate privileges and if your operating system supports
    `unlink' for directories. Because unlinking a directory causes
    any files in the deleted directory to become unreferenced, it is
    wise to `fsck' the filesystem after doing this.

`-f'
`--force'
   Ignore nonexistent files and never prompt the user.
Ignore any
    previous `--interactive' (`-i') option.

`-i'
`--interactive'
   Prompt whether to remove each file. If the response does not begin
    with `y' or `Y', the file is skipped. Ignore any previous
    `--force' (`-f') option.

`--preserve-root'
   Fail upon any attempt to remove the filesystem root, `/', when
    used with the `--recursive' option. Without `--recursive', this
    option has no effect. *Note Treating / specially::.

`--no-preserve-root'
   Cancel the effect of any preceding `--preserve-root'
option.
    *Note Treating / specially::.

`-r'
`-R'
`--recursive'
   Remove the contents of directories recursively.

`-v'
`--verbose'
   Print the name of each file before removing it.

   One common question is how to remove files whose names begin with a `-'. GNU `rm', like every program that uses the `getopt'
function to
parse its arguments, lets you use the `--' option to indicate that all following arguments are non-options. To remove a file called `-f' in the current directory, you could type either:

   rm -- -f

or:

   rm ./-f

   The Unix `rm' program's use of a single `-' for this purpose predates the development of the getopt standard syntax.

   An exit status of zero indicates success, and a nonzero value indicates failure.

FIGURE 6.10   An info page for the rm command.

Installing Programs

Installing programs under Linux is not as standardized as in Windows. Linux users usually install software in one of two ways. The first is to install binary packages via an archive packaged in *.RPM* format or *.DEB /.DPKG* format. The second way to install programs is to compile the program from its source code. Using the actual programming code, a binary is created that can be run as a program. This method relies on the presence of a compiler like *gcc* (GNU Compile Collection) to compile the code into a program sometimes called a binary. This lack of standardization in distribution methods is probably one of the biggest drawbacks to the Linux desktop; programs have to be packaged in multiple ways for all Linux users to take advantage of them. Programs may also have dependencies on software packages such as libraries to be fully functional. If you don't have the libraries installed, you may have to hunt them down and install them before the program will install as desired.

RPM

RPM is a recursive acronym for RPM Package Manager, which is one of the most popular ways to install programs on Linux. RPM-based Linux distributions (e.g., Red Hat, Fedora, Mandriva, SuSE, and Novell) have three distinct elements:

rpm: A binary package that is installed by the RPM package manager. This is how Linux programs are commonly distributed.

RPM: The program used to install the binary package.

RPM Database: The RPM database is a list that keeps track of all the packages installed in the system. The RPM database is similar to the database shown in the Add/Remove Programs dialogue in Windows

Using RPM can be very easy; there are a number of ways to graphically manage the RPM database, or you can access it via a command line. If you choose to install an RPM, most graphical interfaces will prompt you to follow the process, though you can use the underlying text utilities to get the same result.

Command Line RPM Usage

To install a program using rpm you need superuser access to the system. Also, you can only install one program at a time because as RPMs install they update the RPM database. If you are running the update mechanism for your distribution, this will usually lock the database as software is being downloaded and updated in the background. Using RPM is very straight forward and sometimes easier to use on the command line because you will get feedback regarding the supporting packages that may be required by the program.

To install an rpm package you need to use the *–i* switch for install and the name of the package. For example, to install a package called *mypackage.version1.rpm*, you would use the following command:

```
sudo rpm —i mypackage.version1.rpm
```

You may also want to install a package that is on an ftp site. You can install that same package via ftp.

```
sudo rpm —i ftp://www.luckydog.org/pub/rpm/mypackage.version1.rpm
```

As the package downloads, it will install, combining the two steps in one command. To remove an RPM the syntax is very similar, You use the *–e* switch, as in erase. To remove a package called *myprogram.rpm* you would do the following:

```
sudo rpm —e mypackage.rpm
```

There are many other options or switches you can use when installing rpms, but in most cases you will be doing one of three things: installing, removing, or updating.

Note that all the uses of rpm are prefaced with the sudo, or superuser do, command. If you are installing the software and are already logged in as the root user this is not necessary. This command is appropriate here because it allows the user to accomplish single tasks as the superuser without maintaining superuser privileges. The sudo command will also prompt you for a password, so before the command executes the password must be entered correctly. Sudo requires that users be added to the sudoers file, /etc/sudoers, or they will not be able to access sudo. In an administered desktop where help desk personnel make these changes, this is not as common as it would be in a situation where the users administer their own desktop PCs.

APT

APT is an acronym for Advanced Package Tool and is the program used to install programs for Debian-based Linux distributions. The apt tool is considered to be very easy to use and works with either a command line interface or the popular Synaptic GUI package management program. Apt works by checking a list of package repositories held in the */etc/apt/sources.list* file which can be configured to check Internet download sites as well as repositories maintained within your own network. Before you start to install files you should make sure that your sources list is up to date

To install a file with apt you type the following command where *packagename* indicates the name of the package you want to get. For example, as the root user or using sudo, you could choose to install with the following command:

```
sudo apt-get install packagename
```

This will grab not only the program you want but all the packages that depend on that program. You can also remove programs by typing the following command:

```
sudo apt-get remove packagename
```

One of the most attractive features of apt is the ability to upgrade all the packages on your system by using the *apt-get upgrade* or sometime *apt-get dist-upgrade*. The apt-get upgrade command will download all packages on your system that it can find from your repositories list. You can make sure that the list of packages is updated by using the *apt-get update* command which will download all package lists from all potential sources.

Apt has also been ported to the rpm system by former Linux distributor Connectiva, which has since been acquired by Mandrakesoft to form Mandriva. Connectiva took the apt tools and made them work well with RPM distributions. The apt-rpm tools rely on different repositories that contain rpms rather than .deb files, but otherwise the mechanics of both are pretty much the same.

Others

There are some other types of systems for packaging software and building it. For example, the Gentoo Linux distribution uses a system called Portage, which performs many administrative tasks. Basically Portage works in a similar way to RPM from the user perspective, as it checks for the availability of packages and then installs them. However, the technology is very different from RPM, and instead is similar to the ports system used in FreeBSD.

Miscellaneous Package Install Programs

There are a variety of Linux tools that are each a little different based on what distribution you are using. Commonly they are integrated into the update service preferred by your Linux distribution and they may allow you to choose multiple programs to install at once and then sequentially add them and help resolve the dependencies of the Linux.

YUM

YUM is an acronym for the Yellow dog Updater, Modified. YUM has become recently popular because it automatically computes dependencies (libraries and other subprograms needed to support the target program) and makes decisions on how to update those packages. YUM has become a popular tool that complements the Red Hat up2date and other rpm tools or that can be used in lieu of them; if you try the popular Fedora Core Linux distribution, it is likely that you will find that YUM is becoming the solution of choice for package updates and software installation.

Synaptic

Synaptic is a graphical package management program for the apt-get utility. Apt-get is a tool that is normally used with Debian-based distributions. Synaptic is a good blend of the features that Windows users would have access to through the Add/ Remove Programs dialogue in the Control Panel and the Windows Update service.

Archives

Linux users, just like Windows users, often receive files in a compressed format. In Windows it is likely you have downloaded a file with .zip extension and opened it with a program like Winzip. In Linux there are similar types of files. Often a group of files is distributed in an archive that is presented in a *tar* file, which stands for *tape archiver* because of its original use in archiving data to magnetic tape. This is still the most popular way to archive files today. Archives are useful because not only are they a way to bundle files and directories but they can maintain their permissions. To create an archive of the folder *MyDocuments* you would issue the following command:

```
tar —cvf MyDocuments.tar MyDocuments
```

The command `tar` is followed by the parameters or switches, which in this case indicate `c` for create, `v` for verbose, and `f` for file. The `mydocuments.tar` file is the name of the archive you want to create and MyDocuments is the directory that you wish to archive.

You may find that the source codes for some programs are distributed in archives that usually will end in .tar if they are compressed. For example, you might see extenstions such as tar.gz or tar.bz2. The compression is usually done using *gzip*. You can compress files using gzip; when you want to compress an archive you can do that in a single step by adding the z switch. To refer again to the previous example, to create a compressed archive from the MyDocuments folder you would issue the following command:

```
tar —czvf MyDocuments.tar.gz MyDocuments
```

This is probably the way system administrators and command line users will create archives. However, most desktop users will be able to simply right-click on their folders through their file manager of choice and then choose the Compress or Create archive function. In most Linux distributions there will be a helper application that does the work for you. As you can see in Figure 6.11, the right-click menu has an option to compress the file or folder. This is by far the easiest way to create and open archives and requires very little training. It also mimics the way WinZip integrates in Windows.

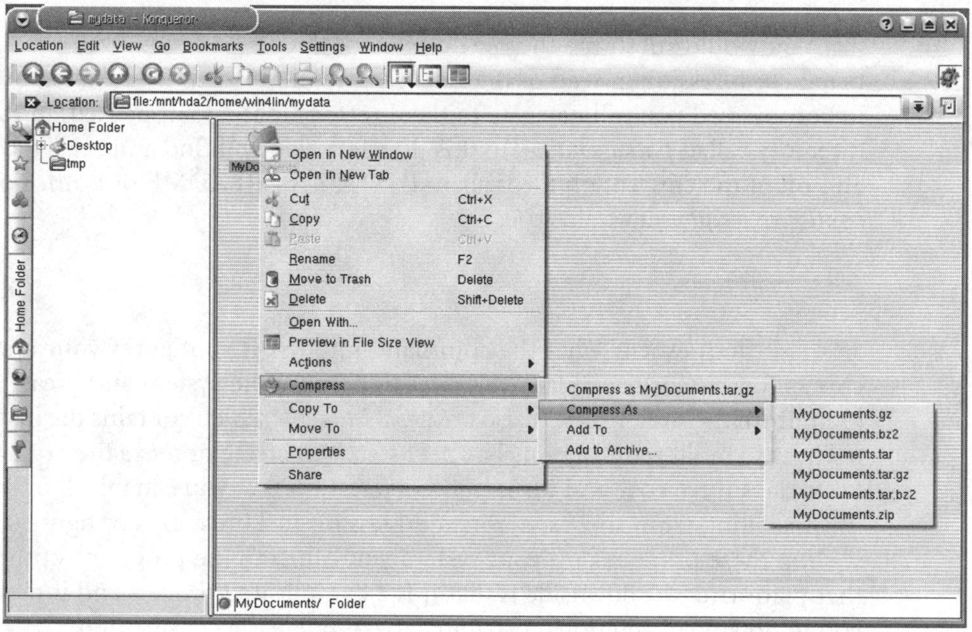

FIGURE 6.11   The compress dialogue in Konqueror for creating archives.

Compiling From Source Code

Often times software will be distributed as source code that requires you to compile the program into an executable program. This process is not difficult but can be time consuming.

The Procedure

You may receive source code in a package that has been compressed. These packages are typically in the following formats: packagename.tar.gz, packagename.tgz, or packagename.bz2. Any of these packages is typically a directory that has been tarred, or combined into one file. The gz or bz2 indicates that the file has been compressed. This is similar to when you zip a file with WinZip under Windows. The programs used to decompress the file are either gzip (for files ending in gz) or bzip (for files ending in bz2). When the program that separates the file again is tar, these packages are often referred to as tarballs. So, for our example called *packagename. tar.gz*, the first step would be to decompress and unpack the file using the following command:

```
tar -xzvf packagename.tar.gz
```

You would substitute the *j* switch for *z* if the file ended in bz2, to address the bzip2 compression instead of the gzip compression which is indicated by z. Once uncompressed you will navigate to the directory that was unpacked, in this case a directory called *packagename*. In this directory you will find a file called *configures* and often the convention files called .INSTALL or README or both. To run the *configure script* you would type:

```
./configure
```

This does exactly what the command implies; it configures your system and checks for system-dependant variables to prepare the system and create the program from the source files. It also creates a *Makefile* which contains the instructions for how to build the program. The next step is to create or *make* the program. This takes the source code and turns it into a program that you can install or run.

Installing from source is a mixed blessing in Linux. By configuring and installing these programs on your system you can compile programs optimized for that platform. The downside is that it is a complicated process and it may require you to download additional programs to complete the compilation.

GRAPHICAL USER INTERFACES

The graphical interfaces to Linux are probably as diverse as any operating system can be. This lack of standardization makes it difficult for some users to move between Linux distributions but you just need to remember that the graphical interface is a complement to, not always a complete replacement for, the command line interface. Using the graphical interface offers point-and-click ease of use, whereas the command line offers extreme flexibility and power. Understanding the core components that make up the graphical interface will also provide a better understanding of how it works, and how you can adapt it for local and remote redisplay.

The X Windows System

The X Windows System, which is sometimes referred to as just X or X11, is the standard graphical interface for the UNIX and Linux operating system. X is not dependent on a physical hardware screen; it's portable so it can be displayed locally on a monitor hooked directly to a PC or transferred over a network to another PC with a local X server or to a thin client device. In Chapter 11, we will discuss thin client technologies that compress the X11 protocol and redisplay it to other network-connected devices.

Window Managers

The X server handles the graphical interface in general, but the actual behavior of those windows is not actually a function of X. The behavior is moderated by a piece of software called a window manager. The window manager will be transparent to most users in the sense that you may never know that it's there, especially when using the Gnome or KDE desktop environments discussed throughout this book. However, this piece of software is very important because it organizes and directs the actions of windows on a Linux desktop, including maximizing and minimizing windows. Also, the windows manager is another modular component of which there are many types. These windows managers may be advantageous because they are lighter in weight, using fewer system resources than a full desktop environment, and could be used on PC hardware that is aging and can no longer run operating systems with higher minimum system requirements. For example, if you are using a lightweight desktop for a kiosk or single application you may want a fast environment. These options would likely fit the bill.

Virtual Consoles and Virtual Displays

As discussed previously, the display and the console are not tied together like they are in Windows. These virtual consoles work independently of each other and allow you to log into a machine in a graphical way, through one of the graphical login managers, or into an independent screen via text mode. You can also log in to numerous virtual desktop environments that are graphical. By default the GUI runs on the seventh virtual terminal; the first Linux terminal is a console terminal and can be navigated to using the ctrl+alt+F1 keys. Each virtual terminal can be accessed by the ctrl+alt+Fn. For example, to switch to the seventh terminal where the GUI environment resides, you would use ctrl+alt+F7.

Virtual Desktops and Workspaces

One of the most useful features that Linux desktop operating systems provide is the ability to create virtual desktops to which you can assign applications. This makes it easy to develop custom workspaces based on specific tasks. For example, you can group applications onto a single workspace for a certain task like authoring documents. You can also assign other less-used applications to another workspace so that when you want to use certain groups you can switch to that desktop. You can create numerous workspaces and move applications around them as shown in Figure 6.12. Every window on the desktop has a right-click menu option that you can use to assign that application to a particular virtual desktop. Or you can assign an application like GAIM (an Instant Messenger Client) to all of them.

FIGURE 6.12 Windows on the Linux desktop can be assigned to different virtual desktops or work spaces.

If you have a large number of applications open at any given time, the ability to have multiple workspaces can be an invaluable feature.

GNOME

The GNOME desktop environment is one of the most popular environments for Linux desktop users and is a common option for Novell Linux Desktop and Red Hat users. It has two main goals: the first is to provide an aesthetically pleasing and easy-to-use desktop environment, and the second is to provide a framework for building applications that support that desktop environment. The GNOME desktop is free and part of the GNU project. Because developers have the freedom to change it and redistribute it in any way, sometimes, depending on who distributes the desktop, different distributions will look a little different from each other. In the case of the following examples, you will see how it's presented in Fedora Core, which is the community-supported project that was originally started as a testing ground for features that may make their way into Red Hat Enterprise Linux. The GNOME desktop is shown in Figure 6.13, with the Start menu in the upper left-hand corner, and bars running across the top and bottom of the screen.

FIGURE 6.13   The GNOME desktop running on Fedora Core.

The GNOME environment is not limited to Linux; it can serve as the desktop environment on other Unix operating systems like Sun Solaris. GNOME is Open Source, so companies can add transparent additions to the environment without need to petition the GNOME project for inclusion or access to integration APIs, etc. In addition, GNOME touts its dedication to a set of human interface guidelines that will help users learn programs faster and accomplish tasks more quickly, and offer an overall pleasing aesthetic.

Configuring the GNOME Desktop

The configuration of the GNOME desktop is pretty simple because most every element you see on the desktop can be right-clicked to spawn a properties option. The two key elements are the actual desktop workspace and the tool bars or panels, similar to what you see in Windows. You will have the option to add or remove panels and add elements to these panels. You can right-click on the GNOME desktop to spawn a menu as shown in Figure 6.14.

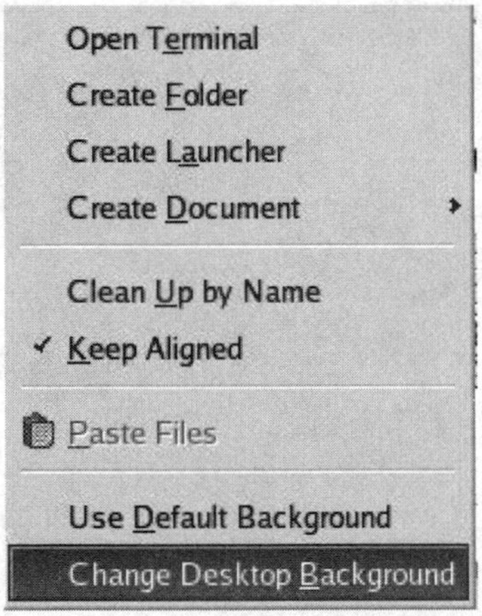

FIGURE 6.14 Right-clicking on the GNOME desktop spawns a menu to aid in configuration.

You can also configure the GNOME desktop by right-clicking on the desktop, which spawns a menu with the following options:

Open Terminal: This dialogue opens a console windows terminal.

Create Folder: Create Folder creates a folder on the GNOME desktop.

Create Launcher: A launcher is analogous to a program shortcut in Windows and launches an application.

Create Document: Templates can be installed to create types of documents.

Paste files: Paste files will change depending on whether you are highlighting files or not. You can copy files and paste them.

Use Default Background: Uses the background set for the system theme.

Change Desktop Background: Allows you to change the Desktop Background to one of the user's choosing.

The desktop also includes a number of icons that function much like Windows icons. As you can see in Figure 6.15, there are a few commonly used icons. The Computer icon is similar to the My Computer icon on a Windows desktop but includes just PC drives and a link to the Linux filesystem, as well as temporarily mounted drives like USB storage devices.

FIGURE 6.15   Common
GNOME desktop icons.

The trashcan is where files are temporarily stored before deletion. This is somewhat misleading as Windows users are used to files automatically going to a Recycle Bin before they are deleted. In Linux, files that are deleted are gone instantly unless you intentionally move them to the trashcan specifically. In Linux, delete means to remove the files permanently.

The Home Folder icon is a link or shortcut to the user's /home/$username/ folder which, like your Windows C:\Documents and Settings\$Usename folder, holds configurations and documents but also potentially programs.

You will also notice in Figure 6.15 that there is an icon labeled 4.1G Media. That is a USB storage device that shows up on the desktop whenever it's mounted. If you click on the Computer icon, you will see that same USB drive along with the CD-ROM drives and the Linux filesystem. This differs from My Computer in Windows because there are no drive letters. For the purposes of comparison you can think of it this way: the filesystem includes the same items your Windows C: drive might, plus any other attached filesystems. In Windows, you might map network drives with corresponding letters. In Linux, you will find all attached filesystems under the filesystem icon, and additional drives mounted over the network will likely be found under */mount* directory.

Panels

Panels are the bars that mark the top and bottom of the GNOME desktop. They can be moved to any side of the screen by dragging and dropping them. Holding down the left mouse button will turn the cursor into a cross with arrows at each end. The panel can then be dropped onto any side of the screen. Right-clicking on the panel will also give the option for altering the properties, as shown in Figure 6.16.

FIGURE 6.16 The Panel Properties dialogue allows you to add elements.

Each panel can have a name, orientation (the side of the screen you want the panel to adhere to), and size (in pixels) for the bar thickness. Also, you can choose to *autohide* the bar so that it disappears until the mouse cursor reaches that side of the screen. The Background tab holds data about the style of the toolbars including the colors (either set individually or acquired from the system theme). Also, the bar can be set to be transparent so only the elements of the bar can be seen. The panel holds a number of different items, including menus, small programs called applets, and launchers which are, as discussed earlier, the shortcuts to program executables.

The GNOME Control Panel

The GNOME Control Panel, as shown in Figure 6.17, is the way you will likely configure your GNOME desktop. The icons within the panel accomplish a number of user-level tasks, such as installing themes and other look-and-feel activities. However, system-wide configurations are established using different tools throughout the system and are not available to nonprivileged users.

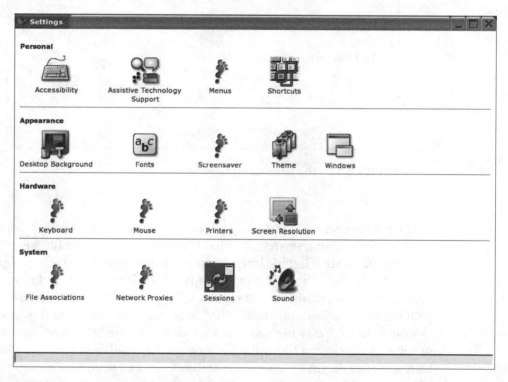

FIGURE 6.17 The GNOME Control panel is a place to set aesthetic elements of the desktop.

Nautilus—The GNOME File Manager

The file manager for the GNOME desktop is called Nautilus. Though not as tightly integrated as Windows Explorer is to Windows, the Nautilus file manager has many of the same capabilities. You can open Nautilus by clicking on the Computer folder as shown in Figure 6.18.

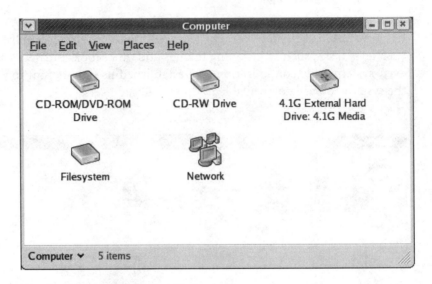

FIGURE 6.18 The Nautilus file browser.

The file browser will most likely be set up with file associations to launch the appropriate application to view the files. For example, an image file will probably open with the GIMP (Graphic Image Manipulation Program), which is a Linux alternative to Adobe's Photoshop program (the GIMP runs on Windows as well). Documents like spreadsheets and reports will open with office programs such as OpenOffice or possibly one of the office suites mentioned later in this chapter. If you would like to change these associations it's fairly straightforward. For example, you can right-click on a file in the file browser view and then choose *Open With*, which will offer the list of known applications that can open that file type (Figure 6.19). You can also choose Open with Other Application to search for an application of your choosing.

Nautilus also gives you a number of customization options that allow you to change the look and feel as well as other behaviors:

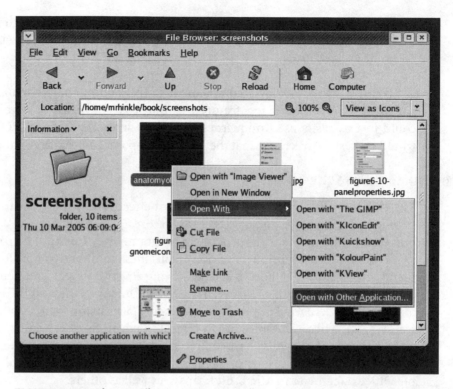

FIGURE 6.19   The Nautilus context menu allows you to choose file associations for opening data files.

Icons and Backgrounds: You can change the background and the icons you use for different types of applications. You can also select a custom icon for a specific file to make it stand out. Icons for the system are usually stored in /usr/share/pixmaps and its subdirectories.

Emblems: You can assign an *emblem* to a file. The emblem will be a small subicon on top of the normal icon. You may want to do this for a favorite or important file. Right-click on the icons you want to add an emblem to and choose properties, then look at the options under the Emblems tab.

Sorting: You can sort files like you can in Windows Explorer by going to the View menu and then choosing View as a List. Then you can click on the title of the column to sort by the parameter that best suits your need.

Web Browsing: Nautilus can function as a simple Web browser and FTP client but with primitive capabilities. Using Firefox or even Konqueror are much better choices.

Music Player: One interesting feature is the ability for Nautilus to function as a music player. Navigate to a directory with MP3s and Nautilus will switch to music player mode.

Nautilus is the GNOME complement to the Konqueror file manager that is part of KDE. Nautilus is less feature rich but it is still highly customizable. You could just as easily use Konqueror as your file manager under GNOME, but it would be best to make sure that the KDE desktop is also installed on that PC.

The GNOME Office Suite

The GNOME office suite is a lightweight but effective way to edit both word processing and spreadsheet documents. The two core applications are AbiWord, a word processor, and Gnumeric, a spreadsheet program. They can both be run on Windows or Linux, so if your final decision entails these solutions you could familiarize users with them on Windows before moving to a Linux environment. When it comes to a pure comparison between Microsoft Office and the GNOME suite, there is a marked difference. The GNOME office suite lacks many of the applications and features that Microsoft Office has to offer, though in some cases that may be just your problem. Users may have simple needs and may be overwhelmed by the bloated Microsoft Office environment. Both Abiword and Gnumeric can open simple Office documents in Microsoft formats, as well as others.

AbiWord—Word Processor

AbiWord is an innovative word processor that, in comparison to Microsoft Word, is very lightweight and fast. It's also available for Windows, Linux, BSD, Solaris, MacOS, BeOS, and QNX. In case you were concerned about standardizing on an enterprise word processing application, AbiWord could feasibly be used for all users. In fact, the minimum requirements of the AbiWord program are rather modest. For example, the minimum system requirements for running AbiWord on Windows are as follows:

■ 486dx or better processor
■ At least 16 MB RAM
■ Windows 95b or later

■ To run it on Linux, the minimum system requirements are pretty basic:

■ GTK+ 2.2 or newer (2.2.4 recommended)
■ At least 16 MB RAM (embedded systems probably won't require more than 8 MB)

- Any processor that supports any of these operating systems (which is, effectively, any processor)
- Optionally GNOME 2.2 (2.4 recommended) [Abisource]

The fact of the matter is that AbiWord's interface is very similar to other common word processors, including cross-platform OpenOffice.org, WordPerfect, and Microsoft Word, as you can see in Figure 6.20. You can import and export to other common file formats, such as Open Office.org and .doc for Microsoft users as well as a host of others. AbiWord also includes a dictionary, mail merge, and some innovative language support that would be useful for language students or international organizations that might need to convert files from one language to another.

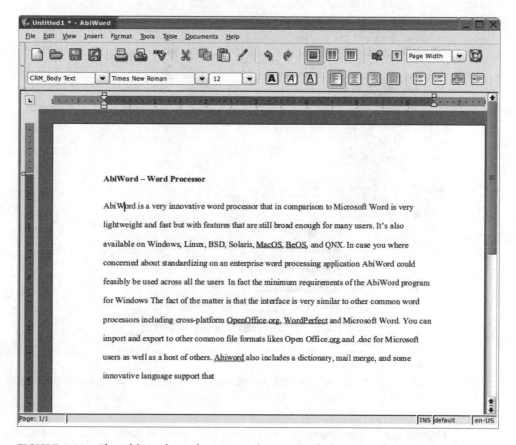

FIGURE 6.20 The AbiWord word processor is a cross-platform word processor with an interface that will be familiar to users of Microsoft Office.

Overall, AbiWord gets overlooked in comparison to other word processors on Linux. It would be a passable choice for authoring many types of word processing documents. Its biggest advantage might be as a full-featured word processor with low resource requirements for Linux desktop users who want to avoid upgrading to newer PCs to address the resource requirements of the large footprint office suites.

Gnumeric–Spreadsheet

Gnumeric is a spreadsheet program that has an interface that's intuitive and consistent with what you might already expect as a Microsoft Excel user. The gnumeric spreadsheet, as shown in Figure 6.21, can author graphs and open spreadsheets that were created in other applications.

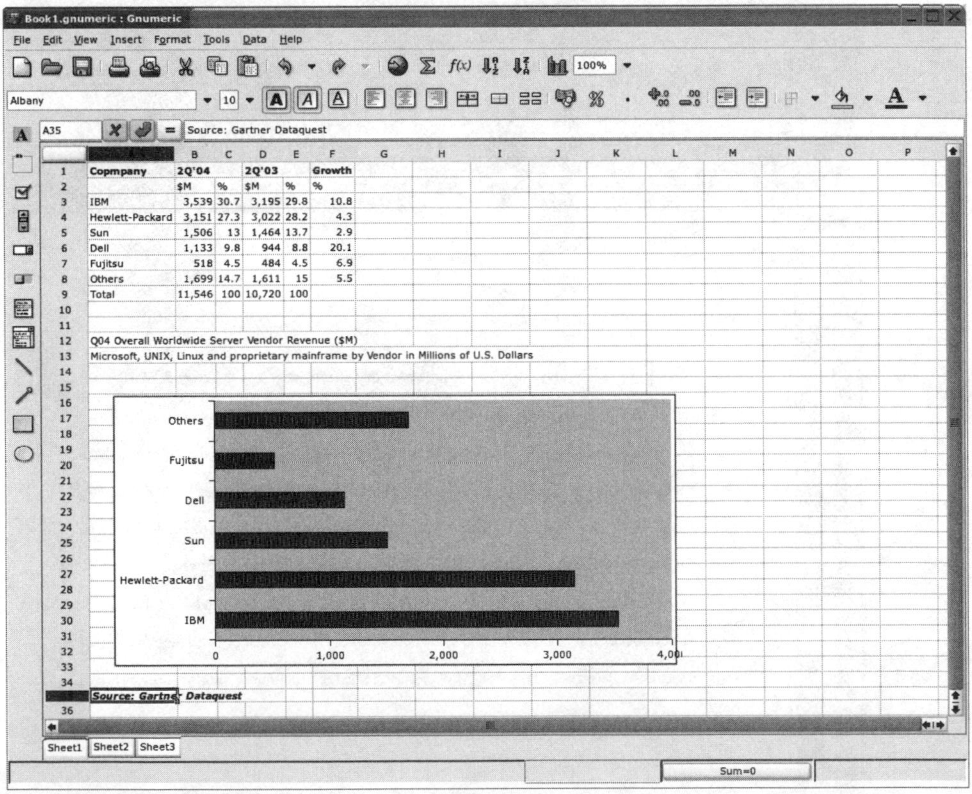

FIGURE 6.21 The Gnumeric spreadsheet looks very similar to those of Windows spreadsheet programs.

In all likelihood Gnumeric is not going to be the spreadsheet program most users will turn to when they start their Linux desktop computing. However, it is a good accompaniment, in the same way Notepad is a good accompaniment to Microsoft Word in Windows.

AbiWord, Gnumeric, and the GNOME-DB project (not discussed in this chapter, but linked in the Other Resources section at the end of the chapter) collectively make up the GNOME desktop suite. All these applications are functional but the standard for office suite for Linux is generally regarded to be OpenOffice.org.

KDE

KDE is a graphical interface designed for use with Linux and Unix systems that was originally developed by Mattias Ettrich, who started much as Linus Torvalds did by posting a cry for help on the Internet (particularly USENET newsgroups) in 1996. Within two years KDE 1.0 was released and grew from there. KDE 2.0 represented an almost complete rewrite of the desktop and was released on October 23, 2000. Amazingly the majority of the work was completed by programmers volunteering their time and their ideas. In fact, the KDE project has over 800 contributors (300 plus of them are part of the language translation team) to make up over four million lines of programming code. KDE can be run on most any Unix environment. KDE is one of the most popular desktop environments because of the broad support for the environment and its extremely in-depth feature set. One caveat on the KDE desktop environment has to do with the architecture under which it is built. KDE is built using Qt libraries supplied by Troll Tech, a company that is important due to the fact that Qt is a complete C++ application development framework that can be used to develop cross-platform applications. Qt applications run natively when compiled from the same source code on Windows, UNIX, MacOS X, and embedded Linux.

Even if you don't choose to migrate to Linux today, looking at technologies like Qt, which can be used to develop Windows applications today and Linux applications tomorrow, makes sense. Using open standards is ideal to avoid the pitfalls of vendor lock in; using toolsets that allow you to switch platforms is just as important. Qt has established itself as a viable software kit for producing open source software. Qt offers multiple licensing schemes, one Open Source and one Commercial. The Qt Open Source Edition is available under the GPL as long as the source code produced with it is also released under the GPL. Those developers who want to develop closed source or proprietary applications are obligated to use the Closed Source Edition of Qt and pay for the licenses.

The KDE project has a few primary goals with regards to KDE. They want to provide the following:

Easy-To-Use Desktop Environment: The KDE desktop environment is very similar to Windows, as it replaces the Start button with a K Menu button and has other conventions similar to Microsoft Windows operating systems.

Reliability and Stability: The desktop should be reliable, without crashes, and allow you to complete your desktop computing without encumbrances that are part of today's commercial offerings.

Free of Charge: The KDE project is a free software project with every line of code falling under the LGPL/GPL licenses.

Though KDE is quite different from a technology standpoint, it will be obvious to most former Windows users how to maneuver around the desktop, as shown in Figure 6.22.

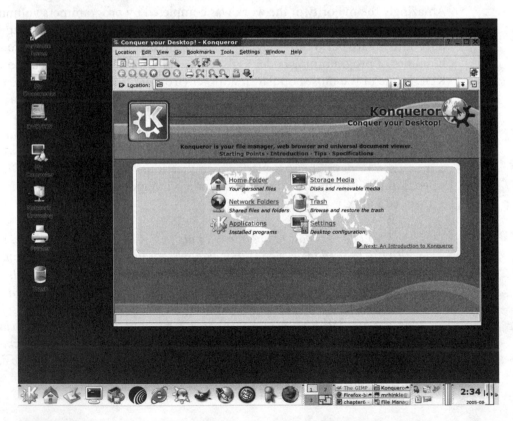

FIGURE 6.22   The KDE desktop is almost identical in structure to the Windows desktop, with a bar across the bottom and icons lined up on the left-hand side.

Configuring the KDE Desktop

KDE uses ASCII-based text files for all its configuration options. This makes it easy to configure KDE using scripts and editors, but as a Linux desktop user you will likely stick to graphical tools to configure the desktop environment.

KDE Control Center

The KDE Control Center is the primary place you will go to customize the KDE desktop environment. It is located under the K Menu, has the heading Control Center, and is comprised of two panels. The left panel holds headings for all the different options on the right, as shown in Figure 6.23. The KDE Control Center also presents more data based on the permissions of the user using it. For example, an unprivileged user basically only has access to his own desktop Look & Feel, while a privileged user like root has access to a broader spectrum of configuration data.

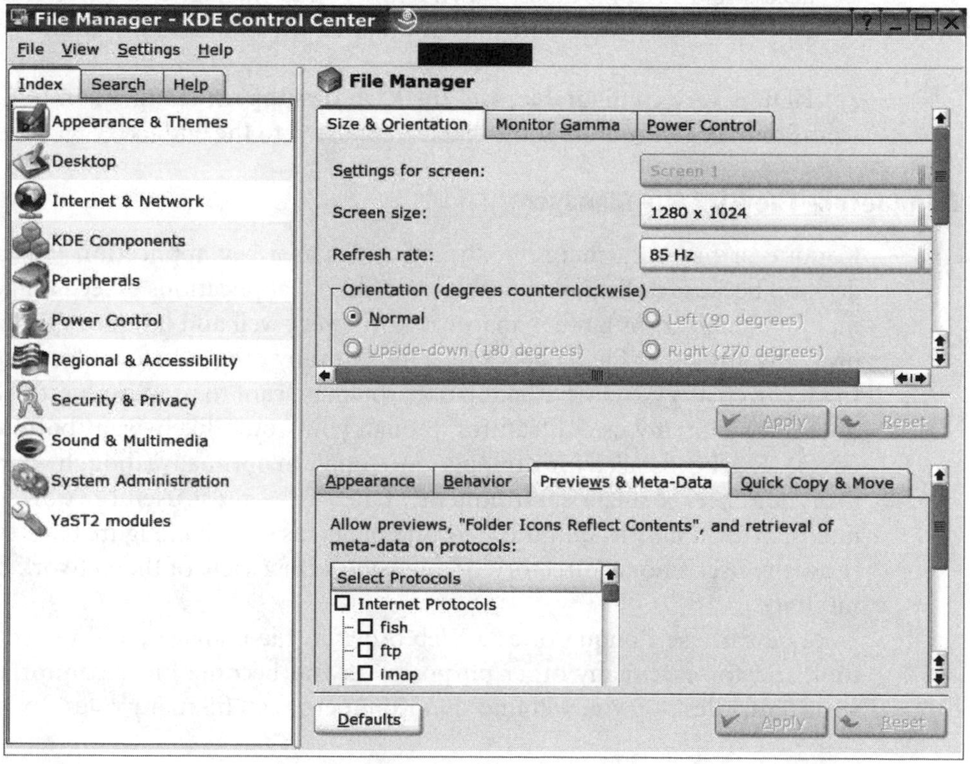

FIGURE 6.23   The use view of the KDE Control Center is the "control panel" for the KDE desktop.

The privileged user can also administer other parts of the system beyond the appearance of the system. In fact, if you are accessing the KDE Control Center from a nonprivileged log in, there will be a button for Administrator Mode and the Apply and Cancel buttons will be grayed out. The administrator, on the other hand, has access to additional settings that include the following:

Internet and Network Settings: This entails settings that affect Web browsing behavior, file sharing, network browsing, and other connectivity issues.

KDE Components: This is where you would associate files with appropriate helper applications, set up services such as printer daemons, and manage the behavior of the file manager.

Peripherals: This control panel is where you manage input devices like digital cameras, mice, joysticks, and KDE display settings.

YaST2:   If you are using a SuSE Linux-based distribution, you will also have access to YaST2 modules, which allow you to manage users and groups, network services, system hardware configuration, and other important settings.

KDE is very configurable, and the KDE desktop, in comparison to GNOME, seems to have many more tools that are apparent to the end user.

Konqueror–The KDE File Manager

Konqueror has been mentioned many times as a key application for the Linux desktop because its flexibility and extensibility in applications exceed that of a normal file manager. As a file manager it works very well and has more features than probably any other file manager for Linux, or any other platform for that matter. In fact, even as a GNOME desktop user you may want to use Konqueror because it does have so many useful features, though you would likely want both KDE and GNOME to be installed for Konqueror to function optimally (though you will only likely log in to a single environment). One of the most useful features of Konqueror is the ability to split the view into panes, as shown in Figure 6.24. Panes can show the user's home directory side-by-side with a view of the network browsing interface.

You can use Konqueror as a Web browser, file manager, and network access tool, and to serve many other purposes. As you become more comfortable with your Linux desktop you will find that Konqueror can fill many roles.

KOffice

The group of applications that make up the KOffice suite is a rather expansive suite of applications that include word processing (KWord), spreadsheets (KSpread),

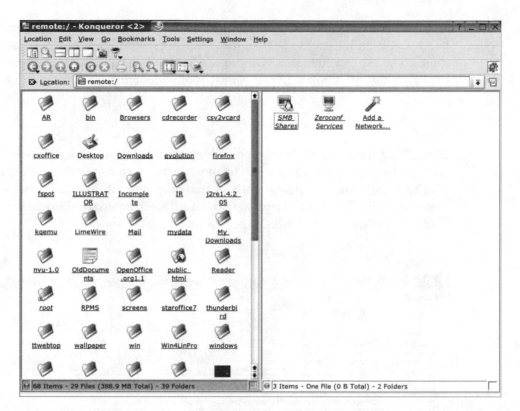

FIGURE 6.24 The Konqueror file manager in multipane mode.

and presentation software (KPresenter), along with a host of supporting applications. These applications all include fairly decent amenities and could handle all the functions of a standard office environment. As with the GNOME Office suite, it is probably more likely you will use OpenOffice.org to service your document needs, but KOffice can open many common document formats.

When it comes to importing and exporting documents from legacy applications running on Windows to native Linux applications, KDE does a fairly decent job. The KDE filters page, http://koffice.kde.org/filters/, privides information about which applications can import or export which file types used by other programs. The importing and exporting of file types, especially those specific to one application over another, is going to provide the biggest challenges to Linux desktop adoption.

It is likely you will find the supporting applications more helpful. *Kivio* is a vector graphics application that can use author-scalable graphics with no degradation and that may be used for illustrating presentations and reports. *KFormula* is a handy application that can be used for authoring scientific and mathematical formulas. The KOffice suite and KDE project do derive some corporate support from the Kompany, a development company that provides cross-platform programming services.

KWord

KWord is a frame-based desktop publishing application which has a fairly robust set of tools (Figure 6.25). It can handle most common document authoring needs. It can save in XML format, and can also read other formats like Microsoft Word's .doc files. KWord's unique feature is that it is a frames-based word processor which lends itself to desktop publishing applications.

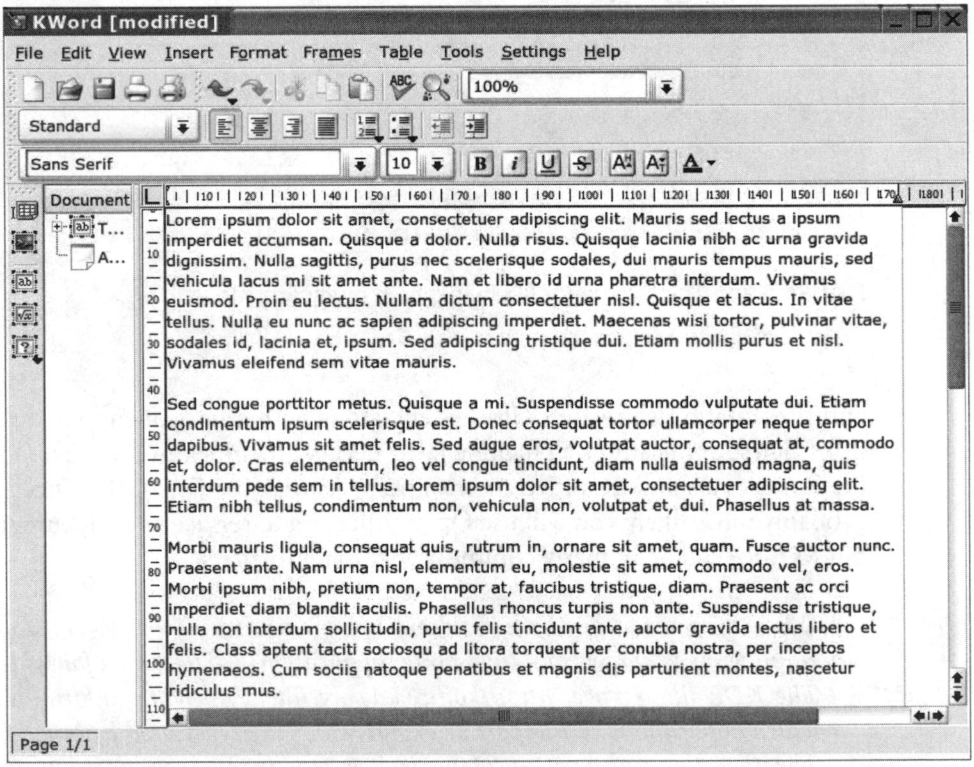

FIGURE 6.25 KWord frame-based word processing application.

KSpread

KSpread is a spreadsheet application and has all the usual features like calculations, but it can do much more. It is scriptable and can complete complex tasks and create author graphs that can be embedded in reports authored in KWord. As shown in Figure 6.26, it comes with templates and can open many file types including Microsoft Excel .xls files.

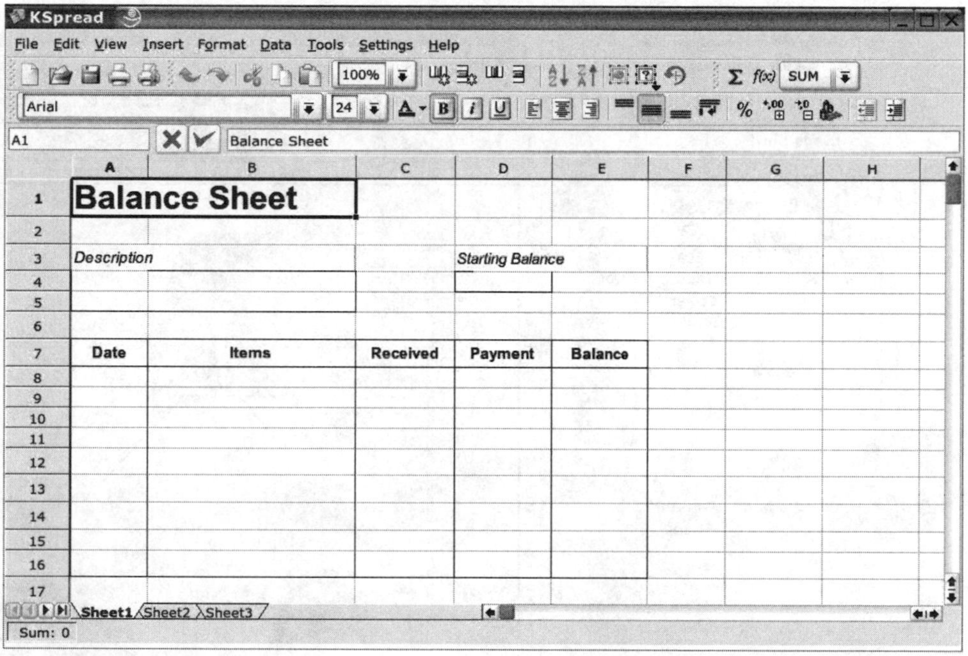

FIGURE 6.26   The KOffice spreadsheet application, KSpread, is a lightweight, easy-to-use spreadsheet application.

KPresenter

KPresenter is a presentation program that is comparable to Microsoft PowerPoint and other presentation-type software. It is well integrated into the KDE desktop. It is probably worth exploring KPresenter as an alternative to PowerPoint, but once again this application will lose out to the OpenOffice.org Impress software as your organization's software of choice.

Kivio

Kivio is a Visio-style program for making diagrams and charts. It has a large library of stencils which are elements for different types of applications like network diagrams and organizational charts. It has a large number of stencil sets, which are the shapes used to create the graphs used in Kivio. In Figure 6.27 you can see an organizational chart made with Kivio and one of it's custom stencil sets.

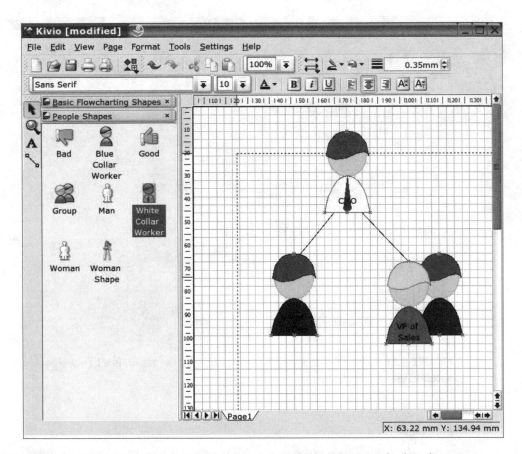

FIGURE 6.27 Kivio can be used to author organizational charts and other diagrams.

The overwhelming reason you would use KOffice is due to its integration into the KDE desktop. It handles most common file formats. It is also free and could save an organization a considerable amount of expense in office suite acquisition costs. However, if you exchange a large number of complex documents between other organizations that use Microsoft Office you may find that there are better options for you, such as OpenOffice.org.

KDE Resources

In addition to the formal part of the KDE distribution, you can search for a large number of additional applications at the KDE-APPS Web site, which give you a searchable database of additional applications based on type, license, and a user-submitted score as to the quality of the application. Most of the applications there are a result of the work of community members and are unencumbered by licensing. Some of them also fill very niche needs that are normally reserved for commercial companies. If you want to add some eye candy or other themes to your KDE desktop, you can visit the KDE-Look site for wallpapers, icons, and desktop themes. These are usually items that are more a source of amusement for desktop users, but in some cases they are very important to give desktops a sense of individuality. The ability to theme the desktop is also a nice touch for companies that provide customer-facing systems.

SUMMARY

The Linux desktop is very configurable; installation and the applications bear many similarities to other operating systems. If you purchase a Linux distribution like Red Hat Linux, Linspire, Xandros, or Novell Linux Desktop, you will likely find much of the information you need in the accompanying user documentation. There may be programs that are available on one distribution that aren't available on others. What is fairly certain is that these distributions will all have similar command line interfaces and graphical user interfaces. You will most likely be using a KDE or GNOME desktop and have to, at some point, make a decision as to which one serves your interests the best. The only guidance we can offer on this is that you should pick the one that works best for you after you have done some research. The differentiators between the two are vast, but in general, the GNOME desktop environment could be characterized as simple and elegant, where KDE is a powerful and full-featured environment. The amount of information available about the Linux desktop environment is voluminous and this text could in no way adequately cover how to use it. Instead, we have focused on how it works and given you a foundation on which to build. By the time you read this book there will likely have been improvements and additions to the desktop that makes it even more diverse. This is good, because it means that the technology is advancing faster than information about it can make it into print.

OTHER RESOURCES

- CERT—*www.cert.org*
- Bash Manual—*www.gnu.org/software/bash/*
- GCC Home Page—*gcc.gnu.org/*
- Midnight Commander—*www.ibiblio.org/mc/*
- Guide to Linux Archive Utility Mastery—*www.oracle.com/technology/pub/articles/calish_archive.html*
- Installing from Source—*www.tuxfiles.org/linuxhelp/softinstall.html*
- GNOME—*www.gnome.org*
- GNOME Accessibility Project—*developer.gnome.org/projects/gap/*
- Introduction to GNOME—*www.gnome.org/learn/intro/2.2/*
- The GNOME Office Home Page—*www.gnome.org/gnome-office/*
- Abiword Home Page—*www.abisource.com*
- Gnumeric Home Page—*www.gnome.org/projects/gnumeric/*
- KDE Home Page—*www.kde.org*
- Konqueror Home Page—*www.konqueror.org*
- KOffice—*www.koffice.org*
- KDE-Apps—*www.kde-apps.org*
- KDE-Look—*www.kde-look.org*

REFERENCES

[Abisource] Abisource, AbiWord: System Requirements. Available online at *http://www.abisource.com/support/require/*

7 Linux Business Desktop Applications

In This Chapter

- Core Applications
- Miscellaneous Business Applications
- Where to Find Additional Applications
- Summary
- Other Resources
- References

Many Linux desktop applications bear similarities to those that are available for Windows users. A large number of these applications are easily downloadable or included with your preferred Linux distribution but don't require software royalties. Admittedly some of these applications are not as well developed or supported as commercial applications, but they offer a significant value when you consider that they provide the functionality that is needed to get the job done. The criticism, if any, that may be aimed at these applications is that they may lack some amenities and nice-to-have features that are not critical to your operations. Also, because many of these applications are cross-platform, such as OpenOffice.org, whether you move to Linux now or later you can run them on Windows first to introduce end users to applications that over time they will be using on a Linux desktop. Once the move to Linux is made this will cut down on the number of new applications users will need to become familiar with. For those applications that you use on Windows today that aren't available on both platforms, such as diagram and flowchart software, desktop publishing and multimedia applications, there are also good native Linux substitutes. Often times these programs benefit from open source community efforts that allow end users to contribute enhancements that are a result of real-life needs, not the vision of a company whose agenda is to sell software and to a lesser degree provide useful applications to their end users.

> **Core Applications:**   Core applications are those applications common to today's business user. They include Web browsers, email clients and office suites. These applications are the primary tools companies use for communications and document creation.
>
> **Secondary Business Applications:**   Secondary business applications are those applications that are used in the enterprise but that are usually specific to smaller groups of users. These applications include desktop publishing, graphing software, and finance applications.
>
> **Miscellaneous Applications:**   These applications may not be critical to the enterprise but are of use to many business users, such as multimedia viewers for viewing training videos or image viewers for organizing presentations.

There is no group of applications that are common to every enterprise, but in general there is a set of applications that are probably used in a high percentage of professional settings. The advantage Linux versions have over many Microsoft Windows applications is independence. Because the application community is so diverse and no one vendor has the advantage of having control over the host operating system, products are not reliant on a single vendor vision that trades convenience for innovation, security, and variety. This chapter is not so much a how-to as it is a guide to where to look for native Linux applications. The documentation for the following applications is best obtained from their Web sites, which are listed in the Other Resources section at the end of this chapter.

CORE APPLICATIONS

Core applications in Linux are those applications that have the broadest appeal to Linux desktop users who need to use their PCs for communication and document creation. This is, of course, keeping in mind that every business is different and some businesses may have industry-specific applications or vertical applications that are unique to their individual industries. These specialized applications are best addressed by the means discussed in Chapter 10. The core applications discussed in this chapter are those that will form the basis for desktop computing and will most likely bring you the most success as logical replacements for Microsoft Office and Internet connectivity. Once you have an understanding of the core applications you can layer in the other applications that will most likely enhance your Linux desktop. Premigration, many of them can have a functional place in your Windows environment. Table 7.1 lists these applications and their ability to be used across platforms.

TABLE 7.1   Listing of Core Applications for Linux Desktop Users

Type of Application	Name	Cross Platform
Email	Evolution	No
	Thunderbird	Yes
Web Browsers	Firefox	Yes
	Konqueror	No
	Opera	Yes
Office Suites	OpenOffice.org	Yes
Graphics	Inkscape (Vector Drawing)	Yes
	GIMP	Yes
Desktop Publishing	Scribus	Yes
	NVU	Yes

Web Browsers

There are many options for Web browsers running under Linux but the discussion for enterprise replacement applications will mainly point to the Mozilla-based Web browsers. These Web browsers are from the program that once reigned as the Internet's most popular browser, Netscape. Over time that position of leadership has been overtaken by Microsoft Internet Explorer, which has the advantages of being tightly tied to the Windows operating system, and of tight system integration and distribution. However, it's the first of these two items that has caused alarm and that makes it a logical target for replacement even before you migrate to Linux. Growing concerns about security with Web browsers are sending users searching for alternatives to Internet Explorer, which, as a popular bridge between the Internet and the operating system, is a logical point of attack for unscrupulous hackers.

Browser Security

One of the most important considerations for active Internet users is the growing number of risks that are emerging on the World Wide Web. These risks include spyware and *phishing* scams that fool users into giving personal data through a variety of deceptions.

Phishing is the practice of deceiving people who are browsing the Web by setting up sites that attempt to masquerade as legitimate Web sites, such as a computer user's bank or other trusted source. Some phishing attempts are made by creating a frames page using a domain that seems to be legitimate, like http://mylinuxbank-security.com, and even displaying the header or other legitimate information from the Web site of the company they are trying to imitate. The Mozilla Firefox Web browser has some features that help fight these types of attempts. When the Load Images for the originating Web site only feature is checked, it can help by alerting the user that images are not being served from http://mylinuxbank.com. When visiting a secure site, the location bar turns yellow to let you know that the site is using SSL encryption. Also, if you look at the bottom right corner of the Firefox browser you will see an icon to the right of the URL that looks like a lock. By clicking on this lock you will be able to see the security properties of that Web site. Phishing schemes can be initiated by emails referring you to a URL that is similar to one you would be familiar with, and you should be skeptical of any such email on any platform, regardless of your browser choice.

The fine-grain controls offered by Mozilla-based browsers are advantageous because they create a barrier of protection around the browser so that there is an early warning system about actions that may be potentially harmful to a desktop user. For example, under the Web Features settings in the Preferences control panel for Firefox, users can choose to only load images from the originating Web site, which could block content from untrusted domains. The Block Pop-up Windows feature is also very popular to prevent windows from popping up with messages that often ask trick questions about wanting to take advantage of special offers which might include downloading third-party software, which is a common way to attempt to deliver spyware to a Windows desktop user.

Internet Explorer Security

If you have used Internet Explorer for any length of time, you may have noticed that it is the mechanism for updating the Windows operating system. You can go to a Web page and have the Web infrastructure scan your system and then determine what components are installed and what components may be updated. This ability is facilitated by Microsoft technologies like VBScript and ActiveX controls, which can be embedded in Web pages and then automatically downloaded and run on your desktop. Linux is impervious to ActiveX threats for the simple reason that there is no way to natively run ActiveX controls on the Linux desktop. The same holds true for the Firefox browser on any platform. ActiveX programs do require some human interaction; they don't download and install without someone accepting them onto the system. Though as click-happy as many users are, they may just accept programs with little regard to their origination and potential functions. In comparison, a similar technology that can accomplish many of the same things is Java. Java is a language used to write programs and it too can be downloaded and run on a PC from a Web page. The difference is that the Java program runs in a secure *sandbox* that provides separation between your host operating system and the program. Java was designed to be platform independent, so it can be ported on a wide array of architectures including Windows and Linux. Also, because it needs to run in a sandbox it may be limited in what it can do, whereas ActiveX is sometimes useful in an intranet environment where ActiveX controls can perform tasks for end users on behalf of system administrators with limited security risk.

One famous, or infamous, ActiveX control was developed by Fred McLain, a programmer in the late 1990s who wrote an ActiveX control that could perform a clean shutdown of Windows 95 by making Windows API calls. The point was that someone could gain that access by including that control in a page, and then when users downloaded it, it would shut down some computers. The ActiveX framework was a replacement for the Windows OLE, which in essence was a Windows software component that could enter the computer via the Web, but, in all fairness, only by the actions of an end user. The problem was that the path to the operating system via the Web offered too few obstacles, making it relatively easy to wreak havoc. Also, in the earlier days of Windows the filesystem and user's permissions were relatively lax, and an end user surfing the Web had access to change most anything on the system. In contrast, Linux has always benefited from a culture that encourages making use of a strong permissions system which limits file access to users and groups. Most Linux users are encouraged to run their operating systems with limited permissions (as nonprivileged users) to prevent disastrous results when accessing the Internet.

Java also has the advantage of being portable across platforms so when making decisions about using Java you can know that Java is supported on a variety of platforms, while ActiveX and VBScript are really only supported under Windows running natively.

Microsoft Internet Explorer uses these technologies and is often at risk as evidenced by the Secunia Advisories issued for IE 6 from 2003–2005, as shown in Figure 7.1.

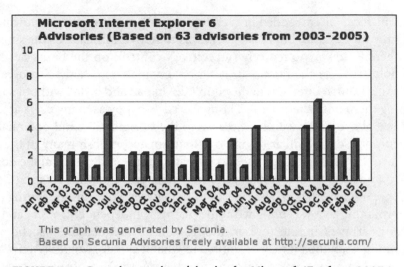

FIGURE 7.1 Secunia security advisories for Microsoft IE 6 from 2003 to February 2005.

Figure 7.2 shows that the real problem is not in the fact that the security flaws existed, but in the amount of time during which there was no solution available. If you look at Figure 7.2 you will see that the solution status for those same 63 advisories was that 32% of them remained unpatched, and 14% of them offered only a partial fix.

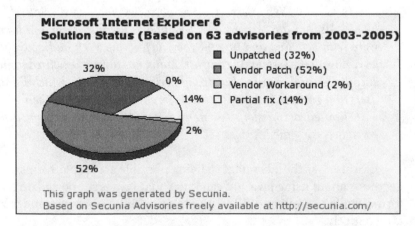

FIGURE 7.2 The graph shows that only 52 percent of the issued security advisories were patched by the vendor, Microsoft.

There are varying degrees of what may be considered security threats. The chart in Figure 7.3 shows the variety of ways that the system may be affected or compromised.

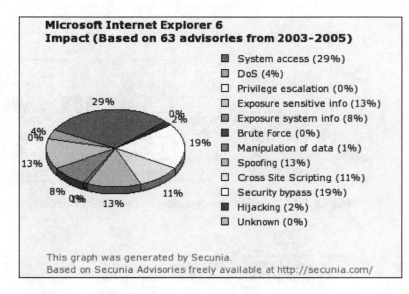

FIGURE 7.3 Graphs show the end result of Internet Explorer exploits including system access and exposure to sensitive information.

Looking at the period from 2003 to 2005, as shown in Figure 7.4, you can see that Firefox reached its 1.x version in the Fall of 2004 and had no data to compare to over the time before its release. You can also factor in the amount of market share that Firefox holds versus Internet Explorer as making it a smaller target for hackers.

An important distinction between the security advisories for the two browsers is in the criticality of the advisories. Due to the relative difficulty of gaining system access or causing widespread damage to the operating system, Mozilla Firefox has had no advisories that were ranked higher than a moderate level as shown in Figure 7.5.

Notice that the vast majority of exploits for Internet Explorer could take place from a remote system, while the Firefox vulnerabilities mainly needed local system access to benefit from the software flaws. That is an interesting consideration for a Web browser because the tool's primary use is to connect to a network. Running a browser other than Internet Explorer was even suggested by the U.S. Government Computer Emergency Readiness Team (US-CERT) in 2004.

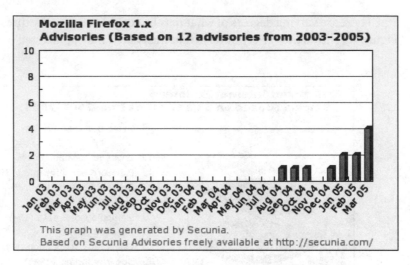

FIGURE 7.4   Secunia security advisories for Mozilla Firefox.

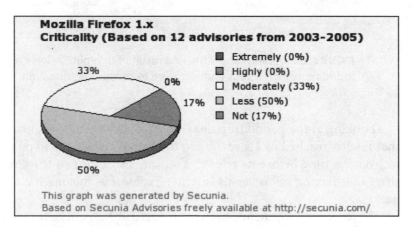

FIGURE 7.5   There were no Mozilla Firefox advisories that ranked
higher than moderate.

*On October 13, 2004, the U.S. Computer Emergency Response Team issued a
warning that stated that Microsoft Internet Explorer did not adequately validate
the security context of a frame. An attacker could exploit this vulnerability by
tricking users regarding the source of a malicious program or script. The proposed
solution was to apply a patch or to disable Active Scripting and ActiveX. Recommendations were also issued for Microsoft Outlook to prevent similar problems.*

One of the most attention-getting suggestions of the report was to explore the use of alternative Web browsers. The report indicated that there were a significant number of technologies relating to the IE domain/zone security model, local filesystem (Local Machine Zone) trust, the Dynamic HTML (DHTML) document object model, the HTML Help System, Mime type determination, the GUI, and ActiveX that had the potential to be security risks. The fact of the matter was that by having such a tightly bundled operating system, a vulnerability in one program led to system-wide concerns. The warning also noted that IE was integrated into Windows in such a way that browser security issues could also lead to operating system exploits. That's not the case with a Mozilla-based browser or other third-party browsers because of the separation of the core OS from the Web browser. Also, Linux users would not be subject to the ActiveX vulnerability because ActiveX cannot be executed natively on Linux.

Firefox Web Browser

Firefox is a cross-platform Web browser that aims to be highly useful and secure. Firefox Web browser is available for Windows, Linux, and Mac OS. Firefox is a product that was based on the popular Mozilla browser project that was started by the release of code and sponsorship from AOL-owned Netscape. Firefox started as an experimental branch of the Mozilla project under the codename Phoenix. Over time Firefox took a leadership position as the marquis product of the Mozilla project. The Firefox logo is an orange fox circling the world as shown in Figure 7.6.

FIGURE 7.6 The Firefox logo.

Firefox offers a set of features that are leading edge and effective in navigating Web pages without coveting too many system resources or facilitating a security breach of your operating system. The features that are most appealing are as follows:

Pop-up Blocking: A built in pop-up blocker lets you decide when to allow a pop-up window to be spawned.

Tabbed Browsing: Tabbed browsing allows Web pages to be opened under tabs under the address bar; pages can be loading in the background as a page is being read.

Live Bookmarks: Lets you read Real Simple Syndication (RSS) news and blog headlines in the bookmarks toolbar; an icon in the lower right corner of the browser will alert you to pages with this capability.

Integrated Search: The Firefox Web browser allows you to submit search engine searches in a box right next to the URL bar, reducing the step of loading a page then submitting a search.

Extensible: Firefox has an extension framework that allows Firefox users to use small add-ons called extensions that provide additional functionality; it also supports themes which allow you to skin your browser to match your personal tastes.

Secure: Firefox doesn't load ActiveX controls and privacy tools which can limit a Web site's ability to set cookies and manage online passwords.

Firefox has many features similar to Internet Explorer, though the terminology is slightly different. The savvy Web surfer may easily discern what terminology in Firefox has an equivalent in Internet Explorer. Examples of these are listed in Table 7.2.

TABLE 7.2   Internet Explorer and Firefox Terminology Translations

Internet Explorer	Firefox
Internet Options—Under the Tools Menu	Options—Under the Tools Menu (in Windows)
Favorites	Preferences—Under the Edit Menu in Linux Bookmarks
Temporary Internet Files	Cache—Usually located in /home/$username/ bookmarks
Address Bar	Location Bar
Refresh	Reload
Save Target As	Save Link As
Copy Shortcut	Copy Link Location

Though the layout is slightly different, the Firefox Web browser functions in basically the same way as Microsoft Internet Explorer, with better security and a few additional features.

Firefox is a product of the Mozilla Foundation that was established in 2003 with support from AOL's Netscape division. The foundation is incorporated as a not-for-profit entity in the state of California with the edict to promote the development, distribution of, and adoption of standards-based Web applications and core technologies. The initial president of the Mozilla Foundation was Mitch Kapor, founder of Lotus Development Corporation and designer of Lotus 1-2-3.

Configuring Firefox

To start configuring Firefox you should go to the Edit-> Preferences menu which is the primary place to change the settings as shown in Figure 7.7.

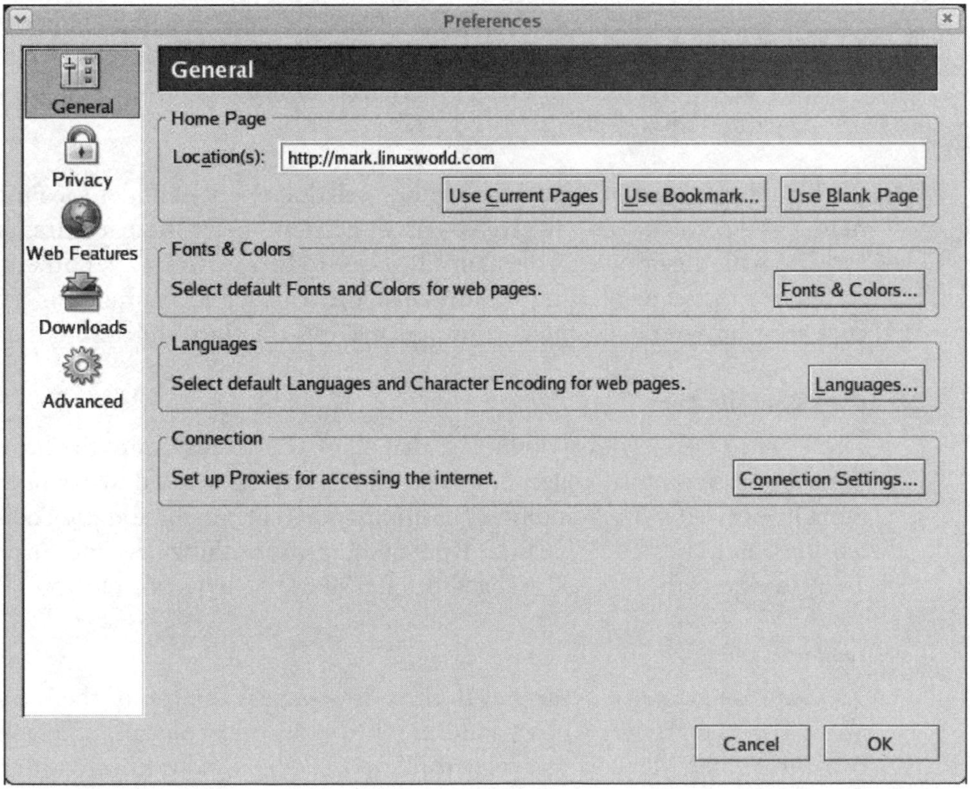

FIGURE 7.7   The Firefox Preferences menu.

There are five groups of settings for configuring Firefox:

General: General is the place to set up your home page, fonts, language support, and proxy information.

Privacy: The privacy area keeps track of where you have been, including the history of Web sites you visited, cookies, and what is in your cache; you can also manage your saved passwords.

Web Features: This is probably one of the most important security settings in Firefox; here you can manage pop-up windows, allowing or and blocking sites; allow Web sites to install software; define what images to load; and enable Java and JavaScript.

Downloads: This is where you specify both where to download files to and the helper applications to deal with files like PDFs, archives, and multimedia files in Web pages; for the new Linux user this is an important setting since you can specify where files go rather than trying to hunt them down in an unfamiliar place later on.

Advanced: The advanced settings are mainly related to the browser's behavior with respect to browsing and how Firefox deals with security certificates; you can choose which security protocols to honor and how trusting you care to be with each Web site.

The Preferences for Firefox are rather well documented under the Firefox help menu, and a quick read will give you an understanding of these features as you go forward with the browser. The main advantage to these settings over other browsers is that, for the security-minded individual, there are a good number of ways to secure your browser and protect your personal information while using the Web.

Other Customizations

There are not only settings in Firefox that allow you to customize the browser, but there is also a complete collection of extensions that can be used to extend the functionality of Firefox. These additional customizations fall into three areas: Toolbars, Extensions, and Themes. While these types of things are nothing new, they may provide a way to extend the browser's capabilities and allow you to tweak it to your liking.

Toolbars

Toolbars are arranged by default in three rows across the top of the browser: the Menu bar, the Navigation bar, and the Bookmarks bar. You can remove the latter two, but not the Menu bar, by going to View->Toolbars and unchecking or checking the toolbars that you want to appear. You can also customize these bars by choosing the Customize option, which gives you the ability to drag and drop the features to the existing toolbar or create a new one with options like cut and paste or functions that launch a new window or tab. The main bar is the Location bar, shown in Figure 7.8, which serves the same purpose as the Address bar does in Internet Explorer.

http://www.luckydog.org/

FIGURE 7.8   The Firefox Location bar is similar to the Address bar in Internet Explorer.

Extensions

Extensions are programs that add on new features to Firefox. These features can be installed through the browser and extend its functionality. The technologies that are used to create extensions include XML, Javascript, DOM, XPCOM, and CSS. To install an extension you can visit the Mozilla Web site and click on an install package. You then need to restart the browser for the extensions to start running. You can see what extensions are installed by going to Tools -> Extensions on your main tool bar. The Extensions control panel will list what extensions are installed, as shown in Figure 7.9.

FIGURE 7.9   The Extensions panel in Firefox also has a link to the Mozilla Update site to add more extensions.

There is an ever-growing quantity of extensions numbering in the hundreds. Some extensions are for entertainment and games, but some are extremely helpful to the migrating Windows user trying Linux. Examples of these include the following:

Bookmark Synchronizer: Bookmark Synchronizer can export your bookmarks and upload them to an FTP server in XML format. That way your legacy Windows Favorites from Internet Explorer can be imported to Firefox running on Windows, then exported to an FTP site where your new Linux installation can synchronize by downloading the XML file it creates. Bookmark Synchronizer is also helpful for users that have a Linux and Windows PC running at the same time or for someone who dual boots Linux and Windows.

AdBlock: AdBlock is an extension that gives finer grain control over Web ads than Firefox's built-in ad blocker's capabilities provide. This is a good example of how Firefox users on any platform benefit from a product that is aimed at protecting your online privacy.

User Agent: User Agent allows Firefox users to change the agent information sent by their browsers. Web sites sometimes make decisions about how to display pages based on this information, or even tell users that if you aren't using a certain version of Internet Explorer the page may not be displayed correctly. Fooling the Web site into thinking Firefox is another browser such as Internet Explorer allows the page to load.

There are more extensions available every day. The extension framework, along with a considerable effort from community developers, isn't necessary for Firefox's success, but they do add a lot of value to the product.

Themes

Themes are a common and often distracting part of desktop computing and companies often have policies prohibiting the addition of third-party software to desktop computers. Firefox also supports themes for its browser, which might be useful for companies that provide customer-facing kiosks and want to include their corporate branding on them.

Firefox Plug-Ins

Firefox supports plug-ins just as Internet Explorer does, though the process for installing plug-ins for Linux browsers is not always as easy as it is for Internet Explorer or Firefox running on Windows. Plug-ins may be installed in one of three locations:

- The location of the Firefox plug-ins directory may vary depending on the way Firefox was installed, but is likely in the /home/username directory.
- A plug-in directory in the Mozilla profiles directory, usually /home/$username/.mozilla/plug-ins/.
- The path pointed to by environment variable MOZ_PLUGIN_PATH. This is the least likely but can be found by typing echo $MOZ_PLUGIN_PATH at a command prompt. No response means that the variable isn't set; otherwise the response may indicate where the path is.

To automate the process of acquiring plug-ins you can use the Firefox Plug-in Finder Service that launches when you come to a page that requires a plug-in to properly display the page, as shown in Figure 7.10.

| Additional plugins are required to display all the media on this page. | Install Missing Plugins... |

FIGURE 7.10   The Firefox plug-in indicator bar appears at the top of a Web page when a plug-in is required to display items on the page.

The plug-in finder service window will indicate whether or not there is a plug-in available for a given program. In many instances, as with Sun Java plug-in and Macromedia Flash Player, the finder will indicate that the plug-in is available for either download and automatic installation. Other times Firefox will launch a page where the plug-in can be downloaded.

Konqueror–Web Browser, File Manager, and More

Konqueror is an integral part of the KDE desktop environment and, while it is a Web browser, it also serves as a file manager and universal viewing application. Though it is part of the KDE desktop it can be run from other desktop environments like GNOME. Regardless, it's one of the better tools available for Open Source due to its versatility. At first glance Konqueror seems to be very similar to Mozilla Firefox, but upon closer inspection it becomes obvious that Konqueror has a broader set of features. It has many similarities to Windows Explorer, but without the security risks associated with having the Web browser/file manager tied so closely to the operating system. Konqueror supports tab-based browsing and has an integrated search bar similar to Firefox. Konqueror uses the KHTML rendering engine, which is also used by Apple's Safari browser. Konqueror has the ability to perform a number of tasks in addition to Web browsing:

File Manager: Konqueror is the most robust of all the graphical file managers for Linux. It has the ability to manipulate files and provide them in a multitude of views.

Customizable Application: Similarly to Firefox, Konqueror can be extended with additional functionality by using Konqueror XML Configuration to add toolbars and other widgets to make Konqueror more useful.

Universal File Viewer: Konqueror can be used to view a host of different file formats. Right-clicking on an image allows you to view the graphics file right in Konqueror. Also, it's possible to view presentations and documents by using the Kparts library.

Figure 7.11 shows how Konqueror can bridge the gap between file manager and Web browser.

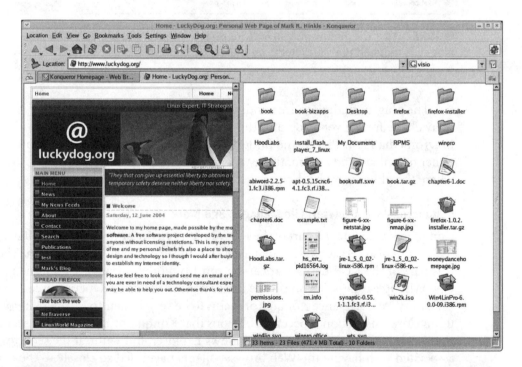

FIGURE 7.11   Konqueror can use a split window view to display Web pages side by side, or a filesystem next to a Web page.

One notable difference is that the settings for Konqueror span the menuing system and may require a little searching as you become familiar with the appropriate ways to tweak the environment. Though there are places throughout the Konqueror menus to tweak different settings, the most central place is under the *Settings* menu. This is where you can configure the look and feel of Konqueror as well as its behavior.

Using Konqueror as a Network Tool

You will get a different presentation when navigating through folders versus going to Web pages. Using the Web view to look at folders can become impractical. The sidebar provides shortcuts and special functions that make it easier to find what you are searching for. You can use Konqueror to both browse local networks or as a graphical SSH tool using the *fish* protocol.

Konqueror makes a fine standards-based browser; it also has some unique features that make it interoperate with Web sites and other parts of your system. You will probably want to use one of the Mozilla browsers like Firefox for most Web surfing, and it's the way you will install plug-ins. The following are some tricks and tips that will help make your Konqueror browsing experience better.

Using Netscape Bookmarks: A helpful feature if you use Netscape or Firefox is to click on the *Bookmarks* menu and then choose *Edit Bookmarks*. There is an option in the *Bookmarks Editor* under *Settings* that allows you to check a box to Show Netscape Bookmarks in Konqueror. This will give you the ability to use the same bookmarks as you do in other browsers.

Using Plug-ins: Installing bookmarks for Konqueror on its own can be done, but it's often easier to use Firefox's plug-in finder service to locate and install plug-ins, and then point Konqueror to them. Once you have the plug-ins installed, go to the Konqueror *Settings* menu and choose *Configure Konqueror*. Choose the *Plug-ins* option; this is where you can add your Firefox or Netscape plug-ins (likely located in /home/$USER/firefox/plugins or /usr/lib/mozilla/ plugins). Once Konqueror has scanned for plug-ins, they should be available while you use Konqueror as a browser.

Browser Identification: Some Web sites try to decide whether you are using Internet Explorer or another browser before they grant you access to make sure that you can see the Web site properly. This is a result of developers and browsers not adhering to a strict standard. You can set your Browser Identification to another browser User Agent by going to *Configure Konqueror* or going to *Tools -> Change Browser Identification* and choosing an option that might give you a shot at browsing these Web sites.

In addition to being useful as a Web browser, Konqueror can function in a number of other capacities as a network tool, including a front end for *ssh* or as an *ftp* client.

Graphical SSH Client: Fish allows users to access another computer's files over SSH and using the Konqueror GUI. SSH is a popular way to connect to Linux computers securely over the network, but it works on the command line, requiring you to know the syntax and then type commands correctly to manipulate files. With Konqueror, you can use Fish in a graphical environment by dragging and dropping files. To access another Linux or Unix server running the SSH daemon type `fish://ip_address` where the IP address is the network address of the other computer. The user will then be accessing the secure conduit between the servers.

FTP Client: Konquerer works just as easily as an ftp client by prefacing your ftp location with the *ftp://* prefix. Konqueror will then prompt you for a username and password if authentication is required.

Other Konqueror Features

Konqueror has many features beyond what you would expect from a Web browser and a file manager. Many of them are the result of the popularity of Konqueror as the heart of the KDE desktop. However, there are a few additional advantages to Konqueror. Konqueror is much more than a Web browser or a file manager; it's one of the core features in the KDE desktop (of course it will run under GNOME as well). For example, if you want to view a document you can enter the location of the file in the Location toolbar and the document will open in a frame in Konqueror. One nice feature is that for comparing documents, you can open them in the Konqueror split screen view and compare them side by side. An additional feature of Konqueror falls under systems management. The FSView tool provides a graphical view of the filesystem. You can access the filesystem view in Konqueror by going to `View -> View Mode -> File Size View` which will give you a view of how much space individual files are taking up, as shown in Figure 7.12.

Konqueror is one of the core technologies (albeit native to KDE) of the Linux desktop, and one that you will find offers extensive capabilities beyond any single application classification.

Opera

Opera has had a reputation as an innovator for many years as a browser on platforms ranging from PC operating systems to mobile devices. While Firefox is the most recent browser darling, Opera has been around for quite some time on both Windows and Linux. The Opera browser has many of the features that Firefox and

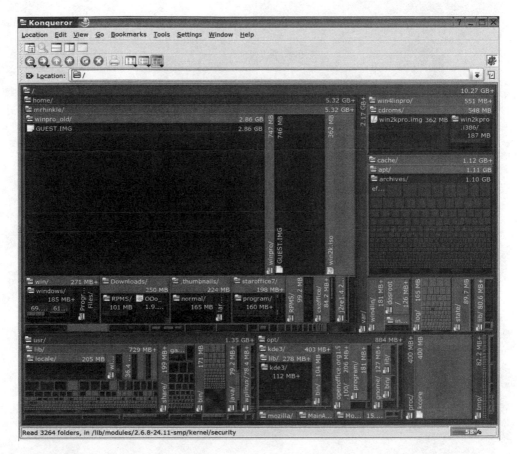

FIGURE 7.12 FSView gives a view of the Linux filesystem space being used from within Konquoror.

Konqueror have, but it also has a reputation as being extremely lightweight from a resource standpoint and innovative, with unique features.

Tiled Browsing or Tabbed Browsing: Opera offers a choice of tile-based or tabbed browsing.

KIOSK Mode: One interesting feature of Opera is its ability to function as an agent to lockdown the desktop.

- The Opera browser is not without restriction. It can be downloaded at no cost other than to endure advertising, as shown in Figure 7.13.

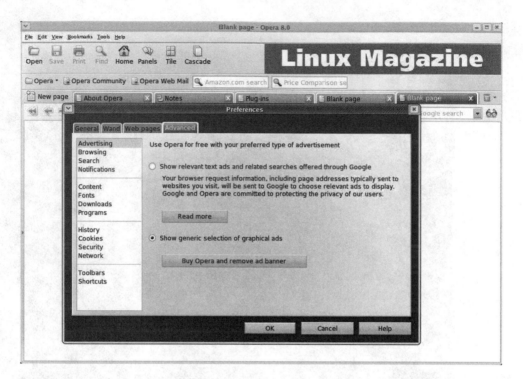

FIGURE 7.13 The Opera Web browser is another cross-platform browser that can be used on Windows before migrating to Linux.

Plug-ins

One of the gotchas for Linux Web browsers is many Web sites use of special plug-ins that are designed to run on Windows. Those plug-ins that are not using a standards-based technology are often unable to function as intended. For the most part, the most common plug-ins, such as Macromedia's Flash plug-in, Adobe Reader, and Real Player, work well. However, you may run into problems with proprietary formats. The support for plug-ins is ever changing, so it is best that you refer to your browser's support site for the latest news.

Installing the Java plug-in for Linux is not the most intuitive process. Sun does provide an RPM for Java plug-ins, but, depending on your type of installation, you may have to create a symbolic link (the Linux equivalent of a Windows shortcut). Linspire has licensed the code that is needed to play Windows Media Player files within the their version of the popular open source Xine multimedia player, and it is possible to play Windows media files within a browser, but not files that are protected by Digital Rights Management. One of the most controversial aspects of multimedia, especially for the Linux desktop user, is the use of Digital Rights Management that is used under Windows and Apple OSX does not work under Linux. You may solve this problem most easily by running a copy of Windows on a virtual machine under Linux. If needs are modest, you could use the Windows Media Player running under Wine, a replacement for the Windows API that runs on Linux and other Unixes.

There are very few places in the enterprise where it's recommended to use Wine, but when it comes to running Windows Media Player files (with the wmv or wmf extension), the Wine project may be your best bet. Though once the upcoming Windows Genuine Advantage is implemented, it may be necessary to validate that Microsoft software is running on a genuine Windows download. You may be prompted to complete a validation process to ensure that you have a genuine copy of Windows.

Email

Email is one of the widely used means of business correspondence. It has the ability to provide an almost immediate means of communication that is not limited by time, so a message can be sent outside of business hours and the sender can be confident that it will arrive and be waiting for the recipient or recipients upon their return to work. It can also provide a cost-effective way for transporting documents and, because of this, it is one of the most heavily relied-on applications that you will use on your desktop. One of the toughest things most businesses will face when migrating to Linux is the adoption of new messaging technologies. Microsoft Outlook, which is tightly tied to the Microsoft Exchange server, has become the predominant messaging and personal information manager for business. You may not be able to break this dependence, and if not, you may want to look at the discussion of how to migrate your native Windows applications to Linux. Otherwise you can find some excellent native Linux applications.

Evolution

Novell's Evolution email client is one of the most popular email and *personal information managers* (PIMs) for Linux. The interface is very similar to the interface used by popular business email client Microsoft Outlook, as shown in Figure 7.14.

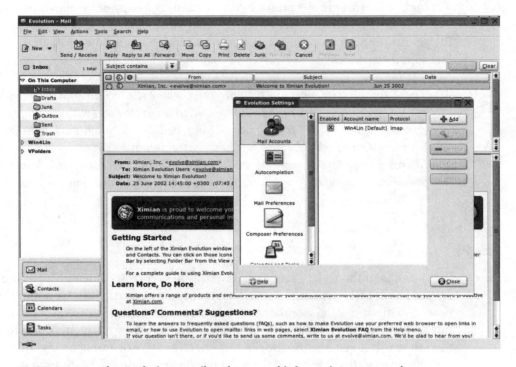

FIGURE 7.14 The Evolution email and personal information manager bears a resemblance to Microsoft Outlook.

The Evolution client also has the ability, through the Ximian Connector, to allow you to connect to Microsoft Exchange servers, which is a unique feature among Linux email clients. Evolution has a few other features that you may want to be familiar with, including Virtual Folders, which allow you to create virtual mail folders that are very similar to the idea of virtual desktop workspaces discussed in an earlier chapter. Virtual folders are a way to save queries in an organized way. In addition to virtual folders, Evolution can be integrated with an email spam filtering project called SpamAssassin which offers a powerful filtering system that can access spam filters outside the program. Many Linux users have developed successful filters by enabling Evolution to access *bogofilter* via a wrapper script and having bogofilter use a statistical process known as the Bayesian technique to make decisions on what is and is not spam. Also, the same is true more recently for the very popular spam filtering software *SpamAssassin*, a project sponsored by the Apache Foundation, producers of the popular open source Web software that we highlighted for server use. SpamAssassin could be used on your Linux desktop in conjunction with Evolution and its mail filters.

Thunderbird

Thunderbird is an extension of the Mozilla project offering a robust email client packed with features and capabilities that rival any commercial application. Also, Thunderbird is available for Windows, Mac OS X, and Linux, so if you are still considering the move to Linux you can try out Thunderbird today on your non-Linux desktop and then still be able to use the same client when you move to Linux. Thunderbird is probably the most advanced of any Linux email client in its spam filtering abilities. Thunderbird has junk mail controls that are very effective in detecting and acting on unsolicited email. Spam can be detected and deleted or stored in a folder for later review in the event of a false positive. Also, Thunderbird has a way to *whitelist* email so that you can be assured that emails from a certain address never get "wrongly imprisoned" by your spam filters. One innovative feature in Thunderbird is the option to use adaptive filters, which can analyze incoming messages and flag those likely to be junk email, as shown in the Figure 7.15

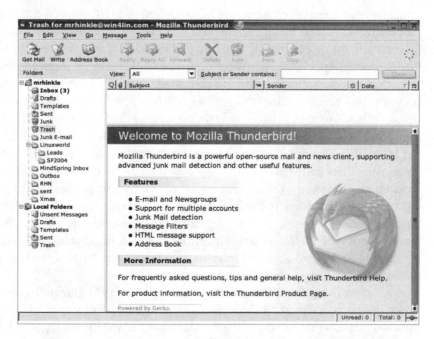

FIGURE 7.15 Thunderbird's adaptive filters learn from previous junk email.

Kmail

Kmail is the KDE email client and it is very popular because it is integrated into the KDE desktop and contact manager (Kontact). Kmail offers all the amenities that you would expect of an email client like support for POP3, IMAP, and SMTP. It also includes an Anti-Spam Wizard and can import email from Evolution, Opera, and Thunderbird. It also has very good filtering capabilities. However, it doesn't integrate email, contacts, and calendar on its own in the same way as Evolution or Outlook.

It's a fact of life for most of us: solicitations to "Make Money Fast" or for "Mail Order Drugstore" or sometimes with offensive or adult content that makes email users blush, especially when a colleague is looking over your shoulder. Spam, which is a slang term for Unsolicited Commercial Email (UCE), has reached epidemic proportions; it clogs your inboxes and saps your productivity. It is not just a Windows or Linux problem, it's an unpleasant fact of life for all users of Internet email. Dealing with spam is not only a Linux problem; it affects users of Mac, Windows, and Unix workstations, as well as cell phone users who utilize email for SMS (short messaging service) text messaging. Every day spammers are scheming to fill your email box with various solicitations for a cadre of products. That's why you should take as many precautions as you can to prevent junk email.

Many of these precautions are independent of platform and can improve your life on the Internet. Being careful who you give your email address to may sound like an obvious precaution, but many people don't guard their email address with the same vigilance as they protect their phone number or their address. Another tactic to prevent spam involves HTML email. Besides the obvious message you see in your mail reader, those who send SPAM often include a way to check that their message is being read so they know that it is likely that future emails sent to that address will be read. They can tell this because these messages usually include a register bit, which is usually a small transparent image that downloads from the sender's Web site when you view the message and then alerts them that you have opened that email. This helps them track which of their messages successfully reaches an end user and qualifies that email address as a target for further advertisements. One way to prevent this is to not download images from the server. Three popular email clients for the Linux desktop, Kmail, Thunderbird, and Evolution, give you the ability to prevent access of Internet resources from the body of the email which defeats this information gathering campaign.

Another thing that Internet email users are all very cognizant of (or should be), from the perspective of a Windows desktop, is the risk of viruses. It is not uncommon to see news stories extolling the damages caused by the latest Windows virus in the news and these viruses cause millions of dollars of damage. However, just because you are running a Linux desktop doesn't mean you should be lax in your approach to email attachments and their hidden payloads. The fact is that a Linux virus doesn't get nearly the bang for the buck as a Windows virus because the Linux desktop user is in the minority. Authors of these malicious programs receive less notoriety by propagating their viruses on the Linux desktop simply because their target is substantially smaller; so the viruses are out there, you just haven't heard about them in the newspapers. Also, if you are running a Linux desktop you may just be an unwitting carrier of viruses; because you would be impervious to a virus that exploits VB script or ActiveX, you may simply be passing it on to a colleague who reads mail on a Windows PC. It is important to take precautions when forwarding on the latest joke, or any document for that matter.

Web-based Email Clients

Because you may be migrating to Linux gradually, you may still be working between two operating systems. So downloading and storing mail on one system and not the other may not be in your best interest while you are in transition, or maybe you have decided to store your email on a server that has scheduled backups. This approach is very advantageous because you can access your email from most any Web browser on numerous platforms. Also, it is a step in the direction of centrally managed applications and data. By keeping data on the server rather than on disparate desktop PCs, you can manage it consistently across an organization, applying spam filtering and virus checking on the server rather than at each individual user's desk. This approach is usually more efficient than each user doing on it on an individual basis. That's why solutions that offer server side management and storage, such as *IMAP* (Internet Message Access Protocol), are valuable; they allow you to access messages as if they where local but require a network connection to do so. There are number of solutions for doing this today, and if you have a POP or IMAP server you can use a number of popular "free" Web interfaces including Squirrel, Neomail, or the full-featured Horde Project. The bottom line is that reducing the complexity of the PC desktop makes it easier to choose what platform you want to use, avoids vendor lock in, and improves your ability to choose how you will accomplish your desktop computing goals.

Scalix Community Edition

Scalix Community Edition is a server-based email and calendaring platform for Linux that is sponsored by Scalix, the company that licensed HP's OpenMail, a robust email platform. Scalix offers commercial products but the community version is freely available and can be upgraded to an Enterprise edition. The Scalix software is a product that can be hosted on Linux server and that offers transparent email capabilities to both Linux and Windows Outlook clients. The advantage of Scalix for Linux users is that the rich Web email client offers an interface similar to Microsoft Outlook's three panes. It also falls into the strategy of managing email purely on the server where system administrators can make wholesale backups of everyone's email and changes to the client are minimized.

Office Suites for the Linux Desktop

OpenOffice.org is an alternative to Microsoft Office suite and includes five core tools: Writer, Calc, Impress, Draw, and Base. There is a word processor, spreadsheet, presentation tool, a drawing program, and a database respectively. This suite was designed so that all the applications have a similar look and feel. The OpenOffice.org suite is the most popular office suite for Linux and is included with most every major Linux distribution. The OpenOffice.org suite components save their files by default in the OpenDocument format, which is an international XML standard for documents. An open standards approach is easier for programs to adhere to because it is well documented, it can be developed without proprietary functions, and it allows other vendors to design programs that can read these open standards-type documents.

OpenOffice.org—An Alternative to Microsoft Office

In earlier versions of Microsoft Word, viruses prevailed by exploiting the macro language (WordBasic) and exploiting Microsoft desktop vulnerabilities. Later versions of Word ask you if you would like to enable macros or not. However, being quick on the draw and clicking through these warnings, as many people do, still may cause problems. If you are still using a Windows desktop you may want to consider using OpenOffice.org on Windows as your primary word processor. The reason for this is that when you receive an attachment that you think might be suspect you can open it in a program that is less likely to be exploited because OpenOffice.org doesn't support Windows macros. OpenOffice.org does have a macro language, but it differs from the one that Word uses. This difference can potentially insulate you from that type of attack. However, as time passes and new packages like alternative office suites gain popularity, they will probably also receive targeted attacks from unscrupulous programmers. In the short term, reading Microsoft Office documents that you receive from unfamiliar sources (or even those that you know), in OpenOffice.org may be a good preventative measure. OpenOffice.org does an excellent job of authoring documents and with each new release becomes a greater threat to eroding Microsoft Office's lead as the most used office suite.

Writer—An Alternative to Microsoft Word

OpenOffice.org Writer is a word processor that is similar to Word and has many of the same features that you would expect from any word processor. It can be used to author very simple documents or complex reports. It has the capability to act as a desktop publishing platform that can save files that are easily edited, complete with a track changes feature, or it can export the documents in PDF format so that documents maintain their look and feel as they migrate from one platform to another. In addition to these formats, Writer can export files to HTML and XML, which, in the interest of true open standards and interoperability, might make your ability to share files even easier either by trading HTML documents or publishing them to the Web. Figure 7.16 shows OpenOffice.org Writer's interface, which is somewhat similar to Microsoft Word, running on Windows. The similarities include underlining of misspelled words and menu bars that perform common formatting functions.

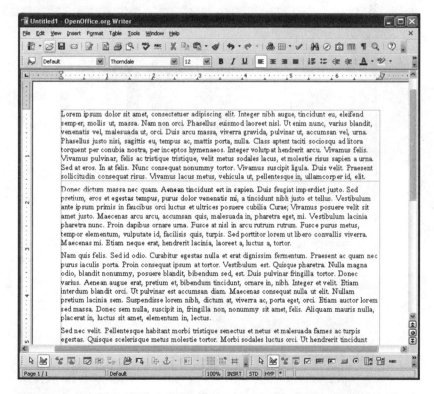

FIGURE 7.16   OpenOffice.org Writer is the word processing program for the OpenOffice.org suite.

Calc–An Alternative to Microsoft Excel

Calc is a spreadsheet program that can create spreadsheets and graphs and save them in a number of formats including the popular XLS format for Microsoft Excel. Additionally, Calc has the ability to poll data sources from databases and then convert the data into a summation or graph. OpenOffice.org's Calc is in many aspects as fully featured as any other program, with some unique features. It has the ability to export right to PDF, as all OpenOffice.org programs do, and it can be run on a number of platforms, making it easier for Windows users to pass Linux users spreadsheets without having to worry about interoperability. Figure 7.17 shows OpenOffice.org Calc with a spreadsheet and graph.

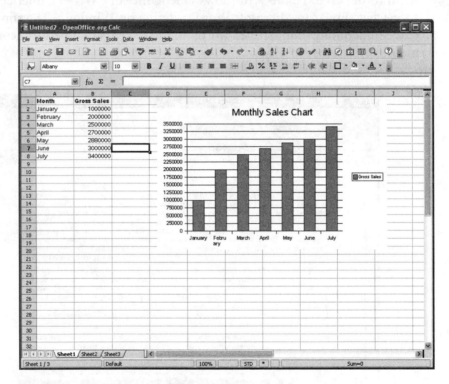

FIGURE 7.17   A Calc worksheet with data and a chart.

Impress–An Alternative to Microsoft PowerPoint

Impress is presentation software that rivals the Microsoft PowerPoint presentation software that is the standard among desktop presenters.

Creating Presentations: The primary use for Impress is to create presentations. The interface is reminiscent of PowerPoint. The program offers multiple views, including *Modify slide layout*, which is similar to the slide sorter in PowerPoint. You can set slide change timing to match speeches that are complemented with presentation software.

Creating Vector Graphics: OpenOffice.org has drawing tools that allow you to add scalable graphics to presentations.

Publishing Presentations in Flash: One extremely useful feature is the ability to publish presentations authored in Impress into a Flash SWF file so that they can be embedded in a Web page.

Of all the presentation software for Linux, Impress is the most likely candidate to replace the functionality provided by Microsoft PowerPoint as shown in Figure 7.18. Interoperability between both OpenOffice.org and PowerPoint is good, but you may notice that presentations that include animations may not translate well between the two packages.

FIGURE 7.18 Impress is presentation software that can open Microsoft PowerPoint documents.

Base—An Alternative to Microsoft Access

Base is a relatively new addition to OpenOffice.org's 2.0 version. One of the long-time complaints about OpenOffice.org was its lack of a database program for desktop users. This has been solved with Base, which let's you create databases and save them in an XML format. It also can import other database formats such as Microsoft Access and MySQL, or any ODBC-compliant database. Figure 7.19 shows the Base interface for creating a database, forms, and reports.

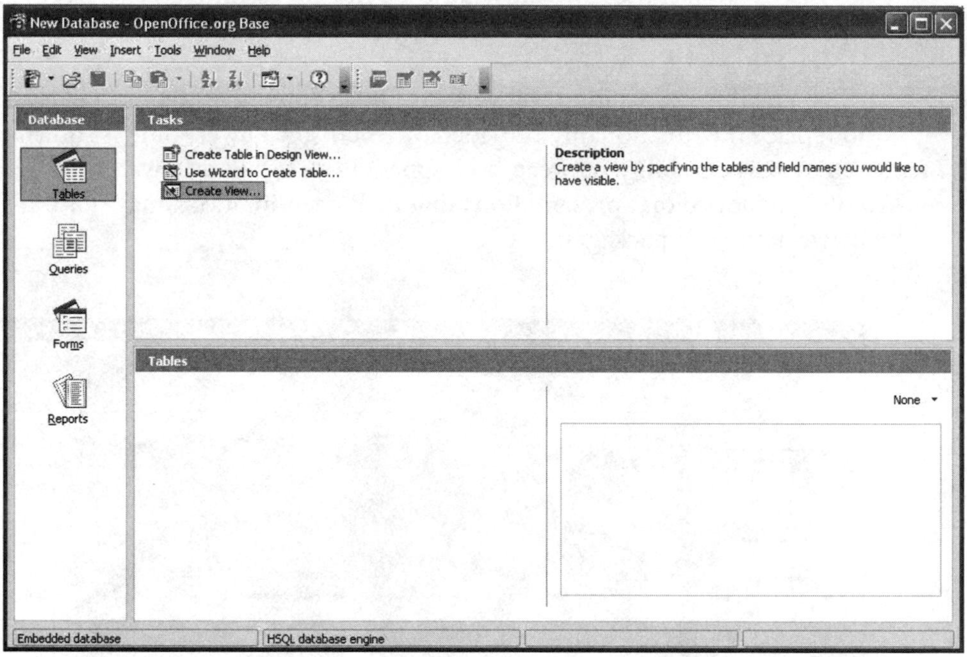

FIGURE 7.19   Base is a database program that can be used to create simple databases.

Other Programs That Are Part of the OpenOffice.org Suite

OpenOffice.org includes a program called *Math* for authoring mathematical equations. These equations can then be inserted as an element into a document authored in Writer or Impress. *Draw* is also a supporting program for the OpenOffice.org suite; it allows you to create graphs or complex drawings and flow charts that are easily inserted into other OpenOffice.org documents.

StarOffice

StarOffice is the Sun Microsystems commercial version of OpenOffice.org. It comes from a common codebase but has some additional features like fonts and templates and the ADABAS database. The value in this product is the commercial support available from Sun and some professional-looking templates. You will find that most features in OpenOffice.org are mirrored in the StarOffice.

MISCELLANEOUS BUSINESS APPLICATIONS

No two businesses are the same, but as a rule, in the large enterprise there are many users who have defined roles. A user may be very focused in his job and have a very specific skill set. In a small business, users are more likely to have to wear many hats. That's why the breadth of applications they use may be quite wide. The desktop applications listed in this section are by no means exclusive, or inclusive of all the needs of the business user, but are good open source alternatives to popular business applications.

Dia—An Alternative to Microsoft Visio®

It's often necessary to have access to flowchart and technical diagram programs, and in the Windows product line Visio fills this role. However, the open source program Dia offers many of those same features and a comprehensive set of shapes to make flowcharts, network diagrams, and other types of illustrations. Dia has its own file format with the extension .dia, but the file is a compressed XML format, so you can choose to not compress the file and try to read it in other programs like Macromedia Dreamweaver. What you will likely find is that you will export documents authored in Dia to an image format that can be read by other programs like PNG, Encapsulated Postscript (EPS), or scalable vector graphics (SVG). Figure 7.20 shows an example of the Dia program creating a network diagram.

Desktop Publishing and Web Authoring

The need to publish documents to share within or between businesses includes marketing collateral or professional-looking reports. There are many high-quality tools that might be similar to what you are already used to, and they are often available to be freely downloaded. Many users never fully realize all the features of these types of programs and would be perfectly happy with the limited but stable features of the desktop publishing and Web authoring programs we'll discuss in this section. For example, in a small business you could use free software to author and save flyers or documents that could be printed at your local copy shop. Web pages could

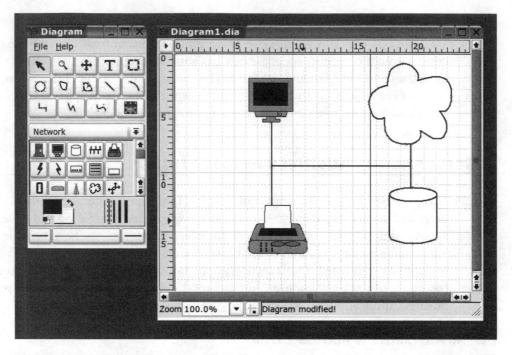

FIGURE 7.20 Dia is a diagram and flowchart authoring tool that can create graphics that can be embedded in office documents.

be authored using the WYSIWIG Web editors in Linux or even on Windows without investing in expensive software that serves both the casual user and the expert alike. Keep in mind that if you buy the state-of-the art desktop publishing suite you may be helping to fund features you will never use, when a simpler, easy-to-use application might do the job just as well.

Scribus

Scribus is a GPL desktop publishing program that is similar to Adobe PageMaker or Quark for Windows and Mac OS. The Scribus desktop publishing program is a page layout program so it doesn't look at elements of the document such as spelling. It simply coordinates where text and graphics are lined up for the purposes of printing. Authoring a brochure or other document might involve a number of free open source software packages, but Scribus can be used to pull them together. For example, if you were creating a four page brochure, you could author the graphics, including logos in the Inkscape vector drawing program, then edit the copy for the brochure in OpenOffice.org Writer, and finally combine these elements in a professional-looking layout using Scribus. You can also export your documents from Scribus. Figure 7.21 shows the Scribus work space with a newsletter template.

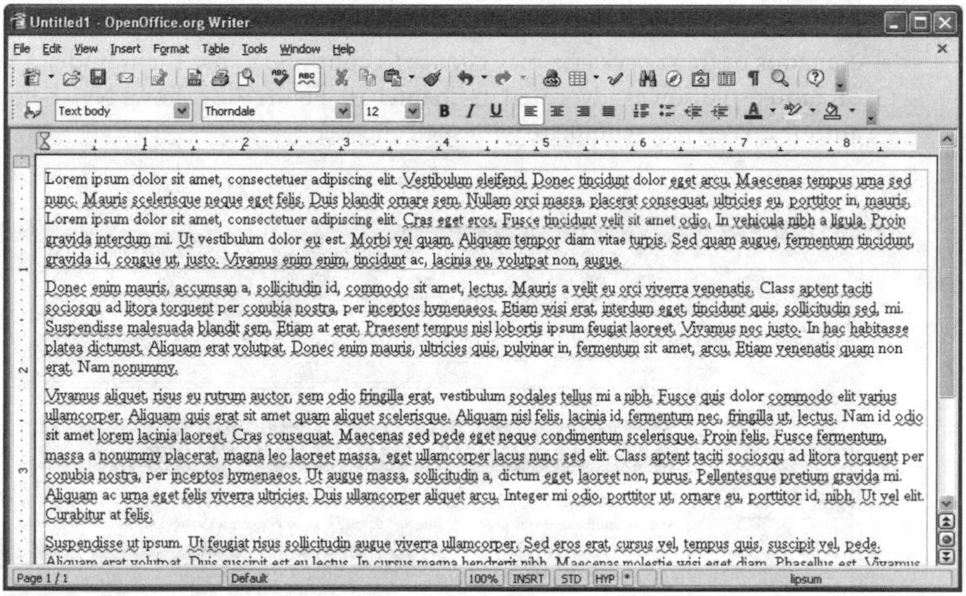

FIGURE 7.21 Scribus can be used to author newsletters that can then be exported to PDF for electronic distribution or printing.

Scribus has features that you would find in commercial applications, and you can extend Scribus for jobs that would normally call for a separate application like Adobe Illustrator. For printing that requires a Color Management System, you can download and install a free program called Little CMS so that document colors can be printed and turn out in the way you expect. Even though Scribus is a fairly robust desktop layout program, you should always check your work in another program like Adobe's Acrobat Reader. This step will ensure that documents really do display as desired and transfer correctly from platform to platform and application to application.

Nvu

Nvu is a Web authoring tool suite sponsored by Linspire, the makers of the popular Linux desktop. The Nvu Web publishing tools are based on the Mozilla Composer code base and have since focused on five areas of improvement: ease of use, WYSIWIG editing, integrated file management, enhanced handling of forms and templates, and extensibility that allows users to add improvements in the form of extensions. Unlike many open source projects, Nvu is backed by the commitments of a company, so there is a likelihood of the project continuing through corporate sponsorship. Also, the Nvu suite is a very good alternative to other commercial packages like Microsoft FrontPage or Macromedia's DreamWeaver, though aficionados of these packages may choose to continue to use them under a Windows on Linux solution as advocated in Chapter 10. Figure 7.22 shows Nvu being used to author a Web page complete with spell checker.

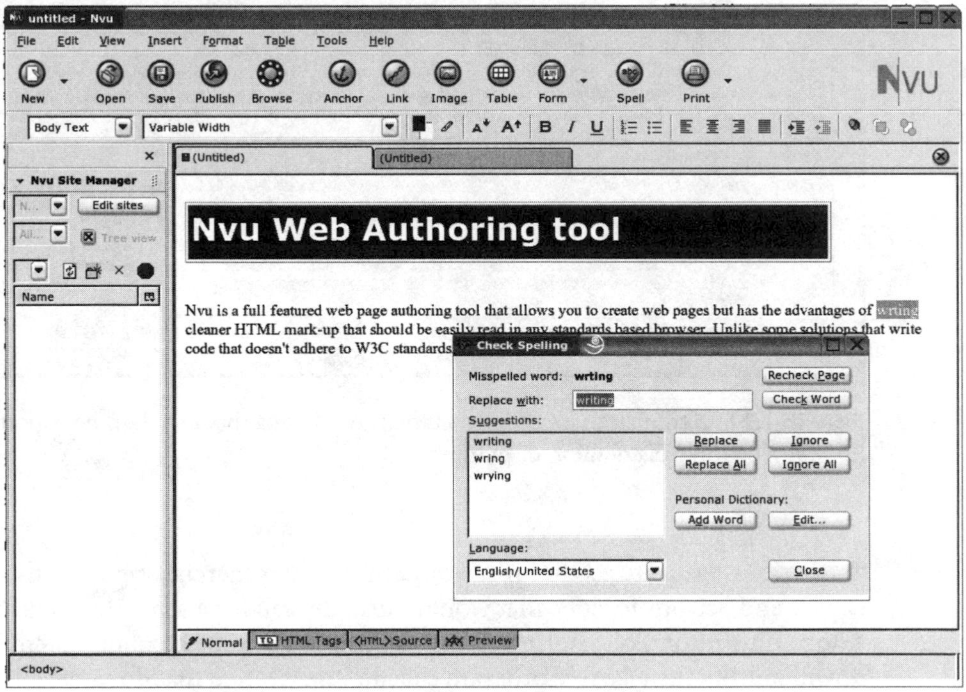

FIGURE 7.22 Nvu is a WYSIWYG HTML editor based on the Mozilla Gecko engine.

Quanta+

Quanta+ is a more fully featured Web development tool that is aimed more at the coder than the layman. It is, however, a robust and useful HTML editor for KDE. It is a very powerful tool for coding Web pages, including those that use PHP. Figure 7.23 shows Quanta+.

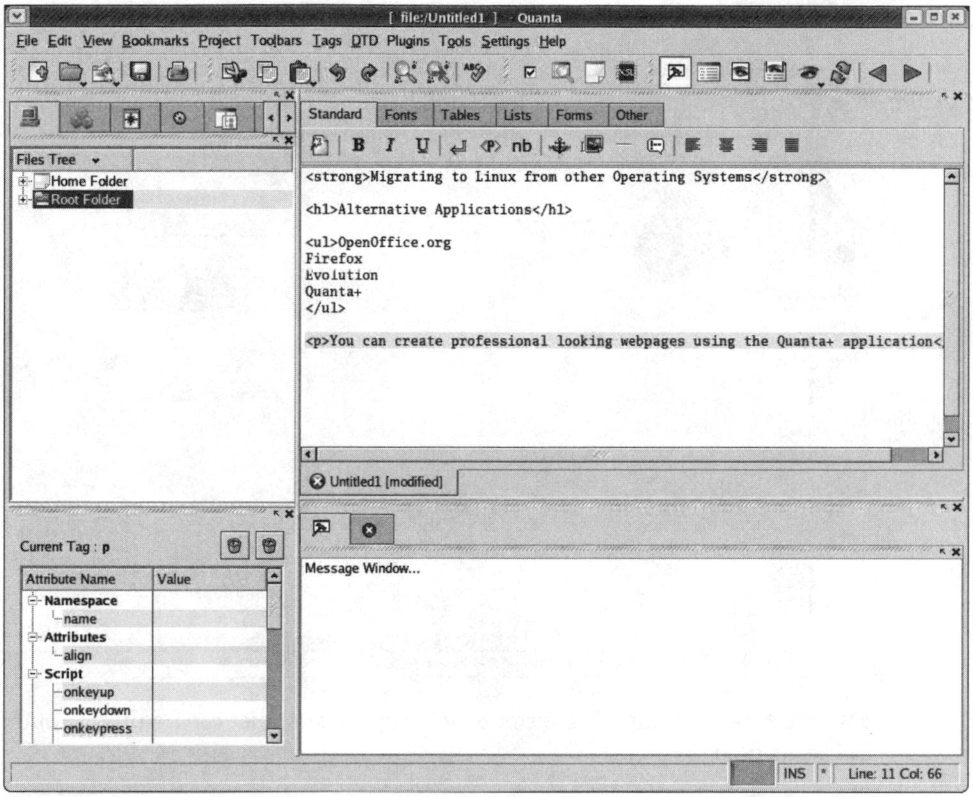

FIGURE 7.23   Quanta+ is a very powerful web development environment.

Inkscape–An Alternative to Adobe Illustrator

Inkscape is a vector drawing program that is similar to Adobe Illustrator or Corel-Draw. It creates images in the open scalable vector graphics format (SVG). You can draw shapes and add fonts to pictures that can be scaled while maintaining the quality of the image as shown in Figure 7.24

The GIMP–An Alternative to Adobe Photoshop

The GIMP (GNU Image Manipulation Program) is very similar to the popular image editing and manipulation program Adobe Photoshop. The GIMP will run on Windows or Linux and is a full-featured Linux image tool capable of creating professional-looking illustrations as well as editing digital pictures. The GIMP has an interface that has a floating toolbar much like Adobe Photoshop or Illustrator as

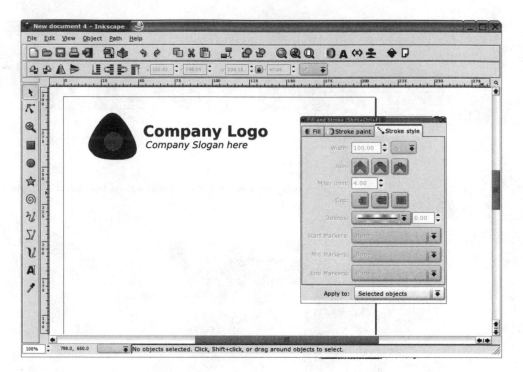

FIGURE 7.24   Inkscape is a vector drawing application that can be used to author diagrams or logos.

shown in Figure 7.25, and filter capabilities to apply special effects to images. The unique feature of the GIMP is its scripting language (Script-Fu) which can be used to create buttons or automate tasks that are repetitive, such as applying a series of operations to an image.

You can also author impressive and unique-looking documents at a fraction of the cost of what you would have to invest in commercial applications. You can, in many cases, use these applications cross-platform to share files that can be read and collaborated on in both Windows and Linux.

Financial

One common complaint about Linux is the lack of financial applications available for both personal and business finance tracking. This is probably one of the most valid criticisms of Linux. Software giant Intuit has the resources to not only produce top-quality software but to develop relationships with financial institutions and to drive commonly used file formats currently open source projects do not. The solution for most organizations switching to Linux will likely be to run their

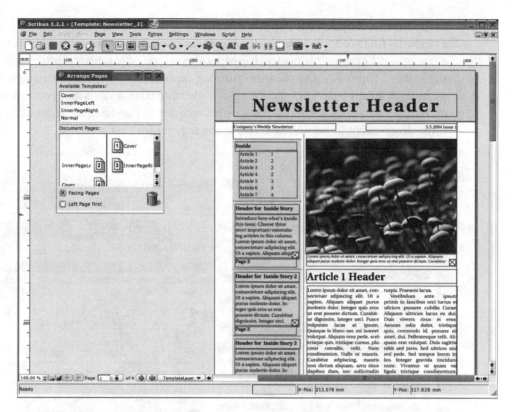

FIGURE 7.25   The GIMP is an image manipulation program that can be used as a substitute for Adobe Photoshop.

financial packages natively on Windows or on a hosted Windows desktop running from within a virtual machine.

GnuCash—Personal and Small Business Finance

GnuCash is a personal and small business finance package that is a fair competitor to Microsoft Money or Inuit's Quicken. GnuCash allows you to track accounts (stock, banking, income, and expenses). GnuCash benefits from development that focuses on modularity and multilanguage support.

Moneydance—Personal Finance Software

Moneydance is a commercial application that provides financial management on multiple platforms including Mac OS X, Windows, Linux, and OS/2. The Moneydance program is supported by Reilly Technologies, LLC, a privately owned company in Richmond, Virginia. Moneydance has most of the features you would expect from a personal finance application including a check registry, account tracking, and visualization and graphing tools to give you an overview of your accounts. Figure 7.26 shows the Moneydance application running on Mac OS X. The information shown includes account balances, upcoming and overdue transactions and reminders, and exchange rate information. Clicking on an account or choosing an account from the drop-down account list will take you to the register for that account.

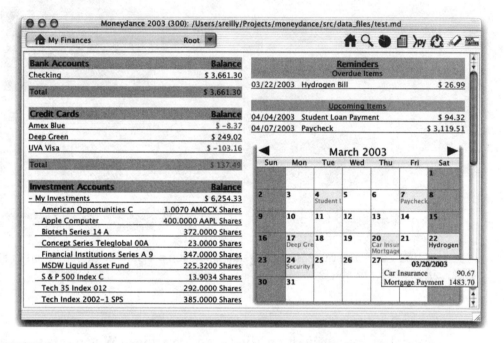

FIGURE 7.26   Moneydance is a cross-platform accounting package shown running on Mac OS X.

ACCPAC–Enterprise Accounting software

ACCPAC is a subsidiary of Computer Associates, which in June of 2002 announced support for Linux with the Pro series of their award-winning accounting package. The ACCPAC Advantage Series has support to run a robust enterprise solution with support on the client desktop. The implementation uses Wine to facilitate the use of a client application on the Linux desktop. They also have the ability to run the accounting server connected to an IBM DB2 database to store data on the server.

You may desire to use an accounting database that is running 100 percent natively on Linux, but the choices are admittedly limited. The stop gap solution for many enterprises will be to evaluate Windows solutions hosted on Linux using methods suggested in Chapter 10. In those cases the solution will entail hosting an existing accounting solution and then, as desired, the accounting package can be migrated to Linux. In some cases, accounting packages like Oracle Small Business Accounting can be used to offer financial packages and client software over the Web rather than running natively over Linux.

Media Players

With the popularity of Web casts and other multimedia methods for delivering training to the desktop, multimedia in business or education can be a requirement. There are a variety of players that can play most application formats natively. The only exception is the Windows Media Format, which requires a proprietary Microsoft codec. This can be overcome using one of the methods mentioned in Chapter 10. There are also issues that surround running multimedia that have less to do with technology and more to do with patents and Digital Rights Management. To an end user these things may not be apparent, as legal issues vary by country and government organization. You should do some research by at least conducting a Web search on issues pertaining to using technologies to play multimedia.

Codec is an abbreviation of the term compressor-decompressor and is the algorithm that is used to compress and decompress a multimedia file such as a song or a movie. It is a tool that takes the file and compresses it for distribution, but then that same codec is needed to uncompress the file so that your media player can play it. Many players come with codecs to read a variety of multimedia types, but some codecs are proprietary and protected by licenses so they cannot be used by open source multimedia programs. Table 7.3 shows a list of file types and common Linux multimedia players.

TABLE 7.3 Multimedia File Formats

Type of File	File Extensions	Player
Music Files	.mp3, .og	XMMS, Juk
Movie Files	.mpeg	Totem, Kaffeine, Xine
Movie Files	.wmv, .wmf	Windows Media Player, Using Wine
Real Player Steaming Video	.rm, .rv	RealPlayer, Helix Player
Quicktime Movies	.mov, .DivX	Apple Quicktime using Wine, MPlayer

Real Player

RealNetworks, which makes RealPlayer for Windows, also makes a Linux version that can be used to play many popular formats including Real Audio, RealVideo 10, MP3, Ogg Vorbis, and others. The RealPlayer is based on the Helix™ Platform, an open source collaborative effort.

Xine

Xine is a free multimedia player for Linux that can be shared with other front ends such as the Kaffeine media player for the KDE desktop. You can use Xine to play a wide variety of file types providing you download the necessary codecs.

You may also resort to using a Windows on Linux solution like Wine to run Windows Media Player on Linux. This solution has the benefit of providing many features such as Digital Rights Management and the appropriate codecs for those files directly from Microsoft. You can also use Wine to run iTunes though you couldn't use it to synch an Apple iPod.

Totem

Totem is the official movie player of the GNOME desktop and uses the Xine multimedia player as a backend. It will likely be the movie player that launches from your GNOME desktop.

Kaffeine

Kaffeine is a multimedia player for KDE that uses Xine for a backend. The Kaffeine multimedia player can play both MP3 audio and video. It can function as a jukebox that can handle music play lists. Kaffeine also has the capability to play and record Digital Video Broadcasting (DVB). Kaffeine can then be used as a digital video recorder to save broadcasts to the hard drive. Figure 7.27 shows the KDE multimedia player, Kaffeine.

MPlayer

MPlayer is a movie player for Linux that plays most popular movie types. It also is reputed to be able to process and play damaged MPEG files that Windows Media Player deems unplayable.

RythmBox and Juk

Listening to music is a popular activity, especially since modern PCs offer robust multimedia capabilities. Linux has music organizers that can create play lists and

FIGURE 7.27   Kaffeine multimedia player is part of the KDE desktop.

spawn music players. RythmBox is a music management application that resembles Apple's iTunes. It is free software and is included with the GNOME desktop, though it can run in any Linux desktop environment providing the required libraries are present. Juk is part of the KDE Multimedia package, and like RhythmBox, it is very similar to the Apple iTunes interface. You can use Juk to manage music lists or to play music. Juk is part of the KDE multimedia package and will likely be present when you install that desktop environment.

WHERE TO FIND ADDITIONAL APPLICATIONS

The number of locations on the Internet to find free software is almost limitless, but that is only mildly helpful unless you know what to look for and can type it into your favorite search engine. The sites listed here are some of the most well supported among Linux enthusiasts and offer a wide variety of applications that can address almost any common desktop computing need.

SourceForge.net

SourceForge is the world's largest open source software development Web site, with over 1,000,000 registered users and nearly 100,000 registered projects. Source-Forge is owned and operated by OSTG, Inc. (Open Source Technology Group, Inc.), a Linux company that had one of the highest-flying initial public offerings in U.S. history. SourceForge.net provides a free hosting and collaborative environment that open source developers and users can use to upload and download software, post comments to forums, read documentation, or track bugs.

Freshmeat.net

Freshmeat.net is also an OSTG Web property, but this site is an index of Unix and cross-platform software. Freshmeat is a content site that highlights software on a daily basis and is complemented by articles about new software packages that are rated with three different criteria: user-supplied quality rating, vitality, and popularity. Users who visit Freshmeat.net can submit a rating on a scale of 1 to 10. Vitality is a function of the age of a project multiplied by the number of announcements and divided by the days passed since the last product release. Popularity is based on a formula that factors the number of visits to the project Web site times the number of subscriptions.

Tucows

As a Windows user you may be familiar with the popular Web site Tucows, which started out as a Windows software distribution Web site. Actually Tucows was originally an acronym for The Ultimate Collection of Winsock Software. Over time, Tucows added additional services including domain name registration services and eventually the inclusion of software for non-Windows software. Today Tucows is one of the biggest software libraries in the world and ISPs worldwide have mirrored the software on the site. Tucows also has a popularity rating system that shows the number of downloads, and there is a rating system that is run by Tucows reviewers.

SUMMARY

There are many, many more applications that your enterprise may need that aren't detailed within this book. Also, the landscape of emerging native Linux applications, including those used in business, expands every day. There is a large grass-roots effort supporting the release of these applications. According to a February 2004 study by Evans Data, over 1.1 million developers in North America have spent some of their time working on open source applications [Evans Data, 2005]. The first wave of applications making its way to mainstream businesses are those that have the broadest appeal, but as more businesses become interested in Linux, new business applications that address vertical markets like health care and manufacturing will emerge. One area where this is already happening is in retail where the needs of the desktop worker are narrowly focused on repetitive tasks like point-of-sale and inventory applications. Organizations with large numbers of workers who do a narrowly defined task like point of sale, order entry, or medical records entry are the most likely candidates for desktop adoption as they have modest needs and more call for high availability and speed. In these cases, relatively simple applications can be ported to the Web.

OTHER RESOURCES

- Internet Exploder FAQ—*http://dslweb.nwnexus.com/mclain/ActiveX/Exploder/ FAQ.htm*
- Secunia Internet Explorer Vulnerabilities—*http://secunia.com/advisories/12889/*
- Firefox 1.x Vulnerabilities—*http://secunia.com/product/4227/*
- Firefox—*www.mozilla.org/products/firefox*
- Firefox Extensions—*https://addons.update.mozilla.org/extensions/*
- Bookmark Synchronizer—*https://addons.update.mozilla.org/extensions/more-info.php?application=firefox&version=1.0&os=Linux&category=Bookmarks&id =14*
- Konqueror—*http://konqueror.kde.org*
- Opera—*www.opera.com*
- Mozilla Plugin Support on Linux (x86)—*http://plugindoc.mozdev.org/linux. html*
- Thunderbird—*http://www.mozilla.org/products/thunderbird*
- Evolution—*www.novell.com/products/evolution*
- Bogofilter—*www.bogofilter.sourceforge.net*
- Spam.Abuse.Net—*http://spam.abuse.net*
- Squirrel Mail—*www.squirrelmail.org*
- Neomail—*http://sourceforge.net/projects/neomail/*
- Horde—*www.horde.org*
- Scalix—*www.scalix.com*
- SpamCop—*http://spamcop.net*
- CAUCE—*www.cauce.org*
- Netscape Plug-in Finder—*http://plugins.netscape.com*
- Dia—*www.gnome.org/projects/dia/*
- Scribus—*www.scribus.net*

- Moneydance—*http://moneydance.com/*
- GNU Cash—*www.gnucash.org*
- AccPac—*www.accpac.com*
- Macromedia Flash Player Download Center Linux—*http://www.macromedia. com/shockwave/download/download.cgi?P1_Prod_Version=ShockwaveFlash&P2 _Platform=Linux&P3_Browser_Version=Netscape4*
- Java Technology on Linux—*http://java.sun.com/linux/*
- PluginDoc for Linux86—*http://plugindoc.mozdev.org/linux.html*
- Linspire DVD Player/ Mplayer—*www.linspire.com/lindows_dvd_info.php*
- Xine—*http://xinehq.de/*
- Windows Media Player in the WineHQ AppDB—*http://appdb.winehq.org/appview.php?appId=131*
- Real Player for Linux—*www.real.com/linux*
- Totem, the Movie Player—*www.gnome.org/projects/totem/*
- Kaffeine Player—*http://kaffeine.sourceforge.net*
- MPlayer—*www.mplayerhq.hu*
- Rhythmbox—*www.rhythmbox.org*
- Juk—*http://developer.kde.org/~wheeler/juk.html*
- SourceForge.net—*www.sourceforge.net*
- Freshmeat.Net—*www.freshmeat.net*
- Tucows—*http://linux.tucows.com*
- KDE-Apps.org—*www.kde-apps.org*

REFERENCES

Evans Data, North American Developer Population Study, "More than 1.1 Million Developers in North America Now Working on Open Source Projects." Availbve online at *http://www.evansdata.com/n2/pr/releases/DPS2004.shtml*, April 28, 2005.

US CERT "Vulnerability Note VU#713878" (October 13, 2004) Available online at *http://www.kb.cert.org/vuls/id/713878*.

Part

III

Supporting the Windows to Linux Migration

L inux migration for an enterprise is a much more intricate process than it is for a single user who decides to forego his or her Windows desktop for another OS. The steps a single user goes through one time may require hundreds or thousands of repetitions for a successful migration in an enterprise or even just a part of a very large enterprise. Besides installing Linux there are many other things you should consider to support a Windows to Linux Migration. In most cases you can use your existing back-office infrastructure to continue to provide file and print sharing, database, Web, and email. If you have come to the conclusion that Linux is good enough for the desktop, though, it stands to reason that your back office could also be run on open source infrastructure hosted on Linux. This move would be complementary because you could make sure to use open standards-based technologies that would be complementary to your new Linux desktops.

Moving data from one platform to another is another hurdle you will need to overcome. Existing users have settings and data that need to be moved to the new environment. Preparations before the move will help to insure interoperability between data created on Windows and later read and manipulated on Linux. The other aspect of data migration includes the physical move of user data. This can be one of the most time-consuming aspects of migration. Distinguishing what data needs to move and then coming up with a plan to move it from one location to another involves planning, but there are a number of tools that can help accomplish this task.

As mentioned early on in this book, one of the most popular reasons given for not moving to Linux is that there are often no applications equivalent to those that you have become dependent on in Windows. Providing a mechanism to migrate those applications can answer your last objection to a Linux migration. Also, planning for the future involves making application decisions that don't tie you too tightly to any one vendor or platform, but instead give you the freedom to move to a more suitable solution if your existing one fails to continue to meet your needs.

If deciding how to migrate data and applications isn't enough, you may also want to reconsider your existing strategy of individual user PCs supported by a help desk that spends more time fixing broken systems then it does improving the quality of your infrastructure. You may look at a hardened desktop environment that is more easily managed and centrally distributed. This change of paradigm is called thin client computing. This is a departure from PCs that run their operating systems locally. A comparable environment can be served from a terminal server to thin client desktop PCs that have fewer moving parts. Failures can be minimized when the system is augmented by a management toolbox that can push user desktops with tight controls to help prevent infection and spread of viruses and the installation of unauthorized software.

8 Back-Office Infrastructure

In This Chapter

- Leveraging Your Existing Infrastructure
- Linux Replacement of Windows Servers
- Open Source Services for Back-Office Infrastructure
- Other Notable Open Source Solutions
- Summary
- Other Resources
- References

Providing the infrastructure to support a Linux, Windows, or even a heterogenous LAN can be accomplished with server infrastructure built on Microsoft Windows products or Linux and open source products. Finding out the advantages and disadvantages of each will be a complement to your Windows-to-Linux desktop migration. If you already have Windows in place, your network needs are stagnant, and you have an investment that you want to preserve, you may want to keep that infrastructure. When it comes time to expand or update your infrastructure, looking at an open source alternative that most importantly supports *open standards* is wise choice. Using products that adhere to open standards may help avoid vendor lock-in, enabling one standards-based solution to replace another should you become unsatisfied with any aspect of your enterprise architecture.

Linux and your Existing Back-Office Infrastructure: You may already have a back-office infrastructure that adequately serves your needs. Linux desktops can take advantage of these systems without any changes. Your primary concern will be with making sure you have acquired the necessary client access licenses to take advantage of these systems.

Replacement of Microsoft Windows Server Operating Systems: Open source software hosted on Linux can provide services almost identical services to those you are familiar with using Windows, but Linux and open source solutions offer many choices that are often unencumbered by the expensive licensing terms associated with many proprietary software packages. You also can choose features a la carte rather than be stuck with the feature set mandated by one vendor.

Open Source and Alternative Services on Linux Servers: If you are looking to replace or enhance the services provided in your enterprise you may want to look at alternatives hosted on Linux servers. There are plenty of free software solutions that offer services equivalent to costly proprietary solutions. There is also a good mix of open source solutions that have the backing of companies; these offer support and costs will mainly fall under labor, training, and support contracts rather than seat licenses.

One of the biggest cost savings you can quantify will be the cost of acquisition of open source solutions. You will also experience savings in administration time and higher availability. A highly available Linux system may only need to be rebooted to apply a new kernel, while Windows Servers may require more frequent reboots, requiring system administrators to attend to these tasks during off hours, an inconvenience often costing additional overtime pay. You should also look at the security aspects of Microsoft Server versus Windows. Additionally, Linux benefits from patch management; because kernel space and user space are distinctly separate, reboots are infrequent. This separation can provide insulation from security exploits; having a server with tight integration between subsystems means that a failure or breach in one system may leave other parts of your installation at risk [Quant, 2005]. Also, consider the results of a survey by Evans Data in July 2004: 92% of respondents indicated that their Linux systems hadn't been infected by a virus; 87% of Linux developers said they had never been hacked, and of the 22% of those who had been hacked, it was by someone with a valid Login ID [Evans Data, 2005]. You may also find that Linux is faster than Windows, as benchmarks by IT Week labs showed that Samba, an open source file and print sharing server that runs on Linux, was 2.5 times faster than Windows Server 2003, and was able to handle four times as many clients as Windows 2000 before performance started to drop [Howorth, 2003]. Overall there is quite a strong case for replacement of Windows Server with Linux running open source packages. Weighing the options regarding when to make the appropriate move to capitalize on these advantages is where you will find the biggest benefits.

LEVERAGING YOUR EXISTING INFRASTRUCTURE

If you already use Microsoft servers in your enterprise to deliver services such as file and print services you can add Linux desktops to your existing infrastructure with very little trouble and without adjusting systems in which you have already invested. Over time you may need to add users or update software, and those events are the times you need to reevaluate your architecture for opportunities. The Microsoft server products work well for a very large majority of LAN and desktop users, though over time upgrades and security risks may cause you to consider alternatives like services hosted on Linux. You will want to make a decision on which fork in the road to take. Microsoft may seem like a safe and easy choice but may not offer the cost savings, performance enhancements, and security features that open source can bring. You should also make sure you really understand the costs associated with one decision over another; server software may seem inexpensive until you factor in downtime and client access licensing.

The Seat Licensing Model

One common complaint about Microsoft and other proprietary solutions is the use of per user or seat licenses. Linux and open source solutions often use a model that is based on per server models that cost the same for support whether you are using 5 seats or 500. Microsoft follows the practice of charging *client access licenses* or *CALs*. Client access licensing, or seat licensing, is a mechanism for charging organizations by use of the software. Microsoft Windows Server on a server with an Intel processor may be able to adequately serve anywhere from 5 to 100 users. Each user on the Microsoft licensing scheme may require additional entitlement licenses to access that server, regardless of any additional value provided by Microsoft. With Microsoft Server 2003 there are also two types of Windows CALs: device based or user based. Device-based client access licenses are for an actual device like a PC that accesses a Windows 2003 server for printing. A user-based license allows every Named User to access the server from different devices throughout the enterprise, so the right to access servers travels with the end user rather than by the device used to access the machine. Database vendors do the same thing, requiring each user, or concurrent user depending on the case, to purchase a seat. In an alternative model, you can install a Linux server with Red Hat or Novell's Linux product, then pay support for installation and updates to the server. The difference is that the price is fixed regardless of the number of users. In some cases the licensing model is by number of CPUs, but still the incremental cost of support versus access licensing still remains attractive, especially as the server reaches full utilization.

Suppliers and actual costs for software may vary; this example takes figures from Microsoft's Web site in April 2005. To accomplish this exercise on your own you should price the number of seats and servers from your preferred vendor. Consider the case of a small company with 100 desktop PC users. The company has the option of installing Windows 2003 Server or Linux. To supply simple file and print services consider a Microsoft Server solution. To acquire Microsoft Windows Small Business Server 2003 with 5 CALs the cost is $599. To license the additional 95 devices, you can buy five 20-pack CALS at a unit price of $1929, for a total of $9645. The total cost of acquisition of the software and licensing would be $10,244. If you want support for this operating system preinstalled, you may be able to receive it from your computer manufacturer or reseller, but if you want to contact Microsoft directly you may be liable for a support charge of $99 for email with a response time of one business day or $245 for a phone call per incident or through some other mechanism. Providing you don't need support you could institute this solution for an acquisition cost of $10,244.

If you wanted to provide file and print services using a commercial version of Linux you could go to Novell, a well-respected software company, and purchase SuSE LINUX Enterprise Server 9 for $349 (to download it). You may buy the installation media and manual for an additional $35. If you want to contact Novell directly for support you can do so for free, 24/7, by electronic means with a four-hour maximum response time for installations. If you want support by phone you can get it by signing up for a support contract with pricing comparable to that of Microsoft.

That's a cost of $374 plus the cost of any support you choose to pay for.

Another option would be to go to the Debian project and download Debian's version of Linux, which is a totally free distribution, and install that on the same hardware that would work for either of the two previous examples. Then set up the services to handle file and print sharing without any acquisition costs other than time and network bandwidth; if you choose to burn the software to CD add a few more cents. For a single instance, the cost of time for the system administrator might approach that of the Novell SuSE LINUX Enterprise Server depending on the administrator's expertise. He also wouldn't have the benefit of a company to resolve issues or give support, but, depending on your level of comfort with Linux, that might be fine. Also, you could use that same server to provide other services like Web or thin client sessions without the need for CALs or, in contrast to a Microsoft product like Terminal Services, Terminal Services CALs. As you scale and add more users your costs don't rise unless you need to add hardware, which is the case no matter which operating system you choose. These incremental savings can quickly add up.

Weigh the factors of cost of acquisition and the labor it takes to do an install when you make your decision. There is some risk that a failed Linux installation could become a money pit with excessive man hours spent troubleshooting problems, but this is a risk of any new IT project. If you do your homework up front, you can determine how much risk you are really taking. One hour of research on the Internet will likely give you a good degree of confidence that this Linux alternative to Microsoft Windows Server products is not a foolish or excessively risky bet.

Heterogenous Network

The reality of most established businesses is that over time IT equipment gets replaced at the end of its usable life, which is staggered depending on the particular system or software package. At these points you replace the systems with new hardware or software or both. These systems may be mail servers, file servers, or desktop PCs. At the point where you are considering replacing systems, you may want to start replacing Windows systems with Linux systems.

Before moving forward with a migration you must address interoperability and integration issues, whether you are an SMB user or a large enterprise. Linux vendors must carry the burden of providing the tools to allow for interoperability between open source solutions and legacy systems. According to a 2005 Yankee Group Study, the North American Linux TCO Survey, 20% of the installed server base worldwide is running Linux. In North America the market share is about 15%. They also noted that the majority of corporate networks are heterogeneous with multiple operating systems, Linux and Windows being the dominant ones. [Ferhst, 2005].

To be more comfortable with Linux as part of your long-term IT strategy, contemplate the replacement of systems as they need it rather than making wholesale changes from Windows to Linux. This allows you to use funds that might have previously been budgeted to replenish commercial databases and operating systems with training for system administrators to be able to administer new Linux systems. That training over time becomes a very small cost as each new server installation can benefit from the acquisition of technical skills by IT personnel. Savings in software acquisition costs may be minor in comparison to the savings garnered by having freedom in vendor choice. In the short term you will probably see modest savings on seat licenses, but the point in moving to an open architecture is breaking vendor lock-in, which allows you to manage your upgrade cycle rather than your software vendor. In addition to competition in products, you may benefit from reduced security incidents and increased PC user productivity. Figure 8.1 shows a heterogeneous network that benefits from both Windows and Linux systems. As it was time to upgrade the company file and print server, a Linux server was put in its place. The decommissioned file server was no longer adequate from a disk space and processing standpoint, but it was more than enough to be used to proxy Internet traffic and provide a basic firewall. When it was time to refresh the desktops in the customer service department, inexpensive white box PCs were used, and the manufacturing floor, which hadn't had computers in the past, received thin client PCs that are cheaper to replace than PCs when they get clogged with dust from the surrounding machinery.

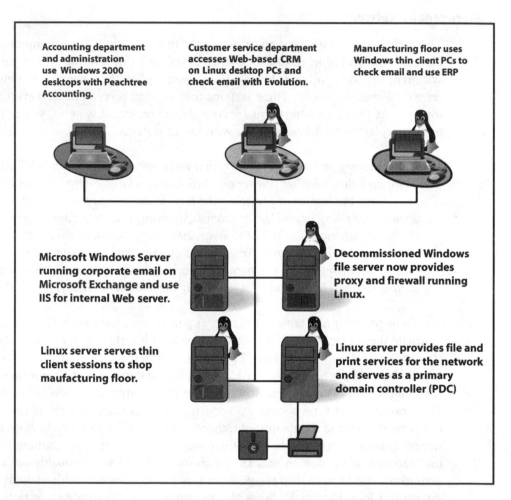

Accounting department and administration use Windows 2000 desktops with Peachtree Accounting.

Customer service department accesses Web-based CRM on Linux desktop PCs and check email with Evolution.

Manufacturing floor uses Windows thin client PCs to check email and use ERP

Microsoft Windows Server running corporate email on Microsoft Exchange and use IIS for internal Web server.

Decommissioned Windows file server now provides proxy and firewall running Linux.

Linux server serves thin client sessions to shop maufacturing floor.

Linux server provides file and print services for the network and serves as a primary domain controller (PDC)

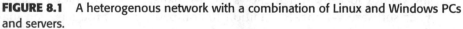

FIGURE 8.1 A heterogenous network with a combination of Linux and Windows PCs and servers.

The point of this hypothetical LAN is to demonstrate that a move to Linux doesn't have to be instantaneous. It can happen as it coincides with business needs and regular events in IT product lifecycles. Decommissioned servers might actually gain a longer useful life when repurposed and used in place of a commercial solution.

LINUX REPLACEMENT OF WINDOWS SERVERS

Replacing a Microsoft Windows Server with a server hosting Linux and open source solutions is a reasonable substitute that can provide similar functionality with very little trouble and potentially less cost. The biggest consideration is the education of the technical personnel that support that server. You can follow two paths: one is to acquire the knowledge internally, the other is to look outside your own IT department for varying degrees of help. You may, in the early stages, choose to hire a system integrator to replace legacy systems with Linux and open source software or acquire a commercially supported Linux package with vendor support.

Linux Server Distributions

Many of the distributors that provide desktop Linux distributions also provide server distributions. You may want to consider using the same vendor for both server and desktop to provide a single point of contact, though it is not necessary. Because Linux servers and desktops use open standards for communication, one company's desktop will be compatible with another company's server products. This is a huge advantage over a Microsoft back office, because if you become disillusioned with one vendor's product you can go to another vendor who still has the same core product but with slightly different presentations and support mechanisms.

General Server Distributions

Linux server and services, regardless of vendor, are likely going to utilize the same core technologies from the operating system kernel to the file and print services. The difference is going to be in the vendor or project that stands behind your choice in distribution, as well as the administrative tools and other value-added features. As with your choice in desktop distribution, your choices will vary and you should shop around as you would with any IT solution. The following distributions all have been successfully used to provide server operating systems.

Novell

Novell offers two distributions for server operating systems. Novell Open Enterprise Server combines NetWare and SUSE Linux Enterprise Server for supporting both NetWare and Linux networks. SUSE LINUX Enterprise Server is a pure Linux solution that can provide enterprise infrastructure for most any enterprise based on open standards. Novell also offers professional support packages for its products.

Red Hat

Red Hat has two server solutions: Red Hat Enterprise Linux AS and Red Hat Enterprise ES. The ES server product is the entry-level product that is limited for use to a certain number of CPUs and total RAM, but it is very suitable for the small enterprise. The AS server product is designed for the larger SMP servers and non-Intel platforms like PowerPC and IBM zSeries. The AS server also differs by offering premium support options for enterprise support contracts. Both server operating systems can take advantage of updates through the Red Hat Network by paid subscription.

Mandriva

Mandriva Corporate Server is a scalable server that, like all the other server offerings, has the same set of services, such as file and print services, but also includes their distribution-specific Security System Management and DrakPark, a Mandriva Linux tool to handle server updates. They plan to keep a twelve to eighteen month upgrade cycle and a five-year product maintenance commitment. Mandriva is a stable and reliable choice for the SMB.

Debian

Debian is one of the most established Linux distributions and, in contrast to the aforementioned Linux distributions, is totally free and backed by an extremely active developer and user community. Its popularity is often credited to its apt package installation system tools that make updating and installing software very easy. The founder of the Debian project, Ian Murdock, is the CTO for Progeny, a Linux consulting company that builds custom versions of Linux based on Debian. They also provide customization and support for other distributions. In a large enterprise, companies like Progeny can help build and provide updates tailored to special software needs. In August 2005, a number of companies announced the Debian Core Consortium Alliance, backed by Linspire, Xandros, MEPIS and others, which are collaborating to develop the commercial Debian-based distribution. Either way you could choose the do-it-yourself approach or be assured that you have support through a company.

These are but a few of many distributions available to replace Microsoft Windows Servers. There are other options but they are usually more task-based, like providing a firewall through the commercially available Astaro Linux.

Specialty Server Distributions

There are hundreds of specialty Linux distributions that might be used for providing forensic data or security services. Depending on your specific need you may be able to find someone who has already solved a problem for you. Many of these distributions are designed with a particular emphasis, such as security, or a single task in mind such as a firewall.

Security-Enhanced Linux (SELinux)   The United States National Security Agency (NSA) sponsors security-enhanced Linux (SELinux) in effort to provide enhanced security features under Linux that mandate access controls and how those controls should be added to Linux. In a nutshell, SELinux is an enhanced Linux kernel that minimizes the amount of privilege programs users need to do their jobs. Confining users to the smallest space needed helps reduce the risk of security exploits. SELinux can be installed into a Linux distribution like Red Hat to enhance the security features that are already present there.

Scyld Beowulf Platform   Scyld is an example of a distribution aimed at providing a standards-based Linux distribution with all the tools to deploy and manage a high-performance Linux cluster that executes large, complex calculations. In research and development facilities, clusters can be cost effective, utilizing commodity x86 servers and Linux with the Scyld tools as a value add.

BlueCat Linux BlueCat Linux   is an embedded Linux from Lynuxworks that can be used in a variety of ways, but in contrast to Scyld, it can also run on small consumer devices. BlueCat provides development and debugging tools as a value-added service.

The purpose of mentioning these specialized Linux distributions is to make you aware that there are many, many options available to you and that if you have a special need that isn't met by one of the mainstream Linux vendors, it may be worth your time to investigate others.

OPEN SOURCE SERVICES FOR BACK-OFFICE INFRASTRUCTURE

Most all of the services supplied by Microsoft Windows server products have a functional equivalent in the infrastructure services provided on Linux. In the history of things, though, Microsoft hasn't always ruled the roost, In fact, for the last 30 years or more, variants of the Unix operating system have played a role in networked computing services. Many of the features originally incorporated into Linux by Linus Torvalds where inspired by the free Unix clone, MINIX, developed by Andrew S. Tanenbaum. The TCP/IP suite of protocols that lets you traverse the Internet was originally developed on Unix. For file and print sharing, Microsoft servers and clients communicate through TCP/IP using the CIFS-SMB (Common Internet File System-Small Message Block) protocol, while Unix servers used a protocol developed by Sun Microsystems called NFS (Network File System). NetBIOS (Network Basic Input Output System) is based on the SMB format that was codeveloped by IBM and Sytec. It soon became a standard and is now referred to as NetBIOS over TCP/IP (NBT). NetBIOS is what provides the ability to browse Windows networks for the names of Microsoft Windows servers. For Linux desktop users to interact with those Microsoft Windows machines they need to use networking software that enables them to communicate using the SMB protocol. The software that is the de facto standard for Unix/Linux users to communicate with Microsoft Windows clients or servers is part of the Samba project. In 1992, Andrew "Tridge" Tridgell, an Australian programmer, was struggling with the problem of making Unix servers look like PC file servers to Windows machines. To accomplish this, Andrew reverse-engineered the SMB protocol and implemented it on Unix. Soon afterwards it was ported to Linux and since then it has become one of the most important pieces of technology for Windows and Unix/Linux interoperability.

Samba File and Print Services

Samba is collectively a set of tools that are useful in file and print sharing and networking using the SMB protocol. The two primary programs that make up Samba are *smbd* and *nmbd*. Together they provide four CIFS services:

File and Print Services: These services are provided by smbd, also called the SMB daemon.

Authentication and Authorization: These services are provided by the SMB daemon that allows users to share printers and file space. Access to file space and printing is controlled by passwords. These shared resources are called *shares*. This is one of the primary functions of Microsoft's Active Directory Server.

Name Resolution: The ability to resolve computer names when connected to a LAN.

Service Announcement: Browsing is also handled by *nmbd,* which works by broadcasting an announcement and then receiving a response from other PCs on the network

These same services are provided by Microsoft Server products but, as discussed earlier, they come with the baggage of client access licensing. The use of Samba as a multiplatform file and print server is without question one of the most widely used and successful open source uses in the enterprise. Because of its popularity it is also one of the best documented. Visiting the Samba Web site will give you links to not only technical documentation but detailed examples of how to set up and configure Samba on your network.

Linux Alternatives to Microsoft Active Directory

It would be inaccurate to say that there is a complete replacement for Microsoft Active Directory; there just isn't and there may never be. The problem is that Microsoft controls both the Windows desktop and the server. Since Samba has to react to changes in these commercial products there is usually a disconnect between the release of a Microsoft server and the ability for the Samba team to match functionality. Samba has yet to be able to control multiple domains from one directory server with the same overall integration as Active Directory.

Directory Services and OpenLDAP

OpenLDAP is an open source Lightweight Directory Access Protocol implementation. LDAP is a universal term for directories that hold information about objects in the database. OpenLDAP can be used as a directory-based authentication system but may not offer as intuitive or polished an interface as Microsoft Active Directory. Samba can be used to join an active directory domain but doesn't offer the single point of administration that system administrators would prefer. Information is organized in an LDAP directory server in a structure that can be accessed quickly, in contrast to databases that might have complex data structure functionality. OpenLDAP can be used as a central authority for network authentication to various resources including users, printing, and file sharing. The reason LDAP is used in lieu of a database is that, as the name implies, it is a lightweight and faster way to access data. OpenLDAP may be important to users who are familiar with Microsoft Active Directory, which can store data in LDAP but does so in conjunction with the powerful Active Directory Server. There is no open source solution with the breadth of features that Active Directory Server offers, but among the commercial offerings Novell's eDirectory comes close. Samba is the closest alternative that can act as a Primary Domain Controller with an LDAP backend.

The desire for a Linux complement or replacement to Active Directory is the remaining requirement that is preventing many organizations from moving to Linux on the desktop. The ideal situation would be for there to be a wholesale replacement complete with migration tools. There is also an alternative to this by expanding the capabilities of Active Directory. One such solution is DirectControl Suite by Centrify, which extends the Microsoft AD identity, access, and policy management to other platforms including Unix and Linux. This feature prevents the current solution of maintaining multiple identity stores Microsoft AD for Windows and OpenLDAP for Linux with Samba to join Linux to the Windows domain. Another promising development is the Red Hat Directory Server, which was also released by Red Hat as the Fedora Directory Server. The need for a Linux alternative to Active Directory may eventually be solved with newer versions of Samba, but it is noteworthy when you look at an open source replacement of your Microsoft server infrastructure that there might not be a complete alternative to your existing back-office servers.

Email and Groupware

Email in business today is critical. The key feature is reliability. Nothing is more frustrating than not being able to receive an important email from a colleague, especially one that affects a deadline. Linux's reputation for uptime and stability are well deserved, which makes it a great choice for redundant mission-critical systems like email servers. The Microsoft messaging solutions are very popular and offer many good features, but have baggage in the form of licensing fees and dependence on Microsoft to anticipate your collaborative needs. Microsoft Exchange does integrate with many Microsoft services including Active Directory. However, this solution requires Microsoft's server platforms (Windows 2003 Server launched in 2003 with full support for Exchange) and the merits of Exchange are also contradicted by the administration headaches and proprietary formats included in mail storage. The consideration that many users have with Exchange is that to take advantage of all the features you must have a client like Microsoft Outlook, which is not available for Linux. The standard answer to a native email client for exchange is Novell's Evolution with connector software to access collaborative features. However, you can get much of the same functionality at a fraction of the cost and without the need for seat licensing using only free software. You may not benefit from some features you enjoy in Outlook, though, such as dragging and dropping email to your calendar or tasks. Users who feel they need to run Outlook might be best served by running that program in a virtual machine environment like Win4Lin or VMware.

There are many open source Linux email solutions including Sendmail, qmail, and postfix. Most of these are adequate email solutions in the SMB if you have the expertise. If you lack the knowledge to set up your mail server unaided or want an enhanced feature set, there are quality messaging solutions like Lotus Mail which you may be familiar with already running on Windows 2003 Server, or there is an emerging crop of commercially supported Linux mail servers and even embedded Linux email appliances.

Free and Open Source Software for Email Servers

Some features that may be advantageous are the collaborative calendaring and newly added chat clients available with Exchange. There are a number of alternative options to choose for Internet email on Linux. They all conform to Internet email standards and protocols, including IMAP, POP3, and SMTP. These solutions are all acceptable for the enterprise because they can handle a large number of email users with minimal resources. Additionally they may support plug-ins for control of SPAM and virus scanning.

You can provide a very robust and highly available mail system by completely using FOSS software. There are tools that include the agents to send and receive mail and packages that support all the common mail protocols like Post Office Protocol (POP), Internet Message Access Protocol (IMAP), and Simple Mail Transfer Protocol (SMTP). There are even free packages to add a Web interface to your mail infrastructure like the popular SquirrelMail Web interface shown in Figure 8.2.

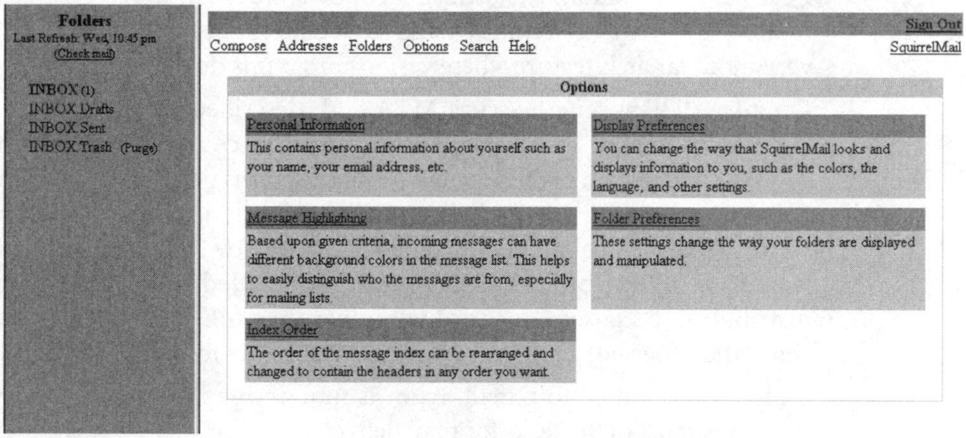

FIGURE 8.2   SquirrelMail is an open source Web-based email client.

SMTP Servers

SMTP is a push type of mail server where users initiate the transfer by contacting the mail server. In the early days of email transfer, Unix-to-Unix Copy Protocol (UUCP) was commonly used to transfer email from machine to machine. As time progressed and email servers where able to have an "always on" network connection, SMTP evolved. SMTP traffic happens over port 25 which will be a consideration for allowing traffic to pass when you set up your open source firewall solution. You can also choose to securely connect over SMTP and require a password to send email. This is a good practice as it helps reduce the chance of your mail server being compromised by unauthorized users. The following mail packages are commonly used as Linux email solutions:

Sendmail: An open source mail transfer agent (MTA) or mail server that routes and delivers email. It is one of the oldest and most widely used email programs and came out of University of California, Berkley, in 1980. Sendmail also has the reputation as being complicated and hard to configure. In the 1990s it suffered from some security problems but has since proven to be more secure. That's one reason why the original author of Sendmail started a company, Sendmail, Inc., that offers a full set of products and services that helped the free software evolve into a secure and professionally supported product. It may not be advisable for new users of Linux to try to tackle the challenges of installing and configuring Sendmail, but if you do, it does have the ability to handle extremely high volumes of email efficiently.

Postfix: Like Sendmail, Postfix is an open source mail server. Postfix has a reputation as an easy-to-administer and secure alternative to Sendmail. It also has a very modular architecture where various programs do different types of work.

Qmail: A lightweight, secure MTA and, described by the qmail project as "not designed to be easy to use, it's designed to be comprehensive." It has a very modular architecture where a number of programs perform the variety of tasks needed to effectively route email. Qmail was also designed specifically as a high-security replacement for Sendmail. It was written by Dan Bernstein and first released in 1996. However, it may not be included in your standard Linux distribution because it does not fall under the GPL; it falls under another license that does not implicitly give the users rights to redistribute and modify.

Exim: In contrast to Qmail, Exim is monolithic in design as one program performs most of the tasks for mail delivery. It's also very popular, included on the Debian Linux distribution, and completely free.

All the listed SMTP options are perfectly decent and scalable ways to handle email. That's only one side of the equation though. In addition to the routing of email, users need a service to retrieve their email; that's where POP and IMAP come in.

POP and IMAP Servers

The factors you may need to consider when looking at the ability for users to retrieve their email as they traditionally have with a Windows mail client like Microsoft Outlook or Eudora is the use of a POP3 or IMAP server, or both. A POP3 (*Post Office Protocol version three*) server allows you to download email from the server to a client over port 110. You can choose to periodically download the email and then delete mail off the server or leave it there. POP email only gives you the ability to have one large mail store.

The other popular option is *Internet Message Access Protocol*, or IMAP, which allows clients to access a remote server and manage mail on the server from their network connections; messages may be cached locally but will still be left on the server until purged. The advantage of this type of protocol over POP for users migrating from a Windows desktop to a Linux desktop is that the mail in an IMAP installation can be left on the server and filed into different directories. Changes made at one PC will be reflected when that user accesses his mail stores from another. If you are migrating a desktop from Windows to Linux you could use an IMAP mail server so that mail is stored remotely, then users can connect once migrated to Linux and still have access to all their mail. IMAP does have one drawback and that is users must be able to access their mail server over a network connection. When setting up your firewall for IMAP you can connect over a secure SSL connection to avoid sniffing of sensitive communications, which happens on port 993, or by default, port 143. There are a number of good open source email servers.

Cyrus IMAP: A result of efforts from Carnegie Mellon starting in the early 1990s, designed to be highly scalable for large enterprise mail systems. Cyrus uses IMAP4 as its core technology but can be accessed as a POP3 server.

QPopper: A widely used POP3 mail server and complementary technology to Sendmail. QPopper has five goals: to provide security, stability, safety, features, and performance. Before installing QPopper on Linux it is advisable to check the QPopper Web site to determine what versions of QPopper are well supported under Linux.

Dovecot: An open source IMAP and POP3 server for Linux and Unix systems with an emphasis on security. Dovecot is also fairly easy to set up and provides good overall performance when compared to other systems.

There is no de facto email server; in many cases, it's a matter of preferences. You can choose to use a completely free solution or rely on commercial vendors who might offer an easy-to-configure and supported mail server that can still benefit from residing on a high-availability Linux server.

Open Source Groupware

Groupware that offers collaborative scheduling and messaging is available for a free download from a number of open source projects. The large enterprise may opt for a commercial package or, depending on its needs, be able to adopt an open source solution. The small enterprise that may not be able to afford a commercial package can easily provide the same tools to their businesses using the packages discussed in this section. The ability to build an infrastructure comparable to large enterprises without investing in expensive commercial systems is one reason why open source is an equalizer for organizations of all sizes who can have competitive tools without a large capital investment.

eGroupWare: A popular Web-based collaboration server that can run on a number of platforms including Linux. The advantage of eGroupWare is that it offers a number of modules that all share a common Access Control List (ACL). eGroupWare can supply calendars (including personal and group scheduling), mail, tasks, notes, and even basic CRM functions. Contacts can be stored on the server. eGroupWare also can be served from a Windows or Linux server, so if you are using a Microsoft Server but don't want to use Exchange, or want to move to a Web-based email interface, eGroupWare is an option.

Hula: A calendar and mail server licensed under the LGPL and MPL public licenses. Hula is sponsored by Novell and was given its start by the donation to the project from Novell of its NetMail source code. The ambition for Hula is to provide a fully functional Web-based server with group calendaring and a rich Web mail client. It also has a built in antivirus scanning for mail and supports SMTP, IMAP, and POP mail servers. The advantage of a solution like Hula is its strict adherence to open standards so that you can avoid being locked into a solution that has proprietary dependencies such as Microsoft Exchange and Outlook or Lotus Notes.

Scalix Community Edition: A calendaring and messaging server that can be downloaded and used for free. It also can be upgraded to a supported enterprise edition that can be covered by a support contract from Scalix or one of its partners.

There is no reason that you can't configure and run and one of the open source mail packages above. Some have companies that support them and provide support as Sendmail Inc. does for Sendmail products. The problem is that they all require a considerable learning curve and you may not want to put such an important service at risk. An incorrectly configured or inadequately secured SMTP server can be used by spammers to send bulk email through your domain. Understanding how to configure the server properly is important. All of the listed solutions are dependent on developer and user communities that provide support via user forums and email lists and documentation published to the Web.

Commercial Email and Groupware Solutions

As is the case with many of the open source applications mentioned in these discussions, where a common need appears among a great number of users, businesses develop support models for those needs. In the case of mail servers, one of the most critical and widespread forms of communication, there are a number of companies that can host their software on Linux, some open source and other proprietary. There is no shame in choosing one over the other, and each one comes with its own set of benefits. The following servers are popular mail packages that can be hosted on Linux.

OPEN-XCHANGE™ Collaboration and Integration Server

OPEN-XCHANGE Collaboration and Integration Server is a groupware solution that lets you store appointments, contacts, tasks, mail, books, documents, and other data and share them among other servers. The OPEN-XCHANGE server can be accessed via a Web browser or KDE Kontact, Apples iCal, and Mozilla Calendar, as shown in Figure 8.3. You can also use it with Microsoft Outlook on Windows by downloading the OXlook plug-in. Open Exchange is supported by Open-Xchange Inc., who previously licensed the software to SUSE Linux AG. Novell now sells OPEN-XCHANGE under the SUSE LINUX OPEN-XCHANGE Server (SLOX) brand.

Bynari Insight Server

Bynari is another solution that allows for collaboration and scalability similar to Microsoft Exchange. The thing that makes Bynari Insight Server notable is that it can be used with Microsoft Outlook to provide many of the calendaring and scheduling features. Insight Server also includes migration tools for Microsoft Exchange so data can be easily moved from legacy Windows servers to Linux.

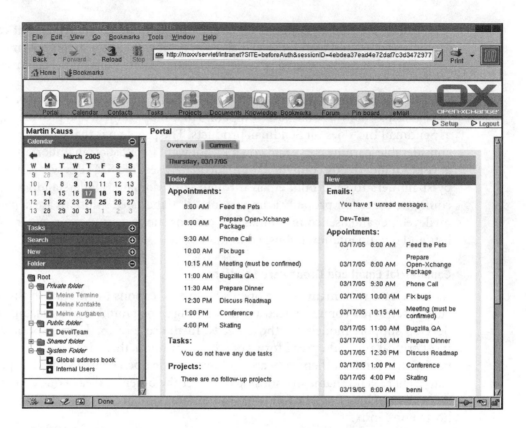

FIGURE 8.3 The Web interface to Open-Xchange Collaborative Server.

Stalker CommunigatePro

Stalker Software is the maker of CommunigatePro, which comes with an enhanced feature set that would require a number of separate open source packages to duplicate, such as secure access, Web-based email, mailing lists, and an easy-to-use administrative interface. You can make changes to your company mail server through a Web browser for remote administration. It's a very affordable solution that requires little expertise and little administrative overhead. CommunigatePro also can run on a number of other platforms besides Linux including Windows.

Many of the mail packages above include plug-ins for mail and viruses but there are also open source alternatives such as ClamAV and SpamAssassin.

Spam Prevention Strategies–SpamAssassin

Email on its own is a great boon for communication; it provides a cost-effective and almost instant medium for exchanging information. It also can be a great productivity-sapping device because it's also a very effective way for advertisers to clog your communication channels. The most popular open source application for server-side spam filtering is SpamAssassin, which allows you to filter email and make decisions on the server, or as a mail agent running locally to qualify email before it reaches your inbox. SpamAssassin has a number of tactics for deciding what is and isn't spam.

Header Analysis: Trying to identify the mail headers of a message for information that might indicate the email message as suspect.

Text Analysis: Text Analysis works much the same way as header analysis, where SpamAssassin identifies patterns that may indicate a message is spam.

Blacklists: Many community organizations provide lists of known spammers and email domains that have been known to send spam. These blacklists can be used by SpamAssassin to filter UCE offenders qualified by a volunteer network.

"Learning" Rules: SpamAssassin also has the ability to "learn" what might be spam and use probability to classify messages as such.

SpamAssassin on a corporate email server can be an effective frontline defense for spam. Based on some training it appends the designation [SPAM] to the subject line preceding the original subject so you can filter those messages to a local folder and check to make sure they are all junk mail and not important. The reason to do this rather than just deleting [SPAM] labeled subjects is to avoid what is known as a "false positive," which means that based on certain criteria the program thinks that the email is spam, when in fact it is a legitimate email, sometimes called *ham*.

Apache–An Alternative to Microsoft Internet Information Server (IIS)

In an April 2005 Netcraft survey of over 62 million Web sites, Apache was far and away the market leader for Web server software with 69.19% of the total market share, followed by Microsoft with 20.55%, and Sun a distant third with 3.04 % [Netcraft, 2005]. Looking back to September 2001, Netcraft also reported that Linux owned 29.6% of the market for Web server operating systems, second behind Windows with 49.6%. As a measure of progress, the Apache project was started 10 years ago and is the pinnacle of open source success. In fact, in August of 1995 the initial Netcraft survey indicated a mere 658 Web sites running Apache. Another interesting statistic comes from the Fortune 100 where a September 2004 survey of Web server operating systems by Netcraft showed 32 of these companies using Solaris, followed by 26 running Windows 200, and 12 running Linux [Netcraft, 2004]. Why the disparity? Maybe the reality is that Apache running alongside Linux, MySQL, and PHP provides the tools that small businesses need to be competitive with companies many times their size. Many of the CIOs of the Fortune 100 might feel more comfortable using something coming from a company with a long track record like Sun or IBM. Though you might consider that IBM supports their popular J2EE application server Websphere as an add-on to Apache.

Mono—An Alternative to Microsoft .NET

Mono is a standards-based open source platform that is focused on running existing .NET or Java frameworks. Novell sponsors the Mono initiative with the objective of enabling Unix developers to build cross-platform .NET applications. In looking at dependencies on Microsoft Internet Information Server, Mono running on Linux servers with Apache may provide an alternative to an IIS and .NET structure.

MySQL—An Alternative to Proprietary Databases

MySQL is billed as the world's most popular open source database and in many circumstances it can easily compete with the likes of Microsoft Access and Microsoft SQL Server. For databases that do nothing but store a large number of records and aren't considered to be high performance, MySQL can and does routinely get the nod over commercial databases like Oracle and DB2. MySQL unseated DB2 as the database of choice for the Associated Press, which was hosting over 600 Web sites for affiliated users across the U.S. [Hall, 2003]. Cost estimates for an alternative Oracle database license by itself was estimated at $300,000, while the whole MySQL solution with servers, programming time, and an annual support license to MySQL AB was only $90,000. MySQL is a freely available database that is backed by a for-profit company, MySQL AB. MySQL is also distributed under a dual licensing model. Users can download the code under the GPL and are then held to those terms, or companies that want to make products that incorporate MySQL into their products can buy a commercial license where change and modifications don't have to be shared.

myPHPadmin

Learning how to manipulate databases through MySQL's command line interface can be daunting and require a steeper learning curve than many new open source users are willing to tackle. That's where tools like myPHPadmin come in. The myPHPadmin Web package requires both a Web server and a PHP to be installed on the server. myPHPadmin, as shown in Figure 8.4, can be used to accomplish most common tasks that a user of a MySQL database would normally accomplish on the Linux command line interface, but from a forms-based interface that helps users overcome the learning curve associated with understanding the syntax for database administration.

FIGURE 8.4   myPHPadmin is an open source, Web-based administration tool for MySQL database.

OTHER NOTABLE OPEN SOURCE SOLUTIONS

No matter what service or solution you want to institute in the enterprise, you will likely find an open source solution to meet the need. Some areas may make sense for you to investigate proprietary offerings. In some cases, such as firewalls, there may be a company that provides an embedded Linux product with easily configurable interfaces. Other times there might be an appliance that has Linux preconfigured and hardened for specific tasks. The following examples are meant to illustrate other places throughout the enterprise where Linux and open source software can solve user problems.

Browser-Based Server Administration with Webmin

Webmin is a browser-based interface to administer Unix and Linux systems. Using any browser, you can manage users, groups, and services on the server. Webmin is a simple Web server that can use forms to submit changes to a Linux server. Webmin's interface has links for configuring Apache Web server, Postfix mail server, and the free PostgresSQL Database server. There are a wide variety of systems settings and services that can be administered through the simple Webmin interface pictured in Figure 8.5.

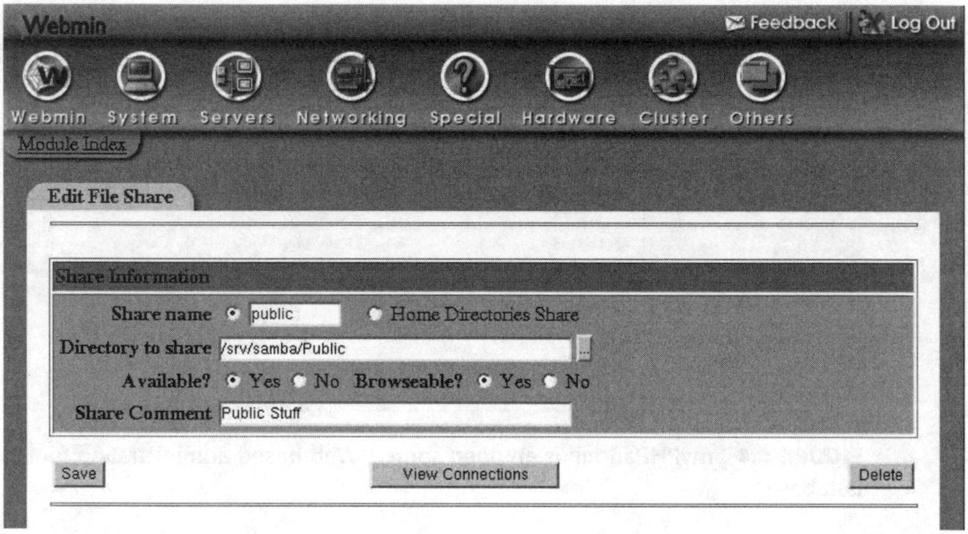

FIGURE 8.5 Webmin provides an easy-to-use interface that doesn't require local access to a server.

YaST–Yet another System Tool

YaST is an open source component of SUSE Linux and the Novell Linux desktop that is very similar to the Control Panel folder in the Windows operating system. The configurations for most every aspect of a SUSE Linux server can be configured from one central point. The YaST tool also can be used to install software and identify and configure hardware. As a desktop configuration tool it shines as well. Figure 8.6 shows YaST with the options to configure network services.

Firewalls

Built into the Linux kernel is the ability to filter network traffic. There are a number of basic open source solutions that utilize IP chains and tables and provide Network Address Translation (NAT), which offers the basic necessities for an office firewall. Additionally, there are many solution providers who offer enterprise class solutions

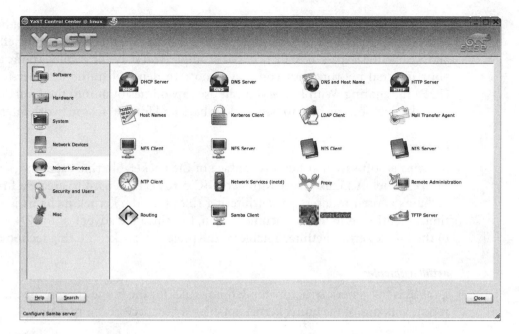

FIGURE 8.6 YaST is a graphical tool that can be used to configure all of the Linux services on a server.

on Linux. It is advisable to look among these providers for solutions. Because of the ever-changing security environment, expertise on security issues seldom adequately exists internal to an IT organization. And despite the use of commercially supported solutions you still may be able to use open source software packages where vendors may be providing services in the form of expertise and support rather than charging software royalties.

Basic Open Source Firewalls

A simple firewall is the first line of defense against unwanted intrusion into your network. In the most basic implementations you could divide the types of networks into two zones: a red zone for danger, and a green zone for a safe zone. The computers behind the firewall are safe in the green zone, and the Internet on the other side of the firewall is the danger or red zone. All traffic over the network is sent in packages, or packets, that are pieces of data. At the beginning of each packet is a header that details what kind of packet it is; the rest of the packet is called the body of the packet and holds the data that is being transmitted. A file, for example, is broken up into packets that are reassembled when they reach their destination.

The practice of *packet filtering* takes the packets and makes decisions about how to route them over the network by looking at the header and deciding on whether to allow each one to pass or to deny it. For example, you may allow email traffic across your internal network, but you may choose to deny all traffic for peer-to-peer (P2P) file sharing. With Linux you can use capabilities built into the Linux kernel to make decisions on how to pass packets back and forth across network interfaces.

ipchains

ipchains is software that takes advantage of the packet-filtering capabilities of the Linux kernel. A Linux server with two NIC cards can be used to create a firewall. ipchains is used to insert packet-filtering rules into the kernel. ipchains is sometimes mentioned in Linux documentation, but since the advent of the 2.4 version of the Linux kernel, netfilter/iptables is the preferred packet filtering technology.

netfilter/iptables

iptables is the generic structure for defining rules for the framework inside the more recent versions of the Linux kernel. iptables is the successor to ipchains.

netfilter

netfilter is the code inside of the Linux kernel that is made up of a list of rules that either accept or drop the packets; accepted packets are allowed to pass through a network interface and dropped packets are rejected.

Open source solutions might be adequate for your needs, but most organizations that don't have security expertise could benefit from commercial support.

Commercially Supported Firewall Products

Security is a sensitive and important subject, especially considering what you might have at risk: financial data, customer records, and other sensitive information. As a do-it-yourselfer, you may not have the expertise to set up your own firewall and security for your network. In these cases you may want to rely on someone with security expertise. You can still take advantage of all the open source programs running on Linux, but decide to obtain versions distributed by companies that can supplement the technology with support and experience.

SmoothWall

SmoothWall Express is an open source firewall distribution based on Linux. It was started in the summer of 2000 with the intention of creating a Linux-based firewall that could be inexpensively implemented on modest hardware. Over time the developers of SmoothWall formed a company to produce commercially supported products that leveraged the open source software. Smoothwall is one of many solutions that are accompanied by an easy-to-use Web interface, shown in Figure 8.7.

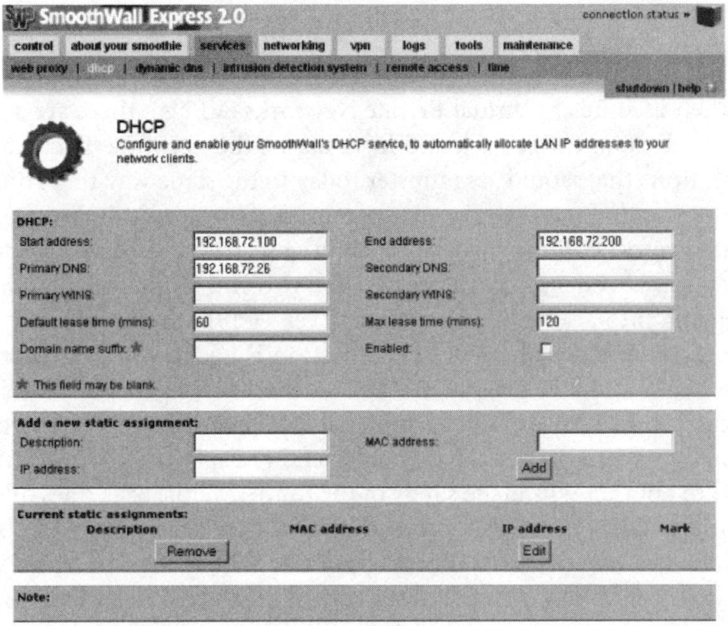

FIGURE 8.7 Smoothwall's Web interface.

Astaro Security Linux

Astaro is a company that makes a commercial version of Linux that provides a number of security features, including firewall, spam blocking and, most recently, spyware protection. It provides intrusion protection by blocking scanning and application-based attacks. Astaro also provides its software preinstalled on security devices that give you a plug-and-play solution.

There are many options for providing Linux firewalls for your private networks, in fact many more than could be discussed here. Some solutions are to write a small footprint image to a floppy disk and then lock the diskette so it can't be written, as is the case with Coyote Linux. In this way the configured firewall cannot be altered once it is configured unless someone can physically access the firewall hardware. The point is that there is a cornucopia of options for firewalls, hosted on Linux and other open source or free operating systems. You need not choose Linux as there are plenty of well-proven solutions available for businesses from SOHOs to large enterprises. Though there is one interesting point to make about Linux and firewalls. Linksys, which was acquired by Cisco, a leading network company, built many of its products using embedded Linux as the operating system and it distributes the firmware for these networking devices directly from its Web site.

Virtual Private Networks

When it comes to Virtual Private Networks (VPNs), there are a number of ways to securely send traffic back and forth across the network. There are not many Linux solutions that would pass muster today in the same way that commercial Windows solutions do for connecting desktop users securely to Windows servers. The solution that is most commonly used for remote secure access is Secure Shell (SSH), which provides an encrypted tunnel between two end points. SSH is a means for remotely logging into a server. SSH operates over TCP/IP and is normally considered to the unsecured telnet protocol. A connection is negotiated by a shared secret key, and then an encrypted session starts. A username and password can be used to authenticate or an RSA or DSA asymmetric key pair. You can *tunnel* traffic using secure shell; so if you needed to you could send redisplay data from X Windows from one PC to another within the safety of the tunnel. While SSH does offer a measure of security, many experts will recommend the IPsec protocol for VPNs. You can compile Linux kernels to include IPSec support, and there is even a free IPsec client for Linux called FreeS/Wan. As legislative issues like HIPAA and Sarbanes-Oxley drive regulations regarding the security of data, Linux users will need to make sure they have taken the precautions needed to provide best efforts to secure their systems. Using these technologies will help provide security even if not required by law.

Squid Proxy Server

A proxy server is a network service that acts as an intermediary between servers on a network. The client connects to the proxy server then requests a network resource, a Web page for example. The proxy then may either process the request or take other action. It may, based on a set of rules, not redisplay the page because of criteria placed on what Web requests are allowed. Proxy servers can also cache content; when various clients on a network request the same page, once it's in cache the server may not need to go download the Web page again, speeding up performance for the end user. Squid is free software that runs on Linux systems. Squid can be used as a gatekeeper to keep bad or inappropriate content from entering the user network.

SquidGuard

Just as SpamAssassin is a set of filters to help block spam, SquidGuard is a plug-in for the Squid proxy server that can be used to provide filtering rules for Squid. If you are providing IT services to a school, you may be mandated by the Children's Internet Protection Act to have a safety policy that includes a technology protection measure on all computers connected to the Internet to protect children from inappropriate content. In an office setting you may need to filter adult content to prevent its spread throughout the office. The advantage to SquidGuard is that you do not need to write all the rules yourself. There are blacklists collected by the Squid-Guard project that can be downloaded and installed into your proxy server. These lists are collected by robots (automated programs) and then collated; you can choose to use all the rules or just some of the rules. You can use them on their own or as a complement to your organizations authorized use policy.

Alternatives to Microsoft Terminal Services

Microsoft Windows Terminal Services can allow multiple users to access sessions on a Microsoft Server that can host individual applications or a complete desktop environment. Most commonly the use of Microsoft Terminal Services is paired with Citrix, a redisplay and management framework that complements the Terminal Services offering from Microsoft. Another way to connect to Microsoft Terminal Services is by using the Remote Display Protocol (RDP). Linux, in conjunction with redisplay technologies, can provide equivalent functions; using Windows on Linux solutions you can even replace the functions that these Windows solutions supply. Chapter 10 and Chapter 11 cover these topics in depth.

Asterisk Server an Open Source PBX

When you consider your IT infrastructure, you may not include your telecom needs in the same group. However, with the growing adoption of Voice Over IP (VOIP), voice traffic is traveling side by side with data traffic. This convergence between voice and data also gives you many freedoms that were in the past confined to analog telephone systems. Asterisk is an open source package that provides a central switching core, with four APIs for modular loading of telephony systems into a single switching network.

ON THE CI

Just because the Asterisk server is an open source project that doesn't mean that a user of the software has no place to turn for support. The Asterisk Project receives a large amount of its support from a company, Digium, that has developed its business around the services and hardware sales related to Asterisk. They are also the primary developer of the software and release their work back into the project. The Digium model then allows other developers to contribute to the code base. Digium makes a good case for a business leveraging open source software on commodity x86 servers. This reduces the cost to the end user who might alternatively be using single-source software and support from the likes of Nortel, Seimens, or Lucent. The soft PBX also has the portability of voice data that can be set to interact with PCs by archiving voicemail or using software-based phone. This opens the door for more services like voicemail storage and backup or value-added software packages that integrate with Personal Information Managers.

SUMMARY

Windows and other operating systems can and do provide adequate back-office services that support today's popular desktop configurations, but they don't just stop there. They may have rapid development tools or administrative interfaces you have become familiar with. Logically you should weigh the costs of retraining and deploying a new system, but you may find in the long run that they are minimal. You also need to think about the seat licensing and the costs you pay for Windows Server and other services and tools. There isn't a best answer for everyone, which is really the point of open source—choice driven by weighing the advantages and disadvantages of each option.

Software licensing and low cost of acquisition are two of the most highly touted advantages of Linux. The operating system is free so that the initial cost of ownership from a software-licensing standpoint is quite a bit less than commercial solutions. Also, the open source model allows organizations to evaluate and change the underlying code should they have that need. Another advantage over commercial operating systems is that open source solutions can be put together from pieces that serve specific needs rather than requiring the user to take the shrink-wrapped solution available to solve a variety of problems. Conversely, if users feel they get value from the commercial vendor, they can take advantage of prepackaged solutions and support contracts provided by companies like MySQL AB, Red Hat, Novell, or others.

Open architecture and true adherence to standards-based computing makes a lot of sense because it offers companies the ability to select competitive solutions from a number of vendors. As noted, the Samba server interacts with Windows servers using SMB-CIFS, but at the end of the day, if all transactions were based on a standard, it wouldn't be necessary for Samba to reverse engineer the protocol and changes made by Microsoft. The litigation between Sun and Microsoft in the mid-1990s over Java is one example. Microsoft embraced Java by breaking the standard and including their changes in their browsers which effectively caused a rift in the ability for users to use what was supposed to be a standards-based technology.

Broad vendor support for Windows has held open source solutions at a disadvantage. The number of vendors supporting open source solutions has been growing rapidly over the years but is still lagging behind Microsoft. The tables are turning as open source makes inroads into the enterprise, taking leadership roles in areas like Web infrastructure. Migrations costs, the cost of removing and redeploying a new operating system, may in the short term overshadow the ongoing maintenance costs of legacy systems. Making the move at a time when you are making changes anyhow can diminish the costs associated with instituting a new solution.

Interoperability with proprietary systems is another problem for open source solutions. Vendors that own both the server and the client technology, as does Microsoft, can add features to their products that make it difficult for other operating systems to interact with them. If you are happy with the performance and cost that your current solutions provide then continue to use them. However, if you are looking to get better value out of your IT budget, then a Linux back-office infrastructure might be the answer.

OTHER RESOURCES

- Red Hat Servers—*www.redhat.com/software/rhel/server/*
- Novell Open Enterprise Server —*www.redhat.com/software/rhel/server/*
- SUSE LINUX Enterprise Server—*www.novell.com/products/linuxenterpriseserver*
- Debian—*www.debian.org*
- Debian Core Consortium Alliance—*www.dccalliance.org*
- Astaro — *www.astaro.com*
- NSA Security Enhanced Linux—*www.nsa.gov/selinux/*
- SELinux for Distributions—*http://selinux.sourceforge.net/*
- Scyld—*www.scyld.com/platform_overview.html*
- Blue Cat Embedded Linux—*www.lynuxworks.com/products/bluecat/bluecat.php3*
- NFS Version 4 Home Page—*www.nfsv4.org*
- Samba—*www.samba.org*
- Centrify—*www.centrify.com*
- Postfix — *www.postfix.org*
- Exim—*www.exim.org*
- Dovecot—*www.dovecot.org*
- Cyrus IMAP Server—*http://asg.Web.cmu.edu/cyrus/*
- Qpopper—*www.eudora.com/products/unsupported/qpopper*

- SquirrelMail—*www.squirrelmail.org*
- eGroupWare—*www.egroupware.org*
- Hula—*www.hula-project.org*
- SpamAssassin—*http://spamassassin.apache.org*
- Linux IPCHAINS Howto—*www.tldp.org/HOWTO/IPCHAINS-HOWTO.html*
- Netfilter/iptables—*www.netfilter.org*
- Astaro Linux—*www.astaro.com*
- Coyote Linux Floppy Firewall—*www.coyotelinux.com/products.php?Product= coyote*
- Red Hat Directory Server—*www.redhat.com/software/rha/directory/*
- Fedora Directory Server Project—*http://directory.fedora.redhat.com/wiki/ Main_Page*
- Linksys GPL Code Center—*www.linksys.com/support/gpl.asp*
- Apache—*www.apache.org*
- The Mono Project—*www.mono-project.com*
- MySQL—*www.mysql.org*
- myPHP Admin—*www.phpmyadmin.net*
- VPN PPP-SSH Mini-HOWTO—*www.tldp.org/HOWTO/ppp-ssh/*
- FreeS/WAN—*www.freeswan.org/*
- Squid—*www.squid-cache.org*
- squidGuard—*www.squidguard.org/*
- SUSE LINUX Openexchange Server—*www.novell.com/products/ openexchange/*
- Open-Xchange—*www.open-xchange.org*

REFERENCES

Evans Data, "More Than 90% of Linux Systems Have Never Been Infected By a Virus," New Evans Data Survey. Available online at *http://www.evans data.com/n2/pr/releases/Linux04_02.shtml*, April 27, 2005.

Fersht, Phllip, "Heterogeneous Linux, Windows Networks Heighten Integration Challenges," Yankee Group. Available online at *http://www.yankeegroup.com/ public/products/decision_note.jsp?ID=13113*, May 20, 2005.

Hall, Mark, Computerworld (October 13, 2003). Available online at *http://www. computerworld.com/databasetopics/data/software/story/0,10801,85900,00.html*, May 24, 2005.

Howorth, Roger, IT Week, "Samba 3 Extends Lead Over Win 2003," (October 14, 2003). Available online at *http://www.itweek.co.uk/news/1144312*.

Microsoft, Pricing and Licensing for Windows Small Business Server 2003. Available online at *http://www.microsoft.com/windowsserver2003/sbs/howtobuy/ pricing.mspx*, November 4, 2005.

Netcraft, "April 2005 Web Server Survey." Available online at *http://news.net-craft.com/archives/2005/04/01/april_2005_Web_server_survey.html*, April 27, 2005.

Netcraft, "September 2001 Web Server Survey." Available online at *http://www.netcraft.com/Survey/index-200109.html#computers*, April 27, 2005.

Novell, SUSE LINUX Enterprise Server: Price list (in U.S. Dolllars). Available online at *http://www.novell.com/products/linuxenterpriseserver/pricing.html*, April 27, 2005.

Quandt, Stacy, "A Comparative Analysis of Linux vs. Windows Capabilities," Quandt Analytics (May 6, 2004).

9 Data Migration and Backups

Migrating data from one platform to another is not a pleasant task no matter if that data is being moved from a Windows to a Linux desktop or from one Windows PC to another. Not only are there considerations in moving data from one PC to another, but there is also a lot of significance in choosing complementary file formats before you migrate to avoid interoperability problems. The steps for data migration start with your application choices; for example, if you have made the commitment to OpenOffice.org on Windows in lieu of Microsoft Office, you will have tackled a considerable hurdle before your migration to a Linux desktop. The physical steps involved with moving from one desktop to another platform are not trivial and could be solved in conjunction with your backup solution. This strategy has two benefits. The first is that it makes sure that any snags you hit during your Linux migration will not result in data loss. The sec-

261

ond is that it gives you a way for moving data from your legacy PCs in the event you want to repurpose them either to fat clients running Linux or to thin clients where your data is migrated to a server anyway. You should consider the following when moving data from Linux:

Format Conversion: You will need to investigate first converting settings and files to Linux-usable formats. For example, Internet Explorer Favorites need to be converted to Bookmarks for use in Firefox or other browsers; word processing and other documents will now need to be opened with native Linux applications that are similar to Microsoft programs. In some cases you can continue to use the same formats, as most Linux office suites can open Microsoft documents with a good degree of reliability. However, you should consider formats that can take advantage of all the formats in a document, which constitutes using XML document formats like the XML OpenDocument format advocated by OpenOffice.org. You may also use an archival strategy where documents can be converted to Portable Document Format (PDF) so that formatting is preserved.

Data Migration: Physically moving application data is going to be one of your most challenging and time-consuming processes especially if the users that are migrating from one platform to another are storing the majority of their data locally rather than on a file server. You can move this data from one platform to another piecemeal but this can be very time consuming. There is a cadre of Linux software vendors that have developed tools to make this process easier and less time consuming.

Backups: The reason for exploring data migration and backups at the same time is due to the similar nature of both tasks: copying and restoring data from a location or media other than your PC. The other reason to consider backups at this point is that you will want to preserve as much of your user-specific data and settings as possible before taking a PC out of service.

The exportation of data and settings is usually the first part of any migration after you have repurposed or installed Linux on new PCs. If you have users who are new to the organization, you likely will be able to skip this step when instituting a Linux desktop environment. You will have to come up with a three-prong strategy to move data. Before getting to this point, hopefully you have already evaluated running Open Source applications natively to mitigate the need for file format conversion. If you have started to back up your files to a Samba file server running on Linux you may have solved much of the problem associated with backups and you may not need to formulate a backup strategy. The process of restoring from backups is very similar to the process you will use to move from Windows to Linux. If you don't use a server strategy, you can use a device or media strategy relying on USB drives or writable CD-ROM media to move data. Whatever method you choose to migrate data, you want to consider not only how the data flows out of Windows but also how it will be transferred back into Linux.

FORMAT CONVERSION

As advocated earlier in this book, moving to programs that run on Windows and support open standards will ease your Windows-to-Linux migration. Adopting open standards before you switch platforms, or even if you never switch desktop platforms, will keep your options open if you decide that one product has become too expensive or a security risk, or if the vendor that supplies the solution is giving you inadequate service. The majority of businesses use Microsoft file formats which have the capabilities to use special features in Microsoft Office, such as indexing, tables, and macros. While these features may be useful, they are not portable. You should consider if there are functions that need to carry over to your Linux migration or if you should consider open formats that can be read by other office products, specifically the ones that you will be using under Linux. You can convert office documents to OpenOffice.org formats by trying to open them under OpenOffice.org in Windows and then saving them in the appropriate format. You will find that OpenOffice.org has relatively good filters for importing documents that can then be saved in a new format like the OpenDocument formats endorsed by the Organization for the Advancement of Structured Information Standards (OASIS). You may also find that spreadsheets with elaborate macros just don't translate well. This is not a reason to terminate your migration plans, but you will likely need to evaluate some Windows-on-Linux solutions to maintain the use of Microsoft Excel on Linux as discussed in Chapter 10. Other solutions may be to create documents that preserve formatting but are not editable by saving them in Adobe's portable document format. You can do this by opening files in Open Office.org and exporting them to PDF. For documents that can't be opened in OpenOffice, you may need a Windows print driver that can print a document to a PDF like Adobe Distiller, or you can evaluate an application like *PDFCreator*, a free print driver for Windows that can create PDFs from virtually any Windows program. The addition of PDFCreator to your arsenal of tools is useful even without moving to Linux, because it gives you a free and easy way to create PDFs from documents you authored in your own applications. PDFCreator requires very little training because it shows up as a printer under Windows, as shown in Figure 9.1

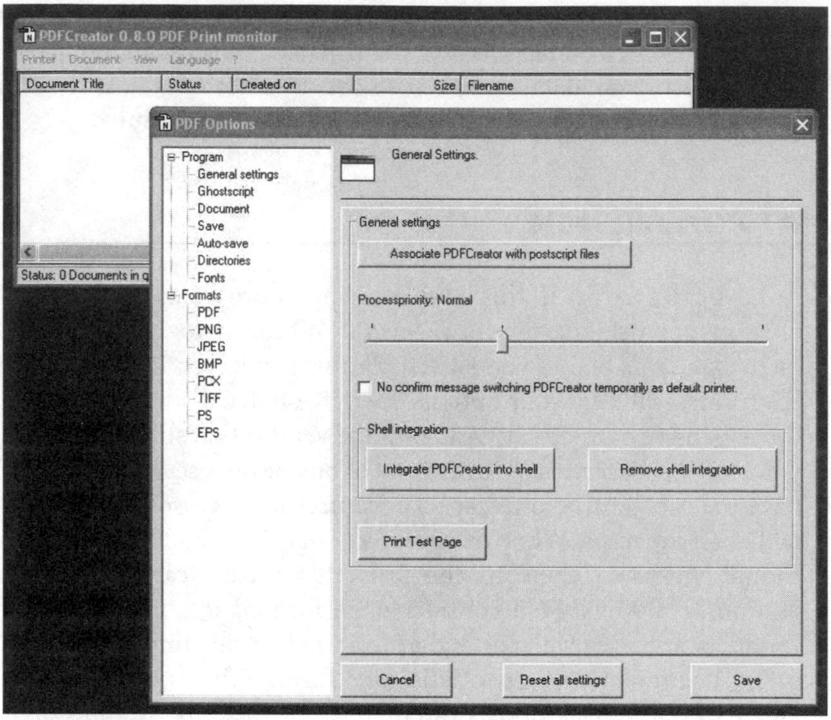

FIGURE 9.1 PDFCreator allows you to print to a special print driver, and print jobs will be captured as a PDF.

The reason for considering PDF as a method for moving documents from one operating system to another is that it will accurately preserve formats rather than being subject to annoying differences in the fonts and other formatting issues that might arise in migrating documents to a new desktop environment.

One area that has received a lot of attention is the idea of an open document standard that can be read by a multitude of office suites. The current adherence to non-common document formats lends itself to users maintaining an allegiance to one suite over another. The practice of using an XML-based document format is the wave of the future. Newer versions of Microsoft Office claim to adhere to an XML standard, but the reality is that unless they adopt a true open document format they will still have the advantage of locking you in to their office suite for 100% compatibility. OpenOffice 2.0 has adopted the OASIS Open Document file format, which is a standardized XML-based file format specifically suited for office applications, including spreadsheets, text, charts, and graphical documents.

Office Documents

Office documents are one of the largest repositories of information the knowledge worker will have. Many of the programs that Linux users have access to, like OpenOffice.org, run on Windows and can open documents from legacy desktop publishing and productivity applications. Before you switch platforms you should seriously consider using OpenOffice.org as your standard office suite. This will give you the ability to test file format compatibility before you make the move to Linux. You will then have the opportunity to make sure your data is accessible in a compatible format on Windows and if not you can try to solve this before you inadvertently lock users out of their files during a Windows to Linux move. Though converting to open source applications on Windows prior to a move to Linux is a good practice, it isn't 100% necessary. Many of the open source office suites will read and write in Microsoft formats with a high degree of accuracy. Table 9.1 offers a translation between Microsoft Office and OpenOffice file extensions.

TABLE 9.1 OpenOffice and Windows File Equivalents

Document type	Application	Document Extension	Template Extension	Microsoft Office Equivalent
Text	Writer	.sxw, .odt	.stw,.ott	.doc .dot
Spreadsheet	Calc	.sxc, .ods	.stc, .ots	.xls .xlt
Drawing	Draw	.sxd, .odg	.std, .otg	n/a
Presentation	Impress	.sxi,.odp	.sti, .otp	.ppt .pot .pps
Database	Base	.odb	n/a	.mdb
Formula	Math	.sxm	n/a	n/a
Master document	Writer	.sxg	n/a	n/a
HTML document	Writer	.html	n/a	.htm

You should note that the core Microsoft Office Suite has a functional equivalent supplied by OpenOffice.org in most every area. The biggest difference you will see between the two are the scripting languages available on one office suite over another for authoring macros.

MIGRATING DATA OFF THE WINDOWS DESKTOP

For existing Windows users, you should develop a strategy to move data from legacy PCs to the Linux PCs. You will likely be migrating office documents, email, and settings. This process, depending on the profile of the user, could be extremely complex. The strategy you may want to consider well before a Linux migration is to get as much data as possible onto a server that is independent of the Windows desktop. This accomplishes three things that are helpful in your Windows migration:

1. Data is now collated in a central location that is easily backed up.
2. Windows PCs can now be repurposed into Linux desktop PCs or thin client machines.
3. Data is in a place from which it can be imported back onto the newly deployed Linux desktop PCs.

Once you get the data off the desktop, the next thing to consider is the format of that data and if it is going to be in a format that can be read by OpenOffice.org or other native Linux applications.

Linux, unlike Windows, is case sensitive, so capitalization is important once the files move. To make things easier in the long run, use the convention of saving everything with all lowercase file names, which will make things easier when you are ready to access documents on Linux. One other consideration is that the seamlessness that exists with spaces in file names under Windows is not handled as elegantly under Linux. Making it a habit to remove spaces from folder and file names, or at least to replace spaces with the underscore, will make it easier for you to type file names in Linux. If you do have file names with spaces, you will use the convention of a backslash to preface a space on the command line.

Centralizing Data for Dual Boot Users

One of the best tips you can get, especially if you are a dual boot user, running Linux and Windows on the same PC, is to create a partition that can be written to from both Linux and Windows with good reliability. If you remember, both Linux and Windows can write to FAT32 filesystems. This is important if you want the ability to access and alter files from both Windows and Linux.

Partitioning for Data Migration

The key for a Windows-Linux migration to work is having all your data in one place that's both readable and write-able for both Linux and Windows. This way you aren't left out in the cold if you can't figure out the nuances of the replacement Linux desktop and applications. You could boot back into Windows and access this natively. If you are using Windows on a FAT32 partition you won't need the data partition but if you are using Windows 2000 or XP on a NTFS partition this step is crucial. Repartitioning is the key to make this all work seamlessly.

For the purpose of demonstration, we'll assume that your hard drive is 60 GB. Your goal will be to repartition the hard drive into three partitions. We will assume that to start with, the PC has Windows XP or 2000 installed on a single partition. Your first step will be to resize the Windows partition to 20 GBs. The next step is to create a FAT32 partition where all your data will live. The third is to create a 20 GB partition where Linux will be installed. You may also have a Linux swap partition that will equal about two times the number of megabytes of RAM you have and a boot partition of less than 100 MB. To keep the numbers easy, we will round the size of three large partitions to 20 GB, though they may be slightly smaller or larger depending on your hard drive size or specific needs.

Once you have created your partitions you should now have three partitions: a Linux partition with your Linux operating system installed, a Windows partition with the Windows operating system installed, and a FAT32 formatted data partition. The next step is to boot into Windows and move your data to the FAT32 partition. You could do this through a long series of manual steps, but there is a much easier way to accomplish this. Use a tool from the Microsoft part of the PowerToys suite called *Tweak UI* to point your My Documents and other special folders to your FAT32 partition. In a system with a single CD-ROM drive and only one other Windows readable partition this will likely be labeled disk drive E:\. You can use the Tweak UI tools to move your *Special Folders* including and most importantly your *My Documents* folder to this FAT32 partition as shown in Figure 9.2.

This will give you the ability to access data in read-write mode once you are booted into Linux. You may want to look for the files your Windows applications use, such as your Outlook .pst file and others, and move them to your FAT32 partition, especially if you are going to use Windows applications on Linux. This may include files for Lotus Notes, ACT!, Goldmine, Quicken, or any other Windows application for which you may not have found a suitable Linux replacement. Once you have used TweakUI and made sure all the information you want accessible from both operating systems in located on your data partition, it's time to boot into Linux.

Any time you move important system folders under Windows you are at risk of causing permanent problems to your Windows system. The Tweak UI tool recommended for these steps is not a supported part of Windows though it is likely you will be able to make the changes with no noticeable problems. However, as is the best practice for anytime you make changes to your system, you should make backups first.

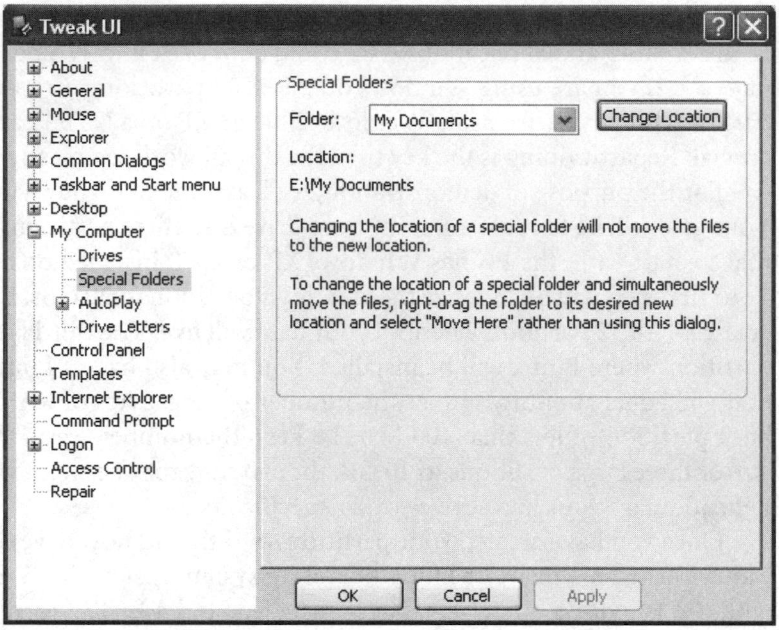

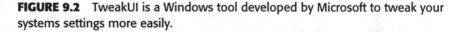

FIGURE 9.2 TweakUI is a Windows tool developed by Microsoft to tweak your systems settings more easily.

Accessing Your Windows Data from Linux

It now is the time to start preparing to do business with Linux. The key here is to make sure that your data migrates along with the applications you need to continue to be productive. The thing that you will need to do once you are booted into Linux is make sure that your Linux OS mounts the FAT32 partition. The reason that it is recommended that you chose to store the data on a FAT32 partition is so that it can be read from both your Window and Linux installations. To mount the partition you will need to edit the /etc/mtab file so that it tells your PC to mount this partition as both readable and writable by Linux. A tool in your Linux distribution may accomplish this but because it's fairly important to the strategy, here are the manual steps for completing this.

To start the mounting process, become the superuser or root by typing su at the command line and then entering the root password. Then you need to figure out where your FAT32 partition is in the Linux distribution. It will be listed as a device in the /dev/ directory. You can figure out which partition contained the data by writing down how much data was on that partition in Windows before rebooting. Once booted into Linux, type the command fdisk –l (the absolute path to this program is /sbin/fdisk but most likely /sbin/ will be in your $PATH and should launch). The results will likely look similar to what you see in Figure 9.3.

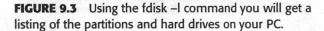

```
[root@localhost mrhinkle]# /sbin/fdisk -l

Disk /dev/hda: 60.0 GB, 60011642880 bytes
255 heads, 63 sectors/track,
7296 cylinders Units = cylinders of 16065 * 512 = 8225280 bytes

   Device Boot    Start      End  Blocks  Id System
/dev/hda1   *       1      1912 15358108+  7 HPFS/NTFS
/dev/hda2         1913     7296 43246980   f Win95 Ext'd (LBA)
/dev/hda5         1913     3824 15358108+  c Win95 FAT32 (LBA)
/dev/hda6         3825     3837  104391   83 Linux
/dev/hda7         3838     7166 26740161  83 Linux
/dev/hda8         7167     7296 1044193+  82 Linux swap
[root@localhost mrhinkle]#
```

FIGURE 9.3 Using the fdisk –l command you will get a listing of the partitions and hard drives on your PC.

In the example, the data partition shown in Figure 9.3 is /dev/hda5. You can then change to the /mnt/ directory and create a directory for your data by entering the following commands.

```
cd /mnt/ <ENTER>
mkdir data <ENTER>
```

Then you need to add following line to /etc/mtab/:

```
/dev/hda5 /mnt/data vfat rw,umask=500 0 0
```

The /dev/hda5 indicates the partition you want to mount. The /mnt/data indicates where you want to mount it. The type of filesystem is vfat, and the rw means that the filesystem should be readable and writable. umask=500 means to use the umask for user 500 (the user mrhinkle for this installation). You can find out what a user's ID number is by listing the users in the /etc/passwd file. The format of the /etc/passwd/ file looks like the output here. Note that username mrhinkle has a user ID of 500.

```
postgres:x:26:26:PostgreSQL Server:/var/lib/pgsql:/bin/bash
desktop:x:80:80:desktop:/var/lib/menu/kde:/sbin/nologin
mrhinkle:x:500:500:Mark R. Hinkle:/home/mrhinkle:/bin/bash
```

These steps can be accomplished a number of different ways, so complete them in whatever way is comfortable for you.

Data Access from Linux

In Windows, most of you already know where your data is stored: in the My Documents folder. If you followed the previous directions you can still access the My Documents folder, but now you can do so in Linux. A practice that may be helpful is to create a link to the My Documents folder that is now on the FAT32 partition. You can even make links to your existing data repositories from the new Linux desktop. You can do this by right-clicking on the desktop and then creating a link to a location that will probably be on the /mnt/data directory that you created earlier. You now have a way to share data from both operating systems.

Office Documents

Office documents are going to be one of the most critical items you will migrate from one platform to another. Before you even start to migrate from Windows to Linux the best practices are to start converting to a transportable format and to start to collect these documents centrally. Getting end users to collate their documents into one place such as their Windows My Documents folder is a good place to start. The next step is to get that data backed up to a file server that you can later access from Linux. This could be a Microsoft Windows Server or a Linux server running Samba. This way, if you have an installation failure your data isn't lost. The same applies if you have a problem with the repartitioning schema that was advocated earlier.

Migrating Email, Calendar, and Contacts

The practice of using server-based email can help ease the burden of a Linux migration because email messages are stored on a server and accessible via IMAP or some other open standard readable by Linux email clients like Evolution or Thunderbird. This makes sure that you will have all your email in a place that can be backed up for the whole enterprise centrally. It also keeps one critical thing off your list of data sources to migrate. It is also useful for transitioning users who might need to use both Windows and Linux desktops for a short time.

Migrating Local Email with Thunderbird

If you need to migrate email stored on the local PC from a Windows user to a Linux user, you can do so in a number of ways. In many cases users will have their mail stored in Microsoft Outlook or Outlook Express. You can migrate email from Outlook's proprietary .pst format to other open formats by using import filters to import the settings and data from Outlook into a more portable format. One tactic is to use the Thunderbird email program on Windows to import settings from Outlook into an open format that can be more easily imported in native Linux installations. When you install Thunderbird under Windows and run it for the first time, a dialogue appears to import settings from Outlook, as shown in Figure 9.4.

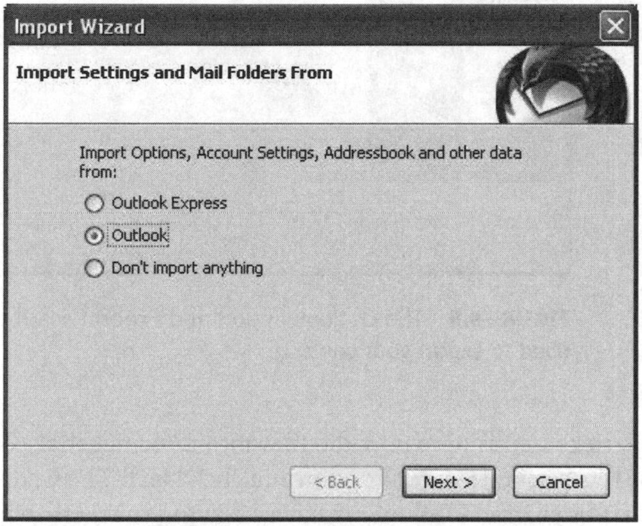

FIGURE 9.4 Thundbird's import email dialogue can import email from Outlook and Outlook Express.

This will then create a profile in Windows for your Thunderbird email. It will also be stored in a format that you can access running Thunderbird on Linux. There is a link to detailed instructions on how to share your Thunderbird settings with both Linux and Windows in the Other Resources section at the end of this chapter.

Migrating Contacts from One Operating System to Another

Your contacts are the lifeblood of your business. They may include vendors or customers, as well as information internal to your company. If you store your contacts in one of the common personal information managers like Outlook or other address book software, you can import them into Evolution through an import filter. You can do this by first going to Outlook and starting the *Import and Export Wizard,* shown in Figure 9.5, by choosing `File-> Import and Export`.

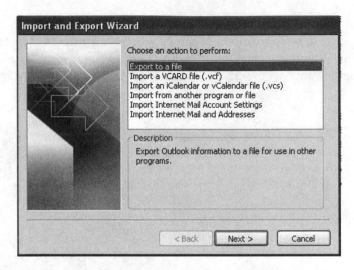

FIGURE 9.5 The Outlook Import and Export wizard can be used to export your contacts.

The next step is to export the files into a format that you can read in Linux. Choose the Export to a file option and click Next. The next step is to choose your contacts folder from Outlook by navigating to your Personal Folders as shown in Figure 9.6

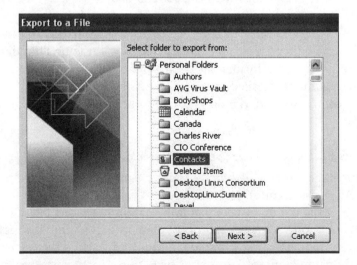

FIGURE 9.6 Choose the data you would like to export, such as contacts, by navigating through your Outlook personal folder.

You can then follow the dialogue to export your contacts into a CSV file that can be imported into your Linux installation. The next step requires you to convert your CSV files to the industry standard vCard that can be read by Evolution personal information and mail client or a number of other mail clients and address books. For this step, you can use a program called *csv2vcard* which is freely downloadable. Once you have converted your files to vCard format you can import them into Evolution using the Evolution Import Wizard. Click on the Contacts button in Evolution and choose `File -> Import` which will launch the Wizard and allow you to import the contacts that have been converted, as shown in Figure 9.7.

FIGURE 9.7 Evolution Import Wizard can be used to bring vCard files into your Evolution email client and PIM.

You can also use the Kontact PIM for the KDE desktop to import files from a number of formats including your CSV file and Windows desktop formats. You can accomplish this by launching Kontact and choosing to Import the csv file that we created earlier. This will allow you to import the CSV file or a Microsoft Exchange address book, as shown in Figure 9.8.

No matter what you used in Windows, there is likely a way for you to export that data and import it into your Linux contact manager. These are the manual ways to export and import mail but the tools discussed later in this chapter that makes the process considerably easier.

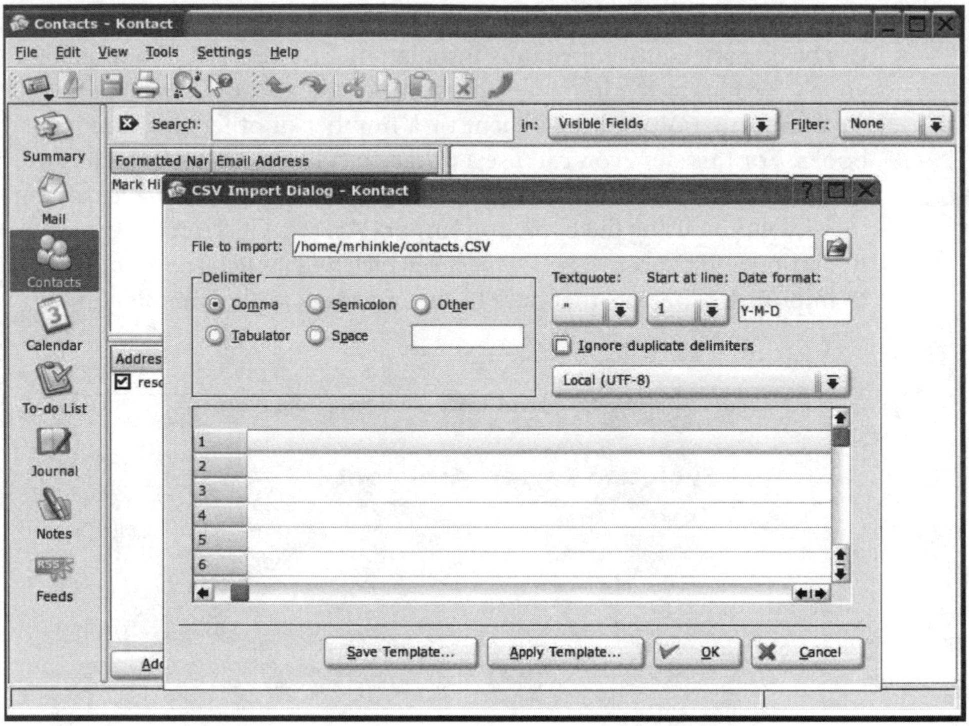

FIGURE 9.8 Kontact can import contacts that were exported from a Microsoft address book.

Converting Favorites to Bookmarks

Internet Explorer stores favorite Web pages as Favorites. The format for Firefox and Mozilla browsers is Bookmarks. By converting to Firefox as your default Windows Web browser, you can already overcome the first hurdle for browser migration, as Firefox can convert Favorites to Bookmarks when it's run on Linux. As advocated earlier, you could migrate those bookmarks to your shared partition or you could use one of two unique extensions available for Firefox.

Bookmark Synchronizer: This extension allows lets you connect to an FTP/WebDav server and synchronize your bookmarks to an XML file that allows you to shuffle the bookmarks back and forth from one operating system to another.

Chipmark: Chipmark lets you take your bookmarks wherever you go. The Chipmark extension lets you access your bookmarks from a server that stores your bookmarks confidentially and securely. Chipmark does this by adding an extra menu on your Firefox browser labeled *Chipmarks* to synchronize your repository of bookmarks. You can use this to export the bookmarks and save them permanently on your Linux desktop.

These tools are nice amenities to help migrate from one platform to another as well as provide a mechanism for telecommuters and other mobile workers to access their data from virtually any location.

Other Applications

We will explore how to migrate applications to Linux in Chapter 10; for now you should note whether or not any applications you use today have proprietary formats. For example, Linux has no direct apples-to-apples replacement for the common financial packages Quicken or Quickbooks made by Intuit. You may want to save your Quicken files in .qif format to be imported by Windows applications running on Linux. When you migrate these data files to Linux you can use the import functions from these applications to reacquire your settings and data in that manner.

Software that Helps You Migrate Settings and Data

There is a whole industry springing up around Windows-to-Linux migration and with that industry are a number of products that can take the settings and data from Windows and move them over to Linux. All these products work in similar ways and offer good results. The differentiators are in the way they move the data and the target platforms they support. When you consider the time it takes to manually make these moves, using one of these automated tools to save time becomes a "no-brainer."

Alacos Linux Migration Agent™

Alacos Linux Migration Agent is one of the more unique ways to migrate data from Windows to Linux because it is designed to do so over a network. Legacy Windows machines run a Windows version of Linux Migration Agent, while a Linux target receives data that is to be migrated. This method is unique and offers the ability to move data to a target machine while the Windows machine is still in service. The Alacos Linux Migration Agent allows you to pick and choose what settings you want to migrate, as shown in Figure 9.9.

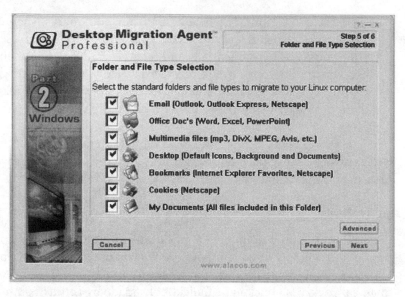

FIGURE 9.9 You can choose to migrate only the settings and data that you want to migrate with Desktop Migration Agent.

One of the most useful features of this product and all the others is the ability to migrate email from Outlook to the email client on Linux. This ability to dissect the .pst file makes things exceptionally easy in comparison to doing a shuffle from Outlook exports to Thunderbird imports and transitioning data from one platform to another. You can also do a direct machine-to-machine copy using a crossover cable connected to the network card on each PC.

Resolvo MoveOver

Resolvo makes a product called MoveOver that does just that—it helps you move the settings from Windows to a native Linux desktop just as Alacos does, but the Resolvo approach is to store the settings in a .zip file that can be stored or written to a CD and then moved over to Linux. The MoveOver Windows-to-Linux migration tool has been released as an open source project, though the open source version only supports certain operating systems. Resolvo has also open-sourced their MoveOver product for Linux to encourage the Linux community to develop the code for different Linux distributions. That is the Achilles heel of MoveOver and all of these automated tools. Every one of these products must develop and test for the settings on each specific Linux distribution as some distributions may store settings and data differently than others. MoveOver's Resolvo has both a default and an advanced interface to export Windows sessions on Linux, as shown in Figure 9.10.

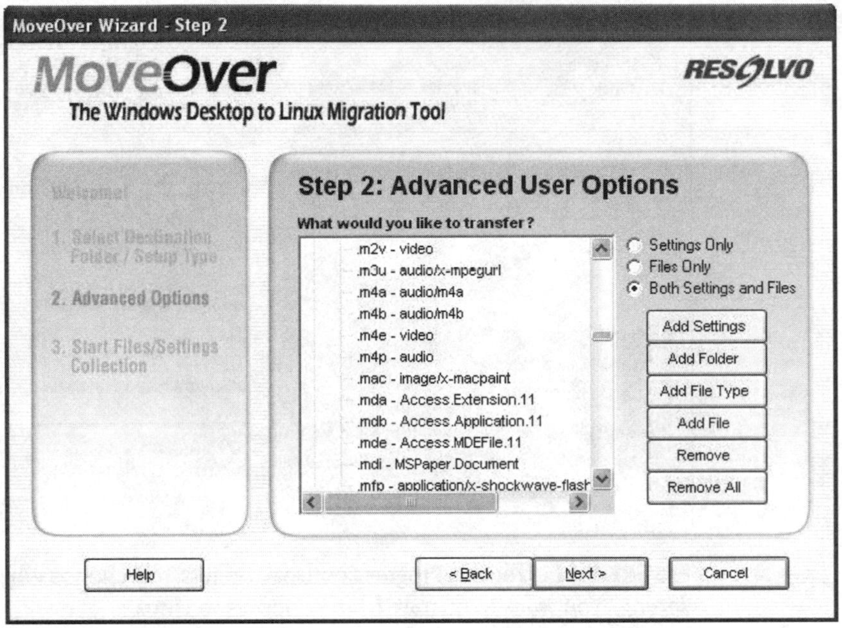

FIGURE 9.10   Resolvo's MoveOver allows you to pick what files move from one platform to another.

Though not every Linux distribution is covered completely by MoveOver, the most common ones like SUSE and Red Hat are targeted by Resolvo.

Versora Progression Desktop

Versora is a software company that specializes in Windows-to-Linux migration on both the server and desktop. Their first products focused on and have great value in migrating data from Microsoft SQL Server and Access to open source databases like MySQL and PostgressSQL. Versora's Progression Desktop product allows you to create a package on Windows of all your files that, once run, can pack up almost all your settings and data and import them into Linux. You can also choose only to move certain aspects of the Windows desktop to create a portable package, as shown in Figure 9.11.

Versora's Progression Desktop works in the same way as Resolvo; it archives the files to be expanded later. With this process you can also keep a backup of your data that over time can provide a snapshot of your premigration data.

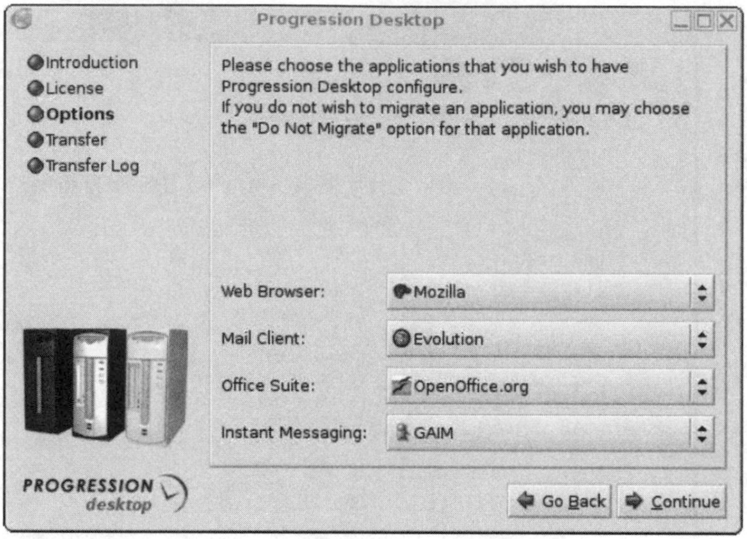

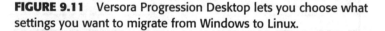

FIGURE 9.11   Versora Progression Desktop lets you choose what settings you want to migrate from Windows to Linux.

Neotek Outlook2Evolution

Outlook2Evolution, or *O2E*, is a solution developed by Neotek to export personal information and mail from Microsoft Outlook and import it to Evolution. The O2E tool, unlike some of the other tools mentioned here, is licensed under the GPL so users can export their data. The O2E tool relies on the presence of Mozilla Thunderbird to do the export and then O2E helps to migrate that data back into your new Linux mail client Evolution. This is once again a little less elegant than the processes of Alacos, Resolvo, and Versora, but it is free, and if you have a light need for moving mail and other PIM data, you can use this tool to assist in data migration.

BACKUPS

There's an old saying that goes, "An ounce of prevention is worth a pound of cure." This phrase could easily have been attributed to a system administrator after a server crash if it hadn't first been attributed to Ben Franklin. More often than not computer users do not take the most basic precautions with our personal computing environments. Backups are probably one of the most important and neglected practices for desktop users. When suffering a PC crash most people will likely wonder with a feeling of dread when their last backup was performed and what the likelihood of recovery is. The bottom line is that there is no foolproof way to keep PCs from crashing, so backups are critical.

Also, if you start to make regular backups you will have a mechanism to migrate data off of the desktop in anticipation of a Windows-to-Linux desktop migration. Ideally you will get to the point that you are confident that all your critical information is stored in a place where it is portable, so even if you choose to stay on Windows, you will have the ability to introduce hardware upgrades without having to suffer.

Data Location

The first step in developing a backup strategy for your data is to figure out where your data lives on your system. By default most all your Linux user data is stored in your /home/$USER directory ($USER means the username you log in to Linux with). Once you confirm that this is where your information is, you can decide how you will make backups—either to media like a DVD/RW drive or a server. By keeping the bulk of your data in one directory, it's easier to keep track of what data needs to be backed up. If you have a relatively small amount of data, 700MB or less, you may just choose to burn data to inexpensive media like CDRs. Using the popular CD burner software *k3b,* you create a data project to copy all your critical files to a DVD or CD. The easy drag-and-drop interface allows you to make copies, but that's only one of many ways to archive your data. You can also copy to a second hard drive or other storage device, or even back up your data over the network. However, the method is not nearly as important as remembering to do it or scheduling the system to do it on a regular basis

Operating System Backups

ON THE CD

One method for creating backups is to use the Knoppix CD-ROM to execute a complete disk copy to an extra hard drive. Now this is not the fastest way to do things but it catches everything on your hard drive, including all your data, and it's very easy to verify the contents of the backup. In this scenario, consider a PC with two hard drives. The first hard drive will be where your operating system resides; the second hard drive is where you will store your data. Not everyone will have a second hard drive, but in the day of cheap storage it's not cost prohibitive to have a second internal or an external hard drive. For a 60 GB hard drive, there are many options well under $100 and because you don't have to invest in backup software it is easy to justify.

How to Back Up Your Hard Drive Using Knoppix

You can create backups of your hard drive in a variety of ways, but copying the entire contents of one local drive to another can create the most thorough backup. To start, you should boot your computer using your Knoppix CD-ROM. You should see both hard drives on your desktop, and if you open your shell you can enter su to gain root (superuser) access. You can also discern which drives are which by their contents, which should be browsable using the Konqueror file manager. Now make sure that after you have determined which hard drive is which by browsing them, that you unmount them so that you can copy one drive to another. One drive is likely to be /dev/hda and the other is probably /dev/hdb; you may need to research them a little more thoroughly to be sure. Then to copy one drive to another you simply type the following command:

```
dd if=/dev/hda of=/dev/hdb
```

Keep in mind that you want to be very confident in the identities of the source and backup drives because if you get the two reversed, the target drive will overwrite the source drive with all your data. Once you have the backup in place, you can use *rsync* to synchronize the two drives going forward. To find out more about rsync, use the *man rsync* command.

Backup Software

There are more solutions for backup than can be covered in this book in adequate detail and you may already have a solution that you are satisfied with, so making a recommendation is probably not necessary. However, you may want to be familiar with a couple of the open source solutions for Linux backup.

Creating Compressed Archives with tar and gzip

The standard way to create an archive is to use the tar utility to combine files and directories into one file. This has been covered in earlier chapters as the way to compress those files, gzip. Though you may find that these utilities are extremely simple to use, they can be part of an overall backup strategy.

Scripting Backups

In your point-and-click environments there are several ways to create backups, but sometimes it's easier to use the command line scripting utilities and scheduling capabilities of Linux to provide reliable automated backups. You can very easily write a script that will automatically create archives of important directories. You can do this manually each time or you can write a simple script to do it for you. By creating a shell script and using the *cron* daemon to schedule its execution, you can feel better about preserving your data.

The steps to create a simple script to execute the backups are pretty straight forward and can be used to make backups of critical directories.

1. The first step is to create a script called *archive* (you may call the script whatever you like). Do this by opening a text editor; gedit or kwrite are the two most common graphical ones depending on whether you are using the GNOME or KDE desktop.
2. Type the following lines in your text editor:

```
#!/bin/shtar czvf $1.$(date +%Y%m%d).tgz $1 exit $?
```

3. Save the file and call it *archive* (no extension is needed)
4. You must then make sure that the file is executable using the chmod command from the command line:

```
chmod 755 archive
```

You now have a script that will save a directory in a compressed archive. To execute the command, type the name of your script proceeded by a dot and a forward slash then a space and the directory name.

```
./archive directory_name
```

Here, `directory_name` is the name of the directory you want to archive. The archive will be in the format of the name of the directory followed by the .tgz extension, which indicates that it has been archived with *tar* and then compressed with *gzip*.

```
directory_name..20050101.tgz
```

Notice that the name has the date (January 1, 2005) in it so you can easily track when you made the backup.

How to Automate Desktop Backups Using the cron Daemon

There are as many ways to back up your data as there are types of data. Here's a quick way to back up your data mirrored in the exact same format that it's stored in your home directory from a command line interface. You will be using two commands: *rsync* and *crontab*. They are probably installed on your system already but you may want to check your distribution documentation.

Rsync is used to synchronize files with another location. In this simple example you will be synching to another directory on the hard drive. In the case of this example, the data will be synchronized from */home/mrhinkle/data/* directory to a drive mounted at */mnt/backups/*.

Cron is a daemon that executes scheduled commands. In this case we are using it to schedule backups, but you can use it to schedule the upload of files to a Web site, to archive mail, or to automate a variety of other tasks.

To start this exercise you will want to type the following at a shell prompt:

```
crontab -e
```

Then add a line in the format below:

```
30 4 * * * rsync -a /home/mrhinkle/data/ /mnt/backups/
```

Keep in mind that the anatomy of a cron file looks like this:

```
30 4 * * *
```

This is the line which indicates the time at which to run the commands further down the line. Of course, your PC needs to be turned on at this time for the backup to run. The first number is the minutes, the second the hour, the next three asterisks indicate day of the month, month of the year, and then the days of the week. Acceptable values here are 0–6 with 0 equal to Sunday; use the wildcard * to indicate every day of the month, month of the year, and day of the week.

The next part is:

```
rsync -a
```

This is the command you will use to copy the incremental changes in data from one directory to another.

Then comes:

```
/home/mrhinkle/data/
```

This is the data you want to synchronize. In this case the data is stored in /home/mrhinkle/data/.

The last part of the line is:

```
/mnt/backups/
```

This is the location you want to synchronize to. In a desktop PC this might be a second hard drive or ideally a remote file server to ensure additional redundancy. Once again, if this is a filesystem that must be mounted you should make sure that it's mounted at the time the cron job runs or else the backup will fail.

Cron comes from the Greek word chronos which means time. Cron is a task scheduling program that runs in the background as a daemon and executes scheduled tasks. These tasks can be a simple command or a very complex scripted procedure such as a full system backup. You could also use cron to schedule a virus scanner to run every night while a PC is unused.

KDar—the KDE Disk Archiver

KDar is the *KDE disk archive tool* that has a graphical interface and is included with the KDE desktop. KDar can perform both complete and incremental backups, where it only saves the delta or changes between your last backup and your next one. KDar is one of the easier backup utilities to use because it does have a rather full-featured interface, as shown in Figure 9.12.

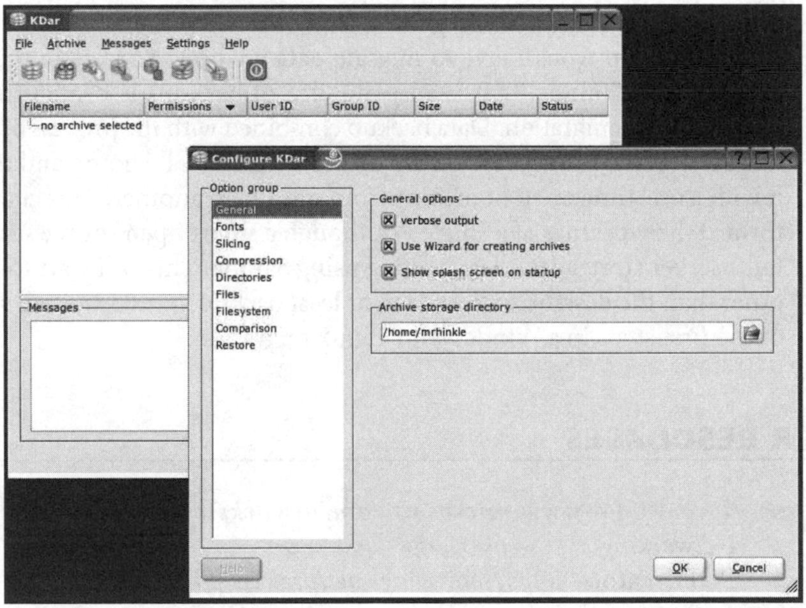

FIGURE 9.12 The KDar graphical backup utility for KDE is an easy-to-use backup utility for the Linux desktop.

You can choose what directory you want to store your backups on. You may also choose to mount a directory on another machine and save your archives in that way. The archives are saved with the extension .dar which is specific to the KDar backup utility.

Unison File Synchronizer

Unison is a file synchronization tool that you can use on Linux, Unix, or Microsoft Windows. You can use this tool to make backups just like you use the rsync utility, but Unison does this through a graphical user interface rather than by issuing more cryptic commands on the shell as rsync does. Unison does have a textual interface for remote usage where graphical access is inconvenient, though.

SUMMARY

Moving data is usually a tiresome chore even when the operating systems are the same. Moving from Windows to Linux may require some compromises in this area, especially when you consider the time needed to make an effective move. As with any of the situations described in this book, you should, whenever practical, try to synch migration of desktop operating systems with other logical and necessary events. For example, migrating from old hardware to a newer PC is a logical time when you would have to migrate data anyhow. Success in this area can be a function of planning, that is why the idea of backups is brought up in the same breath as data migration. Data backup combined with the process of data migration takes a necessary task that you are or should already be doing and then combining it with a one time event of moving from one OS to another. This chapter is oriented toward the workings of a single PC, though a smart open source strategy could entail a server strategy for data hosting using Samba. This will start to provide a place other than the desktop to host data, or least backups, and provide a solution for one of the first steps in a Windows-to-Linux migration.

OTHER RESOURCES

- TweakUI—*www.microsoft.com/ntworkstation/downloads/PowerToys/ Networking/NTTweakUI.asp*
- PDFCreator—*http://sourceforge.net/projects/pdfcreator/*
- csv2vcard—*http://cvs2vcard.sourceforge.net*
- Bookmarks Synchronizer—*https://addons.mozilla.org/extensions/moreinfo.php? application=firefox&category=Bookmarks&numpg=10&id=14*

- Chipmark—*https://addons.mozilla.org/extensions/moreinfo.php?application= firefox&category=Bookmarks&numpg=10&id=666*
- Open Office Document Format—*www.oasis-open.org/committees/office/ faq.php*
- How to Share Mail Between Windows and Linux—*http://texturizer.net/thunderbird/share_mail.html*
- Alacos—*www.alacos.com*
- Resolvo MoveOver—*www.resolvo.com*
- OpenMoveOver—*http://openmoveover.sourceforge.net/*
- Versora Progression Desktop—*www.versora.com*
- Outlook2Evolution Personal Information Migration Tool—*www.neotek.hu/ en/o2e_en.html*
- KDE Disk Archiving—*http://kdar.sourceforge.net*
- Unison—*http://www.cis.upenn.edu/~bcpierce/unison/*

10 Migrating Windows Applications to Linux

The list of reasons to use the Linux desktop includes choice in vendors, progressive software licensing policies, and flexibility of the overall architecture. The biggest detractor from Linux on the desktop other than hardware vendor support is arguably application availability. Applications that may be hard to find are those that fall outside the realm of core applications mentioned in earlier chapters, which included browsers, email clients, and office suites. The "gotcha" with desktop Linux applications is that there may be no functional equivalent to your Windows applications. There are three common solutions to this problem:

Running Windows Applications on Linux: The previous exercise of taking an inventory of Windows application needs and comparing to them to native Linux applications may have left you with some holes in your Linux migration strategy. You can run Windows applications in either a virtual machine that allows the Windows operating system to execute under a specialized piece of software that virtualizes a PC, or you can replace the Windows API and try to run the application without Windows.

Redisplaying Windows Applications from Microsoft Server: You may already have a solution for remotely redisplaying Windows applications through the popular Microsoft Terminal Services extension to Microsoft server products. You may even use the Citrix redisplay framework to extend the capabilities of running Windows securely in a latent network. You could leverage this technology to redisplay those same sessions to Linux desktops.

Porting Applications to Linux: In the long term you will want to consider ways to convert to applications that are native to Linux or run on Linux, or ideally that are platform independent via Web services or a portable architectures like Java.

The ideal solution is to find an equivalent application that can run natively on Linux. For example, substituting OpenOffice.org for the Microsoft Office suite is a logical place to start. Using Firefox in lieu of Internet Explorer is another logical choice. Where you start to run into problems is in specialty applications that might be specific to a vertical industry or an application that was custom developed for your business. The need for Linux versions of these applications doesn't exist yet. Rewriting applications to run on a new platform may never make fiscal sense for niche developers. For example, there are many applications that run on MS-DOS that have yet to be ported to Windows, and they might not continue to run as DOS applications until they reach their end of lives without ever moving to a more modern system. The same situation will exist for Windows applications that may have been perfectly usable running on Windows 95, but won't be moving to Windows XP because it would add very little if any value to their performance. The problem is that these older operating systems at some point may no longer be supported, and PCs may break, and older operating systems may not support the newer replacement hardware.

You may run Windows applications *and* Linux applications side by side, which immediately gives you much broader application choices than either operating system on its own. It also provides you a way to transition to Linux without sacrificing applications and the familiarity of legacy systems. It's inevitable that Linux will continue to broaden its application support, and some enterprises will take measures in their strategic decisions to choose platform-independent applications hosted via the Web. These decisions likely won't play out in a short amount of time but over a number of years. Rather than suffer the opportunity costs of not using Open Source and Linux right now, you can start with a hybrid approach to desktop Linux adoption through the methods discussed in this chapter.

RUNNING WINDOWS APPLICATIONS ON LINUX

Taking all other desktop Linux migration factors under advisement and finding that the only inhibitor for Linux desktop migration is application availability should prompt users to look at ways to extend their investment in Windows software while staging the applications on Linux. You can do this by running the Windows applications on the Linux desktop through software that facilitates the execution of the Windows application or Windows operating system on the Linux desktop. Figure 10.1 shows two such technologies, Win4Lin and Wine, running the Windows operating system and applications on a Linux desktop.

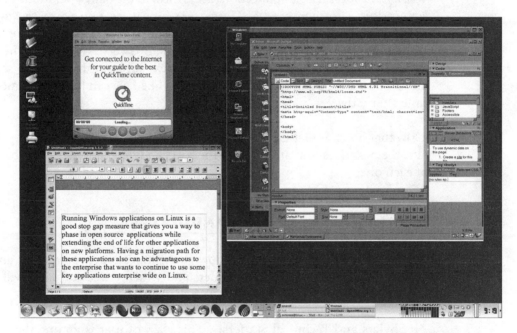

FIGURE 10.1   Win4Lin runs a Windows session as a hosted client on the Linux desktop, while Wine runs applications individually without a Windows operating system.

By staging Windows operating systems and applications as *hosted clients* on Linux you can start to benefit in part from the advantages of Linux listed throughout this book but also from the applications you have already invested in on Windows. You also may realize any of the following benefits.

Limited Retraining Costs: Immersing PC users in a foreign environment may lead to lost productivity while they learn new applications. Though these changes may be minimal for many applications like Web browsers and email, more complex or specialized applications can require more time for users to regain proficiency.

Equivalent Application Availability: There are many vertical or functional applications that include sales contact managers, drafting applications, and medical records software that have no native Linux equivalent. A single vital application can be the reason preventing migration from one platform to another. Windows application solutions can benefit those organizations who otherwise could be realizing the advantages of a Linux application.

Reduced Porting Costs: Enterprises often invest in applications customized to their business. These applications are critical to the daily operations of many enterprises. Also, there are many instances where there is no alternative to these applications. Porting these applications is very costly; that's why looking at migrating applications rather than rewriting them is very attractive in the short term. In the long term, however, running these applications in a Web services model or other platform neutral technology like Java can be a much more viable alternative.

Now that it's clear that Linux can accommodate your Windows desktop applications, the next questions are what are the best candidates and what are the benefits of each one?

WINDOWS ON LINUX DESKTOP CANDIDATES

The variety of uses for desktop PCs includes communication, productivity, and entertainment. It's important then to understand which classes of users will most likely benefit from each type of Windows application on Linux solutions.

Hobbyists and Technical Staffers: This class of user is among the earliest adopters of Linux. They typically have a high tolerance for manipulation and "tweaking" of software and have the skills and desire to customize their desktop operating system. They may have a need for a specialized application not available for Linux. The hobbyist may need gaming software which is probably irrelevant to your enterprise, but the technical staffers may require, for example, drafting applications that lack a Linux equivalent.

Task-Based Workers: The task-based worker usually has relatively modest computing needs, generally including office and communications applications. What they may face as an obstacle are probably proprietary data entry applications such as CRM software, groupware (such as Lotus Notes), and data manipulation applications (e.g., financial applications). In some cases Web-based interfaces lack the same functionality as a native application. The use of a limited interface could slow productivity, so maintaining these data entry and other applications in a Windows environment may provide some advantage. In many cases these users will have one particular Windows on Linux need specific to their market vertical or enterprise.

Education/Shared Workstation Environment: Students and educators are often victims of tight IT budgets and shared workstations. They seldom have a dedicated PC and rely on machines maintained by administrative staff. As new technologies emerge, educators are pressed to teach students on the old software while preparing them to deal with new standards. Hosting Windows applications side by side with Linux applications can provide students the means to learn two types of technology at once.

Government: In government PC installations there is often concern related to the management of systems including installation and software maintenance. Additionally, they often have security concerns. These installations require a strong user-based system to control data and application configurations on PCs. They can also be expansive, as are some agencies of the U.S. government. These institutions may have such a wide user base that they are hard-pressed to adhere to standards without access to legacy Windows applications. Because of the breadth of these organizations, it is likely they will have a variety of Windows applications. In cases where security controls need to be maintained alongside standardized applications, Windows hosted in virtual machines on Security Enhanced Linux (SELinux) could be a very powerful and pragmatic solution.

Knowledge Workers: Knowledge workers are the most demanding class of PC users. These users often require a wide range of applications to complete their desktop. They are, as you saw in earlier chapters, the most complex and risky Linux desktop candidates. They might benefit the most from a hosted Windows session on a Linux desktop.

Windows applications that need to directly access external hardware can be the least likely to be solved by Windows applications running on Linux because the systems that make them plug 'n play (PnP) on Windows are likely to be absent under Linux. Examples of these would be scanners and specialized printers that require software for configuration, or PDAs that run WindowsCE as the operating system and require Windows-based conduits for synchronization. These types of applications will perhaps never have the opportunity to run under Linux, and that should be considered in your strategy when you start to invest in cell phones, PDAs, and other devices that could be reliant on Windows for updates and data exchange. Ideally, just as you evaluated applications that could run natively on Linux, you should look first to devices that can interoperate well with Linux.

HOW TO RUN WINDOWS APPLICATIONS NATIVELY ON LINUX

Running Windows applications on Linux is a key to Linux desktop migration success for many users because while there is a broad range of Linux applications, many legacy Windows applications can hold back migration due to the lack a functional equivalent. That is why finding ways to leverage existing IT investment, increasing the number of available applications available on the Linux desktop, and maintaining the stability of those applications is paramount to Linux desktop success. Also, there is the added benefit of extending the useful life of software and operating systems that you have already invested in. This is a best-of-both-worlds scenario, where Linux desktop users benefit from familiar applications and legacy systems that can be phased out rather than ripped out and replaced. By having a fadeaway strategy you can start to mitigate many of the costs that may otherwise diminish the initial benefits of a Linux migration. This is an often-overlooked aspect of Windows-to-Linux migration. Often analysis of Windows over Linux and vice versa includes an assumption that the change would happen overnight or at least over a short period of time.

There are two approaches to running Windows applications locally on Linux. The first is to try to replace the Windows API and run the Windows application natively on Linux. This is the most ambitious solution because you are trying to run Windows applications without having the intended operating system present. The other way to run Windows applications on Linux is to run a whole instance of Windows in a virtual machine.

Wine—Replacing the Windows API

The technology for replacing the Windows API is called Wine, which is a recursive acronym that stands for *Wine Is Not an Emulator*. The definition of *emulation* is *the imitation of another*, and from the prospective of the application, which is interacting in the same ways as the original Windows API, it is often classified as such. Wine is an open source implementation of the Windows API on top of X and Unix. Wine functions as a compatibility layer that does not require Microsoft Windows, but can use native Windows Dynamic Link Libraries (DLLs). The Wine project was started in 1993 and was sparked by the idea of Sun's Wabi, which was used to run 16-bit Windows applications under Sun Solaris operating systems. Initial discussion involved potentially porting Wabi to Linux, but that never happened. At that point the Wine Project was born. The intended benefit of Wine is that Windows binaries can execute Windows programs without the presence of the Windows operating system and, depending on the software licensing terms, without a copy of Windows. Wine is both a translation layer and a program loader that enables you to run Windows applications on POSIX-compatible operating systems such as Linux. Figure 10.2 shows this approach to replacing the Windows operating system and just keeping the Windows applications.

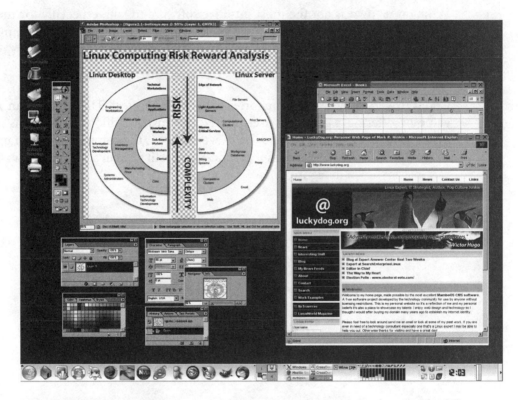

FIGURE 10.2 Wine is shown running Microsoft Excel, Internet Explorer, and Adobe Photoshop without a Windows operating system.

This approach would seem ideal and when Windows applications function as expected, this is a great solution. The risk of using Wine technology is that applications may not run with 100% fidelity of experience under Linux. You are also not running the application under the operating system as intended so you may be at risk of being rejected for support issues by software vendors who have developed and tested their applications for a targeted platform, Windows. Another detractor from running Wine is that applications are not able to take advantage of the normal point-and-click installation methods, Windows' graphical display environment, and other Windows tools that normally support Windows applications running natively. That is why there are a few commercial companies offering support around the Wine specifically adding value by improving the installation and configuration.

Commercial Implementations of Wine

Wine on its own is not the most intuitive software to run, especially for the new Linux user, but the core technology supplemented with support from commercial vendors can be an adequate solution for new Linux desktop users.

CodeWeavers

CodeWeavers is the leading supporter of the Wine project. They provide an added value by offering a graphical user interface to install Windows programs in the Wine framework. CodeWeavers CrossOver Office is the commercial program that wraps around Wine and makes it practical to install a small set of Windows applications, as shown in Figure 10.3.

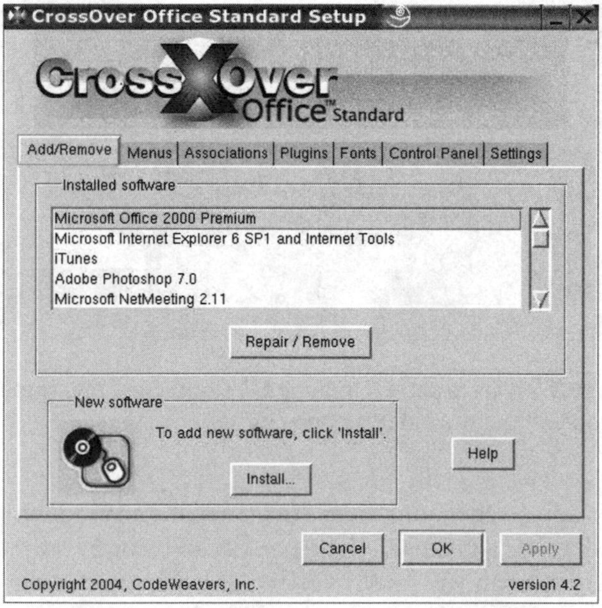

FIGURE 10.3 CrossOver Office is a commercial product paired with Wine that includes a graphical installer to ease the installation of Windows applications.

Support for Windows applications running under CodeWeavers is classified as gold, silver, or bronze, which indicates the expected level of support or end user experience expected for each application.

Gold medal applications install and run as you would expect them to in Microsoft Windows. CodeWeavers expect that their customers can use these applications on an everyday basis with good results, and only minor bugs. As of August 2005 there where 11 gold medal applications in the Codeweavers database:

Office Applications: Word 97/2000, Excel 97/2000, PowerPoint 2000, Word Viewer 97/2000, Excel Viewer 97/2000

Multimedia Applications: Quicktime 6, Flash Player 7

Specialty Applications: Chime

Silver Medal status is awarded to applications that install, and run well enough to be usable. However, in CodeWeavers testing, they find that these applications have significant bugs that prevent them from running flawlessly. As of August 2005 this included 31 applications.

Bronze medal applications install and run, and can accomplish some portion of their fundamental mission. However, bronze applications generally have enough bugs that CodeWeavers recommends that their customers not depend on their functionality. Some applications may be listed as "Not at all" or be unspecified in their database; these applications may not be verified to function even at minimal levels.

Transgaming

Transgaming was formed in 2001 with the intention of running DirectX games under Linux. The flagship Transgaming project, Cedega, provides an installer for running Windows games utilizing Windows Direct X direct hardware access to render 3D games on Linux desktop. They use the WineLib tools to load the Microsoft DirectX libraries for direct hardware access. Business users will likely not have a need for DirectX on Linux but educational institutions might have a call to access Direct X applications for rich multimedia learning applications.

There are a number of other projects that are using the Wine technology to run Windows applications. All focus on helping to integrate and enhance the desktop through the ability to run Windows applications without Linux, though at this time the use of Wine is a relatively risky proposition because each new product release may require additional tweaking to make it run as expected under Linux. The other thing to consider is that each application may need to be configured separately to run under Linux.

Analysis of Wine as a Business Solution

Wine would seem to be the ideal solution for many of your Windows migration needs and if the application runs as intended under Wine then you may have a logical way for Windows applications to be executed. The places Wine would be advantageous to a migrating user are those with a very small number of applications that run at an acceptable level as confirmed by testing. The advantage of the commercial version of Wine is that it helps to install Windows applications and gives some level of support guarantee for specified applications. CrossOver Office, for example, provides a way to facilitate the install dialogue on the Windows desktop, in essence replacing the Add and Remove Programs control panel that Windows users are used to, as shown in Figure 10.4.

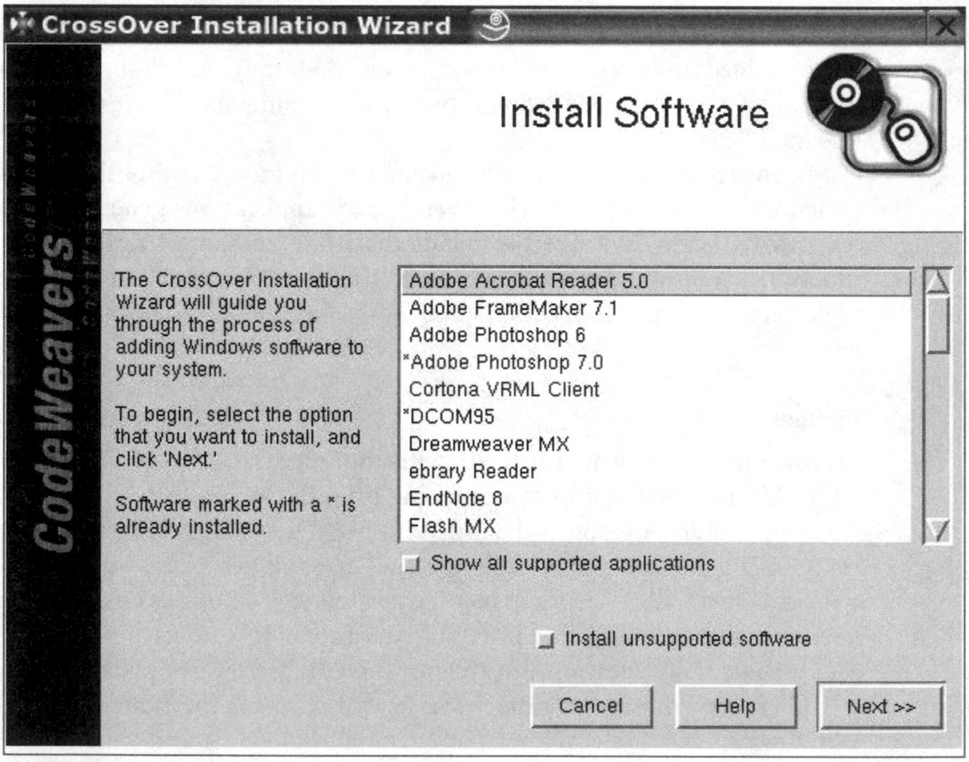

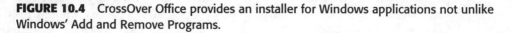

FIGURE 10.4 CrossOver Office provides an installer for Windows applications not unlike Windows' Add and Remove Programs.

Wine might have a better use for enterprises as a porting kit of sorts, where a company specializing in Wine support services, like CodeWeavers, could rewrite a particular Windows application to run under Linux with an acceptable level of compatibility. The cost for this type of porting might make sense for very complex applications that otherwise would be much more expensive to completely rewrite. The other place where a Wine implementation makes sense is in the ability for Wine to execute Windows-only plug-ins under Linux browsers. Running the CrossOver Office product can give you access to both QuickTime and Windows Media Player content by enabling you to run these plug-ins in your Linux browser.

Walt Disney Feature Animation is an example of a Wine success story. Disney started exploring alternatives to its expensive SGI Unix workstations. After doing a comparison between a number of platforms including Windows, FreeBSD, Mac OS X, and Linux, they decided to move to Linux. There were two obstacles to Linux adoption: certain Web plug-ins for Web browsers and a reliance on Photoshop for certain production tasks. Figure 10.5 shows Adobe Photoshop running on the Linux desktop.

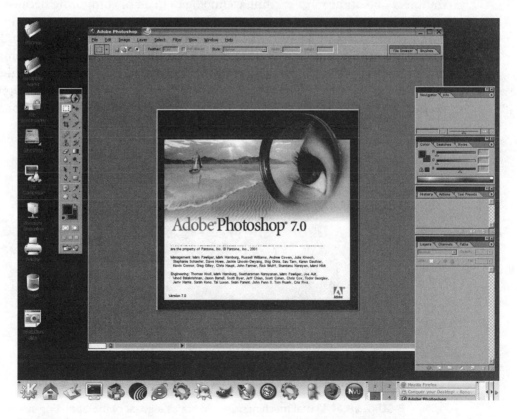

FIGURE 10.5   Adobe Photoshop is supported by CodeWeavers for their customer Disney.

This was one of those situations where Wine made sense; a very limited number of Windows applications needed a migration path and function at adequate levels under Linux. This also helped Disney overcome a final obstacle to Linux adoption, and they were able to move away from an expensive-to-license Unix platform running on costly proprietary hardware.

Virtual Machines to Run Windows PCs

Virtualization means to be created, simulated, or carried on by means of a computer. Virtualization, in the context of this discussion, is the creation by a piece of software of a virtual PC that can host a "guest" operating system. The guest operating system runs inside this virtual machine. However, in this approach the hardware, particularly the processor and memory, are being *double-taxed*. This means that the virtual machine must execute the program that creates the virtual PC, the operating system, and applications that run underneath the application. Virtualization is one of the most exciting technologies in all of computing because it can and does enable users to run multiple copies of operating systems on the same hardware. In cases where server or desktop resources are underutilized and users would benefit from applications that run on two different operating systems, they can do so through using virtual machines. The advantages of virtual machines are that they can create sandboxes on the same hardware which maximize capital investments but still insolate one system from another. Figure 10.6 shows conceptually how a virtual machine interacts with a Linux desktop session.

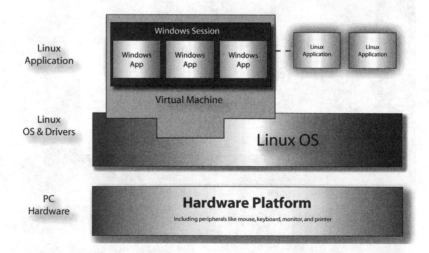

FIGURE 10.6   Virtual machines usually run as a guest of the operating system or are controlled by a layer called a hypervisor that acts as a traffic cop for system resources allocated to the machine and operating system. Hypervisor is a generic term for a facility that provides and manages virtual machines.

The trend for running virtual machines is driven by a desire to get maximum utilization of computing resources. As modern PCs have progressed, processing, storage, and memory have become plentiful, and from a space and power usage standpoint, it can be economical to use virtual machines to reduce costs in the data center or on the desktop.

This trend is not limited to running Windows sessions on Linux, but extends to running Linux on Windows, as was mentioned in a April 2005 article in *Information Week*. Microsoft CEO Steve Ballmer announced increased investment of effort into Intel Virtualization Technology, to enhance and simplify corporate re-imaging of desktops [Rooney, 2005]. It could be speculated that this could result in more of a true multiuser capability in Windows and an extension of its capacity to serve multiple desktop sessions from a single server.

Microsoft Virtual Server 2005 is virtual machine software that enables end users to run multiple Windows operating systems concurrently on the same hardware. This approach could be used to test compatibility for applications before moving from one version of Windows to another, to host legacy Windows NT applications on newer Windows Servers, consolidate server functions onto fewer physical servers, or to be used for software demonstrations. Future versions of Windows operating systems, like the highly touted Microsoft Longhorn/Vista, are speculated to include virtual machine technology. Microsoft, by its actions, is validating this as a trend. Its Achilles heel is that it may only support its own operating systems or may even not embrace a heterogeneous model that would allow both Linux and Windows to run on its products. Additionally, running Windows servers in virtual machines may help separate critical servers from less important ones, but it still leaves you with the same considerations of security, stability, and vendor lock in. What this technology may do for Windows users who want to migrate to Linux is provide a way for them to consolidate Windows systems on a fewer number of servers to make room for Linux in the enterprise.

This may even open the possibility of running Linux sessions on Windows though virtual computing. Leader VMware, a wholly owned subsidiary of EMC, currently has the market cornered for this capability.

Commercial Virtual Machine Software

There are a growing number of software virtualization solutions, especially in the Linux server space, as server consolidation across a hot-swappable and blade architecture becomes more desirable. Virtual machines can be provisioned through software rather than by procuring and installing software on individual machines. Though there are a wide variety of solutions oriented at storage and mainframe provisioning, there are only two technologies that would be acceptable solutions for desktop migration of Windows to Linux, VMware and Win4lin.

VMware

The VMware virtual machine software is typically used for server consolidation but by virtue of its ability to run any Windows operating system on Linux, it is often considered a Windows-on-Linux desktop solution. VMware can run many instances of operating systems designed to run on the IA32 or IA64 platform. This makes VMware a logical choice for running test environments with tens if not hundreds of configurations, rather than setting up individual machines which is expensive in the forms of both time and hardware. VMware is often used to simulate conditions that might be encountered by end users by varying the memory footprint and networking setup. Figure 10.7 shows the Virtual Machine Settings for VMware which are used to set the parameters of the virtual machine.

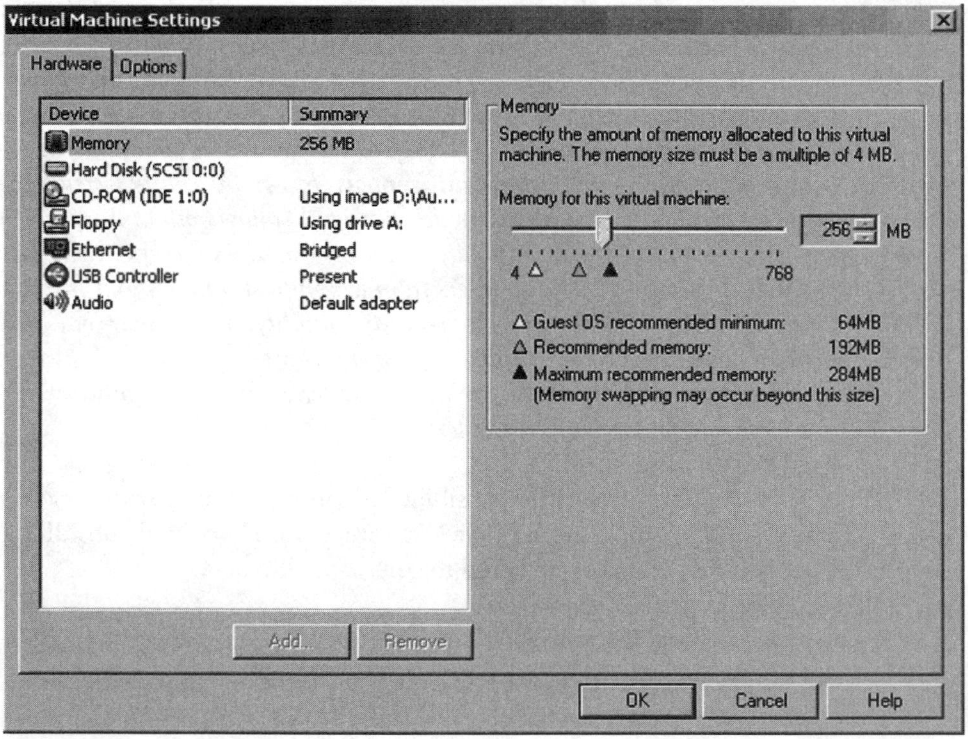

FIGURE 10.7   VMware can allocate resources to the guest operating system through a control panel.

VMware is a highly effective virtual machine infrastructure for software and infrastructure testing environments. It also has a server product line that allows for server consolidation on Intel/AMD hardware including Solaris on x86. VMware's aim is to provide solutions for testing and sales demos and for IT system administrators supporting cross-platform applications including Netware, Linux, Solaris, and Windows. VMware Workstation is also appealing to training organizations that have to provide multiple operating systems from one system and that desire to reset those operating systems back to a baseline after the class is over. Figure 10.8 demonstrates this functionality, where a snapshot of the system can be loaded using the VMware *Teams* function, which can load templates of guest operating systems.

FIGURE 10.8   Choosing a system snapshot under the VMware Teams feature to load a Windows 2000 installation under Linux.

As these features are very impressive the solution is obviously geared to the needs of someone whose specialty exceeds common desktop productivity users. VMware Workstation is a unique product that better serves desktop software testers, allowing them to stage preproduction test environments. This would also be useful to the Windows organization evaluating migration to Linux. VMware Workstation could be a solution for testing and staging Linux operating systems on Windows workstations because Linux sessions could be tested without disrupting productive Windows users. Also, this would give IT decision makers an idea of how Linux installations stack up side by side with Windows. VMware is a very robust virtual machine solution that far exceeds the needs of most desktop users. It includes the following features that are ideal for software testing but would be more than necessary for legacy Windows application migration.

Teams: Users can connect virtual machines with configurable network segments to test multitier applications like those delivered across the Web. Also, using the Teams feature, testers can throttle bandwidth and network conditions to test how applications would perform under those conditions. Browser-based applications are easier to deploy; software, developing, and testing is very difficult. With VMware you can create the whole client server environment on one machine. Many enterprises don't have time to invest in a number of machines to create test environments. Finally, from a resource perspective, VMware Workstation includes a page-sharing feature so that users can share memory pages across virtual machines, reducing memory requirements.

Multiple Snapshots: The VMware snapshot feature can take multiple snapshots of a system at different periods. Regression testing is much easier because going to the point before a bug was introduced can be accomplished by loading previous snapshots.

Cloning: Cloning of virtual machines allows developers to share virtual machines between themselves. You can share not only the whole environment, but also the delta between a virtual machine's base image and the current one, a useful feature when debugging.

In addition to these features, ideal for simulating and duplicating certain user environments, VMware supports guest 64-bit platforms from both Intel and AMD as of spring 2005. For Linux users there is a gtk2-based interface and support for the following additional 32-bit operating systems as a guest or a host: Red Hat Enterprise Linux 4, Red Hat Linux Advanced Server 3, SUSE Linux Enterprise Server 9, SUSE Linux Pro 9.2, Mandrake Linux 10, Sun's Java Desktop System, and Novell Linux Desktop 9. For developers porting applications to these new platforms, VMware could provide an easy-to-administer and flexible test environment.

One useful tip for those users who dual boot both Windows and Linux: you can use VMware to boot from a preinstalled raw disk image. This is helpful for users who want to run the same image simultaneously, for example to run Windows as a process under Linux and have the opportunity to run Windows from the installation they ran natively. This works in reverse as well; a user can execute a virtual machine running a Linux image under Windows. In the scope of an enterprise-wide Linux installation this is not practical, but for a decision maker who has to draw comparisons between the two operating systems or a systems administrator who has to support a mixed operating system environment, it can be a very useful tool.

Analysis of VMware

VMware is one of the most robust and widely deployed virtual machine technologies. VMware is also backed and owned by storage giant EMC. It has a much wider focus than helping to enable Windows on the Linux desktop; its value is really in maximizing the value of hardware by taking full advantage of system resources and offering a disaster recovery and rollback mechanism that is of value in a wide range of applications. Overall VMware is a good technical tool, though it is not geared to seamlessly interact with the other desktop environments. For example, when running VMware the cursor becomes captive of the guest operating system. To release the cursor to the host operating system you must use the Ctrl+Alt keys. File systems are held in separate virtual disk systems or raw images on separate partitions. Users who may need Outlook or Lotus Notes for collaboration wouldn't have the ability to easily access office documents in Linux from a client running on Windows without running some type of file server.

Win4Lin

Win4Lin is focused on the integration of Windows and Linux desktops. The definition of *integration* is a *combination, or the process of combining into completeness and harmony*. In running Windows on a Linux desktop, this is a unique and most desirable way to integrate applications. Win4Lin runs the Windows operating system as a Linux process, sharing resources like any other Linux program. Win4Lin shares the most desirable characteristics with both Wine and VMware. In terms of filesystem integration, the Windows filesystem is stored within the Linux operating system hierarchy in the same format as the Linux files, as you can see in the Konqueror file manager shown in Figure 10.9.

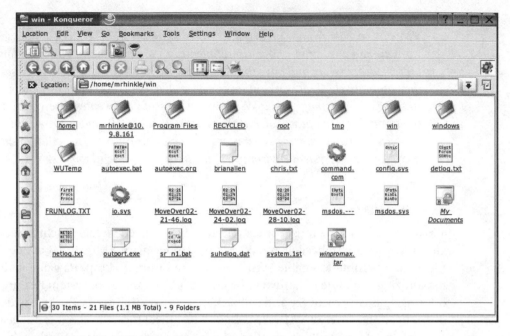

FIGURE 10.9   The Windows filesystem is stored in the user's home directory under Linux when using Windows 98 under Win4Lin 9x.

This allows for the files in the Windows image to be maintained with the same tools that Linux is maintained, allowing administrators to use a consistent set of tools. A Windows session comes into focus on a mouse click just like any other application on the desktop, so there is uniformity in desktop behavior. Additionally, Win4Lin can run only as the user who has permission to run the Win4Lin session. This is true for most all of the Windows-on-Linux solutions, but the special value this brings is that a native installation that becomes compromised by a virus or a worm can compromise the whole PC, whereas running a virtual machine limits the potential damage of a worm or virus to the environment in which it is executed. In a network where spyware, worms, and viruses are running rampant, a virtual machine provides a layer of insulation between system failure and malware.

Because applications and operating systems run as a guest process under Linux, you will find many hot key combinations will not work for Windows or its applications if they are already mapped in Linux. This is true for the Ctrl+Alt+Del sequence used to reboot Windows 98. If you press these keys when running Windows as a guest under Linux, you will likely get the Linux desktop logout dialogue. You should consider this and investigate alternative ways to accomplish these tasks, or consult the documentation for your desktop environment to disable these key sequences on the Linux desktop so that the guest operating system can take advantage of them.

Win4Lin Product Family

The Win4Lin product family is maintained by Win4Lin, Inc., and is a unique way to run Windows applications on Linux. Win4Lin is a commercial product that can execute the whole Windows operating system as a Linux desktop program. There are both single-user versions and multiuser versions of Win4Lin, just as there are single-user versions of Windows and multiuser versions of Windows (Microsoft Terminal Services).

Win4Lin 9X

Win4Lin 9X, as the name implies, runs Windows 95/98/ME operating systems on Linux. Win4Lin 9x works by enhancing the Linux operating system with open source kernel enablers or hooks. Once the Linux host is enabled, Windows sessions can be run on the users desktop. The kernel hooks and low resource requirements for Windows make this one of the fastest ways to run Windows applications on Linux. Also, the Win4Lin boot routine doesn't require a hardware check like running Windows natively, so rebooting the system may take only a few seconds. One other reason why Win4Lin is a good desktop choice is that you can cut and paste from Windows to Linux and vice versa. For example, text from an email received via Microsoft Outlook could be copied and pasted into a document opened natively on Linux.

Win4Lin Pro

Win4Lin Pro is a different architecture than Win4Lin 9x; there is no need to patch the kernel and there is no technical dependency for Windows to run on a certain processor architecture. Win4Lin Pro, like Win4Lin 9x, does store the files for Windows on the filesystem, and system functions like the mouse are integrated into the desktop environment. By moving the mouse out of the Win4Lin window the Linux host system can reacquire the cursor. Win4Lin Pro also has a much broader open source heritage than Win4Lin 9x, as it is based on the QEMU CPU emulator.

Win4Lin Terminal Server

Win4Lin Terminal Server is the same basic program as Win4Lin 9x or Win4Lin Pro in that it runs Windows operating systems. The difference is that it can run multiple Windows operating systems on a Linux server, with one Windows session per user. This would be analogous to the way Windows Terminal Services can run multiple instances of Windows on a Windows server. The difference here is that in a Microsoft model you need to license the server, applications, and client access with very little competition; you also are limited to running just Windows applications. In a Win4Lin Terminal Server model you can run both Linux and Windows applications in a whole redisplayed desktop environment in a thin client model that will be discussed in Chapter 11.

Analysis of Win4Lin

Win4Lin products are a boon to the enterprise with incumbent Windows sessions and software that desires to recycle its existing PCs and start moving forward with Linux desktops. The Win4Lin products are ideal for running Windows on the desktop, but when it comes to peripheral support, like synchronizing PDAs or accessing other specialized hardware, the solution is usually not adequate. The situation that makes the most sense is where an enterprise is willing to migrate to Linux core productivity applications to address 80 percent of their computing needs but also have a variety of legacy applications that they wish to continue to use. Going forward it is inadvisable to continue to invest in Windows applications if your goal is to only institute open standards and have more choices on your desktop, but the reality is that for the foreseeable future there is value in using Windows applications, whether they be in the manufacturing or medical field or necessary for government or education. In these cases, you may find a long and useful life hosting Windows clients on Linux to facilitate these applications while introducing new open source applications and operating systems throughout your enterprise.

CONNECTING TO WINDOWS TERMINAL SERVICES ON LINUX

The ability to execute Windows applications remotely is becoming a more popular and important function for enterprise users, especially partnered with redisplay and management framework, Citrix. The terminal services model is old hat to Unix and Linux users because from the beginning they have benefited from a multiuser architecture where applications could be executed remotely. However, this functionality was not added to Windows until more recently. Distributed or mobile users might have a dependency on Microsoft Terminal Services, but don't fear, you can either continue to use Windows Terminal Services or replace them with alternative technologies.

Microsoft Windows Terminal Services

Microsoft Windows Terminal Services is the extension of the Windows Server architecture that allows multiple users to run an application on a server using a thin client device or piece of software. There are three components that make up Windows Terminal Services. The first is the Terminal Server extension for Microsoft Windows servers. This server processes all the data it receives from the client and redisplays the data back to the client. The communication of this data takes place over the second component, the *Remote Desktop Protocol* or RDP. It is optimized for relaying the data quickly over a network using port 3389 by default. The third component is the client on which Windows is the Windows Terminal Services client; on Linux there are other options.

Windows Terminal Services is Microsoft's answer to running current Windows sessions in a terminal server or client server desktop computing model. At the very least it offers a way for system administrators to remotely connect to Windows servers. You may choose to use Windows Terminal Services to offer a full desktop application or just to publish individual applications to client machines through the use of Citrix. Figure 10.10 shows the interface for configuring the Terminal Services RDP settings.

You also have to consider licensing the Windows Server that hosts the Terminal Server sessions and Terminal Server Client Access Licenses (TSCALs), all which

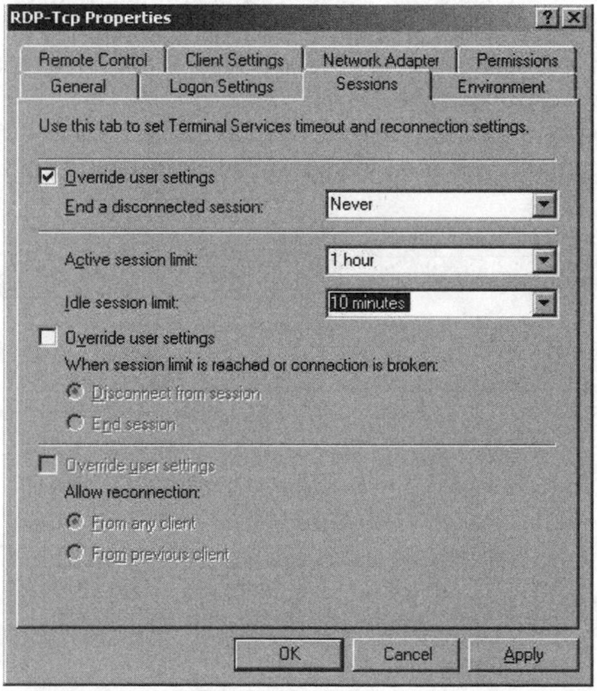

FIGURE 10.10 The screen for configuring RDP for Windows Terminal Services.

can be additive to the cost for your terminal services. Some desktop PCs may include client access licenses but Linux desktops will not; you will need to take measures to ensure that you are able to legally license the session regardless of the platform you access from.

In the theme of recycling, or at least leveraging existing IT infrastructure, Linux desktop users can access their legacy Windows applications by virtue of Windows Terminal Services they have already invested in, but going forward it doesn't seem to be consistent with an open source strategy.

Windows Terminal Services via RDP

Connecting to Windows via the Microsoft Remote Display Protocol, or RDP, is one way to execute Windows applications on Linux. This method has its merits as there is good likelihood that many of your needed Windows applications will run as expected. You will also have the benefit of running Windows on a native installation. There are a couple of solutions for connecting from Linux to an RDP server. One way is to download a client called *rdesktop,* which is an open source desktop connection tool for Linux and Unix. The other popular tool for connecting not only to RDP capable servers but to VNC servers is the KDE Remote Desktop Connection Tool, shown in Figure 10.11.

If you are behind a firewall and are accessing a Windows Terminal Services server from a Linux desktop you will need the KDE Remote Desktop Connection

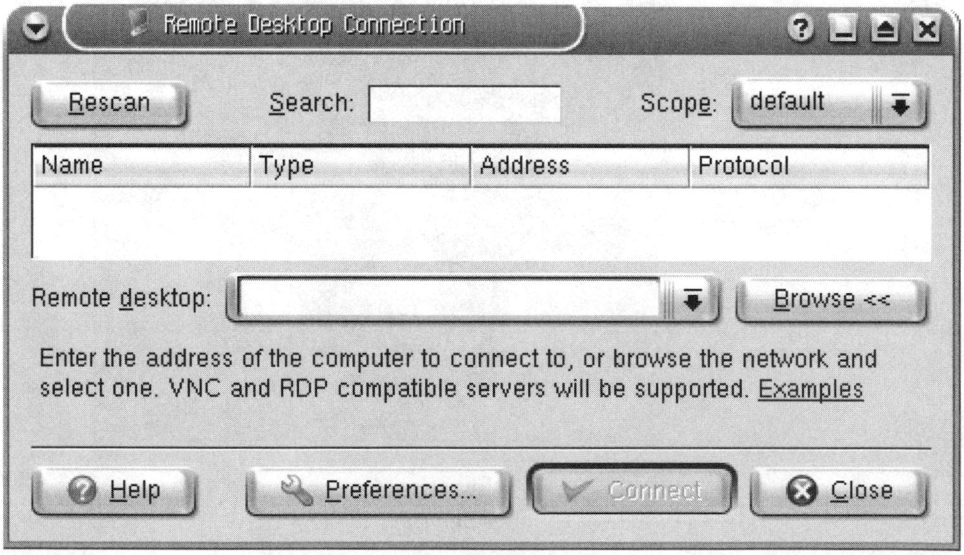

FIGURE 10.11 The KDE Remote Desktop Connection tool is an open source client that can be used to access Microsoft Terminal Services from Linux.

tool or rdesktop. If you are accessing your legacy Windows applications over a WAN or the Internet you should consider products that have stronger security.

Accessing Windows Applications via Citrix

Citrix is a Microsoft Windows–dependent framework for accessing Windows applications. Citrix is a complete management framework that can provide applications securely and over low latency networks. Citrix also supplies a Linux client to connect to Citrix servers via ICA, as shown in Figure 10.12.

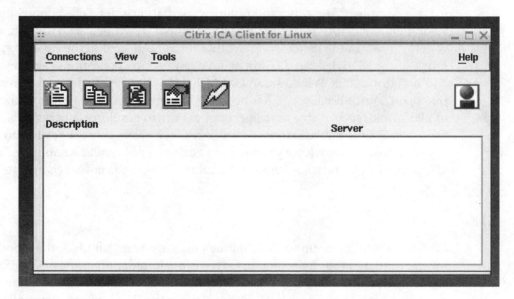

FIGURE 10.12   The Citrix ICA client for Linux.

Citrix, the company, has a large number of products all revolving around accessing Windows systems. The best advice for someone who has already invested in Citrix or Windows Terminal Services is to continue to use that system through its usable life to meet your needs. If you don't have a Citrix or Windows Terminal Services installation, then it would seem counterintuitive for someone who is trying to break dependence on Windows to invest in a Windows server and services to support it.

PORTING WINDOWS APPLICATIONS TO LINUX

Porting applications to Linux is likely to involve one of the potentially biggest costs associated with an enterprise Linux migration, and it is both unlikely and impractical for many organizations to port all their legacy Windows applications to Linux at once. The way to approach porting of applications is to start with the premise that you want to address user needs as well as be practical by leaving yourself the option to take that application to any variety of users desktops on most any platform.

QT

QT is a complete C++ application framework that includes a class library and development tools for cross-platform development developed by Trolltech. QT is widely known in the Linux world because it has been used in the development of much of the KDE desktop. QT can be used to develop applications that run under X11 on Linux, Unix, Windows, and Mac OS. QT is licensed under commercial and free/open source licenses and has been used to develop applications on a number of platforms. Open source developers can use QT to develop applications with the QT Open Source Edition as long as they offer their entire source code to end users. If you choose to not release your source code, then you would be obligated to use QT under the commercial license and would be liable for licensing charges to Trolltech.

GTK+

GTK+ is a multiplatform toolkit. In much the same way that QT is the foundation for the KDE desktop environment, GTK+ is the foundation of the GNOME desktop environment. The GTK+ toolkit is based on a set of libraries for handling desktop requests and building interfaces. You can use the GTK+ to support applications written in not only C/C++ but also in Perl and Python. GTK+ also works well with the GNOME environment and, in conjunction with the Glade GUI builder, you can develop desktop applications in much the same way you do using Microsoft Visual Studio and Visual Basic. The GTK+ interface, unlike Visual Basic, is multiplatform, so you may even choose to build cross-platform applications with the toolkit, though it is likely you will want to consider Web services as a solution going forward as long as users have network access.

REALbasic

REALbasic is a commercial cross-platform software development environment sold by REAL Software that is geared at taking Visual Basic programs into the REAL basic framework and then allowing you to port those programs to Windows, Mac, or Linux without the need for the Microsoft.Net framework. This is an example of a type of tool that could help you in the long-term move to a non-Microsoft-dependent environment; the downside, though, is that it does take you in the direction of a single source vendor once again where you may develop a future dependence on REAL Software

wxWidgets

wxWidgets is an open source C++ GUI framework for developing cross-platform applications on Windows, Linux/UNIX, or Mac OS. The wxWidgets framework has been used since 1992 and has been used to author a number of applications you may be familiar with, including AOL Communicator and Forte Agent, and many you haven't. wxWidgets also is in use by reputable companies like AMD and Xerox USA, and education institutions including Dartmouth Medical School.

Web Services

As computer users have access to a greater level of network access and the need for collaboration grows, there needs to be a fluid way to access applications and share data. The Web is the logical place to do this as it is already the most popular standards-based collaborative environment with a global reach. Interoperability is relatively good as long as Web designers, browser applications, and other access tools adhere to standards. To date, the focus on Web services has been for the most part on push technology, with information being pushed to Web surfers and information being pushed back from surfers in the case of form submittals. This will continue to be a popular way to compute.

One of Microsoft's acquisitions in 2005 was that of Groove Technologies, an online collaborative platform that allows end users to communicate through instant messaging, share files, collaborate in a common environment, and share task-specific program components. While this is a Windows-only technology, it is a good example of the power of networked collaboration and the emergence of a new model, Service-Oriented Architectures (SOAs). Service-oriented architecture is a collection of services that communicate with each other to transfer data or provide other interactive transactions. Information from these services can be sent back and forth using SOAP (which originally was an acronym for Simple Object Access Protocol but that now refers to the method for sending Web Services messages). This is a discussion that could be a volume onto itself, but when investigating a new application you may want to consider whether that application can adhere to an SOA with a Web interface which will break any dependence on the client platform, leaving your options open for your desktop platform of choice.

Mono—A Microsoft .NET Alternative

Mono is a platform for running and developing standards-based applications specifically targeting .NET or Java frameworks. The Mono effort is lead by Novell, and the Mono project lead, Miguel de Icaza, is a Novell employee. The Mono project was born out of the need for providing additional tools to the GNOME desktop, but Mono applications can be executed on Linux, Mac OS, or Windows. The Mono project is worth investigating because it offers an open source alternative to .NET. The idea of Mono is to adhere to the same ECMA standards that Microsoft's .NET adheres to so there is a level of compatibility for .NET applications on Linux.

Web services seems to be the direction that many vendors are following as centralized systems accessible by pervasive technologies like Web browsers make real sense. Strategically you should always weigh what is the best solution for the immediate future versus the best long-term strategic solution. Whenever possible, avoid solutions that have the potential to give you a reduced number of options and alternatives, as this cycle can lead to the pitfalls of vendor lock in and escalating licensing and support costs with no means to escape.

SUMMARY

The ideal situation is one where you don't need to run Windows applications on Linux and you can move to a Linux-only environment. This situation is going to be the exception rather than the rule in a business environment where the majority of desktop users are using Windows. Migrating Windows applications to Linux is a good bridging measure that allows you to move forward with Linux, taking advantage of competition among Linux desktop vendors to keep licensing costs low. Also, you can benefit from the security and stability of Linux, an operating system that has earned its stripes as a highly available security system. A financial windfall of this strategy is that as you move forward you can still leverage investments made in legacy Windows operating systems and applications which could continue to have a productive useful life for many years longer than they would running natively. Over time, as your Linux desktops become capable of handling all your computing needs, Windows virtual machines and applications running on solutions like Wine can be decommissioned much more easily than hardware machines that would require wholesale replacement. This phase-out approach to Windows is a practical way to address Linux migration. The desktop is likely the system in your organization that is both the most pervasive and potentially most disrupted by change. It also can be one of your biggest costs, if not from the aspect of hardware and software licensing, then in maintenance and labor.

OTHER RESOURCES

- Wine—*www.winehq.com*
- CodeWeavers—*www.codeweavers.com*
- Transgaming—*www.transgraming.com*
- Win4Lin—*www.win4lin.com*
- QEMU—*http://fabrice.bellard.free.fr/qemu/*
- VMware—*www.vmware.com*
- Remote Desktop Sharing—*http://docs.kde.org/en/3.4/kdenetwork/krdc/*
- rdesktop: A Remote Desktop Protocol Client—*www.rdesktop.org*
- Microsoft Terminal Services 2003—*www.microsoft.com/windowsserver2003/ technologies/terminalservices/default.mspx*
- Trolltech—*www.trolltech.com*
- GTK+—*www.gtk.org*
- Glade GUI Builder—*http://glade.gnome.org/*
- REAL Software—*www.realsoftware.com*
- wxWidgets—*www.wxwindows.org*
- Mono—*www.mono-project.com/*

REFERENCES

CodeWeavers, Case Study: Walt Disney Feature Animation (June 2003). Available online at *http://ftp.codeweavers.com/pub/crossover/case_studies/DisneyCaseStudy.pdf*, May 10, 2005.

Rooney, Paula, "Microsoft to Launch, License Virtualization for Longhorn," *Information Week* (April 20, 2005). Available online at *http://www.informationweek.com/story/showArticle.jhtml?articleID=160911794*, May 10, 2005.

11 Thin Client Computing

In This Chapter

- Thin Client Overview
- Thin Client and Desktop Implementation Migration Strategy
- Redisplay Software
- Summary
- Other Resources

Thin client computing as it pertains to desktop Linux, is a new take on a relatively old idea. In the days before personal computing there were few computers (which were very expensive) and they needed to be shared by many users. At that time, computer users shared expensive computers through the use of *dumb terminals*. In the mid-1990s Sun and Oracle both preached the virtues of thin clients as the successor to the business PC. That vision has yet to be realized.

The feasibility of this architecture is closer today then ever before, though, through a combination of factors. Bloated PCs are a breeding ground for viruses, spyware, and other security holes. A tightly controlled thin client computing model offers a number of benefits including fine-grained administrative control, security, and high availability. If you choose to move forward with a thin client solution, you should first understand the architecture, so that you can make decisions on how best to introduce a new solution or one that is just complementary to your existing infrastructure. These are the differences between architectures that supplies a wholesale productivity desktop to diskless workstations or just secure access to data stores or legacy Windows applications as a complement to the Linux desktop.

The following discussion will focus on the architecture of a thin client installation including the discussion of a three-tier model encompassing server, redisplay, and client. Once you understand the technology you can focus on where an implementation might best make sense for you and what vendors and open source technologies might provide you with the features you need.

Architecture: Thin client computing relies on client-server architecture. The server is the engine that drives the applications to the thin client. The thin client can be a piece of hardware or software that redisplays activity from the server. Clients can be dumb terminals, PCs, or even handheld devices.

Implementation: Perhaps one of the biggest benefits of thin client infrastructure is that it can be staged and tested well before it reaches the desktop.

Redisplay and Client Solutions: There is a whole gamut of commercial redisplay software and hardware solutions to complement a thin client installation. Once you understand the benefits of a thin client network and the requirements of your user base, your implementation decision will range from do-it-yourself methods to buying solutions that are preassembled to finding a middle point which involves a little of both.

Thin client systems can cut hardware and maintenance costs because they reduce the investment in hardware at the user desktop and because administrative personnel can benefit from a single point of deployment. The mindset that every administrative worker has to have a fully functional desktop may not be correct for your circumstances. Users with repetitive tasks that have modest computing needs may be better served by a thin client computing model. Thin client computing shifts the focus of the hardware upgrade cycle starts to move from desktop to server.

THIN CLIENT OVERVIEW

Most every desktop computer user today is familiar with the PC computing model where user applications are executed on the local PC and data is stored on the local hard drive. This type of computing model is sometimes referred to as *thick client* computing when extended to the network with file or print serving. An alternative to this model is thin client computing, where applications are executed on the server and information is redisplayed over a network to dumb terminals or thin clients that offer input and video display capabilities. This model was necessary when computer processing power was expensive and there was a need to share mainframe computers. However, as computer hardware prices fell the PC became ubiquitous, and subsequently the economics changed, allowing many users access to computers as part of their everyday jobs and/or in their homes. Despite the rise of the inexpensive x86 commodity PC, thin client computing is still alive and well for many who use client-server applications every day by virtue of the World Wide Web. Web services allow many applications that execute on the server to be redisplayed back to the PC via a Web browser. Many applications can embed a thin client viewer on the desktop to allow resources to be network portable. Linux, a multiuser operating system, is ideally suited to both power these thin client solutions as well as operate as an embedded operating system, because it can provide the necessary thin client tools in a small and efficient footprint.

Components of a Thin Client Network

Thin client architecture has at least three components or tiers: server, network, and client. The software components of a thin client network are an application server, a redisplay server, and thin client software. The server or application server is the engine that powers the system. In the case of desktop Linux users, that would be a multiuser server that serves either a full Linux desktop or a single or small contingent of applications. The redisplay server software is what pushes the display information to the end user's desktop. The redisplay server software can reside on the same physical machine or it may be separated out onto its own server or group of servers. The thin client software may be embedded software running on a stateless terminal or it could be a piece of software running on a traditional thick client desktop PC running Windows, Linux, Unix, or Mac OS. Figure 11.1 shows a combination of existing Windows Server technologies and desktops intermingled with Linux.

You can easily host all three parts of the network using Linux as the operating system of the application server. Linux can be the embedded operating system for the thin client device as well as providing routers and firewalls while running the network. You also can mix and match and use a combination of operating systems where an existing Microsoft Terminal Services installation can be accessed from Linux or a Linux server can be accessed from Windows thick client devices.

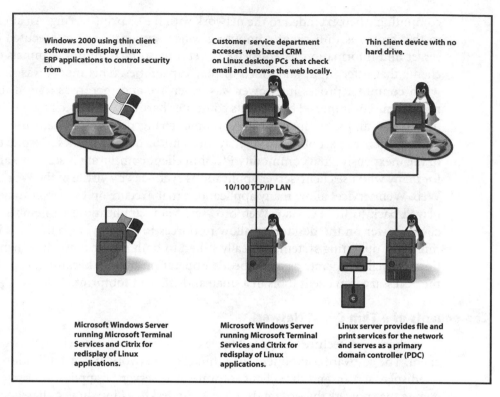

FIGURE 11.1 Sample architecture for a simple LAN-based thin client network may include both Windows- and Linux-based devices.

Server or Terminal Server

The Linux operating system has been developed as a multiuser system with the capability to serve virtual terminals, hence the terminology *terminal server*. Therefore many individual users can log into the server and use the server simultaneously. Individual user configurations can be limited to single applications or a full-blown desktop computing environment. In earlier chapters the modular architecture of Linux was discussed, including the fact that the graphical user interface X Windows was network transparent. X Windows can be the transport to remote display desktop sessions in a thin client environment. Additionally, Linux can allow administrators to limit permissions and grant access to certain applications based on these sessions. You can also limit permission to these sessions from remote machines based on IP address to further enforce security.

Network

The network requirements for thin client GUI implementations depend on a reasonable amount of bandwidth and low network latency to be suitable for everyday use. In a corporate environment, a 10baseT LAN can serve a number of users; as more users are added to the network you may need to monitor to make sure that your network can handle the two-way traffic of redisplay data coming from the server and user input coming from mice and keyboards. Linux server user sessions can be streamed to clients via the X.11 protocol and redisplayed by an X server residing on the client, though the protocol is network intensive and considered *chatty,* with lots of two-way traffic. In less than ideal situations, redisplay technologies can be utilized to improve performance by compressing redisplay data and limiting the screen refresh and redraw rates. Commercial technologies like Tarantella and NoMachine, as well as the popular open source solution Tight VNC, offer such solutions that compress this data and improve performance over X.11 traffic. Because programs are executed on the server, many of these redisplay technologies offer features to reacquire the session so that you can pick up at a point where the connection was severed. For example, a user who works from the office and from home can leave his session active at work and start at exactly the same place he left off at his home PC. In a case where a user runs a large number of queries against a database, reports could be run overnight and results returned to the user's desktop the next morning when the session is reacquired.

Client

Thin client software can reside on a PC or on a device designed for thin client applications, like the diskless workstations often called dumb terminals. These solutions normally provide a mechanism for video redisplay and input. Clients are normally stateless, so data and configuration data is limited or nonexistent. Therefore, if the client is damaged the loss is only in the operating software or hardware, while data and computing environments are preserved. Also, because information no longer resides locally, everyday occurrences such as employee moves and spilt coffee on machines are less disruptive. Replacing a desktop can be as simple as bringing in a low-cost thin client device and connecting it to the network, in contrast to a thick client that might need to have the hard drive imaged, applications reinstalled, and data replicated onto the new PC.

Advantages of Thin Client Networks

It's very easy to make a case for thin client computing from a systems management standpoint. Environments are easily standardized and costs for such systems can be considerably lower than traditional PC environments because the cost is in a server and inexpensive desktop terminals.

Reduced Cost of Desktop Computing Hardware

Thin client PCs usually only serve video and provide input functions. Because technology in these areas doesn't obsolesce as for thick client terminals, the useful life of the device can be many times longer than a traditional PC. Also, because storage is pooled on the server or on storage area networks (SAN), you can benefit from economies of scale rather than having to inefficiently provision storage at each user's desktop. Resources that were once dedicated to single users are now shared over a group; when a user is on a break, or "off the network," a second user can take advantage of those extra processing cycles. Mice and keyboards, monitors and video cards can provide a useful life that is much longer than the rest of the PC, and when they do break down they are relatively inexpensive to replace in comparison with other components like the CPU. Also, thin client servers can be scaled over a blade infrastructure in the data center, where servers can be added incrementally to expand computing resources without interruption to active users.

Centralized Management

Rather than process updates across individual desktop computers, administrators can process system-wide updates on the server. Updating software for many users can be taken care of with one simple installation. To evaluate how valuable this could be to your organization, speak to your IT help desk and ask them how much time they spend on the *SneakerNet*. SneakerNet is the time they spend walking around looking for cubicles to fix user PCs. Not only do they need to find the cubicle but they also need to bring parts, software, and tools to fix the PC. Thin clients are very low maintenance and most of the time formerly spent by administrative staff traveling to and from cubicles can be dedicated to improving the operating environment rather than maintaining it. If something does break, help desk personnel can open user sessions locally at their desks, make fixes, and then allow users to reacquire their sessions at their desks with no travel time required.

Desktop Portability

Because there is little or no personal data kept on thin client devices, users can pull up their computing environment from any network-connected thin client workstation. On the Sun Microsystems campus, users simply carry their employee IDs and embedded smart cards with them, and they can pull up their computing desktops at any Sun Ray workstation on campus, making it possible for employees to travel among connected campuses and pull up their work environments anywhere from a cubicle to a conference room. Sun also benefits by not having to have dedicated offices and workstations for all of their employees.

The same flexibility Sun illustrates on its campus can be applied to telecommuting when empowered by secure WAN redisplay solutions like Citrix or Tarantella. Workers at home can use thin client software on top of their PCs, securely, without the need to maintain a corporate laptop that can take abuse during the commute to and from work. Helping home users maintain their work computing environments can be very difficult for corporate IT departments. By maintaining the environment in the data center they limit problems associated with remote PC maintenance.

High Availability

In businesses where employee downtime has immediate and severe effects, high-availability solutions can save you money. For example, in an inbound sales center it is important that order processing and billing systems are highly available and redundant. During the time that employees' computers are down, they lose productivity. Thin client installations can economically use redundant processing and storage to avoid failures. Consider that in many businesses employee downtime due to IT troubles can be much more expensive than the cheap IT systems that they saved a relatively small amount of money on.

Rapid Deployment

Imagine the case of a large florist whose normal business increases tenfold for Mother's Day, or a large catalog company that quadruples its workforce for the Christmas holiday season. Rapid expansions like this can cause IT headaches. A relatively pain-free solution would be to simply add user accounts to a server farm and plug thin client devices, such as those provided by thin client leader Wyse or Sun's Sun Ray, into Ethernet ports in a cubicle versus installing operating systems and software on hundreds or thousands of PCs. In the case of natural disasters, such as the hurricanes in the southeastern United States, work environments housed safely in hardened telecom facilities could serve displaced workers at a network-connected facility while flood waters receded and infrastructure in the affected areas was repaired.

Standardization and Implementation of Standards

Because the computing environments are virtual, it is easy to standardize the configuration so that all users have the same environment. This is valuable for training purposes as well as in accounting for computing systems and software.

These are all compelling arguments for deploying a thin client environment. Even taken singly, each one has a common motivating factor: in each case they would save organizations money through more efficient use of hardware and centralized management. This is especially true in environments with large numbers of task-based workers who have a relatively narrow breadth of needs.

Disadvantages of Thin Client Networks

Just as there are many advantages to thin client computing models there are also some limitations of thin client computing. For example, thin client devices are dumb terminals; they may not be aware of the addition of new hardware to the thin client because the actual computing and other configurations take place on the server. The caveats to this include the following:

Network Dependence: The biggest consideration for a thin client installation other than specific needs is the quality and bandwidth of the network on which it is delivered. LAN versus WAN delivery may also include considerations of security and encryption to prevent data from escaping the confines of the appropriate parties.

Portable Storage: Flash RAM storage devices that are easily carried around from PC to PC are not ideally supported in a thin client model. Software on the thin client would have to be able to mount the filesystem on the key back to the server filesystem so files could be shared between the two. From a security standpoint this is advantageous as it helps secure data, but it is not convenient for the desktop user to easily move files.

Printing: Because the printing configuration has to happen on the server you have two choices. Configure the print services to print to the appropriate network printer, or map that printing capability from the server to the local device. You may, depending on the technologies you use, be given the option to mount the printers back to a local printer connected to the thin client PC. This is not common but it is possible; the thin client device's USB port or parallel port needs to be available through some mechanism to print back to the locally attached printer, otherwise the best you will be able to do is run a local print daemon and print the information available to that, which may be as basic as a simple screen dump or print screen.

Portable Devices: Portable devices like PDAs and cell phones that synch with personal information devices require synchronization via a USB port or a serial port which the local device may not provide.

When weighing the limitations of thick versus thin client computing, you need to determine if the advantages fit the needs of your end user. If your users require a fair number of peripherals, they may not be great candidates for thin computing. If you have a large number of transaction or task-based workers who don't have a lot of variety in their work or need a large number of peripherals, you probably have a good case for moving to a thin client desktop.

THIN CLIENT AND DESKTOP IMPLEMENTATION MIGRATION STRATEGY

Many organizations that are looking at migrating to Linux on the desktop still think in terms of thick client PCs. The unique aspects of a Windows-to-Linux migration make thin clients an attractive option. The staging of the new Linux infrastructure can be accomplished with no disruption to the end user. Also, replacing the PC with a new thin client device is a simple process that only takes a few minutes at each desktop. Not only does this model offer a relatively easy way to stage and implement a new desktop environment, but it also frees users from their desks. Imagine developing a presentation with supporting documents in your office then walking, with no laptop or CD, to a conference room where there is a thin client terminal to pull up that same information. This model obviously offers flexibility within the office but it also could be extended to any Internet terminal so that employees could telecommute easily or do remote-site presentations for clients, partners, and other employees.

Trial and Pilot Programs

Thin client computing trials need not permanently change any PC other than the server you use to serve Linux. You could simply allow Windows users to receive their Linux sessions on Windows. That way they can dip their toes in the waters of Linux without leaving their Windows security blanket. There are many ways to do this without making irrevocable changes to your infrastructure.

Windows Trial Separation

Changing from Windows to Linux seems to bring an element of finality that makes IT strategists wary because they feel like there is no going back after the change is made. You could do a trial separation to start to gain acceptance of a new operating system by using a Live Linux CD to temporarily convert Windows systems to Linux workstations. This could also be a great way to combat an enterprise virus infection that may normally leave many users without any working environment.

Live Linux CD Connection to Linux Servers

ON THE CD

The Knoppix CD-ROM included with this book has been presented from the viewpoint that it could be a trial CD-ROM for thick client PC users, but in a thin client trial you could use that same Knoppix CD-ROM as a way to temporarily repurpose systems. This would leave the existing thick client installation intact while allowing users to test the Linux environment both locally and by connecting to a Linux terminal server through one of the redisplay clients included on the Live Linux CD.

X Windows on Windows

As discussed earlier, the X Windows system is not tied to a single physical terminal; it can be displayed on any network-connected appliance that has a local X server. You could use a Windows X Server to connect to the Linux server and export the display as an application on your Windows desktop. This solution is more practical when you need access to a single application over the LAN, but is yet another option for starting to integrate Windows and Linux environments.

VNC

Technologies based on the Virtual Network Computing (VNC) software is another option to the X Windows on Window solution, there are both secure and unsecured options for VNC, but VNC does benefit from the compression of the X protocol.

These are only a few options that may be helpful in piloting a thin client installation. You may find that there are more robust commercially available options like Tarantella and a new player, NoMachine.

Phased-in Approach to Migration

It's not practical for most organizations to take a giant leap to a new operating system. However, there will probably be inflection points in the enterprise software life cycle that will make phased-in migration more appropriate. Examples of transition opportunities to start deploying Linux thin client desktops may include the addition of new employees, the end of useful life for thick client workstations that could be easily converted to thin clients, or the time of renewal for your existing operating system. In some cases it may not be necessary or practical to switch all of your systems at once, but by introducing Linux, even gradually, into the desktop computing mix you begin to add a powerful and frugal tool to your infrastructure.

Recycle Thick Client Workstations

One very frugal approach to thin client computing is the recycling method. This method works well when repurposing machines that have outlived their useful life as desktop PCs. Despite having slower CPU speeds, less memory, and limited storage space, these machines are far from useless. The Linux Terminal Server Project, an open source community project, helps breathe new life into what may have been thought of as useless hardware. This organization offers a blueprint for re-purposing aging PCs into thin client devices. They also outline how you could configure a terminal server to serve desktop environments. Granted there will still need to be some investment in servers to drive the LTSP, but in comparison to a thick client model, it's considerably cheaper than upgrading all the desktop PCs in environments when you look at the costs of five or more PCs for task-based users.

Sweet Spots for Thin Client Technology

Early adopters of thin client computing are those who have relatively modest computing needs in the terms of their desktop computing complexity. They typically need their systems to be highly available, cost effective, easy to manage, and possibly mobile. The following functional groups and organizations meet this profile.

Point of Sale (POS)

One of the areas where thin client computing has seen success is in Point of Sale (POS) applications. POS is an ideal solution for thin client because retail often is required to expand and contract with seasonal shopping. Additionally, it's important that these applications are highly available because down time can cause sales losses. IBM understands this and has launched a line of POS systems that run on an end-to-end Linux footprint. Levin Furniture, a western Pennsylvania furniture retailer, is implementing thin client technologies because they like the idea of mobile desktops that can run their Java-based sales applications from any workstation in their showroom. This makes it easier for them to speak to customers but still pull up SKUs and order information from their warehouses.

Call Center

Call centers are places where thin client computing excels. Often, call center employees have specific repetitive tasks. The centers also typically have large numbers of users with identical needs. Many times they require workstations to be shared and used by employees who may sit in a different seat every day. Because of this need for mobility, it's advantageous for them to have a customized but mobile desktop. In a thin client environment users could simply login from any access point and have access to their data and all the tools they need to complete their jobs.

Schools

For all the same reasons that thin client computing makes sense in the call center, it makes sense in schools. Computer users, in this case students, share workstations among as many as seven or eight users a day. Linux has robust user management systems that can be used to create individual virtual desktops for students or to create sessions that rebuild automatically as classrooms turn over groups of students. In the Netherlands, systems integrator Siceroo has helped numerous schools provide this type of infrastructure through Linux and Sun Ray. Each student gets a *smart card* that holds his or her authentication data. Their computer labs are equipped with Sun Ray thin clients. When students arrive at class they can start their work at any stateless Sun Ray workstation. They can then remove their smart card and walk to the teacher's desk and pull up their work via a similar thin client terminal. Schools who are often the beneficiary of donations of older computing equipment are ideal candidates for the Linux Terminal Server Project, or actually an offshoot of this program, the K-12 LTSP for schools.

Branch Infrastructure

Branch infrastructure that employs many small offices where an onsite IT person makes little sense could benefit greatly from a thin client configuration. Thin clients employed at the local branches would have fewer "moving parts" that might break, while complex desktop environments could be maintained in the data center and distributed over the network to remote offices. Additionally, a standard server and user application configuration makes it easy to create uniform implementations that can be easily installed and maintained across a large number of branches. This cookie-cutter and plug-and-play type model has become popular in retail organizations.

Linux Terminal Services

There is no product under Linux called *Linux terminal services* as there is under Windows. Microsoft Terminal Services is the engine that drives Microsoft's version of thin client computing. This is add-on functionality that came after the advent of the Windows server. Linux, on the other hand, was architected in a way that has always lent itself to a terminal server model, where multiple users shared the resources of the operating system either sequentially or concurrently. There are a variety of ways to build a thin client network. At the heart of the network will be a Linux server or a Microsoft Windows Server redisplaying to Linux clients. Figure 11.2 shows the three tiers of a Linux redisplay model using Tarantella, an enterprise redisplay product. Note that you have quite a few options for any tier including running the Windows applications as a guest operating system on Linux. This is a good compromise for enterprises dependent on Windows but no longer willing to host Microsoft servers.

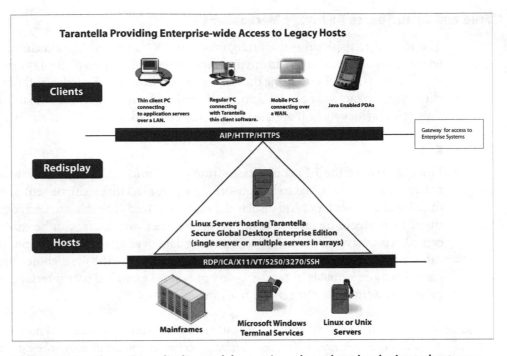

FIGURE 11.2 Three-tier redisplay model can mix and match technologies to best serve your user needs.

Keep in mind that thin client usage in a Linux environment may lend itself to recycling and extending the usable life of hardware that is ailing from limited storage or processing power. You need not recycle though, you can just as easily buy low-cost thin client terminals for desktops that may even have a master configuration control panel and inventory-tracking application.

REDISPLAY SOFTWARE

Redisplay software facilitates the transactions of the processing being executed on the server and the redisplay to a thin client device or software program. Redisplay software normally focuses on compressing and securing traffic between the two endpoints in addition to the obvious task of communication. Some redisplay technologies even allow you to publish a single application rather than a whole desktop environment.

Free and Open Source Redisplay Mechanisms

The idea of redisplay is not a foreign concept to Linux and Unix technical users, who are used to working in an environment where the graphical display can be easily separated from the machine that serves the applications. The idea and use of thin client technology is as old as Unix itself, and with Linux being a cousin to Unix, those similarities make it apparent that Linux is an ideal thin client engine.

X.11

You can forward the X.11 connections from your Linux desktop or server to another machine. X.11 is designed to be network transparent so that it can be sent to any terminal and the user input and display data can be shared. The thing to consider is that the X.11 protocol on its own is not secure and network traffic can be easily intercepted. You may want to consider tunneling data over an SSH connection. In most cases, for a good user experience, X.11 is not going to be the ideal choice for redisplay; it is more valuable in accessing servers when a graphical user interface needs to be used to administer the remote machine.

Most any Linux distribution you use will likely come with an X Windows system from either X.org or XFree86. These X servers are what displays the data to your screen. If you are using Windows, you won't have an X server so you will need to get one to be able to export the X Windows session to the PC. The free software options you have are somewhat limited, but the Cygwin/X software is a port of the X Window System to the Microsoft Windows family of operating systems. This is free software. There are also commercial PC X servers available such as WRQ Reflection Suite, Starnet Communications X-Win32, and Labf's WinAxe.

Linux Terminal Server Project (LTSP)

The Linux Terminal Server Project is not so much a redisplay technology as an add-on for Linux servers to facilitate a Linux thin client network. The LTSP has taken the initiative to partner a lot of technologies together to be a resource for putting a thin client network into practice. In fact, there is no redisplay technology that is unique to LTSP, the difference is just in the presentation. The primary focus is to take diskless workstation nodes and have them connect to the Linux server. LTSP also provides documentation and resources for having the nodes boot from the network so that there is no need to keep any information on the PC. It also cooperates with projects like the EtherBoot project that helps create ROM images that can be downloaded and executed from the network so that PCs can be converted into diskless workstations without the need of a boot medium like a CD or flash card. The instructions for booting a small footprint operating system right into memory makes this is a very efficient and fast way for terminal to become active. You could also buy a commercial thin client device like one made by Wyse to accept connections for your thin client installation. The LTSP is an example of how a community project takes many of the technologies mentioned in this book and provides a recipe that makes it possible for someone with limited capital resources to provide a robust desktop computing experience.

LTSP has been partnered with a Linux distribution to give schools a turnkey Linux installation and simple management framework through the K12 LTSP project, which is based on Fedora Linux and then combined with the LTSP tools. The K12 LTSP is an excellent example of open source collaboration, where a number of products and technologies can be combined to form a vertical solution. The end results are impressive, as schools that are strapped by tight IT budgets are also often the recipient of donated PCs that are no longer of use to the original owner. As productivity workstations they may be too slow for today's computer use, but converted into a thin client device they may have a long and useful life. In conjunction with the project, a very active user community has emerged that shares information and background on how they are using the K12 LTSP to spark ideas in other installations. Of all the thin client technologies mentioned in this book, this is perhaps one of the most popular and is absolutely free except for the cost of your bandwidth and your time.

VNC

VNC stands for Virtual Network Computing and is remote control software that allows you to view the activity on the server with a client or viewer. VNC was developed in the AT&T Laboratories in Cambridge, England, and has become a widely used solution for graphical redisplay on Unix systems. The VNC protocol is a more compressed protocol then X and can be used to redisplay from a variety of platforms. For example, VNC server can be run from a Windows desktop and redisplayed to another Windows desktop or to a Linux desktop. It is sometimes used by Windows administrators as an alternative solution to Windows remote access products like PC Anywhere or GoToMyPC (now owned by Citrix). VNC is supported by Real VNC, a company that was formed by the researchers who worked on it at AT&T labs. There are also spin-offs of the VNC project like TightVNC, which is an enhanced version of VNC that includes additional features, optimizations, and bug fixes. The bottom line is that TightVNC is working to provide better performance through improved compression algorithms and other tweaks.

Commercial Applications

There are many types of free and open source applications that can be used to build a thin client network. There are also many commercial offerings that offer features that go beyond those of community-hosted distributions. You should also consider whether you leverage existing infrastructure like Windows Terminal Service or move to an architecture of Linux application servers running Linux applications. You can even take the middle ground of keeping an end-to-end Linux footprint supplemented with Linux machines running on virtual machines that host Windows.

NoMachine

NoMachine is a relative newcomer to the redisplay market with their NX Server products. NoMachine is extremely fast because of a very good compression algorithm that shrinks the X.11 protocol considerably and then allows it to be redisplayed over even low bandwidth latent networks. NX Server runs on Linux and Solaris operating systems and can be used to redisplay to a variety of operating systems including Windows, Linux, and Mac OS. Figure 10.3 shows a Linux desktop being redisplayed via NoMachine to a Windows XP desktop.

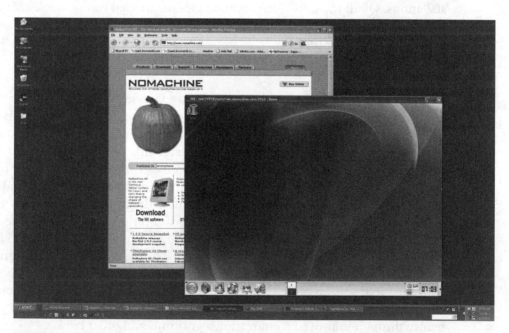

FIGURE 11.3   NoMachine redisplaying a Linux desktop to Windows XP.

NoMachine has taken a suite of Open Source technologies, combined them with commercial tools and provided a network computing solution that can rival Citrix and others. NoMachine works by providing performance enhancements at three levels:

1. **Compression**—NoMachine's NX Server takes the X protocol and compresses the data that would be very high bandwidth running on X Windows without enhancement. The compressed NX Server traffic, by virtue of being compressed, allows it to work even on a 9600 baud modem.
2. **Reduces Network Round Trips**—Exchanges of display data and user input are minimized to decrease round trips or network *chattiness.*
3. **Adaptable**—NX Server can adapt to bandwidth conditions, throttling performance to match network conditions.

NoMachine does release the core libraries of its software to the open source community under GNU General Public License, though its product combines with some proprietary bits to create its commercial solutions. Keep in mind, when comparing a NoMachine solution to Windows RDP, you can use a cost-effective Linux server rather than a Microsoft Windows server that may have a higher cost of acquisition. All functions of the NX Server infrastructure are executed remotely using SSH, and all communications take place under standard SSL public-key cryptography. This way all NoMachine network traffic takes place securely. NoMachine can also be used with a Window Terminal Server by acting as a redisplay server and passing information between the server and the client with a layer of security and performance and no need for Citrix.

Tarantella

Tarantella was the company that once owned SCO Unix until it divested its operating system to Caldera. In May 2005 Tarantella announced that it would be acquired by Sun Microsystems. This was an attractive match because its flagship product, Tarantella Secure Global Desktop, adds management and redisplay capabilities, along with security, to access applications from a wide variety of host operating systems including Windows, Unix, and Linux. This technology will not only help Sun provide technology for pervasive computing from all platforms but will also help bolster its mobile computing strategy.

Tarantella redisplays data using the Adaptive Internet Protocol (AIP), which receives data from hosts and then converts that information so it can be redisplayed natively or over a Web protocol (http or https). Where Citrix does this from

Windows to other hosts, Tarantella provides a solution for heterogenous enterprises that want to access legacy mainframes, Windows servers, and other systems from Linux and Windows desktops as well as mobile devices. Figure 11.4 shows a Tarantella redisplay server running as it fits within an enterprise architecture. Tarantella can be hosted on Linux or Sun Solaris.

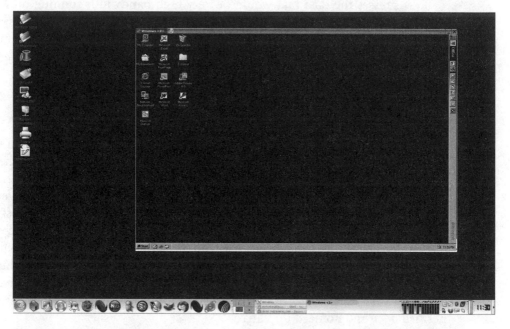

FIGURE 11.4 Tarantella Secure Global Desktop as it fits into an enterprise infrastructure.

Another benefit of the Tarantella authentication is that it can authenticate against any LDAP-compliant directory server (though Microsoft AD and Sun One are the only ones formally supported). Tarantella can play a role in providing a homogenous desktop environment, redisplaying legacy systems to the Linux desktop.

GraphOn

GraphOn is the maker of the Go-Global family of products that can publish Windows or Unix applications to a number of guest operating systems. Its value seems to be in publishing single applications in an ultrathin client configuration. A Windows application could be published to a Linux desktop or vice versa using GraphOn products.

This is not an exhaustive list of thin client software products but covers many bases for deciding what products and solutions could complement a thin client computing environment. Many of these technologies provide an extra layer of security or functionality that is unavailable using a free alternative.

Where some solutions are true thin client and redisplay solutions, some technologies are splitting the difference, allowing a hybrid between thin and thick client. These solutions have the advantages of fast local processing with centralized management. One such technology, produced by Shaolin Microsystems, preaches these virtues under the moniker of "fit clients" rather than a thick or thin client.

Shaolin Microsystems

Shaolin Microsystems makes a product called Aptus that they bill as *fit client* computing. The way Aptus works is that the computing is done on the local machine but all filesystems and applications are mounted over the network. What happens in the fit client model is that the clients boot via PXE boot ROM, an Aptus boot disk that works similarly to the Knoppix Live CD-ROM or a boot loader. Data and applications are housed on the server and mounted over the NFS protocol but still utilize local CPU and memory. The difference here is that by caching information locally a fit client can continue to work even in the event of a server crash. The Aptus solution is a very unique product that brings many of the benefits of thin client computing, including centralized management, but still offers a degree of independence to the client PC.

ON THE CD

Linux Terminal Servers Powered by Windows on Linux Solutions

In Chapter 10, the idea of running Windows applications under Linux was introduced as a way to maintain legacy applications. This idea of extending Windows use on the desktop could translate to a thin client computing mode where Windows and Linux applications could be paired with a redisplay technology like X.11, VNC, NoMachine, or Tarantella hosted on open source architecture to provide an alternative to Citrix.

Win4Lin Terminal Server

Win4Lin Terminal Server is derived from proven technologies developed for Unix-based operating systems over the last 15 years. Users boot Windows 95/98/ME as an application running under the X Window System for Linux. By utilizing the robust services of Linux, Windows performs remarkably well, with increased stability and security. Executing Windows in the application space of Linux helps protect the system from Windows application failures. Layering Windows over the Linux filesystem and networking facilities enhances performance, robustness, and security.

The Win4Lin Terminal Server technology supports a single-user desktop environment, a multiuser server-computing environment, and a remote virtual network-computing environment. Users who use Linux as their primary environment yet still require access to critical Window applications not available natively on Linux will find Win4Lin Terminal Server to be stable and have a better response time over native Windows. Examples of applications with which users report having better performance when using Win4Lin Terminal Server over native Windows or VMware are Microsoft Office, Intuit Quicken, Lotus Notes, and Adobe FrameMaker and Acrobat. Windows can run within a Linux window manager (e.g., KDE or GNOME) on the user's desktop or in full-screen mode on a separate virtual terminal.

Technology Overview—Win4Lin Terminal Server

Executing Windows under Win4Lin Terminal Server provides a number of additional benefits. The Windows installation is easily created, backed up, replicated, and restored. Common Windows corruption problems are either avoided or easily recovered from the point of failure. By providing tight integration with both the Linux filesystem and network stack, there is no need to create separate partitions or configure additional networking services. The Win4Lin Terminal Server software package consists of a set of server processes, kernel loadable modules, and drivers. These facilities combine to create a tightly integrated environment between Linux and Windows. The server processes provide mappings that enable Windows applications to utilize the underlying facilities of the Linux filesystem, networking services, and access to other devices such as the display, keyboard, and mouse. The "enabled" kernel and drivers implement low-level interfaces that define a virtual machine environment that supports the execution of Windows applications. This results in lower system overhead, higher performance, and ease of use.

The Win4Lin Terminal Server package enables Linux to deliver Windows application services over a network. The Linux server executes Windows applications under Win4Lin Terminal Server and uses the remote display capabilities of the X Window System to display applications on the users' desktops. The product uses redisplay technologies to deliver the application to the end user's terminal or workstation.

Win4Lin Terminal Server supports multiple users. Each user has the ability to start a Windows session and receive its own set of processes. Shared drivers support and manage access to the system services. Special kernel hooks (kernel loadable modules that add functionality to the kernel and help to enable the OS for Win4Lin Terminal Server) are implemented to provide virtual memory management services to the VM process as well as special context switch processing and privileged instruction emulation required for Windows. The server processes provide mappings that enable Windows applications to utilize the underlying facilities of the Linux filesystem, networking services, and access to other devices such as the display, keyboard, and mouse. Windows installs and executes transparently on the native Linux filesystem. No special filesystems or file types are required.

Increasing the flexibility of how employees not only get access to critical information, but process, modify, and communicate that information any time, any where drives the adoption of server-based computing in the enterprise. Providing users with information, files, and tools from any network-connected device, wired or wireless, dramatically increases their productivity and efficiency.

The combination of Linux with Win4Lin Terminal Server provides an extremely affordable alternative for users to continue to use their existing Windows licenses and hardware with no loss of application support or performance. When Win4Lin is deployed in a server configuration, the overall cost per user is even more dramatically reduced as installations can take advantage of thin-client technologies and centralized administration of Windows applications.

Win4Lin Terminal Server will run on a LAN as well as in a high bandwidth WAN environment. Several factors make the likelihood of server-based computing (Network Computing) success more promising than efforts in recent past. The first argument for enterprise adoption of server-based computing rests on squeezing out dollars at the desktop. Desktop support is labor intensive. Keeping a desktop productive requires software updates, call center support, hands-on technician support, and user training across a spectrum of functionalities, beyond what a user needs for the job at hand in many cases. Centralizing application management and administration reduces the cost of ownership and increases the flexibility and time-to-update for new user services and applications.

Win4Lin Terminal Server is designed to run on high-performance, low-cost Intel-based servers. Win4Lin takes advantage of the flexibility an open server offers. This solution allows you to easily customize your computing environment to meet your business needs. Enterprises will no longer be held hostage by closed feature sets or anticipation of future releases to solve today's problem. Win4Lin Terminal Server gives you options as to what applications you deploy. It also allows you to leverage the strengths of two operating systems: Linux and Windows.

With server-based computing, client devices, whether thick or thin, have instant access to business-critical applications hosted on the server. This means improved efficiency when deploying business-critical applications. In addition, server-based computing works within the current computing infrastructure and current computing standards, and with the current family of Windows-based offerings. This means improved returns on computing investments—desktops, networks, applications, and training. The end result: server-based computing is rapidly becoming the most reliable way to reduce complexity and total costs associated with enterprise computing.

VMware ACE

VMware ACE is an enterprise desktop management solution that focuses on provisioning and standardizing desktops in virtual machines that can be distributed to remote PCs in a totally secured desktop environment. This allows IT managers to provide a trusted remote PC, albeit virtual, to remote workstations. In this model virtual machines could be distributed in a locked-down environment, blocking access to devices like CD drives and printers. This provides a trusted desktop resource outside the control of an IT administrator but with the assurance that the virtual PC will not be an unsecured conduit into the enterprise. VMware ACE is being billed as a way to consolidate Windows desktops in the data center in much the same way Win4Lin Terminal Server is, and like WTS it can be paired with redisplay technology, though the sessions can take up a greater resource footprint to run the same type of hosted Windows session.

Thin Client Hardware Devices

There are a number of manufacturers that make thin client workstations as well as management software to help configure them to connect to the appropriate servers. Many of the thin client solutions use an embedded Linux operating system, as is the case in the HP t5515 thin client, while you could make your own thin clients out of commodity and recycled PCs. There is a competitive market for these devices. The following vendors are all trusted makers of thin client devices:

Wyse: Wyse is the world's largest supplier of network-centric computing solutions. It offers a range of devices that can service Linux thin client networks. It also specializes in software (Wyse Rapport®) that can manage desktop devices.

Neoware: Neoware, like Wyse, makes both thin client devices and software. Its software and devices are comparable to those of Wyse. Neoware differentiates itself as an aggregator of thin client technologies. Over the last several years it has acquired not only small niche players but IBM's NetVista hardware division.

Sun: Sun makes a very innovative line of thin client devices that are designed for Unix redisplay; these devices also include the ability to authenticate using a smart card.

HP: HP is another source of thin client devices. It has a full line of thin clients that use both embedded Linux and embedded Windows software.

The benefit of using a thin client vendor is not only in the procurement of hardware but also in the opportunity to learn from its expertise in installing and designing thin client networks.

SUMMARY

Users love their PCs and love the control they have over their desktop computers. A switch to Linux might be an administrator's dream but a knowledge worker's nightmare. If you have done a thorough needs analysis before moving from one platform to another, you should have an accurate idea of the real need of the end user versus the perceived need. That needs analysis should also provide the guidance you need to decide if thin client computing is a good fit for your environment.

Today's computing industry has become a race for more processing power at the cheapest price. For enterprises looking to reduce the cost of desktop hardware without sacrificing performance, thin client computing can significantly enhance these users' computing environments and the effectiveness of system administrators. It also gives you portability to take your computing environments from one desktop to another or to allow remote access to sensitive data without leaving your servers unprotected. This additional layer provides flexibility but can also provide security by adding another gateway with limited scope into your enterprise.

OTHER RESOURCES

- Tarantella—*www.tarantella.com*
- Citrix—*www.citrix.com*
- VNC—*www.realvnc.com/*
- Tight VNC—*www.tightvnc.org*
- GraphOn—*www.graphon.com*
- Sun Ray—*www.sun.com/sunray/*
- Linux Terminal Server Project—*www.ltsp.org*
- Etherboot—*http://etherboot.sourceforge.net*
- Windows Server 2003 Terminal Services—*www.microsoft.com/windowsserver 2003/technologies/terminalservices/default.mspx*
- K-12 Linux Terminal Server Project—*www.k-12Ltsp.org*
- Cygwin X—*http://x.cygwin.com/*
- X-Win32—*www.starnet.com/products/*

- WinAxe—*www.labf.com/winaxe/index.html*
- WRQ Reflection—*www.wrq.com/products/*
- Shaolin Aptus—*www.shaolinmicro.com/product/aptus/*
- Win4Lin Terminal Server—*www.win4ln.com*
- VMware Ace—*www.vmware.com/products/desktop/ace_features.html*
- Wyse—*www.wyse.com*
- Neoware—*www.neoware.com*
- Sun Ray Thin Clients—*www.sun.com/software/index.jsp?cat=Desktop&tab=3&subcat=Thin%20Clients*
- HP Thin Client Devices—*http://h18004.www1.hp.com/products/thinclients/index_t5000.html*

12 Additional Resources

In This Chapter

- Web Sites
- Mailing Lists and Forums
- Usenet News
- Consultants
- Summary
- Other Resources
- References

You should now have a good overview of the capabilities of the Linux desktop and have the tools to research and make a decision on whether a new platform and its complement of open source software is the right solution for your organizational or personal computing needs. Linux has grown and continues to grow through a community made up of developers, companies, governments, and other groups, as well as of individuals, all of whom are looking to help Linux and their own interests. This collegial attitude among Linux users creates a sort of global village, where despite the language you speak or country in which you live, it is likely you will find someone willing to help you become successful with your Linux installation. Many of these resources wouldn't exist without the ability to communicate effectively and cheaply via the Internet and include the following:

Web Sites: There are a number of Web sites dedicated to Linux that provide both documentation and interactive help free of charge to those seeking Linux knowledge.

Mailing Lists: Mailing lists are one of the oldest and most effective ways to ask questions and give feedback. Many open source projects rely heavily on mailing lists for development discussion, feedback, and user support.

Usenet Newsgroups: Usenet news is one of the oldest forms of communication on the Internet. This giant bulletin board is a global forum for discussions and archives of those discussions.

Users Groups: As mentioned in earlier chapters, Linux Users Groups can be an invaluable source of information and resources for installation and other expertise.

Consultants: Many enterprises today use consultants to solve their knowledge gaps whether those gaps are in IT, manufacturing, or some other aspect of a business.

There really is no shortage of information available to the resourceful user who has the ability to search the Web effectively. However, sometimes it is good to have a guide to Linux attractions on the Web, especially when a search for "Linux desktop" in Google yields a whopping 30,400,000 results.

WEB SITES

Probably the best place to find information specific to a problem you have is to use Google to search for that *specific information* on the topic you are trying to solve, but if you are looking for information on a general topic then it is helpful to have a guide. If you are looking to build your knowledge of the Linux desktop and find a support structure that is only a Web browser away, then frequenting the Web sites listed in this section is a good way to build your own expertise and to find information relevant to your desktop Linux issues. Many of these Web sites offer a Real Simple Syndication (RSS) feed that you can subscribe to, to quickly browse headlines for information relevant to you and your enterprise.

The Mozilla Firefox browser offers the ability to read RSS feeds right in your Web browser. When you visit a Web page with an RSS feed you will see an orange icon with arced lines in the lower right-hand corner of your Web browser. You can click the icon to bookmark the feed and then read the articles via your Bookmarks menu in Firefox.

LinuxQuestions.org—*www.linuxquestions.org*

LinuxQuestions.org is a user-supported Web site that revolves around forums where Linux users can pose questions about their Linux problems and receive answers from fellow Linux users. There are over 150,000 registered users and well over 1 million posts discussing topics ranging from software to hardware compatibility to *newbie* questions for those who are not yet familiar with Linux. LinuxQuestions also sports original content and reviews of Linux products such as Linux distributions, books, and magazines. If you are looking for a friendly environment to pose a question about the Linux desktop, this is an excellent free resource.

There are numerous discussions on this Web site that might be helpful to someone migrating from Windows to Linux. The interactive forum format also allows you to expand upon the question and ask for additional clarification. Here are some examples of articles that might be helpful to someone researching migrating Windows to Linux:

- "Configuring XFree86 for a Nonspecific Linux Distribution." Available online at *http://www.linuxquestions.org/questions/answers.php?action=viewarticle&artid=16*
- "Newbies' Guide to the Small Home LAN." Available online at *http://www.linuxquestions.org/questions/answers.php?action=viewarticle&artid=316*
- "Samba and SuSE Linux as a PDC." Available online at *http://www.linuxquestions.org/questions/showthread.php?s=&threadid=273458&highlight=samba*

DesktopLinux.com—*www.desktoplinux.com*

DesktopLinux.com is a blog-type Web site that is a good source of Linux desktop news. The blog format is a collection mainly of links to other Web sites peppered with original content submissions from the DesktopLinux reader community. There is also a very active Linux reader Web site with many timely and relevant posts and links to issues that affect enterprise Linux desktop users. Examples of content found on this site include the following:

- "Red Hat unveils multipage document viewer." Available online at *http://www.desktoplinux.com/news/NS8900220249.html*
- "Guest Editorial: A Constructive Critique of Debian Linux." Available online at *http://www.desktoplinux.com/articles/AT7588639943.html*
- "The Best Free Desktop Linux . . . and How to Make It Better." Available online at *http://www.desktoplinux.com/articles/AT3135712364.html*

Linux Documentation Project—*www.tldp.org*

The Linux Documentation Project (LDP) is a volunteer-driven documentation project tasked with maintaining documentation to supplement the Linux experience. The LDP offers a number of types of documentation:

Guides: A guide is typically the longest type of document that focuses on a subject matter area. For example, one guide is a Linux dictionary that might help with your new Linux vocabulary.

FAQs: FAQs or Frequently Asked (and answered) Questions have been popular since the early days of the Internet. The LDP FAQ section seems to be the most dated and widely flung source of information. Check the dates of FAQs because they may be less relevant than when they were first published.

HOWTOs: The Linux HOWTOs are, as the name implies, detailed instructions on *how to* accomplish certain tasks or troubleshoot problems.

Man Pages: Man pages are the text-based help pages for Linux commands used on the system console that are available by using the *man* command followed by the name of the command with which you need help.

All documentation is available under the GNU Free Documentation Licenses, so you are welcome to incorporate these documents into training manuals for your staff as long as you maintain the license.

Examples of documentation that would benefit a migrating Windows-to-Linux user include the following:

- "Introduction to Linux, A Hands-on Guide." Available online at *http://www.tldp.org/LDP/intro-linux/html/index.html*
- "Samba Authenticated Gateway HOWTO." Available online at *http://www.tldp.org/HOWTO/Samba-Authenticated-Gateway-HOWTO.html*
- "The Linux FAQ." Available online at *http://www.tldp.org/FAQ/Linux-FAQ/index.html*

Linux.com—*www.linux.com*

Linux.com is part of the Open Source Technology Group, which is a collection of IT-related sites including NewsForge and Slashdot. In the Linux community these are without a doubt some of the most popular Linux Web sites. Linux.com is designed to be a resource to help provide a collection of resources to make your Linux experience a success. You will find articles like the following there:

- "My Workstation OS: SUSE Professional." Available online at *http://distrocenter.linux.com/distrocenter/05/01/06/2023224.shtml?tid=127&tid=128*
- "A Killer App: PDF Editor." Available online at *http://applications.linux.com/applications/05/01/06/0612209.shtml?tid=49&tid=47*
- "Windows to Linux Migration Guide." Available online at *http://enterprise.linux.com/article.pl?sid=04/07/23/2219257*

NewsForge–*www.newsforge.com*

NewsForge, the Online Newspaper for Open Source, is also part of the OSTG network and is a portal for open source news and content that is complementary to Linux. Often, content that appears on Linux.com is linked from NewsForge. However, NewsForge is one of the best places to get up-to-date Linux information either through a browser or RSS feed. Examples of information that might be relevant to new users of Linux appear here via user-contributed articles or from the NewsForge editorial staff.

- "Securing Your Workstation with Firestarter." Available online at *http://www.newsforge.com/article.pl?sid=04/12/20/1737201*
- "Building a Distro." Available online at *http://www.newsforge.com/article.pl?sid=04/12/22/1557226*
- "My workstation OS: My own." Available online at *http://www.newsforge.com/article.pl?sid=04/12/22/1624253*

Slashdot–*www.slashdot.org*

Slashdot is among the most popular Linux Web sites. The terminology *slashdotted* refers to the power of the readership of that site to overwhelm a Web site with traffic once a link is posted to the Slashdot front page. The Slashdot community is made up of Linux and open source enthusiasts who "metamoderate" or qualify content via an online voting system. The Slashdot Web site is very heavily driven by user feedback and submissions and often is a place to find heated reactions rather than objective information. This is a sharp contrast to sites that rely on unbiased journalism. Getting the Slashdot perspective and reading the feedback allows readers to obtain a wide variety of opinions on technologies, though they are seldom unbiased. Examples of discussions that may be of value to a migrating business desktop user include the following:

- "Linux + Windows Single Sign-On." Available online at *http://linux.slashdot.org/linux/05/01/05/1336224.shtml?tid=172&tid=201&tid=106*

- "SLES9 vs. Windows Server 2003 in a Windows Network." Available online at *http://linux.slashdot.org/article.pl?sid=04/10/23/199202&tid=190&tid=163&tid =143&tid=201&tid=218*
- "Linux Desktop Migration Cookbook from IBM." Available online at *http://linux.slashdot.org/article.pl?sid=04/12/17/1951219&from=rss*

Freshmeat–*www.freshmeat.net*

Freshmeat is a portal that maintains the Web's largest index of *Nix and cross-platform software. Freshmeat plays host to thousands of applications, many released under open source licenses and providing a bazaar of applications that are freely downloadable for use on Linux and other platforms. Examples of articles and information that may be of value for enterprise Linux users are listed here:

- "Spam Filters." Available online at *http://freshmeat.net/articles/view/964/*
- "Computer Cloning with Partition Image." Available online at *http://freshmeat.net/articles/view/1375/*
- "Configuring a Transparent Proxy/Webcache in a Bridge using Squid and ebtables." Available online at *http://freshmeat.net/articles/view/1433/*

SourceForge–*www.sourceforge.net*

SourceForge is the world's largest repository for open source software development. While Freshmeat is an index for software, many of the projects stored on this Web site are sponsored by VA Software, which also owns the OSTG. SourceForge gives open source developers access to a storage and Web presence for their Open Source projects as well as collaborative software tools from VA Software. SourceForge.net offers presences for over 90,000 projects and boasts just under 1,000,000 registered users. Some of SourceForge's most popular open source programs that can be downloaded without royalties include the following:

- BitTorrent, a P2P file sharing utility that is often used to download free Linux CDs over a P2P network rather than from overworked ftp servers. Available online at *http://sourceforge.net/projects/bittorrent/*
- WebCalendar, a PHP application used to maintain a calendar for individuals or groups on an intranet. Available online at *http://sourceforge.net/projects/webcalendar/*
- PDFCreator, a program that can create PDF-format documents from virtually any Windows program. Available online at *http://sourceforge.net/projects/pdfcreator/*

SearchEnterpriseLinux–*www.searchenterpriselinux.com*

SearchEnterpriseLinux strives to supply IT professionals with the latest developments in enterprise Linux technologies, products, and industry issues. Their Linux-specific search engine provides targeted results on Linux developments from prescreened Web sites. Their Expert Technical Advice section provides question and answer sessions from Linux experts. In addition to these features, SearchEnterpriseLinux also provides newsletters, original articles, and links to the best information (in their opinion) on the Web that addresses enterprise Linux concerns. Examples of information and articles that can be found on the SearchEnterpriseLinux Web site include the following:

- "Mandrakesoft Trail Could Lead to Corporate Linux Desktop." Available online at *http://searchenterpriselinux.techtarget.com/originalContent/0,289142, sid39_gci1042384,00.html*
- "Ask the Experts." Available online at *http://searchenterpriselinux.techtar get.com/ateExperts/0,289622,sid39,00.html*
- "Ways to Choose Linux & Keep Microsoft, Part 2." Available online at *http:// searchenterpriselinux.techtarget.com/originalContent/0,289142,sid39_gci1041942 ,00.html*

DesktopOS–*www.desktopos.org*

DesktopOS is a relatively new Web site that was started in November 2003, but similarly to LinuxQuestions.org it supplies a number of forums that are particularly oriented to the transitioning Windows-to-Linux user. Most of the content takes the format of user testimonial and the site is a good place to find opinions on certain desktop Linux topics.

- "Two Years Before the Prompt:, A Linux Odyssey." Available online at *http:// www.desktopos.com/modules/wfsection/article.php?articleid=32*
- "Unofficial Ubuntu Starter Guide." Available online at *http://deskto pos.com/ubuntu-starter-guide/*
- "Linux Desktop and Operating Systems." Available online at *http:// www.desktopos.com/modules/newbb/index.php?cat=2*

MAILING LISTS AND FORUMS

Mailing lists and Forums are a common way to share information about a topic; most every open source project has at least one or two for both users and developers of these software packages. Most of these lists are can be subscribed to using only an email program, but some have a Web interface that will send an email to verify your intentions to subscribe. Archives are historical accountings of mailing lists and often migrate to forums; even if you come to the Linux scene late you may be able to take advantage of past Linux discussions by searching these archives.

USENET NEWS

Usenet news is a worldwide discussion system comprised of groups called newsgroups and, to carry the metaphor further, each post to a newsgroup could be called an article, though typically they are referred to as messages. Participants post to newsgroups with information that is then threaded into a discussion. Each thread typically indicates an exchange of information, often in a questions and answers format.

Google offers an interface for searching newsgroups. The Web site http://groups-beta.google.com/ indicates that the site is a beta product, but it's very good for searching Usenet posts through a Web browser.

Examples of Usenet groups that may be of benefit to the desktop Linux user include the following:

comp.os.linux.development.apps: Focusing on writing applications for Linux including porting Windows applications to Linux.

comp.os.linux.advocacy: Discussion in this group centers on the benefits of Linux over other operating systems.

comp.os.linux.networking: Networking and communications are discussed as they relate to the Linux operating system.

Netiquette of Usenet

Netiquette, or *internet etiquette,* is a very important part of newsgroups. Enjoying the privilege of participating in Usenet dictates a certain level of decorum that usually the most knowledgeable and experienced posters follow and expect of other users. Understanding the rules of Usenet netiquette will improve your chances of getting responses to your questions. You should understand what constitutes a good question and what the expected topic of the Usenet group is. If the group topic is not directly related to your question consider carefully whether your post will be well received. Also, if your question may be addressed by multiple groups, beware of simply broadcasting it to all that might be relevant. This is called cross-posting. Be very sure that you are only posting to relevant groups and that you cast your question within the framework of the groups. Read all discussions in progress, which are called threads. Make sure that if your topic is relevant, you post within the thread, or start a new thread if none of the existing ones are germane to your question.

Asking Good Questions

Also make sure that you ask good questions. You will increase your chances of polite, thorough replies to your question if you ask detailed, well-mannered questions. Give as much information as you can. Include the specifications of your equipment and software and any actions that you might have taken. Here's a good checklist for getting answers to your questions.

Be clear and concise: State your problem as plainly as possible.

Choose the right forum: Make sure to do some research into the topic being addressed in a forum, and make sure your question is on topic.

State your expected outcome: For example, if you want to play MP3s on your Linux desktop make sure that you say that. "I am using SUSE 9.3, on a Toshiba Satellite laptop with an Intel A97 chipset, and I would like to be able to play MP3 files using Amarok. Right now I get an error /dev/dsp in use. Can you please give/tell me what steps I need to follow to troubleshoot the problem?"

Do some research first: At the very least type your question into a search engine and convey that in your question. You are likely to get help if you demonstrate that you have put forth a sincere effort first.

Be courteous: Ask nicely, and follow the netiquette of the forum, and you will likely get the answer or at least a courteous response.

This is good advice whether you are asking in a newsgroup or a Web board. Make sure not to take out your frustration with a problem on a group of people who might be willing to help you.

Linux Users Groups (LUGs)

Of all the methods for obtaining help from qualified sources one of the most useful can be the Linux Users Groups. These were discussed in some detail in Chapter 2.

The following directories contain links to Linux Users Groups worldwide:

- Linux.org's Linux User group list—*http://www.linux.org/groups/*
- Groups of Linux Users Everywhere (GLUE)—*http://glue.linuxgazette.com/*
- Linux Users Groups Worldwide—*http://lugww.counter.li.org/*

CONSULTANTS

There are a number of ways for you to acquire Linux desktop knowledge as pointed out earlier in this chapter. You can acquire it or hire it. Depending on your specific circumstances, one may be more attractive than the other. The best thing you can do when hiring expertise is to check references that may come from within your local Linux Users Group or from other businesses. Understanding what certifications are available, as discussed in earlier chapters, might serve as a qualifier. Also, large enterprise services companies like IBM have consulting services that can ably supply enterprise support for Linux.

SUMMARY

One of the greatest advantages of the Internet is the relatively cheap and easy medium it provides for sharing information among those with common interests. Also, because information can be uploaded in a variety of formats and presentation is flexible, automated systems can archive and search the information effectively. No one book could adequately address your concerns and provide all the information that you need for a successful Linux migration, but the intent, at least of this book, is to provide you a map to how you can successfully migrate from Windows to Linux. Using this book in conjunction with resources on the Internet can provide you an easy-to-understand guide for migrating Windows and Linux applications.

The one thing that you should take away from this text is that a wholesale migration to Linux in one fell swoop is probably not going to yield any short-term savings. Open source solutions, especially in the larger enterprise, have to be integrated as part of a long-term strategy. Making evaluations of open source solutions at the time of new systems deployment or technology refreshes is one way to mitigate the costs of acquisition and migration. These are costs that the enterprise would be spending IT dollars on anyway.

Open Standards are Better: When choosing any system, whether it be proprietary, commercial Open Source, or even free and Open Source, dealing with open standards lowers the bar for entry into the sector. In an area where there is high demand for product and there are low barriers to overcome (as in the World Wide Web), competition can flourish. This helps prevent a single vendor from gaining the lion's share of the market and continues to allow innovation.

Common Code Base with Multiple Vendors: In the Microsoft world, they own the operating system and can integrate their products on top of it. They can tune the stack to complement their products. Other vendors competing with them don't have that kind of access or the resources to develop and market their own operating systems. In the open source market many vendors can leverage core development and focus on the amenities that benefit their own products, focusing their development dollars on value-added features rather than expected core functionality.

Single Source Solutions and Vendor Lock-In are Expensive: By locking yourself into products that are single source, you don't benefit from a competitive market. If you require a feature or upgrade you are obligated to do business with only one organization. In an open source market it is easier to move from one vendor to another because ideally they sell products that have common components. There may be fewer barriers or devices to keep you married to one vendor over another.

Linux is a good desktop operating system for the reasons stated above. It also may not be the best solution for you today, but it could be tomorrow. So it bears taking the time to research and come to understand what your computing options are and what benefits they might yield.

OTHER RESOURCES

- Linux Dictionary—*www.tldp.org/LDP/Linux-Dictionary/html/index.html*
- LinuxQuestions.org—*www.linuxquestions.org*
- DesktopLinux.com—*www.desktoplinux.com*
- Linux.com—*www.linux.com*
- Slashdot—*www.slashdot.org*

- NewsForge—*www.newsforge.com*
- RFC 1855—Netiquette Guidelines—*www.faqs.org/rfcs/rfc1855.html*

REFERENCES

Pang, Albert, "Consolidations of Enterprise Applications Vendors Alter Software Industry in 15-Month Buyout Frenzy," (April 2005). Available online at *http://www.idc.com/getdoc.jsp?containerId=33219.*

Appendix

A Software Licenses

Many of the licenses governing the software discussed in this book are novel in the sense that they afford the end user many freedoms that proprietary software does not. The idea of these licenses is to offer other parties the opportunities to improve and innovate upon previous designs. The following five licenses have all been developed in that spirit.

The following sections are facsimiles of these licenses for the reader's evaluation. In no way does any material herein constitute legal advice of these licenses, and users of software governed by these licenses should seek their own counsel. For a comprehensive list of open source licenses the nonprofit Open Source Initiative (OSI) certifies software under the OSI Certified Software program.

GNU PUBLIC LICENSE

The GPL public license was invented by Richard Stallman to prevent free code from being adopted and made proprietary. His solution was to provide a way to copyright software and then release it to be shared, making sure that the terms of the release transferred those same rights to others. The GPL is probably the most notorious and radical software license today because it completely changes the paradigm of licensing.

License Maintainer: Free Software Foundation, Inc.
License URL: http://www.gnu.org/licenses/gpl.txt

GNU GENERAL PUBLIC LICENSE
Version 2, June 1991
Copyright (C) 1989, 1991 Free Software Foundation, Inc.
59 Temple Place, Suite 330, Boston, MA 02111-1307 USA

Everyone is permitted to copy and distribute verbatim copies of this license document, but changing it is not allowed.

Preamble

The licenses for most software are designed to take away your freedom to share and change it. By contrast, the GNU General Public License is intended to guarantee your freedom to share and change free software—to make sure the software is free for all its users. This General Public License applies to most of the Free Software Foundation's software and to any other program whose authors commit to using it. (Some other Free Software Foundation software is covered by the GNU Library General Public License instead.) You can apply it to your programs, too.

When we speak of free software, we are referring to freedom, not price. Our General Public Licenses are designed to make sure that you have the freedom to distribute copies of free software (and charge for this service if you wish), that you receive source code or can get it if you want it, that you can change the software or use pieces of it in new free programs; and that you know you can do these things.

To protect your rights, we need to make restrictions that forbid anyone to deny you these rights or to ask you to surrender the rights. These restrictions translate to certain responsibilities for you if you distribute copies of the software, or if you modify it.

For example, if you distribute copies of such a program, whether gratis or for a fee, you must give the recipients all the rights that you have. You must make sure that they, too, receive or can get the source code. And you must show them these terms so they know their rights.

We protect your rights with two steps: (1) copyright the software, and (2) offer you this license which gives you legal permission to copy, distribute and/or modify the software.

Also, for each author's protection and ours, we want to make certain that everyone understands that there is no warranty for this free software. If the software is modified by someone else and passed on, we want its recipients to know that what they have is not the original, so that any problems introduced by others will not reflect on the original authors' reputations.

Finally, any free program is threatened constantly by software patents. We wish to avoid the danger that redistributors of a free program will individually obtain patent licenses, in effect making the program proprietary. To prevent this, we have made it clear that any patent must be licensed for everyone's free use or not licensed at all.

The precise terms and conditions for copying, distribution and modification follow.

GNU GENERAL PUBLIC LICENSE
TERMS AND CONDITIONS FOR COPYING, DISTRIBUTION AND MODIFICATION

0. This License applies to any program or other work which contains a notice placed by the copyright holder saying it may be distributed under the terms of this General Public License. The "Program", below, refers to any such program or work, and a "work based on the Program" means either the Program or any derivative work under copyright law: that is to say, a work containing the Program or a portion of it, either verbatim or with modifications and/or translated into another language. (Hereinafter, translation is included without limitation in the term "modification".) Each licensee is addressed as "you".

Activities other than copying, distribution and modification are not covered by this License; they are outside its scope. The act of running the Program is not restricted, and the output from the Program is covered only if its contents constitute a work based on the Program (independent of having been made by running the Program). Whether that is true depends on what the Program does.

1. You may copy and distribute verbatim copies of the Program's source code as you receive it, in any medium, provided that you conspicuously and appropriately publish on each copy an appropriate copyright notice and disclaimer of warranty; keep intact all the notices that refer to this License and to the absence of any warranty; and give any other recipients of the Program a copy of this License along with the Program.

You may charge a fee for the physical act of transferring a copy, and you may at your option offer warranty protection in exchange for a fee.

2. You may modify your copy or copies of the Program or any portion of it, thus forming a work based on the Program, and copy and distribute such modifications or work under the terms of Section 1 above, provided that you also meet all of these conditions:

a) You must cause the modified files to carry prominent notices stating that you changed the files and the date of any change.

b) You must cause any work that you distribute or publish, that in whole or in part contains or is derived from the Program or any part thereof, to be licensed as a whole at no charge to all third parties under the terms of this License.

c) If the modified program normally reads commands interactively when run, you must cause it, when started running for such interactive use in the most ordinary way, to print or display an announcement including an appropriate copyright notice and a notice that there is no warranty (or else, saying that you provide a warranty) and that users may redistribute the program under these conditions, and telling the user how to view a copy of this License. (Exception: if the Program itself is interactive but does not normally print such an announcement, your work based on the Program is not required to print an announcement.)

These requirements apply to the modified work as a whole. If identifiable sections of that work are not derived from the Program, and can be reasonably considered independent and separate works in themselves, then this License, and its terms, do not apply to those sections when you distribute them as separate works. But when you distribute the same sections as part of a whole which is a work based on the Program, the distribution of the whole must be on the terms of this License, whose permissions for other licensees extend to the entire whole, and thus to each and every part regardless of who wrote it.

Thus, it is not the intent of this section to claim rights or contest your rights to work written entirely by you; rather, the intent is to exercise the right to control the distribution of derivative or collective works based on the Program.

In addition, mere aggregation of another work not based on the Program with the Program (or with a work based on the Program) on a volume of a storage or distribution medium does not bring the other work under the scope of this License.

3. You may copy and distribute the Program (or a work based on it, under Section 2) in object code or executable form under the terms of Sections 1 and 2 above provided that you also do one of the following:

a) Accompany it with the complete corresponding machine-readable source code, which must be distributed under the terms of Sections 1 and 2 above on a medium customarily used for software interchange; or,

b) Accompany it with a written offer, valid for at least three years, to give any third party, for a charge no more than your cost of physically performing source distribution, a complete machine-readable copy of the corresponding source code, to be distributed under the terms of Sections 1 and 2 above on a medium customarily used for software interchange; or,

c) Accompany it with the information you received as to the offer to distribute corresponding source code. (This alternative is allowed only for noncommercial distribution and only if you received the program in object code or executable form with such an offer, in accord with Subsection b above.)

The source code for a work means the preferred form of the work for making modifications to it. For an executable work, complete source code means all the source code for all modules it contains, plus any associated interface definition files, plus the scripts used to control compilation and installation of the executable. However, as a special exception, the source code distributed need not include anything that is normally distributed (in either source or binary form) with the major components (compiler, kernel, and so on) of the operating system on which the executable runs, unless that component itself accompanies the executable.

If distribution of executable or object code is made by offering access to copy from a designated place, then offering equivalent access to copy the source code from the same place counts as distribution of the source code, even though third parties are not compelled to copy the source along with the object code.

4. You may not copy, modify, sublicense, or distribute the Program except as expressly provided under this License. Any attempt otherwise to copy, modify, sublicense or distribute the Program is void, and will automatically terminate your rights under this License. However, parties who have received copies, or rights, from you under this License will not have their licenses terminated so long as such parties remain in full compliance.

5. You are not required to accept this License, since you have not signed it. However, nothing else grants you permission to modify or distribute the Program or its derivative works. These actions are prohibited by law if you do not accept this License. Therefore, by modifying or distributing the Program (or any work based on the Program), you indicate your acceptance of this License to do so, and all its terms and conditions for copying, distributing or modifying the Program or works based on it.

6. Each time you redistribute the Program (or any work based on the Program), the recipient automatically receives a license from the original licensor to copy, distribute or modify the Program subject to these terms and conditions. You may not impose any further restrictions on the recipients' exercise of the rights granted herein. You are not responsible for enforcing compliance by third parties to this License.

7. If, as a consequence of a court judgment or allegation of patent infringement or for any other reason (not limited to patent issues), conditions are imposed on you (whether by court order, agreement or otherwise) that contradict the conditions of this License, they do not excuse you from the conditions of this License. If you cannot distribute so as to satisfy simultaneously your obligations under this License and any other pertinent obligations, then as a consequence you may not distribute the Program at all. For example, if a patent license would not permit royalty-free redistribution of the Program by all those who receive copies directly or indirectly through you, then the only way you could satisfy both it and this License would be to refrain entirely from distribution of the Program.

If any portion of this section is held invalid or unenforceable under any particular circumstance, the balance of the section is intended to apply and the section as a whole is intended to apply in other circumstances.

It is not the purpose of this section to induce you to infringe any patents or other property right claims or to contest validity of any such claims; this section has the sole purpose of protecting the integrity of the free software distribution system, which is implemented by public license practices. Many people have made generous contributions to the wide range of software distributed through that system in reliance on consistent application of that system; it is up to the author/donor to decide if he or she is willing to distribute software through any other system and a licensee cannot impose that choice.

This section is intended to make thoroughly clear what is believed to be a consequence of the rest of this License.

8. If the distribution and/or use of the Program is restricted in certain countries either by patents or by copyrighted interfaces, the original copyright holder who places the Program under this License may add an explicit geographical distribution limitation excluding those countries, so that distribution is permitted only in or among countries not thus excluded. In such case, this License incorporates the limitation as if written in the body of this License.

9. The Free Software Foundation may publish revised and/or new versions of the General Public License from time to time. Such new versions will be similar in spirit to the present version, but may differ in detail to address new problems or concerns.

Each version is given a distinguishing version number. If the Program specifies a version number of this License which applies to it and "any later version", you have the option of following the terms and conditions either of that version or of any later version published by the Free Software Foundation. If the Program does not specify a version number of this License, you may choose any version ever published by the Free Software Foundation.

10. If you wish to incorporate parts of the Program into other free programs whose distribution conditions are different, write to the author to ask for permission. For software which is copyrighted by the Free Software Foundation, write to the Free Software Foundation; we sometimes make exceptions for this. Our decision will be guided by the two goals of preserving the free status of all derivatives of our free software and of promoting the sharing and reuse of software generally.

NO WARRANTY

11. BECAUSE THE PROGRAM IS LICENSED FREE OF CHARGE, THERE IS NO WARRANTY FOR THE PROGRAM, TO THE EXTENT PERMITTED BY APPLICABLE LAW. EXCEPT WHEN OTHERWISE STATED IN WRITING THE COPYRIGHT HOLDERS AND/OR OTHER PARTIES PROVIDE THE PROGRAM "AS IS" WITHOUT WARRANTY OF ANY KIND, EITHER EXPRESSED OR IMPLIED, INCLUDING, BUT NOT LIMITED TO, THE IMPLIED WARRANTIES OF MERCHANTABILITY AND FITNESS FOR A PARTICULAR PURPOSE. THE ENTIRE RISK AS TO THE QUALITY AND PERFORMANCE OF THE PROGRAM IS WITH YOU. SHOULD THE PROGRAM PROVE DEFECTIVE, YOU ASSUME THE COST OF ALL NECESSARY SERVICING, REPAIR OR CORRECTION.

12. IN NO EVENT UNLESS REQUIRED BY APPLICABLE LAW OR AGREED TO IN WRITING WILL ANY COPYRIGHT HOLDER, OR ANY OTHER PARTY WHO MAY MODIFY AND/OR REDISTRIBUTE THE PROGRAM AS PERMITTED ABOVE, BE LIABLE TO YOU FOR DAMAGES, INCLUDING ANY GENERAL, SPECIAL, INCIDENTAL OR CONSEQUENTIAL DAMAGES ARISING OUT OF THE USE OR INABILITY TO USE THE PROGRAM (INCLUDING BUT NOT LIMITED TO LOSS OF DATA OR DATA BEING RENDERED INACCURATE OR LOSSES SUSTAINED BY YOU OR THIRD PARTIES OR A FAILURE OF THE PROGRAM TO OPERATE WITH ANY OTHER PROGRAMS), EVEN IF SUCH HOLDER OR OTHER PARTY HAS BEEN ADVISED OF THE POSSIBILITY OF SUCH DAMAGES.

END OF TERMS AND CONDITIONS

How to Apply These Terms to Your New Programs

If you develop a new program, and you want it to be of the greatest possible use to the public, the best way to achieve this is to make it free software which everyone can redistribute and change under these terms.

To do so, attach the following notices to the program. It is safest to attach them to the start of each source file to most effectively convey the exclusion of warranty; and each file should have at least the "copyright" line and a pointer to where the full notice is found.

Copyright (C) <year> <name of author>

This program is free software; you can redistribute it and/or modify it under the terms of the GNU General Public License as published by the Free Software Foundation; either version 2 of the License, or (at your option) any later version.

This program is distributed in the hope that it will be useful, but WITHOUT ANY WARRANTY; without even the implied warranty of MERCHANTABILITY or FITNESS FOR A PARTICULAR PURPOSE. See the GNU General Public License for more details.

You should have received a copy of the GNU General Public License along with this program; if not, write to the Free Software Foundation, Inc., 59 Temple Place, Suite 330, Boston, MA 02111-1307 USA

Also add information on how to contact you by electronic and paper mail.

If the program is interactive, make it output a short notice like this when it starts in an interactive mode:

Gnomovision version 69, Copyright (C) year name of author Gnomovision comes with AB-SOLUTELY NO WARRANTY; for details type `show w'. This is free software, and you are welcome to redistribute it under certain conditions; type `show c' for details.

The hypothetical commands `show w' and `show c' should show the appropriate parts of the General Public License. Of course, the commands you use may be called something other than `show w' and `show c'; they could even be mouse-clicks or menu items--whatever suits your program.

You should also get your employer (if you work as a programmer) or your school, if any, to sign a "copyright disclaimer" for the program, if necessary. Here is a sample; alter the names:

Yoyodyne, Inc., hereby disclaims all copyright interest in the program `Gnomovision' (which makes passes at compilers) written by James Hacker.

<signature of Ty Coon>, 1 April 1989

Ty Coon, President of Vice

This General Public License does not permit incorporating your program into proprietary programs. If your program is a subroutine library, you may consider it more useful to permit linking proprietary applications with the library. If this is what you want to do, use the GNU Library General Public License instead of this License.

GNU LESSER PUBLIC LICENSE (GLPL)

The GNU Lesser Public License was released in June 1991 and was originally named the GNU Library General Public License; it was renamed in 1999. Richard Stallman, founder of the Free Software Foundation, described the new license as a "strategic retreat" because the organization's preference was for all software associated with the GPL to be free, but they also realized that certain proprietary libraries could benefit free software. Their solution was to become tolerant of linking to this software and hope that in the long run free libraries would be authored to make this practice unnecessary.

Maintainer: Free Software Foundation Inc.
License URL: http://www.gnu.org/copyleft/lesser.txt
GNU LESSER GENERAL PUBLIC LICENSE
Version 2.1, February 1999
Copyright (C) 1991, 1999 Free Software Foundation, Inc.
59 Temple Place, Suite 330, Boston, MA 02111-1307 USA

Everyone is permitted to copy and distribute verbatim copies of this license document, but changing it is not allowed.

[This is the first released version of the Lesser GPL. It also counts as the successor of the GNU Library Public License, version 2, hence the version number 2.1.]

Preamble

The licenses for most software are designed to take away your freedom to share and change it. By contrast, the GNU General Public Licenses are intended to guarantee your freedom to share and change free software--to make sure the software is free for all its users.

This license, the Lesser General Public License, applies to some specially designated software packages--typically libraries--of the Free Software Foundation and other authors who decide to use it. You can use it too, but we suggest you first think carefully about whether this license or the ordinary General Public License is the better strategy to use in any particular case, based on the explanations below.

When we speak of free software, we are referring to freedom of use, not price. Our General Public Licenses are designed to make sure that you have the freedom to distribute copies of free software (and charge for this service if you wish); that you receive source code or can get it if you want it; that you can change the software and use pieces of it in new free programs; and that you are informed that you can do these things.

To protect your rights, we need to make restrictions that forbid distributors to deny you these rights or to ask you to surrender these rights. These restrictions translate to certain responsibilities for you if you distribute copies of the library or if you modify it.

For example, if you distribute copies of the library, whether gratis or for a fee, you must give the recipients all the rights that we gave you. You must make sure that they, too, receive or can get the source code. If you link other code with the library, you must provide complete object files to the recipients, so that they can relink them with the library after making changes to the library and recompiling it. And you must show them these terms so they know their rights.

We protect your rights with a two-step method: (1) we copyright the library, and (2) we offer you this license, which gives you legal permission to copy, distribute and/or modify the library.

To protect each distributor, we want to make it very clear that there is no warranty for the free library. Also, if the library is modified by someone else and passed on, the recipients should know that what they have is not the original version, so that the original author's reputation will not be affected by problems that might be introduced by others.

Finally, software patents pose a constant threat to the existence of any free program. We wish to make sure that a company cannot effectively restrict the users of a free program by obtaining a restrictive license from a patent holder. Therefore, we insist that any patent license obtained for a version of the library must be consistent with the full freedom of use specified in this license.

Most GNU software, including some libraries, is covered by the ordinary GNU General Public License. This license, the GNU Lesser General Public License, applies to certain designated libraries, and is quite different from the ordinary General Public License. We use this license for certain libraries in order to permit linking those libraries into non-free programs.

When a program is linked with a library, whether statically or using a shared library, the combination of the two is legally speaking a combined work, a derivative of the original library. The ordinary General Public License therefore permits such linking only if the entire combination fits its criteria of freedom. The Lesser General Public License permits more lax criteria for linking other code with the library.

We call this license the "Lesser" General Public License because it does Less to protect the user's freedom than the ordinary General Public License. It also provides other free software developers Less of an advantage over competing non-free programs. These disadvantages are the reason we use the ordinary General Public License for many libraries. However, the Lesser license provides advantages in certain special circumstances.

For example, on rare occasions, there may be a special need to encourage the widest possible use of a certain library, so that it becomes a de-facto standard. To achieve this, non-free programs must be allowed to use the library. A more frequent case is that a free library does the same job as widely used non-free libraries. In this case, there is little to gain by limiting the free library to free software only, so we use the Lesser General Public License.

In other cases, permission to use a particular library in non-free programs enables a greater number of people to use a large body of free software. For example, permission to use the GNU C Library in non-free programs enables many more people to use the whole GNU operating system, as well as its variant, the GNU/Linux operating system.

Although the Lesser General Public License is Less protective of the users' freedom, it does ensure that the user of a program that is linked with the Library has the freedom and the wherewithal to run that program using a modified version of the Library.

The precise terms and conditions for copying, distribution and modification follow. Pay close attention to the difference between a "work based on the library" and a "work that uses the library". The former contains code derived from the library, whereas the latter must be combined with the library in order to run.

GNU LESSER GENERAL PUBLIC LICENSE

TERMS AND CONDITIONS FOR COPYING, DISTRIBUTION AND MODIFICATION

0. This License Agreement applies to any software library or other program which contains a notice placed by the copyright holder or other authorized party saying it may be distributed under the terms of this Lesser General Public License (also called "this License"). Each licensee is addressed as "you".

A "library" means a collection of software functions and/or data prepared so as to be conveniently linked with application programs (which use some of those functions and data) to form executables.

The "Library", below, refers to any such software library or work which has been distributed under these terms. A "work based on the Library" means either the Library or any derivative work under copyright law: that is to say, a work containing the Library or a portion of it, either verbatim or with modifications and/or translated straightforwardly into another language. (Hereinafter, translation is included without limitation in the term "modification".)

"Source code" for a work means the preferred form of the work for making modifications to it. For a library, complete source code means all the source code for all modules it contains, plus any associated interface definition files, plus the scripts used to control compilation and installation of the library.

Activities other than copying, distribution and modification are not covered by this License; they are outside its scope. The act of running a program using the Library is not restricted, and output from such a program is covered only if its contents constitute a work based on the Library (independent of the use of the Library in a tool for writing it). Whether that is true depends on what the Library does and what the program that uses the Library does.

1. You may copy and distribute verbatim copies of the Library's complete source code as you receive it, in any medium, provided that you conspicuously and appropriately publish on each copy an appropriate copyright notice and disclaimer of warranty; keep intact all the notices that refer to this License and to the absence of any warranty; and distribute a copy of this License along with the Library.

You may charge a fee for the physical act of transferring a copy, and you may at your option offer warranty protection in exchange for a fee.

2. You may modify your copy or copies of the Library or any portion of it, thus forming a work based on the Library, and copy and distribute such modifications or work under the terms of Section 1 above, provided that you also meet all of these conditions:

a) The modified work must itself be a software library.

b) You must cause the files modified to carry prominent notices stating that you changed the files and the date of any change.

c) You must cause the whole of the work to be licensed at no charge to all third parties under the terms of this License.

d) If a facility in the modified Library refers to a function or a table of data to be supplied by an application program that uses the facility, other than as an argument passed when the facility is invoked, then you must make a good faith effort to ensure that, in the event an application does not supply such function or table, the facility still operates, and performs whatever part of its purpose remains meaningful.

(For example, a function in a library to compute square roots has a purpose that is entirely well-defined independent of the application. Therefore, Subsection 2d requires that any application-supplied function or table used by this function must be optional: if the application does not supply it, the square root function must still compute square roots.)

These requirements apply to the modified work as a whole. If identifiable sections of that work are not derived from the Library, and can be reasonably considered independent and separate works in themselves, then this License, and its terms, do not apply to those sections when you distribute them as separate works. But when you distribute the same sections as part of a whole which is a work based on the Library, the distribution of the whole must be on the terms of this License, whose permissions for other licensees extend to the entire whole, and thus to each and every part regardless of who wrote it.

Thus, it is not the intent of this section to claim rights or contest your rights to work written entirely by you; rather, the intent is to exercise the right to control the distribution of derivative or collective works based on the Library.

In addition, mere aggregation of another work not based on the Library with the Library (or with a work based on the Library) on a volume of a storage or distribution medium does not bring the other work under the scope of this License.

3. You may opt to apply the terms of the ordinary GNU General Public License instead of this License to a given copy of the Library. To do this, you must alter all the notices that refer to this License, so that they refer to the ordinary GNU General Public License, version 2, instead of to this License. (If a newer version than version 2 of the ordinary GNU General Public License has appeared, then you can specify that version instead if you wish.) Do not make any other change in these notices.

Once this change is made in a given copy, it is irreversible for that copy, so the ordinary GNU General Public License applies to all subsequent copies and derivative works made from that copy. This option is useful when you wish to copy part of the code of the Library into a program that is not a library.

4. You may copy and distribute the Library (or a portion or derivative of it, under Section 2) in object code or executable form under the terms of Sections 1 and 2 above provided that you accompany it with the complete corresponding machine-readable source code, which must be distributed under the terms of Sections 1 and 2 above on a medium customarily used for software interchange.

If distribution of object code is made by offering access to copy from a designated place, then offering equivalent access to copy the source code from the same place satisfies the requirement to distribute the source code, even though third parties are not compelled to copy the source along with the object code.

5. A program that contains no derivative of any portion of the Library, but is designed to work with the Library by being compiled or linked with it, is called a "work that uses the Library". Such a work, in isolation, is not a derivative work of the Library, and therefore falls outside the scope of this License.

However, linking a "work that uses the Library" with the Library creates an executable that is a derivative of the Library (because it contains portions of the Library), rather than a "work that uses the library". The executable is therefore covered by this License. Section 6 states terms for distribution of such executables.

When a "work that uses the Library" uses material from a header file that is part of the Library, the object code for the work may be a derivative work of the Library even though the source code is not. Whether this is true is especially significant if the work can be linked without the Library, or if the work is itself a library. The threshold for this to be true is not precisely defined by law.

If such an object file uses only numerical parameters, data structure layouts and accessors, and small macros and small inline functions (ten lines or less in length), then the use of the object file is unrestricted, regardless of whether it is legally a derivative work. (Executables containing this object code plus portions of the Library will still fall under Section 6.)

Otherwise, if the work is a derivative of the Library, you may distribute the object code for the work under the terms of Section 6. Any executables containing that work also fall under Section 6, whether or not they are linked directly with the Library itself.

6. As an exception to the Sections above, you may also combine or link a "work that uses the Library" with the Library to produce a work containing portions of the Library, and distribute that work under terms of your choice, provided that the terms permit modification of the work for the customer's own use and reverse engineering for debugging such modifications.

You must give prominent notice with each copy of the work that the Library is used in it and that the Library and its use are covered by this License. You must supply a copy of this License. If the work during execution displays copyright notices, you must include the copyright notice for the Library among them, as well as a reference directing the user to the copy of this License. Also, you must do one of these things:

a) Accompany the work with the complete corresponding machine-readable source code for the Library including whatever changes were used in the work (which must be distributed under Sections 1 and 2 above); and, if the work is an executable linked with the Library, with the complete machine-readable "work that uses the Library", as object code and/or source code, so that the user can modify the Library and then relink to produce a modified executable containing the modified Library. (It is understood that the user who changes the contents of definitions files in the Library will not necessarily be able to recompile the application to use the modified definitions.)

b) Use a suitable shared library mechanism for linking with the Library. A suitable mechanism is one that (1) uses at run time a copy of the library already present on the user's computer system, rather than copying library functions into the executable, and (2) will operate properly with a modified version of the library, if the user installs one, as long as the modified version is interface-compatible with the version that the work was made with.

c) Accompany the work with a written offer, valid for at least three years, to give the same user the materials specified in Subsection 6a, above, for a charge no more than the cost of performing this distribution.

d) If distribution of the work is made by offering access to copy from a designated place, offer equivalent access to copy the above specified materials from the same place.

e) Verify that the user has already received a copy of these materials or that you have already sent this user a copy.

For an executable, the required form of the "work that uses the Library" must include any data and utility programs needed for reproducing the executable from it. However, as a special exception, the materials to be distributed need not include anything that is normally distributed (in either source or binary form) with the major components (compiler, kernel, and so on) of the operating system on which the executable runs, unless that component itself accompanies the executable.

It may happen that this requirement contradicts the license restrictions of other proprietary libraries that do not normally accompany the operating system. Such a contradiction means you cannot use both them and the Library together in an executable that you distribute.

7. You may place library facilities that are a work based on the Library side-by-side in a single library together with other library facilities not covered by this License, and distribute such a combined library, provided that the separate distribution of the work based on the Library and of the other library facilities is otherwise permitted, and provided that you do these two things:

a) Accompany the combined library with a copy of the same work based on the Library, uncombined with any other library facilities. This must be distributed under the terms of the Sections above.

b) Give prominent notice with the combined library of the fact that part of it is a work based on the Library, and explaining where to find the accompanying uncombined form of the same work.

8. You may not copy, modify, sublicense, link with, or distribute the Library except as expressly provided under this License. Any attempt otherwise to copy, modify, sublicense, link with, or distribute the Library is void, and will automatically terminate your rights under this License. However, parties who have received copies, or rights, from you under this License will not have their licenses terminated so long as such parties remain in full compliance.

9. You are not required to accept this License, since you have not signed it. However, nothing else grants you permission to modify or distribute the Library or its derivative works. These actions are prohibited by law if you do not accept this License. Therefore, by modifying or distributing the Library (or any work based on the Library), you indicate your acceptance of this License to do so, and all its terms and conditions for copying, distributing or modifying the Library or works based on it.

10. Each time you redistribute the Library (or any work based on the Library), the recipient automatically receives a license from the original licensor to copy, distribute, link with or modify the Library subject to these terms and conditions. You may not impose any further restrictions on the recipients' exercise of the rights granted herein. You are not responsible for enforcing compliance by third parties with this License.

11. If, as a consequence of a court judgment or allegation of patent infringement or for any other reason (not limited to patent issues), conditions are imposed on you (whether by court order, agreement or otherwise) that contradict the conditions of this License, they do not excuse you from the conditions of this License. If you cannot distribute so as to satisfy simultaneously your obligations under this License and any other pertinent obligations, then as a consequence you may not distribute the Library at all. For example, if a patent license would not permit royalty-free redistribution of the Library by all those who receive copies directly or indirectly through you, then the only way you could satisfy both it and this License would be to refrain entirely from distribution of the Library.

If any portion of this section is held invalid or unenforceable under any particular circumstance, the balance of the section is intended to apply, and the section as a whole is intended to apply in other circumstances.

It is not the purpose of this section to induce you to infringe any patents or other property right claims or to contest validity of any such claims; this section has the sole purpose of protecting the integrity of the free software distribution system which is implemented by public license practices. Many people have made generous contributions to the wide range of software distributed through that system in reliance on consistent application of that system; it is up to the author/donor to decide if he or she is willing to distribute software through any other system and a licensee cannot impose that choice.

This section is intended to make thoroughly clear what is believed to be a consequence of the rest of this License.

12. If the distribution and/or use of the Library is restricted in certain countries either by patents or by copyrighted interfaces, the original copyright holder who places the Library under this License may add an explicit geographical distribution limitation excluding those countries, so that distribution is permitted only in or among countries not thus excluded. In such case, this License incorporates the limitation as if written in the body of this License.

13. The Free Software Foundation may publish revised and/or new versions of the Lesser General Public License from time to time. Such new versions will be similar in spirit to the present version, but may differ in detail to address new problems or concerns.

Each version is given a distinguishing version number. If the Library specifies a version number of this License which applies to it and "any later version", you have the option of following the terms and conditions either of that version or of any later version published by the Free Software Foundation. If the Library does not specify a license version number, you may choose any version ever published by the Free Software Foundation.

14. If you wish to incorporate parts of the Library into other free programs whose distribution conditions are incompatible with these, write to the author to ask for permission. For software which is copyrighted by the Free Software Foundation, write to the Free Software Foundation; we sometimes make exceptions for this. Our decision will be guided by the two goals of preserving the free status of all derivatives of our free software and of promoting the sharing and reuse of software generally.

NO WARRANTY

15. BECAUSE THE LIBRARY IS LICENSED FREE OF CHARGE, THERE IS NO WARRANTY FOR THE LIBRARY, TO THE EXTENT PERMITTED BY APPLICABLE LAW. EXCEPT WHEN OTHERWISE STATED IN WRITING THE COPYRIGHT HOLDERS AND/OR OTHER PARTIES PROVIDE THE LIBRARY "AS IS" WITHOUT WARRANTY OF ANY KIND, EITHER EXPRESSED OR IMPLIED, INCLUDING, BUT NOT LIMITED TO, THE IMPLIED WARRANTIES OF MERCHANTABILITY AND FITNESS FOR A PARTICULAR PURPOSE. THE ENTIRE RISK AS TO THE QUALITY AND PERFORMANCE OF THE LIBRARY IS WITH YOU. SHOULD THE LIBRARY PROVE DEFECTIVE, YOU ASSUME THE COST OF ALL NECESSARY SERVICING, REPAIR OR CORRECTION.

16. IN NO EVENT UNLESS REQUIRED BY APPLICABLE LAW OR AGREED TO IN WRITING WILL ANY COPYRIGHT HOLDER, OR ANY OTHER PARTY WHO MAY MODIFY AND/OR REDISTRIBUTE THE LIBRARY AS PERMITTED ABOVE, BE LIABLE TO YOU FOR DAMAGES, INCLUDING ANY GENERAL, SPECIAL, INCIDENTAL OR CONSEQUENTIAL DAMAGES ARISING OUT OF THE USE OR INABILITY TO USE THE LIBRARY (INCLUDING BUT NOT

LIMITED TO LOSS OF DATA OR DATA BEING RENDERED INACCURATE OR LOSSES SUS-
TAINED BY YOU OR THIRD PARTIES OR A FAILURE OF THE LIBRARY TO OPERATE WITH
ANY OTHER SOFTWARE), EVEN IF SUCH HOLDER OR OTHER PARTY HAS BEEN ADVISED
OF THE POSSIBILITY OF SUCH DAMAGES.

END OF TERMS AND CONDITIONS

How to Apply These Terms to Your New Libraries

If you develop a new library, and you want it to be of the greatest possible use to the public, we recommend making it free software that everyone can redistribute and change. You can do so by per-
mitting redistribution under these terms (or, alternatively, under the terms of the ordinary General
Public License).

To apply these terms, attach the following notices to the library. It is safest to attach them to the start
of each source file to most effectively convey the exclusion of warranty; and each file should have at
least the "copyright" line and a pointer to where the full notice is found.

<one line to give the library's name and a brief idea of what it does.>

Copyright (C) <year> <name of author>

This library is free software; you can redistribute it and/or modify it under the terms of the GNU
Lesser General Public License as published by the Free Software Foundation; either version 2.1 of the
License, or (at your option) any later version.

This library is distributed in the hope that it will be useful, but WITHOUT ANY WARRANTY; without even the implied warranty of MERCHANTABILITY or FITNESS FOR A PARTICULAR PUR-
POSE. See the GNU Lesser General Public License for more details.

You should have received a copy of the GNU Lesser General Public License along with this library; if
not, write to the Free Software Foundation, Inc., 59 Temple Place, Suite 330, Boston, MA 02111-1307
USA

Also add information on how to contact you by electronic and paper mail.

You should also get your employer (if you work as a programmer) or your school, if any, to sign a
"copyright disclaimer" for the library, if necessary. Here is a sample; alter the names:

Yoyodyne, Inc., hereby disclaims all copyright interest in the library `Frob' (a library for tweaking
knobs) written by James Random Hacker.

<signature of Ty Coon>, 1 April 1990

Ty Coon, President of Vice

That's all there is to it!

MOZILLA PUBLIC LICENSE

The Mozilla Public License was used to overcome some limitations of the Netscape Public License which was used to take the parts of the source code from the Netscape products into the public domain. The Mozilla Foundation has inherited Netscape's rights to some source code that was originally licensed under the Netscape Public License.

Maintainer: The Mozilla Foundation

URL: http://www.mozilla.org/MPL/

MOZILLA PUBLIC LICENSE

Version 1.1

----

1. Definitions.

1.0.1. "Commercial Use" means distribution or otherwise making the Covered Code available to a third party.

1.1. "Contributor" means each entity that creates or contributes to the creation of Modifications.

1.2. "Contributor Version" means the combination of the Original Code, prior Modifications used by a Contributor, and the Modifications made by that particular Contributor.

1.3. "Covered Code" means the Original Code or Modifications or the combination of the Original Code and Modifications, in each case including portions thereof.

1.4. "Electronic Distribution Mechanism" means a mechanism generally accepted in the software development community for the electronic transfer of data.

1.5. "Executable" means Covered Code in any form other than Source Code.

1.6. "Initial Developer" means the individual or entity identified as the Initial Developer in the Source Code notice required by Exhibit A.

1.7. "Larger Work" means a work which combines Covered Code or portions thereof with code not governed by the terms of this License.

1.8. "License" means this document.

1.8.1. "Licensable" means having the right to grant, to the maximum extent possible, whether at the time of the initial grant or subsequently acquired, any and all of the rights conveyed herein.

1.9. "Modifications" means any addition to or deletion from the substance or structure of either the Original Code or any previous Modifications. When Covered Code is released as a series of files, a Modification is:

A. Any addition to or deletion from the contents of a file containing Original Code or previous Modifications.

B. Any new file that contains any part of the Original Code or previous Modifications.

1.10. "Original Code" means Source Code of computer software code which is described in the Source Code notice required by Exhibit A as Original Code, and which, at the time of its release under this License is not already Covered Code governed by this License.

1.10.1. "Patent Claims" means any patent claim(s), now owned or hereafter acquired, including without limitation, method, process, and apparatus claims, in any patent Licensable by grantor.

1.11. "Source Code" means the preferred form of the Covered Code for making modifications to it, including all modules it contains, plus any associated interface definition files, scripts used to control compilation and installation of an Executable, or source code differential comparisons against either the Original Code or another well known, available Covered Code of the Contributor's choice. The Source Code can be in a compressed or archival form, provided the appropriate decompression or de-archiving software is widely available for no charge.

1.12. "You" (or "Your") means an individual or a legal entity exercising rights under, and complying with all of the terms of, this License or a future version of this License issued under Section 6.1. For legal entities, "You" includes any entity which controls, is controlled by, or is under common control with You. For purposes of this definition, "control" means (a) the power, direct or indirect, to cause the direction or management of such entity, whether by contract or otherwise, or (b) ownership of more than fifty percent (50%) of the outstanding shares or beneficial ownership of such entity.

2. Source Code License.

2.1. The Initial Developer Grant.

The Initial Developer hereby grants You a world-wide, royalty-free, non-exclusive license, subject to third party intellectual property claims:

(a) under intellectual property rights (other than patent or trademark) Licensable by Initial Developer to use, reproduce, modify, display, perform, sublicense and distribute the Original Code (or portions thereof) with or without Modifications, and/or as part of a Larger Work; and

(b) under Patents Claims infringed by the making, using or selling of Original Code, to make, have made, use, practice, sell, and offer for sale, and/or otherwise dispose of the Original Code (or portions thereof).

(c) the licenses granted in this Section 2.1(a) and (b) are effective on the date Initial Developer first distributes Original Code under the terms of this License.

(d) Notwithstanding Section 2.1(b) above, no patent license is granted: 1) for code that You delete from the Original Code; 2) separate from the Original Code; or 3) for infringements caused by: i) the modification of the Original Code or ii) the combination of the Original Code with other software or devices.

2.2. Contributor Grant.

Subject to third party intellectual property claims, each Contributor hereby grants You a world-wide, royalty-free, non-exclusive license

(a) under intellectual property rights (other than patent or trademark) Licensable by Contributor, to use, reproduce, modify, display, perform, sublicense and distribute the Modifications created by such Contributor (or portions thereof) either on an unmodified basis, with other Modifications, as Covered Code and/or as part of a Larger Work; and

(b) under Patent Claims infringed by the making, using, or selling of Modifications made by that Contributor either alone and/or in combination with its Contributor Version (or portions of such combination), to make, use, sell, offer for sale, have made, and/or otherwise dispose of: 1) Modifications made by that Contributor (or portions thereof); and 2) the combination of Modifications made by that Contributor with its Contributor Version (or portions of such combination).

(c) the licenses granted in Sections 2.2(a) and 2.2(b) are effective on the date Contributor first makes Commercial Use of the Covered Code.

(d) Notwithstanding Section 2.2(b) above, no patent license is granted: 1) for any code that Contributor has deleted from the Contributor Version; 2) separate from the Contributor Version; 3) for infringements caused by: i) third party modifications of Contributor Version or ii) the combination of Modifications made by that Contributor with other software (except as part of the Contributor Version) or other devices; or 4) under Patent Claims infringed by Covered Code in the absence of Modifications made by that Contributor.

3. Distribution Obligations.

3.1. Application of License.

The Modifications which You create or to which You contribute are governed by the terms of this License, including without limitation Section 2.2. The Source Code version of Covered Code may be distributed only under the terms of this License or a future version of this License released under Section 6.1, and You must include a copy of this License with every copy of the Source Code You distribute. You may not offer or impose any terms on any Source Code version that alters or restricts the applicable version of this License or the recipients' rights hereunder. However, You may include an additional document offering the additional rights described in Section 3.5.

3.2. Availability of Source Code.

Any Modification which You create or to which You contribute must be made available in Source Code form under the terms of this License either on the same media as an Executable version or via an accepted Electronic Distribution Mechanism to anyone to whom you made an Executable version available; and if made available via Electronic Distribution Mechanism, must remain available for at least twelve (12) months after the date it initially became available, or at least six (6) months after a subsequent version of that particular Modification has been made available to such recipients. You are responsible for ensuring that the Source Code version remains available even if the Electronic Distribution Mechanism is maintained by a third party.

3.3. Description of Modifications.

You must cause all Covered Code to which You contribute to contain a file documenting the changes You made to create that Covered Code and the date of any change. You must include a prominent statement that the Modification is derived, directly or indirectly, from Original Code provided by the

Initial Developer and including the name of the Initial Developer in (a) the Source Code, and (b) in any notice in an Executable version or related documentation in which You describe the origin or ownership of the Covered Code.

3.4. Intellectual Property Matters

(a) Third Party Claims.

If Contributor has knowledge that a license under a third party's intellectual property rights is required to exercise the rights granted by such Contributor under Sections 2.1 or 2.2, Contributor must include a text file with the Source Code distribution titled "LEGAL" which describes the claim and the party making the claim in sufficient detail that a recipient will know whom to contact. If Contributor obtains such knowledge after the Modification is made available as described in Section 3.2, Contributor shall promptly modify the LEGAL file in all copies Contributor makes available thereafter and shall take other steps (such as notifying appropriate mailing lists or newsgroups) reasonably calculated to inform those who received the Covered Code that new knowledge has been obtained.

(b) Contributor APIs.

If Contributor's Modifications include an application programming

interface and Contributor has knowledge of patent licenses which are reasonably necessary to implement that API, Contributor must also include this information in the LEGAL file.

(c) Representations.

Contributor represents that, except as disclosed pursuant to Section 3.4(a) above, Contributor believes that Contributor's Modifications are Contributor's original creation(s) and/or Contributor has sufficient rights to grant the rights conveyed by this License.

3.5. Required Notices.

You must duplicate the notice in Exhibit A in each file of the Source Code. If it is not possible to put such notice in a particular Source Code file due to its structure, then You must include such notice in a location (such as a relevant directory) where a user would be likely to look for such a notice. If You created one or more Modification(s) You may add your name as a Contributor to the notice described in Exhibit A. You must also duplicate this License in any documentation for the Source Code where You describe recipients' rights or ownership rights relating to Covered Code. You may choose to offer, and to charge a fee for, warranty, support, indemnity or liability obligations to one or more recipients of Covered Code. However, You may do so only on Your own behalf, and not on behalf of the Initial Developer or any Contributor. You must make it absolutely clear than any such warranty, support, indemnity or liability obligation is offered by You alone, and You hereby agree to indemnify the Initial Developer and every Contributor for any liability incurred by the Initial Developer or such Contributor as a result of warranty, support, indemnity or liability terms You offer.

3.6. Distribution of Executable Versions.

You may distribute Covered Code in Executable form only if the requirements of Section 3.1-3.5 have been met for that Covered Code, and if You include a notice stating that the Source Code version of the Covered Code is available under the terms of this License, including a description of how and where You have fulfilled the obligations of Section 3.2. The notice must be conspicuously included in any notice in an Executable version, related documentation or collateral in which You describe recipients' rights relating to the Covered Code. You may distribute the Executable version of Covered Code or ownership rights under a license of Your choice, which may contain terms different from this License, provided that You are in compliance with the terms of this License and that the license for the Executable version does not attempt to limit or alter the recipient's rights in the Source Code version from the rights set forth in this License. If You distribute the Executable version under a different license You must make it absolutely clear that any terms which differ from this License are offered by You alone, not by the Initial Developer or any Contributor. You hereby agree to indemnify the Initial Developer and every Contributor for any liability incurred by the Initial Developer or such Contributor as a result of any such terms You offer.

3.7. Larger Works.

You may create a Larger Work by combining Covered Code with other code not governed by the terms of this License and distribute the Larger Work as a single product. In such a case, You must make sure the requirements of this License are fulfilled for the Covered Code.

4. Inability to Comply Due to Statute or Regulation.

If it is impossible for You to comply with any of the terms of this License with respect to some or all of the Covered Code due to statute, judicial order, or regulation then You must: (a) comply with the terms of this License to the maximum extent possible; and (b) describe the limitations and the code they affect. Such description must be included in the LEGAL file described in Section 3.4 and must be included with all distributions of the Source Code. Except to the extent prohibited by statute or regulation, such description must be sufficiently detailed for a recipient of ordinary skill to be able to understand it.

5. Application of this License.

This License applies to code to which the Initial Developer has attached the notice in Exhibit A and to related Covered Code.

6. Versions of the License.

6.1. New Versions.

Netscape Communications Corporation ("Netscape") may publish revised and/or new versions of the License from time to time. Each version will be given a distinguishing version number.

6.2. Effect of New Versions.

Once Covered Code has been published under a particular version of the License, You may always continue to use it under the terms of that version. You may also choose to use such Covered Code under the terms of any subsequent version of the License published by Netscape. No one other than Netscape has the right to modify the terms applicable to Covered Code created under this License.

6.3. Derivative Works.

If You create or use a modified version of this License (which you may only do in order to apply it to code which is not already Covered Code governed by this License), You must (a) rename Your license so that the phrases "Mozilla", "MOZILLAPL", "MOZPL", "Netscape", "MPL", "NPL" or any confusingly similar phrase do not appear in your license (except to note that your license differs from this License) and (b) otherwise make it clear that Your version of the license contains terms which differ from the Mozilla Public License and Netscape Public License. (Filling in the name of the Initial Developer, Original Code or Contributor in the notice described in Exhibit A shall not of themselves be deemed to be modifications of this License.)

7. DISCLAIMER OF WARRANTY.

COVERED CODE IS PROVIDED UNDER THIS LICENSE ON AN "AS IS" BASIS, WITHOUT WARRANTY OF ANY KIND, EITHER EXPRESSED OR IMPLIED, INCLUDING, WITHOUT LIMITATION, WARRANTIES THAT THE COVERED CODE IS FREE OF DEFECTS, MERCHANTABLE, FIT FOR A PARTICULAR PURPOSE OR NON-INFRINGING. THE ENTIRE RISK AS TO THE QUALITY AND PERFORMANCE OF THE COVERED CODE IS WITH YOU. SHOULD ANY COVERED CODE PROVE DEFECTIVE IN ANY RESPECT, YOU (NOT THE INITIAL DEVELOPER OR ANY OTHER CONTRIBUTOR) ASSUME THE COST OF ANY NECESSARY SERVICING, REPAIR OR CORRECTION. THIS DISCLAIMER OF WARRANTY CONSTITUTES AN ESSENTIAL PART OF THIS LICENSE. NO USE OF ANY COVERED CODE IS AUTHORIZED HEREUNDER EXCEPT UNDER THIS DISCLAIMER.

8. TERMINATION.

8.1. This License and the rights granted hereunder will terminate automatically if You fail to comply with terms herein and fail to cure such breach within 30 days of becoming aware of the breach. All sublicenses to the Covered Code which are properly granted shall survive any termination of this License. Provisions which, by their nature, must remain in effect beyond the termination of this License shall survive.

8.2. If You initiate litigation by asserting a patent infringement claim (excluding declatory judgment actions) against Initial Developer or a Contributor (the Initial Developer or Contributor against whom You file such action is referred to as "Participant") alleging that:

(a) such Participant's Contributor Version directly or indirectly infringes any patent, then any and all rights granted by such Participant to You under Sections 2.1 and/or 2.2 of this License shall, upon 60 days notice from Participant terminate prospectively, unless if within 60 days after receipt of notice You either: (i) agree in writing to pay Participant a mutually agreeable reasonable royalty for Your past and future use of Modifications made by such Participant, or (ii) withdraw Your litigation claim with respect to the Contributor Version against such Participant. If within 60 days of notice, a reasonable royalty and payment arrangement are not mutually agreed upon in writing by the parties or the litigation claim is not withdrawn, the rights granted by Participant to You under Sections 2.1 and/or 2.2 automatically terminate at the expiration of the 60 day notice period specified above.

(b) any software, hardware, or device, other than such Participant's Contributor Version, directly or indirectly infringes any patent, then any rights granted to You by such Participant under Sections 2.1(b) and 2.2(b) are revoked effective as of the date You first made, used, sold, distributed, or had made, Modifications made by that Participant.

8.3. If You assert a patent infringement claim against Participant alleging that such Participant's Contributor Version directly or indirectly infringes any patent where such claim is resolved (such as by license or settlement) prior to the initiation of patent infringement litigation, then the reasonable value of the licenses granted by such Participant under Sections 2.1 or 2.2 shall be taken into account in determining the amount or value of any payment or license.

8.4. In the event of termination under Sections 8.1 or 8.2 above, all end user license agreements (excluding distributors and resellers) which have been validly granted by You or any distributor hereunder prior to termination shall survive termination.

9. LIMITATION OF LIABILITY.

UNDER NO CIRCUMSTANCES AND UNDER NO LEGAL THEORY, WHETHER TORT (INCLUDING NEGLIGENCE), CONTRACT, OR OTHERWISE, SHALL YOU, THE INITIAL DEVELOPER, ANY OTHER CONTRIBUTOR, OR ANY DISTRIBUTOR OF COVERED CODE, OR ANY SUPPLIER OF ANY OF SUCH PARTIES, BE LIABLE TO ANY PERSON FOR ANY INDIRECT, SPECIAL, INCIDENTAL, OR CONSEQUENTIAL DAMAGES OF ANY CHARACTER INCLUDING, WITHOUT LIMITATION, DAMAGES FOR LOSS OF GOODWILL, WORK STOPPAGE, COMPUTER FAILURE OR MALFUNCTION, OR ANY AND ALL OTHER COMMERCIAL DAMAGES OR LOSSES, EVEN IF SUCH PARTY SHALL HAVE BEEN INFORMED OF THE POSSIBILITY OF SUCH DAMAGES. THIS LIMITATION OF LIABILITY SHALL NOT APPLY TO LIABILITY FOR DEATH OR PERSONAL INJURY RESULTING FROM SUCH PARTY'S NEGLIGENCE TO THE EXTENT APPLICABLE LAW PROHIBITS SUCH LIMITATION. SOME JURISDICTIONS DO NOT ALLOW THE EXCLUSION OR LIMITATION OF INCIDENTAL OR CONSEQUENTIAL DAMAGES, SO THIS EXCLUSION AND LIMITATION MAY NOT APPLY TO YOU.

10. U.S. GOVERNMENT END USERS.

The Covered Code is a "commercial item," as that term is defined in 48 C.F.R. 2.101 (Oct. 1995), consisting of "commercial computer software" and "commercial computer software documentation," as such terms are used in 48 C.F.R. 12.212 (Sept. 1995). Consistent with 48 C.F.R. 12.212 and 48 C.F.R. 227.7202-1 through 227.7202-4 (June 1995), all U.S. Government End Users acquire Covered Code with only those rights set forth herein.

11. MISCELLANEOUS.

This License represents the complete agreement concerning subject matter hereof. If any provision of this License is held to be unenforceable, such provision shall be reformed only to the extent necessary to make it enforceable. This License shall be governed by California law provisions (except to the extent applicable law, if any, provides otherwise), excluding its conflict-of-law provisions. With respect to disputes in which at least one party is a citizen of, or an entity chartered or registered to do business in the United States of America, any litigation relating to this License shall be subject to the jurisdiction of the Federal Courts of the Northern District of California, with venue lying in Santa Clara County, California, with the losing party responsible for costs, including without limitation, court costs and reasonable attorneys' fees and expenses. The application of the United Nations Convention on Contracts for the International Sale of Goods is expressly excluded. Any law or regulation which provides that the language of a contract shall be construed against the drafter shall not apply to this License.

12. RESPONSIBILITY FOR CLAIMS.

As between Initial Developer and the Contributors, each party is responsible for claims and damages arising, directly or indirectly, out of its utilization of rights under this License and You agree to work with Initial Developer and Contributors to distribute such responsibility on an equitable basis. Nothing herein is intended or shall be deemed to constitute any admission of liability.

13. MULTIPLE-LICENSED CODE.

Initial Developer may designate portions of the Covered Code as "Multiple-Licensed". "Multiple-Licensed" means that the Initial Developer permits you to utilize portions of the Covered Code under Your choice of the NPL or the alternative licenses, if any, specified by the Initial Developer in the file described in Exhibit A.

EXHIBIT A — Mozilla Public License.

``The contents of this file are subject to the Mozilla Public License Version 1.1 (the "License"); you may not use this file except in compliance with the License. You may obtain a copy of the License at http://www.mozilla.org/MPL/

Software distributed under the License is distributed on an "AS IS" basis, WITHOUT WARRANTY OF ANY KIND, either express or implied. See the License for the specific language governing rights and limitations under the License.

The Original Code is _____. The Initial Developer of the Original Code is _____. Portions created by _____ are Copyright (C) _____ _____. All Rights Reserved.

Contributor(s): _____.

Alternatively, the contents of this file may be used under the terms of the _____ license (the "[___] License"), in which case the provisions of [_____] License are applicable instead of those above. If you wish to allow use of your version of this file only under the terms of the [____] License and not to allow others to use your version of this file under the MPL, indicate your decision by deleting the provisions above and replace them with the notice and other provisions required by the [___] License. If you do not delete the provisions above, a recipient may use your version of this file under either the MPL or the [___] License."

[NOTE: The text of this Exhibit A may differ slightly from the text of the notices in the Source Code files of the Original Code. You should use the text of this Exhibit A rather than the text found in the Original Code Source Code for Your Modifications.]

Sun Industry Standards Source License (SISSL) The Sun Industry Standards Source License was developed so that certain standards remain intact for a product while the source code remains open and royalty free. License Maintainer: Sun Microsystems Inc. License URL: http://www.openoffice.org/licenses/sissl_license.html Sun Industry Standards Source License (SISSL)

1.0 DEFINITIONS

1.1 "Commercial Use" means distribution or otherwise making the Original Code available to a third party.

1.2 "Contributor Version" means the combination of the Original Code, and the Modifications made by that particular Contributor.

1.3 "Electronic Distribution Mechanism" means a mechanism generally accepted in the software development community for the electronic transfer of data.

1.4 "Executable" means Original Code in any form other than Source Code.

1.5 "Initial Developer" means the individual or entity identified as the Initial Developer in the Source Code notice required by Exhibit A.

1.6 "Larger Work" means a work which combines Original Code or portions thereof with code not governed by the terms of this License.

1.7 "License" means this document.

1.8 "Licensable" means having the right to grant, to the maximum extent possible, whether at the time of the initial grant or subsequently acquired, any and all of the rights conveyed herein.

1.9 "Modifications" means any addition to or deletion from the substance or structure of either the Original Code or any previous Modifications. A Modification is:

B. Any new file that contains any part of the Original Code or previous Modifications.

1.11 "Patent Claims" means any patent claim(s), now owned or hereafter acquired, including without limitation, method, process, and apparatus claims, in any patent Licensable by grantor.

1.12 "Source Code" means the preferred form of the Original Code for making modifications to it, including all modules it contains, plus any associated interface definition files, or scripts used to control compilation and installation of an Executable.

1.13 "Standards" means the standards identified in Exhibit B.

1.14 "You" (or "Your") means an individual or a legal entity exercising rights under, and complying with all of the terms of, this License or a future version of this License issued under Section 6.1. For legal entities, "You" includes any entity which controls, is controlled by, or is under common control with You. For purposes of this definition, "control" means (a) the power, direct or indirect, to cause the direction or management of such entity, whether by contract or otherwise, or (b) ownership of more than fifty percent (50%) of the outstanding shares or beneficial ownership of such entity.

2.0 SOURCE CODE LICENSE

2.1 The Initial Developer Grant

The Initial Developer hereby grants You a world-wide, royalty-free, non-exclusive license, subject to third party intellectual property claims:

(b) under Patents Claims infringed by the making, using or selling of Original Code, to make, have made, use, practice, sell, and offer for sale, and/or otherwise dispose of the Original Code (or portions thereof).

(c) the licenses granted in this Section 2.1(a) and (b) are effective on the date Initial Developer first distributes Original Code under the terms of this License.

(d) Notwithstanding Section 2.1(b) above, no patent license is granted: 1) for code that You delete from the Original Code; 2) separate from the Original Code; or 3) for infringements caused by: i) the modification of the Original Code or ii) the combination of the Original Code with other software or devices, including but not limited to Modifications.

3.1 Application of License.

The Source Code version of Original Code may be distributed only under the terms of this License or a future version of this License released under Section 6.1, and You must include a copy of this License with every copy of the Source Code You distribute. You may not offer or impose any terms on any Source Code version that alters or restricts the applicable version of this License or the recipients' rights hereunder. Your license for shipment of the Contributor Version is conditioned upon Your full compliance with this Section. The Modifications which You create must comply with all requirements set out by the Standards body in effect one hundred twenty (120) days before You ship the Contributor Version. In the event that the Modifications do not meet such requirements, You agree to publish either (i) any deviation from the Standards protocol resulting from implementation of Your Modifications and a reference implementation of Your Modifications or (ii) Your Modifications in Source Code form, and to make any such deviation and reference implementation or Modifications available to all third parties under the same terms as this license on a royalty free basis within thirty (30) days of Your first customer shipment of Your Modifications.

3.2 Required Notices.

You must duplicate the notice in Exhibit A in each file of the Source Code. If it is not possible to put such notice in a particular Source Code file due to its structure, then You must include such notice in a location (such as a relevant directory) where a user would be likely to look for such a notice. If You created one or more Modification(s) You may add Your name as a Contributor to the notice described in Exhibit A. You must also duplicate this License in any documentation for the Source Code where You describe recipients' rights or ownership rights relating to Initial Code. You may choose to offer, and to charge a fee for, warranty, support, indemnity or liability obligations to one or more recipients of Your version of the Code. However, You may do so only on Your own behalf, and not on behalf of the Initial Developer. You must make it absolutely clear than any such warranty, support, indemnity or liability obligation is offered by You alone, and You hereby agree to indemnify the Initial Developer for any liability incurred by the Initial Developer as a result of warranty, support, indemnity or liability terms You offer.

3.3 Distribution of Executable Versions.

You may distribute Original Code in Executable and Source form only if the requirements of Sections 3.1 and 3.2 have been met for that Original Code, and if You include a notice stating that the Source Code version of the Original Code is available under the terms of this License. The notice must be conspicuously included in any notice in an Executable or Source versions, related documentation or collateral in which You describe recipients' rights relating to the Original Code. You may distribute the Executable and Source versions of Your version of the Code or ownership rights under a license of Your choice, which may contain terms different from this License, provided that You are in compliance with the terms of this License. If You distribute the Executable and Source versions under a different license You must make it absolutely clear that any terms which differ from this License are offered by You alone, not by the Initial Developer. You hereby agree to indemnify the Initial Developer for any liability incurred by the Initial Developer as a result of any such terms You offer.

3.4 Larger Works.

You may create a Larger Work by combining Original Code with other code not governed by the terms of this License and distribute the Larger Work as a single product. In such a case, You must make sure the requirements of this License are fulfilled for the Original Code.

4.0 INABILITY TO COMPLY DUE TO STATUTE OR REGULATION

If it is impossible for You to comply with any of the terms of this License with respect to some or all of the Original Code due to statute, judicial order, or regulation then You must: (a) comply with the terms of this License to the maximum extent possible; and (b) describe the limitations and the code they affect. Such description must be included in the LEGAL file described in Section 3.2 and must be included with all distributions of the Source Code. Except to the extent prohibited by statute or regulation, such description must be sufficiently detailed for a recipient of ordinary skill to be able to understand it.

5.0 APPLICATION OF THIS LICENSE

This License applies to code to which the Initial Developer has attached the notice in Exhibit A and to related Modifications as set out in Section 3.1.

6.0 VERSIONS OF THE LICENSE

6.1 New Versions.

Sun may publish revised and/or new versions of the License from time to time. Each version will be given a distinguishing version number.

6.2 Effect of New Versions.

Once Original Code has been published under a particular version of the License, You may always continue to use it under the terms of that version. You may also choose to use such Original Code under the terms of any subsequent version of the License published by Sun. No one other than Sun has the right to modify the terms applicable to Original Code.

7.0 DISCLAIMER OF WARRANTY

ORIGINAL CODE IS PROVIDED UNDER THIS LICENSE ON AN "AS IS" BASIS, WITHOUT WARRANTY OF ANY KIND, EITHER EXPRESSED OR IMPLIED, INCLUDING, WITHOUT LIMITATION, WARRANTIES THAT THE ORIGINAL CODE IS FREE OF DEFECTS, MERCHANTABLE, FIT FOR A PARTICULAR PURPOSE OR NON-INFRINGING. THE ENTIRE RISK AS TO THE QUALITY AND PERFORMANCE OF THE ORIGINAL CODE IS WITH YOU. SHOULD ANY ORIGINAL CODE PROVE DEFECTIVE IN ANY RESPECT, YOU (NOT THE INITIAL DEVELOPER) ASSUME THE COST OF ANY NECESSARY SERVICING, REPAIR OR CORRECTION. THIS DISCLAIMER OF WARRANTY CONSTITUTES AN ESSENTIAL PART OF THIS LICENSE. NO USE OF ANY ORIGINAL CODE IS AUTHORIZED HEREUNDER EXCEPT UNDER THIS DISCLAIMER.

8.0 TERMINATION

8.1 This License and the rights granted hereunder will terminate automatically if You fail to comply with terms herein and fail to cure such breach within 30 days of becoming aware of the breach. All sublicenses to the Original Code which are properly granted shall survive any termination of this License. Provisions which, by their nature, must remain in effect beyond the termination of this License shall survive.

8.2 In the event of termination under Section 8.1 above, all end user license agreements (excluding distributors and resellers) which have been validly granted by You or any distributor hereunder prior to termination shall survive termination.

9.0 LIMIT OF LIABILITY

UNDER NO CIRCUMSTANCES AND UNDER NO LEGAL THEORY, WHETHER TORT (INCLUDING NEGLIGENCE), CONTRACT, OR OTHERWISE, SHALL YOU, THE INITIAL DEVELOPER, ANY OTHER CONTRIBUTOR, OR ANY DISTRIBUTOR OF ORIGINAL CODE, OR ANY SUPPLIER OF ANY OF SUCH PARTIES, BE LIABLE TO ANY PERSON FOR ANY INDIRECT, SPECIAL, INCIDENTAL, OR CONSEQUENTIAL DAMAGES OF ANY CHARACTER INCLUDING, WITHOUT LIMITATION, DAMAGES FOR LOSS OF GOODWILL, WORK STOPPAGE, COMPUTER FAILURE OR MALFUNCTION, OR ANY AND ALL OTHER COMMERCIAL DAMAGES OR LOSSES, EVEN IF SUCH PARTY SHALL HAVE BEEN INFORMED OF THE POSSIBILITY OF SUCH DAMAGES. THIS LIMITATION OF LIABILITY SHALL NOT APPLY TO LIABILITY FOR DEATH OR PERSONAL INJURY RESULTING FROM SUCH PARTY'S NEGLIGENCE TO THE EXTENT APPLICABLE LAW PROHIBITS SUCH LIMITATION. SOME JURISDICTIONS DO NOT ALLOW THE EXCLUSION OR LIMITATION OF INCIDENTAL OR CONSEQUENTIAL DAMAGES, SO THIS EXCLUSION AND LIMITATION MAY NOT APPLY TO YOU.

10.0 U.S. GOVERNMENT END USERS

U.S. Government: If this Software is being acquired by or on behalf of the U.S. Government or by a U.S. Government prime contractor or subcontractor (at any tier), then the Government's rights in the Software and accompanying documentation shall be only as set forth in this license; this is in accordance with 48 C.F.R. 227.7201 through 227.7202-4 (for Department of Defense (DoD) acquisitions) and with 48 C.F.R. 2.101 and 12.212 (for non-DoD acquisitions).

11.0 MISCELLANEOUS

This License represents the complete agreement concerning subject matter hereof. If any provision of this License is held to be unenforceable, such provision shall be reformed only to the extent necessary to make it enforceable. This License shall be governed by California law provisions (except to the extent applicable law, if any, provides otherwise), excluding its conflict-of-law provisions. With respect to disputes in which at least one party is a citizen of, or an entity chartered or registered to do business in the United States of America, any litigation relating to this License shall be subject to the jurisdiction of the Federal Courts of the Northern District of California, with venue lying in Santa Clara County, California, with the losing party responsible for costs, including without limitation, court costs and reasonable attorneys' fees and expenses. The application of the United Nations Convention on Contracts for the International Sale of Goods is expressly excluded. Any law or regulation which provides that the language of a contract shall be construed against the drafter shall not apply to this License.

EXHIBIT A - Sun Standards License

"The contents of this file are subject to the Sun Standards

License Version 1.1 (the "License");

You may not use this file except in compliance with the License. You may obtain a copy of the

License at _____.

Software distributed under the License is distributed on an "AS IS" basis, WITHOUT WARRANTY OF ANY KIND, either express or implied. See the License for the specific language governing rights and limitations under the License.

The Original Code is _____.

The Initial Developer of the Original Code is: Sun Microsystems, Inc..

Portions created by: _____

are Copyright (C): _____

All Rights Reserved.

Contributor(s): _____

EXHIBIT B - Standards

The Standard is defined as the following:

OpenOffice.org XML File Format Specification, located at http://xml.openoffice.org

OpenOffice.org Application Programming Interface Specification, located at http://api.openoffice.org

BERKLEY SOFTWARE DEVELOPMENT LICENSE

The Berkley Software Development (BSD) license was used to put software developed at the University of California, Berkley into the Public Domain. The BSD or BSD-like licenses today allow users to take BSD licensed software and modify it or redistribute it without including the source code. This makes this code very attractive for commercial use though this stipulation makes it incompatible with the GNU Public License

License Maintainer: Originally the University of California

License URL: http://www.opensource.org/licenses/bsd-license.php

The BSD License

<OWNER> = Regents of the University of California

<ORGANIZATION> = University of California, Berkeley

<YEAR> = 1998

In the original BSD license, both occurrences of the phrase "COPYRIGHT HOLDERS AND CONTRIBUTORS" in the disclaimer read "REGENTS AND CONTRIBUTORS".

Here is the license template:

Copyright (c) <YEAR>, <OWNER>All rights reserved.

Redistribution and use in source and binary forms, with or without modification, are permitted provided that the following conditions are met:

THIS SOFTWARE IS PROVIDED BY THE COPYRIGHT HOLDERS AND CONTRIBUTORS "AS IS" AND ANY EXPRESS OR IMPLIED WARRANTIES, INCLUDING, BUT NOT LIMITED TO, THE IMPLIED WARRANTIES OF MERCHANTABILITY AND FITNESS FOR A PARTICULAR PURPOSE ARE DISCLAIMED. IN NO EVENT SHALL THE COPYRIGHT OWNER OR CONTRIBUTORS BE LIABLE FOR ANY DIRECT, INDIRECT, INCIDENTAL, SPECIAL, EXEMPLARY, OR CONSEQUENTIAL DAMAGES (INCLUDING, BUT NOT LIMITED TO, PROCUREMENT OF SUBSTITUTE GOODS OR SERVICES; LOSS OF USE, DATA, OR PROFITS; OR BUSINESS INTERRUPTION) HOWEVER CAUSED AND ON ANY THEORY OF LIABILITY, WHETHER IN CONTRACT, STRICT LIABILITY, OR TORT (INCLUDING NEGLIGENCE OR OTHERWISE) ARISING IN ANY WAY OUT OF THE USE OF THIS SOFTWARE, EVEN IF ADVISED OF THE POSSIBILITY OF SUCH DAMAGE.

Links
The Open Source Initiative – www.opensource.org
GNU Public License - www.gnu.org/licenses/gpl.txt
GNU Lesser Public License - www.gnu.org/copyleft/lesser.txt
Mozilla Public License - www.mozilla.org/MPL/
Sun Industry Standards Source License - www.openoffice.org/licenses/sissl_license.html
BSD License - www.opensource.org/licenses/bsd-license.php

References

GNU Bulletin Volume 1, no.10 (June 2000) Available online at http://www.gnu.org/bulletins/bull10.html#SEC6

Appendix

B Linux Distribution Competitive Analysis

As a Windows desktop user the decision of what version of Microsoft Windows to use was probably a relatively easy decision. In today's desktop PC landscape, the decision mostly lies in which version of Windows XP to use (typically preinstalled by your hardware manufacturer). In contrast, desktop Linux offers you a variety of choices that extends into the hundreds. These different presentations of Linux are called *distributions*, or *distros* for short on the discussion boards. Desktop Linux choices are provided by Novell and small companies you have probably never heard of like MEPIS and Xandros, or even by community groups like Debian or Gentoo that lack any formal corporate backing. These distributions have a lot in common; they all use the same kernels though they may be patched differently. They probably have many of the same applications, though they may be offered in variety of configurations. That's why you should consider your needs and find the one that best meets your requirements. This is the real contrast to Windows or even Apple operating systems; with Linux you can make a list of your needs then you pick which distribution is right for you. You may pay for support only if you need it, once you have found a distribution with your desired feature set you pay only for the media (CD or DVD) and then if there is no seat licensing (per seat subscription options are frequently available depending on the distribution), use that media to install the operating system on many machines without fear of being out of licensing compliance. This idea may be considerably different to those who are used to the one-size-fits-all Windows operating system. To make some basic assumptions on how to proceed with your desktop Linux evaluation, the discussion in this appendix has been broken down into the following groups of Linux:

Enterprise: These types of Linux distributions are provided by companies with established track records and publicly available financial information. CIOs and IT Directors can then make judgments about the vendors' financial health and ability to provide future services.

Small and Medium Business (SMB): The SMB Linux distributions are those that have the capability to serve a fairly substantial enterprise though they might be considered more of a risk as a result of coming from a relatively small company or one not proven in its ability to provide enterprise-grade solutions. These companies may not have the financial means or track record of one of the large enterprise players, but that is not to say that these solutions are without merit. The distributions are mentioned because they hold some of the most innovative features in desktop Linux or provide exceptional value. They also may be of value when paired with a blue chip services organization like IBM Global Services or other consulting firms.

Notables: The distributions in this category are listed because they could be used in the enterprise or the SMB but have a limited or unverifiable track record or lack a formal corporate backer. Often, despite this, they might serve your desktop computing needs or provide some novelty that would be more advantageous than others.

Making a decision on the desktop distribution can be daunting but the following analysis should at least give you a good cursory overview of where to look and what distributions might best fit your individual needs.

Distrowatch.com is one of the most up-to-date and comprehensive sources of information on Linux distributions. The Distrowatch Web site shows popularity of Linux distributions by visitor input. First published in May 2001, the Distrowatch Web site is a good collation of articles on various Linux distributions both well-known and obscure. Each Linux distribution has its own home page with links to download sites and just as importantly reviews. Recent news is posted to the Web site under a news section, and there is a short synopsis as well as a package listing for each distribution. If you are in the process of researching a Linux distribution for use on the desktop, this is one of the best places to start.

LARGE ENTERPRISE LINUX DISTRIBUTIONS

Enterprises have different needs then those of smaller organizations. Enterprises, for the purposes of this discussion, are those that have at least hundreds of desktop PC users but more likely thousands. A poor decision with regards to enterprise infrastructure may yield problems that could easily run into the hundreds of thousands if not millions of dollars. That's why the considerations of the large enterprise must be more farsighted and undertaken with more caution. With large risk should come larger reward; taking the initiative to undertake a Windows-to-Linux migration could yield great savings for a large company or government organization. Bearing that in mind, the following analysis gives a conservative overview of the Linux desktop, recommending vendors that have the means to provide enterprise-grade services.

Red Hat

Red Hat (see Figure B.1) was founded in 1993 under the name ACC Corp. In a very short time the name of the company became Red Hat Software. Today the company has the most recognized Linux brand and has the leadership role in the industry for the enterprise, boasting customers throughout the Fortune 500. Red Hat software has many advantages, from deep financial resources to a proven track record. Red Hat has clients who have successfully instituted Linux infrastructure throughout data centers in financial organizations like UBS Financial and government entities like the U.S. Department of Energy Labs.

Company URL: *http://www.redhat.com*

Year Founded: 1993

Publicly Traded: NASDAQ: RHAT

Desktop Products: Red Hat Enterprise Linux WS, Red Hat Desktop, Fedora (Red Hat–sponsored community version of Linux)

Complementary Products: Red Hat Network, Red Hat Enterprise Linux ES

Pricing: $179—Basic Edition Red Hat Enterprise Linux WS, $299—Standard Edition Red Hat Enterprise Workstation, $2500—Red Hat Enterprise Desktop (10 desktop entitlements). All prices as of April 2005.

■ Red Hat's desktop offerings benefit from its heritage as an enterprise server solution. Red Hat Enterprise Linux is the family of server software that has been making inroads into the corporate data center for many years. Red Hat's desktop products benefit from the stability and security that has already been built in to the server products. Features include the inclusion of high-end data storage performance that would be of benefit to the technical workstation user. Security features are one of the real selling points of Red Hat Enterprise Linux, as the distribution includes Security Enhanced Linux (SELinux) which is a complement to discretionary controls put in place by system administrator; SELinux provides a level of security built right into the Linux kernel. Features that are expected of a desktop distribution are also included; Red Hat products include the following applications:

Core Productivity Applications: Firefox Web browser, Evolution email client, and OpenOffice.org productivity suite.

Multimedia Applications: RhythmBox (music jukebox), HelixPlayer (Open Source media player), and Totem (movie player).

Desktop Environment: Red Hat has chosen to include the GNOME desktop environment punctuated with a set of Red Hat–specific tools.

Developer Tools: There are a large number of development tools available for Red Hat distributions, including the GCC compiler toolchain.

■ Overall the Red Hat Linux desktop environment is conservative in its choices with few of the cutting-edge features that might be included in more progressive distributions. If those tools are a consideration it may be wise to look at the Red Hat–spawned and community-maintained Fedora Core.

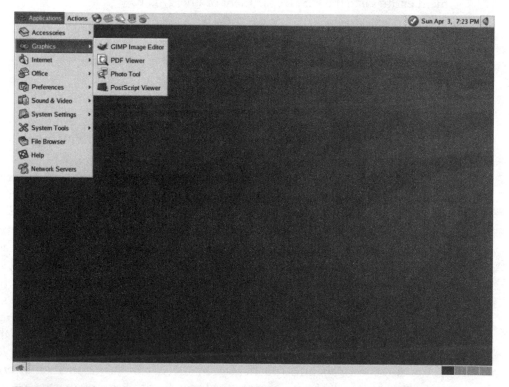

FIGURE B.1 The Red Hat Enterprise Linux is based on the same software as their reputable server offerings.

Products

Red Hat products are tightly tied to a support model where users receive updates from a trusted source rather than through an unqualified supplier at large on the Internet. This service is what Red Hat sells as a complement to open source software, which includes updates and installation support on top of a carefully packaged Linux distribution. Red Hat users can either purchase desktop operating systems with updates that they receive from an Internet connection, or they can receive their updates from a bundled server that resides on the customer site. For highly secure installations, the updates can be delivered from physical media to an update server hidden in a secure internal network. In government installations where controlling the entry of software into the network is important, this model is obviously advantageous.

Red Hat Enterprise Linux WS

Red Hat Enterprise Linux WS is an excellent choice for the Unix workstation user who is converting to Linux. This conversion allows users to take advantage of inexpensive x86 hardware while enjoying functionality comparable to what they were used to with a Solaris or SGI workstation. Red Hat Enterprise Linux WS offer the advantage of centralized management, security, and support for large-memory client systems and up to two CPUs. Red Hat Enterprise Linux is a good solution for large deployments of technical workstations because many of the tools users already are familiar with under commercial Unix are easily ported to the Linux architecture.

Red Hat Enterprise Desktop

Red Hat Enterprise Desktop would be usable for the knowledge worker who has little reliance on Windows applications. This Red Hat solution can span a variety of industries but is best suited for the technical workstation user or knowledge worker that requires primarily core productivity applications or those available via Web services. The Red Hat Desktop product comes bundled with desktop management capabilities and a locally hosted Red Hat Network Proxy. The Proxy downloads the updates for the desktops from a trusted source, Red Hat itself, and makes them available to the desktops on the local network. The Satellite model keeps all desktop update infrastructure on site so there is no reliance on an outside network (updates can come on physical media or via download).

Fedora Core

Fedora Core is not an official Red Hat product offering; instead it is the result of a community sponsored project where Red Hat worked with the community to provide a proving ground for emerging technologies. The release cycle is more aggressive than Red Hat Enterprise Linux and unlike the Red Hat official products, the Fedora Core software is much more *bleeding edge* as it includes the latest Linux desktop technologies that can be tested here first and then adopted into the Red Hat product line. In 2005 Red Hat spun-off the Fedora project into its own foundation so the similarities between the two may start to disappear over time

Novelties

The thing that makes Red Hat unique is that it is an execution company which is very conservative and dependable in its release cycle and the quality of product. The desktop offers much of the same functionality as other Linux distributions. However, Red Hat is a large company with call centers and it does provide support contracts with 24/7 response. It does extensive testing and is considered to be rock solid in data center applications. That same stability filters down to the desktop products.

Kickstart

In addition to Red Hat's ability to execute, it does provide some unique technologies that are Red Hat–specific, like *kickstart* which enables you to start an unattended Linux installation by setting up a configuration file (the kickstart file) and then starting the installation via CD-ROM, a local hard drive, or over the network but without the need to attend the install and answer specific questions. This feature is very useful when it's necessary to install a large number of identical workstations.

Red Hat Network (RHN)

The Red Hat Network is the name of Red Hat's update service, which offers an updater that allows you to pick and choose software to be updated. RHN also offers three types of modules that extend the RHN service. The Update Module allows you to easily install system software, the Management Module allows you to group systems using role-based permissions, schedule updates, and develop custom content channels (groupings of Linux packages), and the Provisioning Module helps manage *kickstarts* and create system snapshots for rollback.

Summary

- If you are looking for a complete end-to-end Linux solution with good back office solutions, Red Hat is a good choice. The desktop environment has all the options that an average knowledge worker would require. The place that Red Hat falls short is in the more advanced options for Linux power users. Their solution for Windows applications compatibility is to use Citrix ICA for connecting to Microsoft Terminal Services or to use Wine for running Windows applications with a replaced API. Where they shine is in the ability to deploy their solution with enterprise support and updates. Their bundles include access to the popular Red Hat Network which is a subscription-based service that provides updates to end users much like Windows Update does for Microsoft Windows users. They also have good documentation and there are support options that include live 24x7 support.

Product Pages

Red Hat Enterprise Linux WS—*www.redhat.com/software/rhel/client/*
Red Hat Enterprise Desktop—*www.redhat.com/software/rhel/client/*
Fedora Core—*http://fedora.redhat.com*
Red Hat Network—*http://rhn.redhat.com*

Novell

Novell is the one of the more interesting Linux distribution companies because they have been a recognized supplier in enterprise IT for many years. Until 2003 Novell had been selling its Netware operating system primarily with infrastructure tools that revolved around identity, management, and security. In 2003 it acquired German Linux distribution maker SUSE and started to meld SUSE Linux products with its own (see Figure B.2).

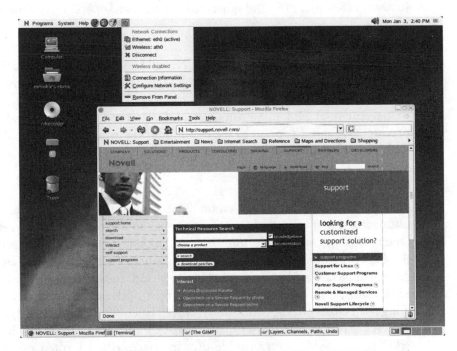

FIGURE B.2 Novell Linux Desktop offers the benefits of SUSE Linux with Novell's management capabilities.

Company URL: *http://www.novell.com*

Year Founded: 1983

Publicly Traded: NASDAQ: NOVL

Desktop Products: Novell Linux Desktop, SUSE Professional Linux

Complementary Products: Novell Open Enterprise, Novell Linux Enterprise Server, ZENworks, eDirectory, Evolution, Mono

Pricing: Novell Linux Desktop—$35 for media, $50 upgrade protection. SUSE LINUX Professional 9.3 Strong Encryption with media $99.95. Geographical pricing available. All prices as of April 2005.

Novell's products are some of the more innovative of the enterprise Linux distributions by virtue of its acquisition of SUSE and Ximian (a desktop Linux software company with strong ties to the GNOME foundation). Novell entered the Linux market through acquisition but it acquired two well-respected Linux companies. SUSE had a strong reputation for supporting multiple platforms. Using the *autobuild* system it can quickly build the same operating system for different architectures including non-x86 platforms like SPARC and PowerPC (PPC). Novell also has excellent hardware support and is a strong choice for companies that want to repurpose a variety of hardware (SPARC, PPC, and others) to one standard operating system, Linux.

Products

Novell has two desktop Linux brands, Novell Desktop Linux and SUSE Linux Professional. The Novell Linux Desktop (NLD) is designed for the general desktop user and leverages Novell infrastructure products like eDirectory and ZENworks for management. SUSE Linux Professional (SLP) is a more aggressive and full-featured product that should appeal to the desktop power user, though it would be suitable for almost any skill level of computer user.

Novell Linux Desktop (NLD)

Novell Linux Desktop is focused on desktop productivity. It includes the core applications that Linux desktop users should expect: Firefox for Web browsing, OpenOffice.org, and Evolution for email. NLD also benefits from readiness to use the ZENworks Linux management server, where systems administrators push updates from a central location. NLD benefits from the expertise of the GNOME and KDE teams; it directly employs a fair number of these open source developers. By tying itself closely to the community, Novell can offer the community the resources to develop packages that filter their way back into Novell products. The idea behind NLD is to provide a very simple user interface with a limited number of menu choices at the start. There are few user options but at the discretion of the systems administrator, any number of additional applications can be pushed out.

SUSE Linux Professional (SLP)

SUSE Linux Professional is marketed to the Linux power-user and home enthusiast or hobbyist. The SLP release cycle is also more aggressive, with a 6-month cycle versus an 18-month to 24-month cycle for NLD. Besides being more aggressive with product releases, SLP includes a large number of packages and offers access to the powerful YaST system administration tool. SLD is also a powerful operating system, well suited to the mobile user as hardware support even for more exotic hardware specific to laptops, which is recognized in most cases. SLD also includes some of the newer Linux tools for desktop users including Beagle (an indexing and search tool similar to Google's Desktop Search) and F-spot (an open source digital photo management application). Figure B.3 shows the SUSE Linux Professional Desktop.

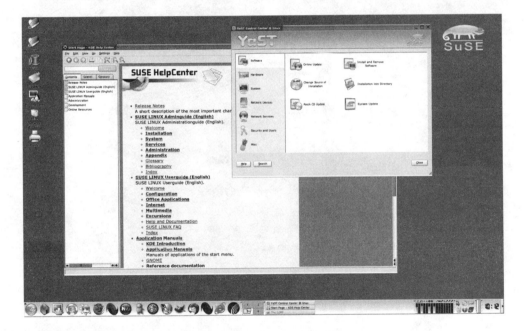

FIGURE B.3   SUSE Linux Professional Desktop.

Novelties

Novell includes a number of progressive tools with its releases that are at the forefront of Linux desktop technologies. Though many of these features are available for other platforms now, they are included by default with SUSE Linux and SUSE Linux.

YaST–Yet another Systems Tool

YaST is Novell's open source Linux system management tool that is similar to the Windows Control Panel. Almost every setting for the system, including hardware and software installation, network services, and security, can be administered from a single interface, as shown in Figure B.4.

FIGURE B.4   Novell's Open Source YaST system administration tool.

Beagle–A Document Index and Search Tool

Beagle indexes documents, email, Web History, Instant Messaging conversations, and a host of other files like images, music files, and even Microsoft Format documents. This tool is similar to the popular Windows desktop search tool developed by Google. Considering that Windows users are not going to be familiar with the conventions of where documents might be stored in Linux, this is yet another beneficial feature to the Windows user migrating to an unfamiliar Linux operating system.

Network Interface Switcher

The ability to switch between network interfaces is an extremely useful tool for Linux users in comparison to the variety of ways this is accomplished across all distributions. The Novell Linux distribution has a Network Switcher that sits on the GNOME toolbar and allows wireless users to choose between active interfaces, making switching from Ethernet to a wireless connection painless. In many distributions this is not readily apparent and requires the use of command scripts to bring down one interface and raise another.

Legal Indemnification

Novell provides legal indemnification in the case of intellectual property suits that might arise from any party making claims against the code that may become mingled into its Linux products.

Extras

SUSE Linux includes the new Xen virtualization package and a rather extensive software catalog including dedication to both the GNOME and KDE desktop environments. A full installation can take up quite a bit of disk space but you will be apt to find applications that address most of your needs, even if only marginally.

In the enterprise class of Linux desktops, Novell is rather progressive and offers a full suite of tools to support a successful desktop Linux installation. They also employ quite a few of the core developers for projects that support the Linux desktop like GNOME and KDE.

Summary

Novell is one of the largest IT companies in the world with perhaps the largest number of total resources applied to a successful Linux desktop product. It also has a large and established customer base that uses Windows and NetWare and will need to cater to the expectations of these customers to attract them to its newer products. Because it already has a powerful set of tools for LAN computing including management tools, email servers, and identity/security tools that are enterprise grade, it is in one of the strongest positions to produce an enterprise Linux desktop. It also has a unique blend of technical expertise acquired from Linux companies SUSE and Ximian to ensure that it has adequate internal knowledge to develop and improve its offerings.

Product Pages

Novell Linux Desktop—*www.novell.com/products/desktop/*
SUSE Linux Professional—*www.novell.com/products/linuxprofessional/*
Beagle—*www.gnome.org/projects/beagle/*

Sun Microsystems

Sun understands Unix through its development and ownership of the popular Unix operating system Solaris. It is also used to providing large enterprise support and solutions. Sun has tremendous research and development resources and its coffers are quite full and able to fund additional products. It has started to make forays into Linux and Open Source by coming out with a desktop Linux distribution, Sun Java Desktop (see Figure B.5), and by investing in StarOffice and then turning the source code over to the community for development under the OpenOffice.org project. With Sun's support, OpenOffice.org is one of the leading cross-platform alternatives to the Microsoft Office franchise.

Company URL: *http://www.sun.com/software/javadesktopsystem/*

Year Founded: 1982

Publicly Traded: NASDAQ: SUNW

Desktop Products: Sun Java Desktop System

Complementary Products: StarOffice, Sun Control Station, numerous infrastructure products and hardware that work with UNIX or Linux

Pricing: $100 per year—Sun Java Desktop System (including StarOffice)

Sun is no stranger to open source software. As early as 1984 it introduced and licensed NFS to the industry and has made many other contributions to the IT community without royalties. It has also open sourced its Solaris operating system under the Common Development and Distribution License.

Sun Java desktop was originally released for Linux but has since been included with Solaris 10. The future of Sun JDS as a Linux platform remains to be seen as the Solaris and Linux desktops could be in competition. Approach this distribution with caution as it is unclear whether Sun JDS on Linux factors into Sun's long-term strategy.

Products

Sun's Java Desktop System exists for both Linux and Solaris, and both leverage the GNOME desktop environment along with Java add-ons.

Sun Java Desktop System for Linux

The Sun Java Desktop System is a very simple desktop presentation with very few applications installed by default. The advantage is that the desktop has a very lim-

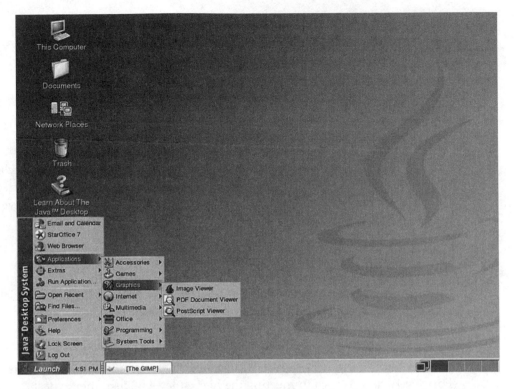

FIGURE B.5   Sun Java Desktop leverages Sun's Java brand and technology for JDS.

ited but simple to understand interface so as not to confuse new users. The real future in the Sun Java Desktop is in the ability for it to be managed. Sun lists the following systems administration features for Sun Java Desktop System:

Policy-Based Configurations: The ability to harden the desktop to prevent corruption and improve uptime.

Centralized Deployment: Deploy patches and software to multiple desktops, increasing the productivity of the systems administrator.

Inventory: The Sun Java Desktop also includes inventory collection capabilities to keep track of the software installed on individual assets.

The way Sun endeavors to provide these and many other features is through the Sun Control Station, which is aimed at simplifying the tasks needed to administer desktops from a central location. The strategy also includes the management of the Solaris workstation and servers so technology that is being developed as Sun JDS evolves will already be in practice for Unix workstations.

Novelties

Sun has the benefit of being an industry leader that has solved a number of problems for its legacy non-Linux solutions like Solaris. It can take the benefit of its experience and leverage it across its new Linux offering, the Sun Java Desktop. Sun is also looking to the future of desktop computing with its emphasis on thin client computing.

Java Installed

Because Sun is leveraging its Java brand, it includes the Java packages including plug-ins for the Web browsers and Java installed and configured in the desktop environment. There are also Java applications like games and a Java Media Player that are unique to this distribution.

StarOffice™

Sun produces the StarOffice suite and has donated the code to the community in the form of the OpenOffice.org office suite. The Sun JDS includes commercial support and backing of Sun Microsystems for StarOffice.

Enterprise Support

Sun has a huge technical support organization that provides support to many of the Fortune 1000. It is used to meeting the highest level of customer expectations and does so on a daily basis. As an enterprise user you may already have support contracts with Sun and may have an idea of what its commitment to customer satisfaction and service is. That's an important reason why you may want to consider Sun over others.

Summary

The Sun Java Desktop System is a solid, well-thought-out desktop system and Sun has the experience and resources to provide an enterprise class of support. Sun seems to suffer from a slight case of schizophrenia, as it would seem that Linux would be in competition with its Solaris workstation products. If you want to run a mixed environment of Solaris and Linux workstations, though, it would be a single point of contact for support and could prevent interoperability problems.

Product Pages

Sun Java Desktop—*http://www.sun.com/software/javadesktopsystem/*

SMALL AND MEDIUM BUSINESS (SMB) LINUX DISTRIBUTIONS

The criteria for small and medium business distributions for the purposes of this discussion include not only a desktop but also a complementary back-office solution, though any Linux or even Windows LAN infrastructure would just as well serve the functions necessary for Linux desktop users. The products in this category all have decent interoperability with Windows users within the enterprise as well as customers and suppliers from outside the organization. These distributions may also offer innovations and features that a more conservative large enterprise distribution might lack.

Mandriva

Mandriva is the company that was formerly known as Mandrakesoft. In April 2005 it announced the acquisition of Connectiva, a prominent Linux distribution from Brazil with good traction in South America. The Mandrake heritage was one of community commitment, ease of use, and robust desktop features. Mandrake was also known for delivering its software in value-added bundles that combine core Linux distributions with additional commercial or dedicated-use applications like firewalls.

Company URL: *http://www.mandriva.com*

Year Founded: 1998

Publicly Traded: Euronext: MAKE.PA

Desktop Products: Mandriva Linux Desktop for Businesses, Mandriva Move

Complementary Products: Mandriva Corporate Server, Mandriva Club, value-added bundles for various types of users

Pricing: Mandriva Linux Desktop for Businesses $89 Euros

Products

Mandriva products (see Figure B.6) are reputed to be some of the easiest and most intuitive for Linux desktop users. Mandriva's strength beyond ease-of-use has been good support for all types of PC hardware. It also is at a point where it is moving to an annual release cycle that will be less disruptive to users who might have been forced to upgrade more frequently. It also offers corporate and per incident support so that users who need it can get guaranteed service-level agreements. Since acquiring the South American Linux distribution Connectiva in 2005, it may also benefit from some unique technologies in the future, like Connectiva's highly touted apt-rpm.

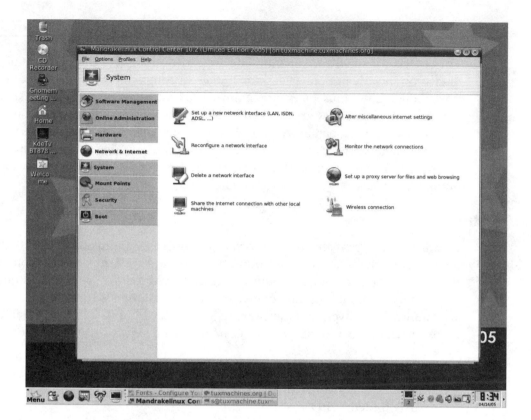

FIGURE B.6 Mandriva Linux combines the technology and benefits from the merging of Mandrakesoft and Connectiva.

Mandriva Linux Corporate Desktop

Mandriva includes all the usual core productivity applications as well as a commitment to maintain a product for up to five years for its desktop product. The provision for interaction with the Mandriva Linux Corporate server offers a good end-to-end desktop and LAN computing solution.

Mandriva Move

Mandriva Move is a Live CD version of the Mandriva operating system and functions in much the same way the companion CD-ROM to this book functions. Pairing Mandriva Move and a USB flash key is a very effective alternative to a laptop when another PC is available. This method allows you to take your applications and operating system with you anywhere on the Live CD, and your data on your flash drive.

ON THE CD

Novelties

The Mandriva desktop Linux installation, as a result of its loyal customer base, has often pushed the leading edge of Linux technology to meet the demand of its enthusiastic constituency.

Mandriva Linux Tools

Mandrake includes their "Drake" tools that leverage open source technologies to make configuration of the desktop very easy. Examples of these tools include DiskDrake, a partitioning tool, and RPMDrake, a package installation tool that uses the URPMI tools (urpmi and urpme).

Value-Added Software for Windows Compatibility

Mandrake includes a demo of CrossOver Office standard version to run some Windows applications on the local system and an *ICA client* to connect Citrix® server. Finally it includes NX Client to connect to a NoMachine NX server so you can acquire a thin client session from either Windows or Linux.

Summary

Mandriva is a worthwhile distribution to investigate due to a good track record as a desktop distribution. Over the past few years Mandriva has started to release more products to provide server support for their distributions, mainly for LAN infrastructure like file and print services along with security applications like firewalls.

Xandros

Xandros (see Figure B.7) is based on the initial development done by Corel, the makers of Word Perfect and other popular desktop productivity applications. In 2001 Xandros acquired Corel Linux Business Divisions development team. Since then Xandros has developed a highly functional Linux desktop that former Windows desktop users will likely find intuitive. The start bar is relatively simple and the menuing includes names that make sense to the inexperienced user. One benefit for the migrating user is that there are plenty of tools that are specifically helpful to the migrating Windows user, including built-in support for Windows applications through CodeWeaver's Wine implementation and authentication for Windows Active Directory Servers.

Company URL: *http://www.xandros.com*
Year Founded: 2001
Publicly Traded: No

Desktop Products: Xandros Desktop Version, Xandros Business Desktop OS

Complementary Products: Xandros Desktop Management Server

Pricing: Desktop OS (Includes CrossOver Office Plugin and Sun Star Office)—$129, Xandros Community Version—Free Download

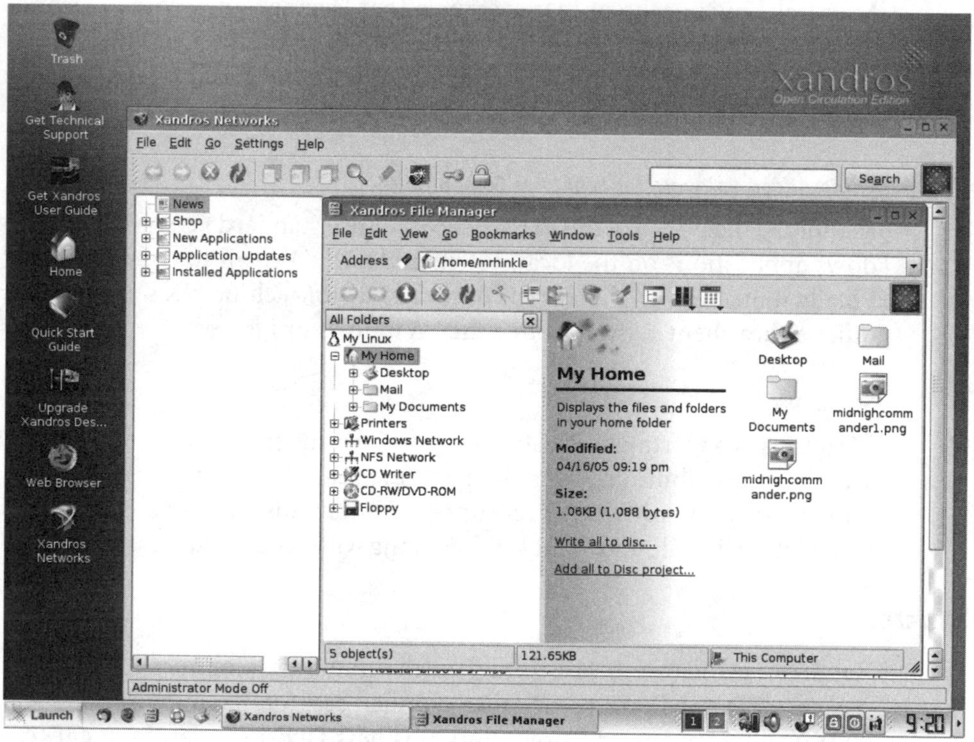

FIGURE B.7   Xandros offers simple installation and a custom file manager.

Products

The Xandros Desktop products all have a common set of features and are based on a highly customized version of the KDE desktop environment. However, Xandros has focused on features within the distribution that are not Open Source but complement the desktop, including a proprietary file manager and other tools like CD burner software as value-added applications not available to other distributions.

Xandros Business Desktop

While there are a variety of bundles organized around the Xandros desktop core Linux distribution, the Xandros Business Desktop has been tailored for business users. Integration with Active Directory makes it easy to deploy Linux desktops alongside Windows desktops without disrupting already productive users. The inclusion of the CodeWeavers product is another nice addition if you need to run Windows applications that are supported under Wine. If you have Windows 98 licenses and applications that you would like to reuse, the Xandros Networks includes a demo of Win4Lin 9x which allows you to run Windows 98/ME as a program under Xandros. Of all the Linux distributions, Xandros offers some of the best options for legacy Windows users.

Novelties

While many Linux distributors are satisfied to use open source applications throughout their distribution, Xandros has chosen to include proprietary programs to handle important functionality like file management and CD burning. Its presentation is as good and in many ways better than some open source alternatives found on Windows.

Easy Installation

Xandros has an easy five-click install that is very streamlined and sacrifices a variety of options for speed and ease of use. Xandros' installation is extremely simple with an automatic installation and detection of existing Windows installations.

Active Directory Server and Windows NT PDC Authentication

Xandros provides specific features in its Windows Networking Control Center that configure clients to authenticate against Windows Primary Domain Controllers (PDC), as shown in Figure B.8.

Xandros File Manager (XFM)

The Xandros file manager is unique to Xandros Linux distributions and, starting back with Corel Linux, it has been a primary focus of this Linux distribution. The Xandros file manager is as simple to use and robust as anything you might find on Mac or Windows. The interface includes drag-and-drop capabilities to share files across networks using FTP or Windows network shares.

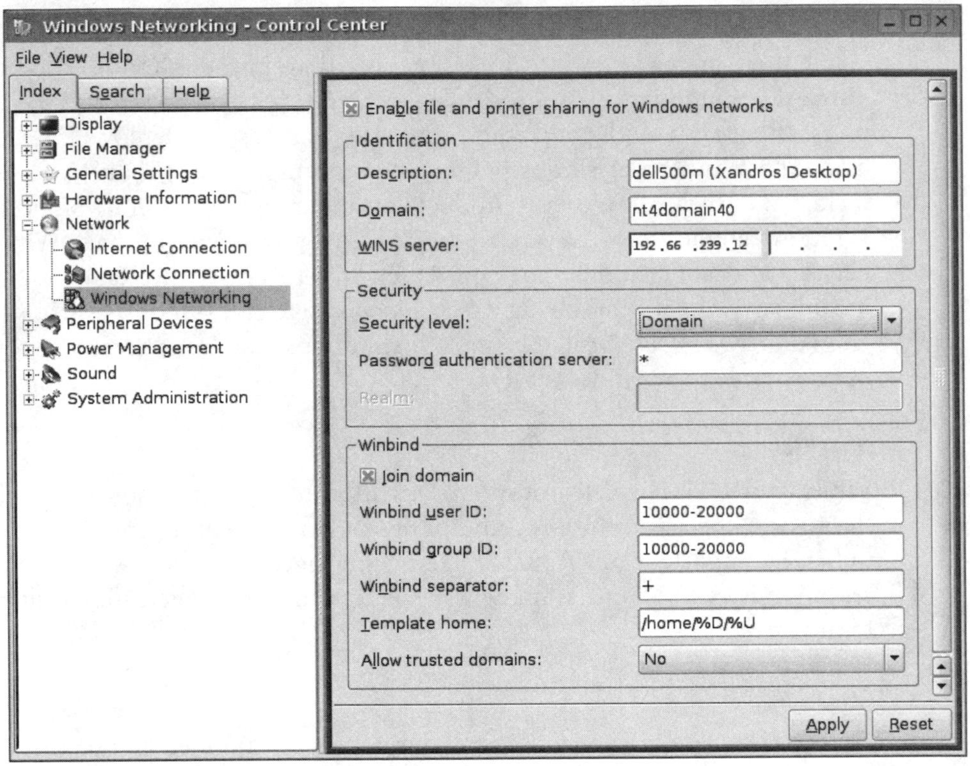

FIGURE B.8 The Xandros Windows Networking Control Panel makes configuration of Linux clients under Windows domain servers easy.

Xandros Disc Burner

The Xandro Disc Burner is integrated into the Xandros file manager and has much of the functionality that Windows users who are familiar with Roxio Easy CD Creator would recognize. Right-click menus give users the option to write files to CDs. The Xandros Disc Burner can also copy disks and erase rewritable disks.

Inclusion of CodeWeavers CrossOver Office

Xandros also includes a copy of CodeWeavers CrossOver Office preinstalled so users who have supported Windows applications can run them natively under Linux using the CodeWeaver's implementation of Wine.

Included StarOffice

Xandros includes a copy of the commercial StarOffice Suite from Sun that includes all the capabilities that OpenOffice.org does but with commercial support. At one point in time this might have been a bigger selling point, but with advances in OpenOffice.org the inclusion of StarOffice is nice but holds relatively little advantage to most users.

Overall the Xandros distribution has the capability to replace a Windows desktop environment.

Summary

The Xandros is a great choice for desktop operating systems if you want easy-to-use features and the ability to process updates to the desktop through the Xandros Desktop Management Server. All management for updates to the desktop can be processed through the graphical user interface.

Linspire

Linspire (see Figure B.9) is very unique compared to all the other distributions and gathered a lot of infamy as a result of a lawsuit with Microsoft over its initial name, Lindows. In 2004 the lawsuit resulted in a settlement that required Lindows to become Linspire. Despite the renaming, Lindows has remained a favorite distribution among new Linux users. The Linspire interface is very clean and reminiscent of Windows XP with a bottom of the screen launch bar and a *system tray* on the lower right-hand corner.

Company URL: *http://www.linspire.com*

Year Founded: 2001

Publicly Traded: No

Desktop Products: Linspire

Complementary Products: Click N Run Warehouse

Pricing: $49.95 Linspire 5.0, Linspire 5.0 with CNR service $89.95 as of April 2005

Products

Linspire focuses on providing a user experience that is equivalent or better to the one a Windows home user would have, with little, if any, need to delve into complicated command line configurations or special tools. Linspire has also spent time improving applications that may be open source but didn't quite offer the quality of experience Windows desktop users have come to expect.

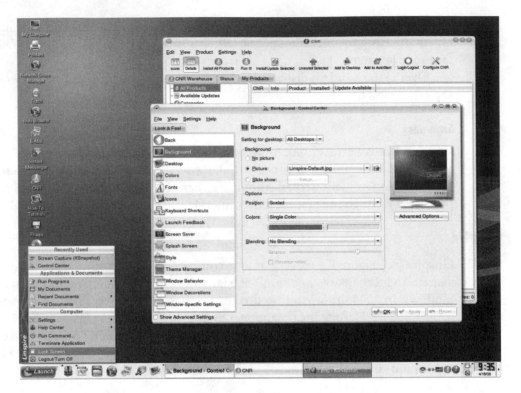

FIGURE B.9 Linspire has an interface very similar to Windows XP.

Novelties

Linspire really caters to the computer novice, making Linux accessible to the least-skilled desktop user. Its interface and presentation is as good as any desktop distribution and benefits from an active user community that provides plenty of feedback.

Click N Run (CNR) Software Service

The CNR Service offers one-click install of thousands of Linux applications. The optional service also alerts Linspire users to the availability of updates in much the same way that Windows Update updates your Windows PC. However, the CNR software service collates applications that are not solely maintained by Linspire. This overcomes one of the most difficult problems with Linux in application installation and distribution compatibility. CNR has one of the most comprehensive collections of desktop software that requires no more than a single click to install. The only downside to this approach is that the user and groups permissions that most distributions rely on are not as strictly enforced for Linspire users.

"L" Applications

Linspire adds a lot of value by taking open source applications and creating their own branded applications for specific desktop tasks. Their *Lsongs* music player, shown in Figure B.10, is very similar to Apple iTunes but runs on Linux.

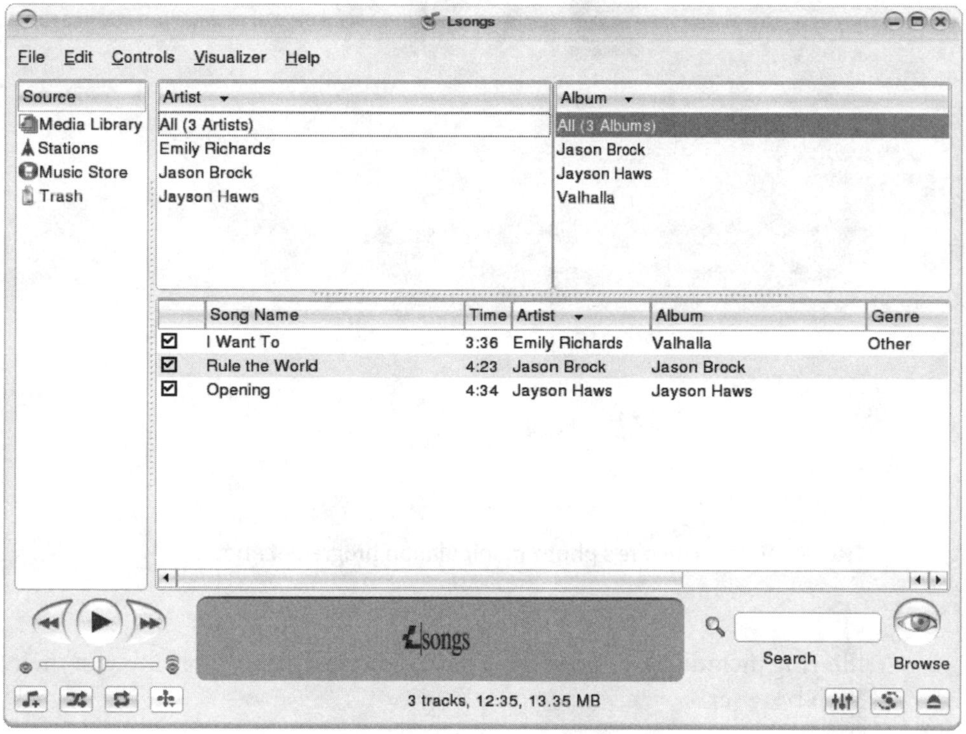

FIGURE B.10   Linspire's Lsongs is an easy-to-use Linux music jukebox that is comparable to Apple's iTunes.

Linspire has done the same with a Linux photo manager dubbed LPhoto that makes it simple to manage digital photographs. The interface allows users to create Web pages out of photo albums and send email or print all from one interface, shown in Figure B.11

Family-safe Features

Linspire also offers a number of safety features in its product. Members get additional protection though at an additional purchase price through the use of Virus-Safe (powered by Vexira Antivirus), SurfSafe (powered by Cerberian), junk email

FIGURE B.11   Linspire's photo manipulation program, LPhoto.

filtering included for free in the email client, and pop-up blocking in their Linspire Web browser.

Summary

Linspire really shines for organizations that don't have on-site IT personnel. Updates can be processed through the easy-to-use CNR Software Service, and most features are well documented. The reason that Linspire falls into the SMB category is that in lieu of an on-site server updates can be processed on the desktop through a simple one-click mechanism. For file and print sharing and other needs, either a Linux server or more likely an embedded Linux device would be an ideal complement along with hosted services for Web and email. The downside is that Linspire does not advertise telephone support but does offer premium online support for its CNR subscribers and Linspire Insiders. Because of the variety of third-party software applications that are tested and easily installed, and dedication to a high quality of testing and interoperability, Linspire would be a decent choice for SOHO users.

NOTABLES

Linux distributions that fall into the notable category could include a very long list. Not withstanding, the following distributions all offer advantages and have obtained a following that merits recognition when investigating a Linux distribution.

Debian

The Debian project was started in 1993 by Ian Murdock and has since flourished among the technical workstation crowd. It has also served as the basis for many other distributions like Xandros and Knoppix, which is included on the companion CD-ROM, that leverage its *apt* package manager software that is both easy to update and resolves dependencies for other libraries automatically. Debian is probably one of the most widely used Linux distributions today because of its governing doctrine of community responsibility. Debian is governed by a "social contract" that mandates Debian will remain 100% free software and that the software will be given back to the community, they won't hide problems, and that their priorities are their users and free software. In the event that they choose to distribute nonfree software, they will distinguish it as such and make sure that it is separate from the Debian software distribution.

Company URL: *http://www.debian.org*

Year Founded: 1993

Publicly Traded: No

Desktop Products: Debian

Pricing: Free download, media and support available from various sources

■ Debian really doesn't have desktop software because the distribution can be adapted for whatever use makes the most sense to the end user. Debian has been used in server installations and as a desktop platform with considerably frequency.

Novelties

■ The novelties of Debian are more the result of a community's effort to meet their own needs. The hassles of installing software that may have dependencies past the core program like compilers, libraries, and other programs became a source of contention for Debian users, so they chose to use a package management system that could resolve these dependencies and easily install software. That's really a benefit when compared to other distributions that may not distribute binaries or that cannot distribute binaries bundled with other packages.

Apt–Advanced Packaging Tool

Apt is regarded as one of the most efficient and practical ways to install Linux packages and managed dependencies. Apt works by checking a list of software sources which are archives located on the Internet (or that can be set up locally) and then downloads not only the package but any packages that it may be dependent on (usually software libraries).

Hardware Support

■   Another benefit of the Debian community is its contribution and ability to provide a large array of hardware drivers. Debian's hardware support is the envy of both commercial and community-driven Linux distributions. The only downside is that as a community group they have very little bargaining power to supply propriety drivers for specialized hardware.

Guarantee of Freedom

When you choose a single vendor you may be at their mercy when it comes time for upgrades or new features. They control the product roadmap and you are obligated to follow their mandates or be at risk of being unsupported and hung out to dry. The Debian social contract ensures that you will not be forced into a price gouging upgrade cycle. Since it will always be free you know that your costs will not rely on acquisition but maintenance. That is helpful to those companies that have been forced into an upgrade cycle by their vendor and had to upgrade at times when it was extremely trying to their business.

Summary

■   Debian may not have the same level of support that Linux vendors supply but their user forums are extremely active, often providing answers to questions posted in less than one hour. Also, once installed it is extremely easy to manage. In many cases, if Debian isn't your choice for a desktop distribution it may be a good choice as a server operating system. Debian also has one of the most extensive public users lists on the Internet, outlining how they are using Debian in businesses, educational institutions, nonprofits and governments around the world. It's likely that if you are looking for a reference local to you, you will be able to search their database for a company using Debian in your local area —*www.debian.com/users/*.

Gentoo

Gentoo Linux wouldn't be classified as a beginner's desktop. The focus of this distribution is its highly adaptable and optimized architecture. The Gentoo distribution is a more Spartan approach to desktop Linux as all software is chosen and installed by the user. Because of this near limitless adaptability Gentoo is often called by its makers a *metadistribution*.

Project URL: *http://www.gentoo.org*
Year Founded: 2003
Publicly Traded: No
Desktop Products: Gentoo Linux
Complementary Products: Gentoo Linux
Pricing: Free download

Gentoo Linux

Gentoo Linux can be used as a desktop Linux distribution or as a server. That is the real unique feature of Gentoo, it's often adopted by users who like to tweak and optimize their systems. Gentoo has many similarities to Debian from an organization and social point of view. The differences are mainly in how the software is built.

Novelties

Gentoo is unique in comparison to many distributions because it is driven purely by a community that holds itself to the standard of its own Gentoo Social Contract. The Gentoo Social Contract is very similar to the Debian Social Contract. The Gentoo Social Contract mandates that the software is and will remain free, so there is no chance of the project deciding to close its doors to the user base.

Portage

Portage is the software distribution for Gentoo Linux. To get all the latest updates you can issue the emerge –synch command to update your locale Portage tree. The Portage tree is a collection of scripts that Gentoo Linux uses to install packages or programs for Gentoo Linux. Portage can be used for simple installation of updates or for more complex installations used to control versions.

Summary

Gentoo is probably not the most intuitive distribution to use for your first foray into desktop Linux, but it does hold many advantages for the technologist who wants to control the desktop. It's also one of the most well-supported open source projects, with a loyal fan base and extensive documentation.

MEPIS

MEPIS (see Figure B.12) is a relatively new distribution that has gained a lot of attention as an easy-to-use Linux distribution that is built on the Debian distribution with a number of enhancements. The most notable enhancement is the ability to run either as a Live filesystem CD or to be installed to a hard drive.

Company URL: *http://www.mepis.org*

Year Founded: 2003

Publicly Traded: No

Desktop Products: SimplyMEPIS

Complementary Products: None

Pricing: Download—Free, CD $9.95, annual download subscriptions for all MEPIS versions

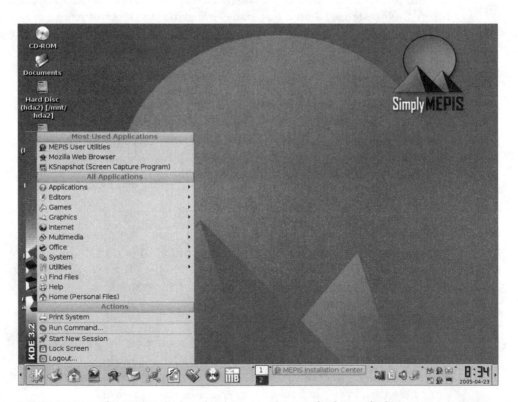

FIGURE B.12   The MEPIS desktop makes use of a tweaked KDE desktop.

The reason that the MEPIS CD is being mentioned alongside others with such widespread support is that it's a new breed of simple to use software that doesn't make the user wade through an intimidating mountain of software. SimplyMEPIS picks one application for each task and installs that in the beginning. Overtime more applications can be added if the user so desires, but it's not necessary. The goal of MEPIS is to provide a simple functional desktop without the noise associated with some distributions that might package as many as four or five applications for the same task, such as Web browsers or email. MEPIS also benefits from a rabidly loyal fan base of users that have chosen to staff the Web site *www.mepislovers.org*. The complementary Web site offers free support through forums and IRC (as do many distributions) but their quick rise to popularity has shown that end users really wanted this type of distribution.

Novelties

MEPIS is unique in the sense that's its very simple and easy to use. It's designed as a functional desktop, not necessarily as a Windows replacement, and doesn't adhere to any style guidelines that many other Linux distributions have tried to follow.

Easy Program Installation

MEPIS has tweaked the installation interface to make it easy to install software through KPackage that leverages Debian apt tools, but does so with a menu-driven interface based on K Package, a KDE package management interface.

MEPIS System Center

MEPIS provides an easy-to-use configuration center that is very simple (see Figure B.13). It provides a central control panel to adjust common settings, while the user control panel is very simple to use and meant to be intuitive to all levels of PC user.

LiveCD Functionality

ON THE CD Similar to the Knoppix companion CD-ROM included with this book, Simply-MEPIS is a bootable Live CD that allows you to run Linux from CD before making a decision.

Summary

MEPIS is one of the most promising Linux distributions because of its relatively low cost and its simple aim to provide core desktop functionality rather than trying to address an overly broad number of features.

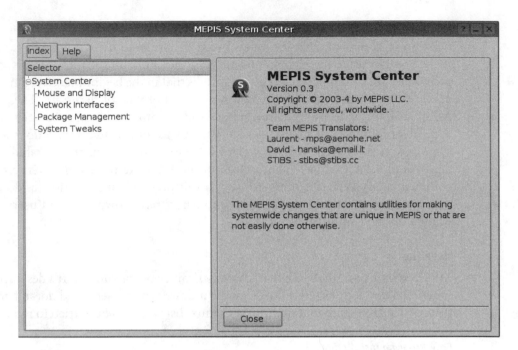

FIGURE B.13 The MEPIS configuration center.

SUMMARY

It should be apparent by the number of Linux distributions listed here that there are many, many choices. This gives you a lot of freedom in your vendor and the price, if any, you decide to pay for your desktop operating system. You will also find that there are many options at your disposal. Recommending any one distribution over another is somewhat like recommending a suit of clothes without knowing someone's size. The best advice you can get is to take your own needs and shop them around to the list of vendors to find the one that fits best.

C Case Studies

When it comes to implementing IT systems there is often a disconnect between theory and practice. So hearing anecdotes from organizations that have successfully implemented Linux and open source systems in their enterprises is a helpful way to see how a plan becomes part of a projection environment. The case studies contained within this appendix are examples of companies, governments, and educational institutions that have successfully used both commercial and free/open source software on Linux to save money and improve their computing environments.

CASE STUDY I—SOFTWARE COMPANY SAVES $400–$500 PER DESKTOP

Mindbridge CEO Scott Testa Remembers His Epiphany

Mindbridge, the makers of IntraSmart, a software suite for intranet applications, always purchased PC clones for desktop machines. The cost of the hardware came to about $250 each without the operating system. Testa suddenly realized that they spent twice as much on the desktop software as they did on the hardware, including the operating system, office suite, and Windows client access licenses. He knew something was wrong with this picture. Through a gradual process, almost all of the 50+ employees are now running a Linux desktop.

A Bottom-up Organic Process

For Mindbridge, the impetus to migrate began with the system administrators. Light unofficial use of Linux in the organization early on gave some of the IT staff a chance to get some experience. Linux began to spread on the server side as the company grew, then some technical users wanted Linux workstations. Eventually, Red Hat

Linux on the desktop became standard issue for the technical users. A few reluctant technical users were given two desktops, one Windows and one Red Hat Linux, with a KVM switch (a keyboard, video, mouse switch—a box that allows a single set of peripherals to be used with multiple computers) to help them make the transition. It was a useful crutch for Windows users getting used to the Linux desktop.

Testa acknowledges that it has become easier over time to migrate people to Linux, and he sees almost no resistance to the change now. All staff in support, sales/telemarketing, and administration are now using Linux on the desktop—some Lindows (a user-friendly Linux distribution), most Red Hat. The last users to move from Windows were the telemarketers, who used a CRM package that only ran on Windows. Their CRM vendor happened to be in the process of migrating development from a Windows-specific client to a browser-based client. The telemarketers were able to migrate once the new CRM client was released, because the new client was platform-neutral.

The biggest problem Testa has seen in Mindbridge's move to Open Source has been compatibility between OpenOffice.org and Microsoft Office. Early on, they had trouble opening complex Word documents sent to them from outside the company. He says that these problems are getting much better now that OpenOffice.org is more mature. He has always liked the easier PDF generation of OpenOffice.org, though, and considers it more professional to send to customers than Word format.

Mindbridge achieved savings of between $400 and $500 per desktop with a wide-scale migration to Linux.

Open Source Products Used

- Red Hat Linux for most desktops
- Lindows for some desktops
- OpenOffice.org office suite
- Evolution email client
- IBM's Eclipse Java development environment
- CVS source code control

Software Development on Linux

Software development is Mindbridge's core business, and they trust it to Linux and open source programmers' tools. As a Java shop, they have standardized on IBM's Eclipse development environment and CVS for source code control. Most of what they utilize is either free or low cost, and they have found that they did not need to sacrifice the quality of the tools to realize the cost savings. The programmers have mostly been using Red Hat since 1998. One caveat they have discovered is that for the programmers' tools they are using, Linux takes more memory than an equivalent Windows workstation.

Doing the Practical Thing

At Mindbridge, they don't view themselves as Microsoft bashers or Linux zealots. It was a matter of simple economics. Testa estimates that they save between $400 and $500 per new desktop by using Linux. As the company grows, and desktop machines are purchased for new employees, Linux has become the practical choice. Testa believes that open source migration was easier for them as a software company because they are relatively tech-savvy. Being a relatively young company, they also lacked the legacy systems that tie many organizations to Windows. The primary driving force has been the cost.

For Mindbridge, movement in the IT industry toward browser-based clients helped them migrate to Linux. According to Testa, "Open Source is not a fad—it's a trend, especially with vendors releasing browser-based products. Who cares what the underlying operating system is when the applications are delivered over the Web!"

CASE STUDY II—PATIENCE PAYS OFF IN A CONSERVATIVE IT ENVIRONMENT

Joel Sweatte knows that it's harder to introduce Open Source into traditionally conservative environments. As the head of Unix systems at National Commerce Bank, a Southeastern U.S. regional bank, he has slowly introduced Linux into the banking Web portal myCCB.com, a critical production system that he manages at the bank. In a follow-the-leader industry, he sees his role as a patient adviser. According to Sweatte, "My strategy is to stay current, and watch for opportunities to spread Linux. All I can do is make upper management aware of the options."

The Right Test Project Can Convince Colleagues

Sweatte advises using Linux on new systems that will be in front of people, so they become accustomed to them and therefore convinced of the value of Open Source. At National Commerce, he had two older HP systems running iPlanet, a proprietary Web and application server, for an e-commerce application on myCCB.com. Sweatte's team left one untouched, and replaced the other with Linux and IBM's Websphere application server on an Intel PC, at a savings of about $22,000. He then ran them side by side as a test. The team measured the performance of both, and found that the relatively inexpensive Linux PC was faster. While not a rigorous benchmark test, it was proof to Sweatte that he didn't need to upgrade the HP hardware in order to achieve acceptable performance at a significantly lower cost.

They disconnected the HP, and now run the entire application on one machine. The total savings is the $33,000 per year maintenance on the HP systems, minus a one-time charge of $5,000 for the Linux PC hardware. Sweatte did not purchase an outside support contract for the Linux servers.

No One Notices the Infrastructure

Sweatte went to the district warehouse, and took ten old PCs that were packaged for recycling. He built a few good systems with the parts from those rejected machines. He then created a large file drop box using SquirrelMail, a free open source email system, to compensate for the low file size limits in the regular corporate email system. This system is used to upload large files, so they don't have to be sent via corporate email. He slipped the dropbox system in under the radar, and it has since become a production system.

As Sweatte says, "We took machines literally off the scrap heap, built a good system, and it has become a production system that everyone depends on. It has never broken. When things just work, no one pays attention."

"Most of the time, you already have some Linux in the organization, but no one has been paying attention. We already had Sendmail, but ignored it since it was so reliable. We ignored Linux because it just worked. We have never had major problems—Linux just doesn't fail here."

National Commerce Bank saves approximately $33,000 per year in maintenance costs with a migration from HP to Linux servers for an e-commerce application.

Open Source Products Used

- Sendmail
- Turbo Linux
- Red Hat Linux
- SquirrelMail

Resistance from Lower Ranks of IT

Sweatte supports about 3,000 email users on seven Microsoft Exchange servers. He knows he could run this on two Linux servers—one as a primary server and one as a failover for high availability. He could even reuse the hardware from the existing servers. But in a conservative IT environment, he is getting too much resistance to the proposal to get approval. Much of the resistance is coming from the system administrators who have specialized in Microsoft products and who may fear that changes in the industry will leave them without the right skills. "Even though it will cost lots of money to keep Microsoft Exchange servers, and they won't work as well, the company doesn't want to change." Upper management simply doesn't know enough about Linux yet to trust it as an alternative. The banking industry tends to follow the curve of technology change, not lead it.

According to Sweatte, the trick to working in conservative environments is to be relentless and don't give up. "Stay with the technology, and know it. Make it relevant to the company. Work on places where you can get it in, and get it accepted." He knows that the Linux systems he has in place now work well and save money. His strategy moving forward is to keep looking for ways open source software can further benefit the company. The proof he has seen that Linux is cheaper and more reliable have turned him into the resident Linux evangelist.

CASE STUDY III—MANUFACTURING COMPANY CONVERTS TO LINUX DESKTOPS IN 120 DAYS

Jeff Whitmore, the IT Manager at guitar manufacturer Ernie Ball, didn't have time to plan a multiyear phased migration to open source software. The CEO of the company dictated a move away from Microsoft on short notice, so Whitmore sprang into action and started looking at options for Linux on the desktop. An IT staff of four migrated almost 80 desktops to Linux in less than 120 days, from initial mandate to research to deployment.

The Impetus for Change

After a disgruntled employee reported to the Business Software Alliance (BSA) that Ernie Ball was out of compliance with Microsoft licensing, BSA personnel appeared at their offices with federal marshals and conducted an audit. They were found to be about 10% out of compliance, and eventually negotiated a hefty penalty fee of more than $1,000 per desktop. They were then given 120 days to get into compliance. Microsoft ran advertisements in the local market making an example out of the company, prompting the CEO's decision to migrate to Linux rather than purchase more licenses.

Back to the Future: X Terminal Sessions

Whitmore's staff spent the first 30 days researching options, and decided to use thin clients on the desktops. They first looked at specialized thin client hardware appliances, but decided they would be able to use their existing PCs. The next 30 days were spent learning how to deploy and administer thin client Linux desktops with X terminal sessions.

The remaining time was spent deploying the desktops. For a time, Whitmore was worried that they wouldn't make the deadline, but his staff of four finished the task with four days to spare.

All user data for 80 desktops is stored on one Intel-based Linux server. It's a heavy-duty 850 MHz, dual-processor server from Dell with built-in redundancy. The desktops are older PCs loaded with a stripped down copy of Linux, and no user access to the local drive. All applications and user data is delivered in an X terminal session. In a terminal session setup, all the work of running "desktop" applications is done on the server, and just the interface is delivered to the client. The company purchased an expensive Cisco switch to handle the network load. The server and switch were by far the largest expenditure of the migration, but Whitmore thinks in retrospect that the switch may be more than they really need given their network traffic.

The company saved a significant amount of money by reusing older desktop hardware as X session terminals. Many desktops are 233 MHz machines from 1999 and 2000, and none is over 500 MHz. Performance is fine for an X session. According to Whitmore, "Most desktop environments are simple—they just need word processing, spreadsheets, email, and a browser. The desktop doesn't have to be complex to meet user requirements."

Guitar manufacturer Ernie Ball was pushed to quickly migrate almost all of their desktops to Linux, and found that supporting their users is much easier without Microsoft.

Open Source Products Used

- Custom version of Linux for thin clients
- Red Hat Linux to serve data to thin clients
- DOS emulator for Linux to run an industry-specific application
- Evolution email client
- OpenOffice.org

Finding Linux Applications

The trickiest part for Whitmore was finding the Linux applications needed to replace some of the industry-specific Windows products. Ernie Ball uses CNC (computer numeric control) machines for carving wood in the manufacturing process, and they were controlled by a DOS emulator on Windows. They were able to substitute a DOS emulator on Linux after some research. They also control a buffing robot that reads a chip in the guitar to determine how to buff each guitar. The IT staff wrote a Linux-based application to replace the existing Windows application in this instance.

On the desktop, the biggest complaint from users was that they had to give up Microsoft Outlook. At the time of their desktop migration, the Evolution email client was not available, so they used Netscape mail. When Evolution came out, everyone breathed a sigh of relief, since it is made to mirror the functionality and look of Microsoft Outlook. It is now the company standard. OpenOffice.org was the office suite choice from the start. They encountered some problems sharing files with the outside world at first, but they have worked them out as OpenOffice.org matured.

Their last remaining Windows server requirement involves timeclock polling software. Because they have production floor workers, the company maintains multiple physical timeclock machines. Windows software polls and manages the data, and there is no Linux substitute for their current setup. Whitmore will eventually replace the timeclock machines with new equipment that features an open API for accessing data. With an open API, his staff will be able to write their own customized software to interface with the timeclocks.

An Informal Network of Gurus

Ernie Ball never spent money on outside Linux training. Whitmore was already running SCO Unix for his business application servers, and Linux for a Web server. Since his staff all had Unix experience, they were able to pick up Linux quickly. He has also seen the proof that Linux takes fewer administrators. Because of time spent by two staff members at a new facility, they have reduced the support staff at the main offices by half. With Windows, Whitmore is sure that they would have needed more people.

The IT staff approached end user acclimation by empowering employees to help each other. Regular nontechnical users who were especially comfortable with technology were chosen to act as informal helpers for their peers, and were trained by IT staff first. Then these informal gurus assisted their colleagues. Employees have gotten used to the changes, and now look to Open Source for their home computers. Whitmore's staff has been asked to burn CDs of OpenOffice.org for employees to take home, and it's a service they are happy to provide, because the office suite is freely distributable.

Fewer IT Headaches

The actual migration went smoother than Whitmore expected, and he claims that his life is much easier since the transition. He likes having total control of all the data. Users do not have access to a local drive, so they can't lose data. When someone deletes his entire home directory, Whitmore doesn't bat an eye. "No problem—we just restore it from yesterday's backup!"

The IT staff uses xosview, an open source tool that displays system stats (*http://sourceforge.net/projects/xosview/*), to check on systems across the network. They can monitor CPU usage and processes, and kill a process remotely if necessary. Administration has become a lot easier. The desktops don't die anymore, and there are no more blue screens. Whitmore's advice to IT managers thinking of deploying Linux on the desktop: "Do it! My life has been a lot easier since we did this. Bite the bullet and accept the initial pain of the learning curve. Once you do, it's so much easier."

CASE STUDY IV—LOCAL GOVERNMENT SAVES $27,000 WITH SQUID/SQUIDGUARD

Justin Smith thinks in practical terms. As CTO for Guilford County Government in North Carolina, budgetary concerns were the driving factor in his consideration of open source technologies. Smith achieved an estimated savings of $27,000 per year by replacing just two servers on the edge of his network, and began to train his staff for future Linux deployments.

Taking the Plunge

Smith was already using some Linux in the environment for noncritical systems. They were running a Linux-based backup system for an Oracle database and operated a Web-cam (video camera connected to the network) on a Linux server, but they were nervous about expanding into more critical functions.

As the economy got worse, the budget drove them to look seriously at possible cost-cutting measures. Smith had been already been thinking about Linux for some time. When his support contract for SurfControl (a proprietary Web proxy, Web content filter, and spam filter) was up for renewal, Smith looked for a way to replace it with Open Source. He and his staff began an informal discussion about the ROI of using Linux for the task. They decided that it was a no-brainer since they could end up saving a significant amount, especially on the proxy and filter software. Smith was convinced that Linux could replace their current system, but he needed to show a proof of concept. Smith took advantage of leftover money at the end of the budget cycle to find out if Linux would work as well. That way he'd get his proof of concept, but he didn't have to give up part of his budget in case it didn't work.

Smith successfully replaced the Windows-based SurfControl server with Squid/SquidGuard and SpamAssassin (Web content and spam filters discussed in

Chapter 8) on Linux. They chose to target the Web proxy as the first production system to move to Linux because they were having a few problems with the product and were not getting timely support from the vendor. Given how much he paid for the support contract for SurfControl, Smith just didn't think he was getting a good deal for the money. After the conversion, they found that performance was better with the new system as well.

The second production system they targeted was the Sendmail relay and spam filter. By using SpamAssassin on Linux, Smith was able to completely remove the SurfControl product from two separate servers. His support contract for the Windows-based Sendmail relay was expensive, so Smith was glad to be able to drop it, too.

Smith found that support was less expensive and timelier from a local consulting company that specialized in open source products. That company introduced him to inexpensive high-availability service on Linux servers. For not much more than the cost of the hardware, they were able to set up both servers with a redundancy system using Heartbeat, open source software used to set up failover service. The previous systems did not have failover capability, so Smith was able to achieve a level of service not previously available.

Guilford County, NC saves about $27,000 per year with just two Internet infrastructure migration projects.

Open Source Products Used:

- Red Hat Linux servers
- Squid/SquidGuard
- Sendmail
- SpamAssassin
- Heartbeat for failover control

The Savings

The cost savings is a big win for Guilford County. Smith estimates that they save $12,500 per year for the proxy server and $15,000 per year for the mail server. Most of this savings comes from replacing expensive proprietary products and support, and the rest from replacing Windows on the servers. The open source products they chose are all available at no cost, so the only expense was in consulting fees to deploy and support. Overall, it adds up to a savings of about $27,000 per year for two Internet infrastructure projects.

Getting Help

Smith had Unix experience on staff, and he had light Linux experience himself. Expert support for any potential migration was an issue for Smith, and he needed to know that he would have the help required to ensure a smooth transition. He hired a consulting company to research software, perform the deployment, and provide support, taking pressure off the IT staff. They didn't have to have in-depth knowledge to maintain the systems on a daily basis, and could learn from the consultants who performed the deployment and provided support.

Smith believes that some local government organizations may have more Linux experience already, and may be able to do their own proof of concept. It all depends on the amount of time you have available and staff skills.

A Smooth Transition

The transition was actually smoother than Smith expected. He had an idea of what to use as replacement software, but he depended on the consultant to make sound recommendations. The only thing Guilford County's 2000 users noticed was a slightly different error message when they tried to reach a Web site that was blocked. The Web content filter took a little time to get properly adjusted, because the public health workers need access to sites that most corporations would choose to block, such as information about illegal drugs. Once the settings were right for their needs, Smith's staff found administration a breeze.

Sanctioned for Government Use

In 2003, the chief information officer of the U.S. Department of Defense issued an agency-wide memo sanctioning the use of Open Source for department systems. Word of the memo circulated in the local government IT community, and Smith thinks that it is likely to make a difference in the rate of open source adoption for departments like his. "We'll see a more rapid adoption in government at all levels now. The DOD statement means that Open Source is taken more seriously in government in general, and now you don't have to worry about being an outcast since it's been officially approved."

Smith's advice to his peers is to look for where it makes sense to deploy in your particular environment. "I'm not for one operating system over another. I just want everything to work smoothly. You have to know your environment, and you have to gauge where it will make sense for you."

CASE STUDY V—VOLUNTEER EFFORT SAVES A
CHARTER SCHOOL $145,000

Systems integration professional Mark Fowle had two kids in a Holly Springs, NC, charter school, and was active on the board of directors and the technology committee. When the school moved to a new facility, Fowle saw an opportunity to help them upgrade some systems at a reduced cost using Open Source. He proposed Linux for new servers, and the StarOffice office suite on new Windows desktops. Fowle was able to provide Web and email services at no additional cost beyond the hardware, avoiding expensive outside services. With a little volunteer help from the local Linux Users Group, Fowle eventually saved the school nearly $145,000 over two and a half years. He continues to assist them with technology decisions and support, and is currently working on migrating some desktops to Linux.

Making the Case for Linux

With the typical limited budget of a school, the obvious first reason to look at Open Source was licensing cost savings. But Fowle also promoted the idea that students would be better served if they gained experience with a variety of systems.

The case for Linux had to be built slowly. The school administration tended to view computers from the point of view of brand names rather than function, and Fowle recognized this as a sign of a heavy dependence on Windows. He worked to help them rephrase the issues in practical terms of what they actually needed. Once Fowle was able to turn their attention to the underlying purpose of each machine, they became interested in open source alternatives because of the budgetary impact. Finally, several designs were created and presented to the board for review.

Implementation

The design that was selected allowed Fowle to start by building a Linux server as a primary domain controller to authenticate the existing Windows NT, 2000, XP, and 98 desktops and provide a security layer.

Fowle started with the servers primarily because they would be the most important and the most expensive if implemented with proprietary software. The firewall was first, then the primary DNS server and finally the Web server. He made choices on substitutes for previously used products. Native DNS (Bind 9) was used instead of a Microsoft solution, and Apache was used instead of Microsoft IIS. The Windows version of StarOffice replaced Microsoft Office on some PCs. Instead of using a Cisco Pix firewall or utilizing services from the Internet service provider, Fowle opted for Linux and MonMotha for firewall protection.

The next phase of the school's migration plan is to move some of the older Windows 98 and NT desktops to Linux. Installation of programs such as OpenOffice.org or StarOffice will allow the students to experience non-Microsoft tools and broaden their skills. Fowle believes this gives them a better overall understanding of text processing, spreadsheet, and graphic presentations, rather than rote memorization of menus and keyboard shortcuts. Of course, the license savings continues to be the key factor.

The Community Partners Charter High School in Holly Springs, NC, saved approximately $145,000 over two and a half years with a series of open source migrations.

Open Source Products Used

- StarOffice
- BIND 9 for DNS
- MonMotha for firewall

Staffing Challenges

Fowle acknowledges that trained staff can be a problem in smaller IT environments. The only person on staff at the school who provided computer support did not have sufficient skills to maintain Linux. Fowle became the volunteer technology director and reported to the school's board of directors.

Over time, Fowle has educated the school's operations directors to do some low-level administration and support. He has found plenty of free, highly competent support from his local Linux Users Group and open source developers around the world. According to Fowle, "You just need to know where to find help, whether free or paid support. Expert help is out there—the first step is to know how to find it."

The Power of Volunteers

Fowle's efforts to help his children's school goes far beyond attending PTA meetings. But with a vision for solving computing problems with the most practical means available, he successfully integrated open source products into a Windows environment and saved the school a bundle. Your local Linux Users Group would also probably be willing to help your children's school with someone acting as liaison and coordinator. Because there is so much interest in grassroots open source advocacy, expert users and system administrators are more than willing to help in cases like this Holly Springs, NC, charter school.

CASE STUDY VI—STATE GOVERNMENT LEADS THE WAY WITH LAMP

Jim Willis, Director of e-Government Services for the Rhode Island Office of the Secretary of State, was a consultant for the state when he implemented an online database using open source tools. The ability to use open source technologies was a condition of his hiring, and the state has benefited as a result of his leadership.

Putting Linux in Plain View

The first project Willis undertook was an online rules and regulations database available to the public and other government agencies. It was the proof that open source tools could deliver value for less. The whole project was delivered for $40,000 with Willis working alone part-time for four months. Because the new online database faced the public, it was the perfect test for open source value.

Willis was promoted to Director of e-Government after the next election of a new Secretary of State, and he took on the role of advising other agencies on the use of Open Source. A high-level member of the new Secretary's staff was well versed in Open Source, and encouraged a more open attitude toward Willis' proposals. A trend of working to improve efficiency in IT has also worked in favor of open source adoption.

The LAMP Development Model

A major trend has emerged in Internet development utilizing four open source tools or platforms: Linux for the operating system, Apache for the Web server, MySQL for the database, and PHP, Perl, or Python for the custom code (LAMP). Willis used these tools for the rules and regulations database, and was able to complete the project in less time than other development models would have allowed.

Willis has been consistently pleased with the performance of the MySQL database. It is running on a Dell server with Red Hat preinstalled, with almost perfect uptime. MySQL was also included in the Red Hat installation. Agencies use a custom PHP form to upload their regulation files in PDF format. Willis was already familiar with PHP, so it was a natural choice. Some freely available Perl code was adapted to provide certain functions as well, but the vast majority of development occurred using PHP.

A big advantage of Open Source is that help is easier to find. Willis recommends developing staff who are able to find the solutions to problems, because no one has memorized how to handle every situation. You just have to know where to look. "I've called Red Hat for support just once, when I was getting started. Google is really the first line of support."

The State of Rhode Island Secretary of State's office saves between 6 to 10 hours per week of support time with a migration to Linux and a Web-based email solution, instead of Microsoft Exchange and Outlook.

Open Source Products Used

- Red Hat Linux
- Apache Web server
- MySQL database
- PHP Web scripting language
- Courier IMAP, QMail
- SquirrelMail

Saving Time is More Important Than Saving Money

After his initial success with the rules and regulations online database, Willis looked for other ways to use open source software. He started by replacing an Exchange server with Courier IMAP and QMail on Linux, open source email systems, and replacing Outlook with SquirrelMail, a Web-based email client. Users were having trouble with Outlook, and his staff was spending too much time supporting it. Willis picked the email system as a good migration candidate because he knew it would save both money and time. It took Willis' team two days to migrate the mail server. They saved money in licensing costs by replacing Windows and Microsoft Exchange, but the biggest benefit has been the free time to devote to other projects. Willis says that he saves between 6 to 10 hours per week of support time with the new system. The reliability of open source software on Linux is allowing him to pursue other projects that will benefit the public.

Cost is still an issue, of course. Before starting on any migration to Open Source, Willis does an informal analysis to find out how much it will save the state. In his case, it's sufficient justification to proceed.

Web Servers and Databases

The next step was to start migrating Web servers and database servers. Willis had several Microsoft IIS servers that needed to be upgraded. By now, his staff was familiar with Apache, so they used Linux and Apache as a replacement for Windows and IIS. There was one glitch, however. They had previously written Active Server Pages that needed to be converted to PHP and Perl.

According to Willis, when you have applications "write" code for you, rather than code by hand, it's hard to know later what you've done. This made it somewhat difficult to convert the applications. They tried some conversion tools, such as asp2php. It worked sometimes, but Willis found that it was easier to rewrite the applications. Most of them were just database query scripts, which were easy to rewrite, and took about 3–4 days per script. All of the servers that Willis' team has already converted have paid for themselves already.

Advice for Other States

Now other states are asking Jim Willis for advice in adopting Open Source. His advice for getting started is to take on a small migration project first to prove to colleagues that it will work. "Don't pick something critical for the first project. Pick a server that provides an important service, though, that people will be able to see in action."

He generally plans a migration when one of two things happen: he is tired of always supporting a problem system, or he needs to purchase an upgrade.

CASE STUDY VII—OPENNMS FOR MANAGED HOSTING COMPANY

When Rackspace Managed Hosting started in 1998 to lease Internet colocated servers to customers, they went with Linux almost everywhere in an effort to keep costs down. In fact, heavy use of Linux was standard in the low-margin managed hosting sector. According to IT Manager Eric Evans, "People would be surprised by how much they would save if they went with Linux."

Linux Servers and a Mix of Desktops

Evans supports a little under 200 servers for internal company use. Evans put all of the internal services that he could on Linux servers, including email, file servers, print servers, DNS, and network monitoring. Only the financial application server and the sales force automation server remain on Windows, because the vendors do not yet have Linux versions. Linux comprises about 80% of internal servers.

Of the approximately 9,000 customer servers, Evans estimates that 60 percent are Linux, reflecting demand for cheaper Web solutions. Some customer services that Rackspace provides, such as domain registration and a customer portal, are also on Linux servers. The mandate to use Open Source whenever possible extends to the service provider role as well. Rackspace only uses Windows servers for applications for which there is no Open Source substitute.

According to Evans, more attention is paid to IT expenditures now that Linux has shown its value to the organization. "Any time we need to deploy Windows, we choke on the price, and have to work harder to get the approval. Open source deployments are typically time, hardware, and that's about it."

Rackspace employs a large support department, so a sizable percentage of desktop users are technology-savvy. Although the officially supported desktop is still only Windows XP, employees are permitted to install whatever they want on their desktops as long as they give up support from the IT department. As a result of the loose rules, many technical employees have installed Linux. The IT department ensures that basic services such as printing will work for both operating systems, resulting in a hybrid desktop environment.

Everyone in engineering runs Microsoft Office on CrossOver Office (discussed in Chapter 10), an emulator for a subset of Windows applications. According to Evans, "CrossOver Office is nearly flawless, and it's about as close as you can get to natively running Microsoft Office on a Linux workstation. I bought the plug-in first to play Quicktime videos, but was skeptical. But it worked great, so I spent $60 on it for the full version." Evans likes it better than OpenOffice.org because he has absolute compatibility with Windows users now and in the future. And he was surprised that Microsoft Office is faster on CrossOver running on Linux than it is on Windows.

Most nontechnical employees run Windows XP. Evans doesn't run Microsoft Active Directory, though. Instead, he uses a SAMBA primary domain controller, backed by openLDAP as a Windows domain controller. A Linux server is used for all authentication. Evans concedes that he probably sacrificed some functionality with this choice, but found that it didn't actually matter for Rackspace. The bells and whistles that were sacrificed were not really needed. Evans and his staff also know that they can authenticate anything against LDAP, since it's an open standard. Open standards have always been preferred at Rackspace whenever possible, to keep options open in the long term.

OpenNMS Saves Big

Rackspace doesn't have exact figures on how much a Linux migration saved, because they didn't migrate. But they are very aware of how much can be saved with specialized tools that run on Linux. OpenNMS, an open source network monitoring tool, is used internally for the approximately 200 company servers.

And the cost savings are huge. Evans looked at OpenView, a proprietary competitor to openNMS from HP. But OpenView can cost tens or hundreds of thousands of dollars, depending on the installation. For Rackspace's needs, this product would cost about $200,000 to $250,000 just for internal network monitoring and reporting with $10,000 per year in maintenance costs. To use OpenView for their customers' servers was simply out of the question because the costs were too high. OpenNMS is a comparable open source free network monitoring tool. Rackspace purchases support from Blast Internet Services, the maintainers of OpenNMS, for just a few thousand dollars per year. The savings are dramatic.

There is a trade off for the savings, however. The HP product requires less on-going administrative effort because the tools are mature. Evans expects automation to improve as more administration tools are added to openNMS. The positive side is that Rackspace has some influence over what goes into the product. His staff is working now to expand openNMS so they can use it for network monitoring of their customers' servers. They will contribute their efforts to be incorporated into future versions of openNMS. Their code will help other users of the product, but it also benefits Rackspace by removing the burden of supporting the enhanced code.

Rackspace Managed Hosting saved over $200,000 by using openNMS for network monitoring rather than a proprietary product. They continue to save several thousand dollars per year in support.

Open Source Products Used

- Red Hat Linux
- openNMS for network monitoring
- BIND 9 for DNS
- Sendmail and Postfix email servers
- SAMBA primary domain controller
- OpenLDAP for Windows domain controller
- CrossOver Office (proprietary product) to run Microsoft Office on Linux

Supporting Open Source Deployments

Evans finds that they have far lower administrative overhead with Linux than with Windows. "It's part of the Unix paradigm. We've seen as high as a 50–1 effective server to system administrator ratio with Linux, but only 20–1 for Windows. Our average has probably been 35–1 or 40–1 on Linux."

Evans hasn't had much of a problem finding Linux expertise. "When I received applications, they came from Monster.com and our Web site job postings. Rackspace is known as a desirable place to work because it is a startup, and employees have some freedom to run Linux on desktop. Linux enthusiasts are happy to be here."

When asked what advice he has for IT Managers thinking about a move to Linux, his basic message is that it's not as hard as you may think. "People overestimate the complexity of migrating to Linux. FUD (fear, uncertainty, and doubt) would have it that Linux is extremely complicated to set up and use, but that's just not the case. Even good Windows or network administrators pick it up. Linux is becoming more mainstream and mature, and is a perfectly capable platform for infrastructure, databases, etc. Don't fear it."

CASE STUDY VIII—CITY GOVERNMENT SAVES WITH THIN CLIENTS

Kenosha, Wisconsin, a city of 80,000 on the shores of Lake Michigan, has embraced thin client computing with Linux to reduce total IT expenditures. An IT staff of four supports 250 users with a trimmed total IT budget of $500 per desktop per year.

Thin Clients with No Moving Parts

Microsoft Windows never gained a foothold at the City of Kenosha. They were always a Unix shop, with a mainframe serving character-based applications to Unix workstations. City applications were written in COBOL running on the mainframe, and later on SCO Unix. When PCs running Windows were becoming the standard desktop, the city decided that they didn't want to go in that direction. They wanted to keep the IT staff small, and they knew that Windows on the desktop would mean increased demand for support. They also didn't want to spend the money when they had a perfectly good solution already. It really came down to a matter of finances.

Because the Unix workstations were working well for them, they decided to stick with Unix. But the hardware needed to be replaced, so they started shopping around for a less expensive way to keep their current systems.

The IT staff settled on Neoware (formerly Human Design Systems) thin client stations to replace the older Unix workstations. With flash RAM and no moving parts, maintenance was greatly simplified. The staff wanted to keep the desktop as maintenance-free and inexpensive as possible and thin clients fit the bill. The City of Kenosha does not pay for a support contract on the desktops, and they haven't needed it. One of the clients was even in service for 12 years before being retired, a feat that would have been impossible with a PC. As IT Director Ruth Schall says, "There's nothing that can go wrong with the desktops, so maintenance is much cheaper than PCs would have been."

The thin client stations now run a stripped down version of Linux provided by Neoware. Red Hat Linux on a server from Penguin Computers delivers data to the clients over a 100 Mbps network. The city's COBOL applications run on the Linux server. COBOL development continues today using TIP IX, a COBOL development environment for Linux. They have found no difference between running COBOL on the mainframe and on Linux, except that Linux is actually faster.

Basic Productivity Software on the Desktop

The desktops run a basic window manager, and the city has standardized on custom menus. Evolution is used for the email client. Users love it because it looks like Microsoft Outlook, which most use at home. The city originally used the Netscape browser, but switched to Phoenix (now called Firefox), a fast browser based on the original Netscape (Mozilla) code. It has a clean design, and ties in well with Evolution.

The standard office suite has been Corel WordPerfect for Linux. Because this version of WordPerfect is no longer in development, the city is beginning to migrate users to OpenOffice.org. According to Tig Kerkman, IT Systems Administrator for the city, they originally planned to migrate to Sun Microsystems' StarOffice. But OpenOffice.org has made such great strides that he now considers it a better choice. They are not in a hurry to migrate the office suite, however, because they are not incurring any new costs with WordPerfect. Because WordPerfect is still entrenched in the legal profession and government, there is still an active community providing support online. But good compatibility with Microsoft Office documents was still missing.

 The City of Kenosha, Wisconsin supports a user base of 250 with a total IT budget of $500 per desktop per year.

Open Source Products Used

- Red Hat Linux to serve thin clients
- Customized version of Linux on Neoware thin client hardware
- Evolution
- Corel WordPerfect and OpenOffice.org
- Phoenix Web browser
- CodeWeavers Crossover Server Edition to share a limited number of Microsoft Office licenses
- TIP/IX for COBOL development on Linux

Ensuring Compatibility with Microsoft Office Documents

The city chose CodeWeavers Crossover Server Edition to allow users access to Word, Excel, and PowerPoint when needed to view documents sent from outside the organization. According to Schall, CrossOver Office is critical because it ensures 100 percent compatibility with the important Windows applications.

Five licenses of Microsoft Office are enough to handle outside documents. The license cost is low, and relative to actual need within the organization. To ensure compliance with the Microsoft licensing, only five users are allowed access at one time. The Linux server running CrossOver actually launches the application, which is accessed by the thin client stations as needed.

Kerkman has been very pleased with the help available from CodeWeavers. When they had a printing problem, for example, they were able to work with a real expert to get the problem solved quickly. He says that support has been phenomenal.

Doing More with Less

Schall is amazed at how much they can do with so few people and so little money. She knows that other government organizations with the same number of users require significantly more IT staff and money than she does at Kenosha. One reason for the increased efficiency is that they don't spend time cleaning up after email viruses that affect Microsoft Outlook. As Schall says, "They fall like undetonated bombs on our servers. It's not a problem."

Her team of three has always written and maintained customized software for the city, rather than purchasing off-the-shelf products. They get exactly what they need, but pay less for it. According to Schall, this is only possible because their Linux systems are so reliable that they have time for development instead of putting out fires.

Advice to Other Municipalities

As Kerkman says, "Don't be afraid of Linux. The system administration side is easier. Here, two people handle the entire desktop support, installation, everything, for 250 users." His advice is to start using it as your mail server, or as your gateway to the Internet to gain experience. Then move to the desktop, but don't emphasize the operating system. "Don't tell the users they are running Linux. Tell them, 'This is your desktop,' and that it's what they need to do their job."

Schall also notes that a lot of management is worried about bringing in Linux because they are worried about finding support and knowledgeable employees. "But you have access to dozens of people with the answers, whereas when you pay for support, it is frequently poor. Although you don't have formal support with many open source products, help is out there and it's of good quality." The IT staff at Kenosha were never satisfied with commercial support anyway. "We knew more than they did. We have not had any major problems with Linux."

CASE STUDY IX—LINUX THIN CLIENTS BEST CHOICE FOR 1,200 REMOTE USERS

When the North Carolina Cooperative Extension needed to overhaul the computer system for 1,200 users in multiple remote locations, Systems Programmer Administrator Janyne Kizer found that Linux on thin clients was the best solution.

The North Carolina Cooperative Extension is a joint effort between the state of North Carolina, most of the state's one hundred counties, and NC State University. Each participating county has an office that accesses the system, which serves a network of agricultural support staff. 4H agents, state agricultural agents, plant pathologists, entomologists, and other staff make use of the network to assist farmers with agricultural management. Ninety servers are spread around the state to support 1,200 users, with some as far as six hours' drive from the IT support staff's location.

From Solaris, to Problems with a Windows Test Deployment

The decision to use thin clients had been made long ago, because the Cooperative had been using Solaris on thin clients from NCD. When it was time for a large-scale upgrade, the original plan was to switch to Windows terminal servers. But to make Windows terminal servers work, many of the workstations would have to be upgraded, making the move more costly than expected. The team started the process anyway, and set up ten Windows servers as a pilot.

The servers were set up to synchronize their Active Directory settings, but problems were encountered. Many of the counties still had low bandwidth connections, and because the servers had trouble synchronizing under those conditions, there were some days when some users couldn't log in at all. Eventually, it became clear that a Windows deployment wouldn't work within the limitations of available network speed and current number of IT staff. The team found that the network infrastructure simply wasn't adequate to support Windows terminal servers. With state and local government budget constraints, upgrading the networking wasn't an option. According to Rhonda Conlon, Director of Extension Information Technology at NCSU, the network cost alone to upgrade to T-1 speeds would have been nearly $65,000 per month. So when the team turned to Linux, it wasn't primarily because of the cost savings of software licensing. They were simply looking for a solution that would work within their existing environment so they wouldn't have to upgrade the network.

Linux Thin Clients Did the Job

With Unix experience, it was natural to turn to Linux. Kizer and her staff decided to test Linux terminal servers on the existing thin client systems. If it worked, then they would deploy Linux for the whole system. They chose Red Hat from a short list of about three distributions. One factor was that Red Hat was based in their home state, and they liked the idea of using a North Carolina company. There was also a campus computing environment at NCSU already using Red Hat, and they wanted to take advantage of existing expertise.

They put together the basic applications that users would need, then put out some beta test servers. They had the first site up within six weeks. Next, they installed Linux servers at five sites. Everything worked just as they needed, so they deployed a total of 90 servers to complete the overhaul.

The thin client hardware, some of it seven years old, was easily reused with minor memory upgrades. Red Hat was chosen as the distribution provider, along with StarOffice, BlueFish (HTML editor), GAIM (AOL-compatible instant messenger client), Mozilla for Web browsing and email, the Netit text editor, and GIMP (Photoshop-like program).

Kizer tried to maintain continuity wherever possible, so as not to change everything all at once. Users were already familiar with Netscape browsing and email, for example, so going to Mozilla was easy for them. The Extension purchased a support contract for StarOffice.

According to Kizer, "We are a very small department, with one system administrator, two support people, and two part-time undergraduates working the help desk. We are able to handle 90 remote servers and 1,200 users. We would have needed many more people to handle a Windows deployment, but we couldn't hire people because of budget constraints. Linux solved a lot of problems for us."

 The North Carolina Cooperative Extension provides Linux desktops on diskless thin client hardware with all the office basics for 1,200 remote users scattered around the state.

Open Source Products Used

- Red Hat Linux on diskless workstations
- Mozilla for Web browsing and email
- StarOffice
- BlueFish for HTML creation
- GAIM for instant messaging
- GIMP for image editing
- Netit for basic HTML editing in plain text

As Conlon says, "We were willing to spend the money on Windows, but we couldn't make it work with the network infrastructure. When we factored in other things such as additional support costs, hardware upgrades, etc., then it was clear that we needed to go with Linux." In the end, the North Carolina Cooperative Extension enjoyed significant savings. Conlon's estimate of the initial license savings is about $368,000. The ongoing license savings is about $150,000 per year.

User Acceptance

User acceptance has been a bit of an issue, but Kizer believes some of it is simply the resistance to change that is common in government environments. "A user recently got upset that a file he created at home in Microsoft Word wouldn't open in StarOffice. When we looked at it, we found that it wouldn't open in Word, either. Because the software was new to him, he was quick to blame StarOffice, when the problem was really a corrupt file." She has found that users will sometimes complain in a general way about their new systems, but when asked what work-related tasks they are unable to do, they don't have specific complaints.

End users receive training from their local office technology liaison and from several trainers employed by the state. The IT staff gave a series of train-the-trainer sessions, and the training staff did the rest. The local technology liaisons also help users with issues. None of the IT staff has received any formal training in Linux.

Support Issues

The only real problem uncovered after deployment of the new system was solved in house. When some remote sites ran into problems printing from an envelope feed, Kizer uncovered the source of the problem as an incomplete printer driver. Her team solved the problem themselves by fixing the driver, and submitted it the Linux community. You don't have to be an expert Linux kernel hacker to improve the operating system. With access to the source code, you can make changes to meet your requirements, and bug fixes will benefit the community at large.

The free support has been the best available for Kizer's team, but they have also purchased support from more than one open source vendor. Her strategy in keeping current on technical issues is to read technical books and magazines, and become active on the local Linux User Groups lists. Kizer is lucky to have two groups nearby with plenty of expertise—NC State has one on campus, and there is also a very active group nearby in Research Triangle Park, North Carolina.

"My Life is Easier Now"

Kizer's advice to other technical managers thinking of migrating to a Linux thin client solution is to go ahead and do it if you can. "It just makes your life a lot easier. It's supereasy to support, with great disaster recovery. When we started this project, we typically had an average of 100 problem tickets open at any given time. Now that we have made the switch, we have under 25 open tickets at any given time. We probably spend as much time supporting the 100 on-site Windows users as we do the 1,200 off-site users. The system is very stable."

CASE STUDY X—GRUPPO VENTAGLIO ITALIAN TOUR OPERATOR USES THIN CLIENT

Viaggi del Ventaglio is Italy's leading holiday resorts and vacation tour operator. Based in Milan, Italy, Ventaglio provides vacation tour packages and also manages resort properties worldwide. Requirements for reliable information exchange are critical in the travel industry. It is even more crucial when working with widespread property management and reservations. To provide a level of customer satisfaction that makes for repeat clients, Ventaglio must also provide a world-class information system that can ultimately become a competitive advantage. Being in the travel business not only requires Ventaglio to react quickly to their customers needs but also be able to bring their data and applications to a variety of locations in Italy and throughout the world. Win4Lin Terminal Server is a key part of their IT strategy.

> **Company:**   Established in 1976, Viaggi del Ventaglio is Italy's leading tour operator in the holiday resorts segment. The company is also the nation's second-ranking general tour operator, arranging vacations for more than 541,000 clients.
>
> **Challenge:**   Ventaglio's resorts and offices are located throughout the world. Individual branches need access to central IT systems, which include legacy applications as well as critical Microsoft® Office® applications. These programs must be available to remote "desktops" over a WAN.
>
> **Solution:**   Win4Lin Terminal Server delivers Ventaglio's business-critical applications from Linux® systems deployed on a combination of HP® and IBM® servers. Combining Win4Lin terminal Server with Tarantella® Internet application delivery technology makes applications available to users throughout the Ventaglio enterprise.
>
> **Benefits:**   Desktop applications are easily standardized and consolidated from Ventaglio's central IT department in Milan. Application servers are configured redundantly to minimize downtime. Computing power is centralized, resulting in saved resources. Inexpensive thin client PCs are deployed at remote locations. With Linux, system administration is inexpensive and flexible for Ventaglio. When Desktop hardware fails, it is simply replaced with identical thin client hardware.

The Challenge: Cost-Effectively Delivering Windows Applications Over a WAN to Widespread Offices and Resorts

Ventaglio tour operators throughout the company network need access to centralized Windows® applications as well as central databases. Win4Lin Terminal servers along with Tarantella Web-enabling technology allow Ventaglio employees to access these applications securely through a Web browser over the Internet.

Implementing Win4Lin Terminal Server

Shyam Sundaresen, Chief Information Officer of Ventaglio, deploys all the Windows applications centrally in the Ventaglio data center in Milan, Italy. These Windows applications run on Linux servers running Win4Lin Terminal Server. These terminal servers are then attached to the Tarantella Enterprise 3 product that serves these Windows sessions and non-Windows applications securely anywhere, to any client regardless of location. Users connect via thin client network-connected devices or Java-enabled browsers running on most platforms (Windows, Mac, Linux/Unix). Both data applications and Windows productivity applications such as Microsoft Office are delivered from one central computer system. Upgrades and maintenance are administered from a central support office.

IT Cost Savings with Win4Lin Terminal Server Products

Not only does Ventaglio save on hardware by centralizing all IT services, they are also able to utilize their existing Windows 95/98 licenses in this configuration without adding NT servers and Windows 2000/XP licenses. The power and flexibility of distributing Windows applications using Linux servers is a key advantage. Equally, this configuration results in much lower resource requirements, with better performance than on a comparable Windows 2000 platform.

Summary

By using a thin-client computing model on Linux architecture, Ventaglio has solved a complex computing problem that required Win4Lin technology.

CASE STUDY XI—LINUX APPLICATIONS FOR HOMELESS SERVICES AGENCY

DESC lacked many alternatives to their computing needs. They wanted to migrate to thin clients to standardize desktops, simplify system administration, and be able to manage a growing user base without adding more IT staff. Linux was already their core sever platform; due to the cost-effectiveness and reliability of their server solution they wanted Linux to be the base for their terminal server as well. At the same time, they had a continuing need to run Windows-only applications such as PageMaker, Publisher, Internet Explorer, and Microsoft Office, so it was imperative they had a 100 percent reliable Windows application environment.

Organization: Downtown Emergency Service Center (DESC) works to end homelessness for disabled and vulnerable people. DESC provides emergency shelter, clinical services, and permanent, supportive housing. DESC is one of the largest multiservice centers for homeless adults in the Pacific Northwest.

Challenge: Like all charitable organizations, money spent on operating expenses such as IT limits the amount of resources available to help those in need. DESC staff use computers for a variety of purposes, including email, word processing, and spreadsheets, as well as Web-based applications to operate and manage the agency. The IT challenge was to provide these computing resources with minimal drain on the organization's budget, so that staff would have the tools necessary to help clients get into housing and end their homelessness.

Solution: DESC already used Linux as their primary server platform, so a Linux desktop solution aligned well with their focus on streamlining. DESC wanted a desktop solution that was easy to standardize and control but could also provide Windows applications familiar to their staff such as Adobe PageMaker, Microsoft Publisher, and Microsoft Office applications.

Most DESC desktops ran Windows 98, usually on older hardware. Upgrading all their desktops would have involved significant expense. These older machines, however, could still perform well as thin clients. DESC wanted to use LTSP as their application-server platform. However, without a viable approach to their legacy applications, this solution could not be implemented. They investigated several Windows-on-Linux solutions with varied results. VMware wasn't well suited to the task, because they didn't need an entire virtual machine and the memory requirements were impractical. DESC also considered both the free and commercial versions of WINE (CrossOver Office by CodeWeavers), but the application compatibility was limited.

 "Win4Lin was the ideal solution because it gave us virtual Windows machines that were almost identical to the physical Window machines we were already running."

System Architecture

DESC provides housing, shelter and/or clinical services to approximately 5,000 disabled and vulnerable homeless adults each year. DESC has approximately 165 full-time employees (including 3 full-time IS staff), and an annual operating budget of $8.5 million. DESC operates 346 units of housing (with more in development), and operates shelter programs with a capacity of 278 people per night. DESC offers a continuum of clinical services ranging from street outreach and engagement to long-term case management. They are licensed as both a mental health and a chemical dependency provider. (More information is available at *www.desc.org.*)

At The Morrison (DESC's central location), there are approximately 70 workstations (the agency has 120 desktops across four locations). The infrastructure in this location is comprised of several Linux servers for file and print sharing, authentication, internal Web applications, a Postgres database server, and an application/terminal server running LTSP. They also have a Windows 2003 server (accessed by Windows Terminal Server clients) that runs their accounting software. Approximately 40 of their workstations either run LTSP or are dual-booted with Windows 98. The legacy Windows 98 machines are being phased out and migrated to LTSP.

Summary

Win4Lin Terminal Server has played a key enabling role in DESC's efforts to streamline computer administration through LTSP. Running Win4Lin has allowed DESC to proceed with migration to Linux and LTSP while providing a familiar Windows environment, and a safety net for running Windows applications whenever they are needed.

CASE STUDY XII—SUN RAY THIN CLIENTS FOR NETHERLANDS' SCHOOLS

Siceroo's goal was to install a stable, flexible and low-cost ICT (Information, Communications, Technology) infrastructure in schools throughout the Netherlands and to help the schools implement and use it.

Company: Siceroo, a systems integrator in the Netherlands, implements state-of-the-art and cost-effective ICT (Information and Communication Technology) solutions for thousands of primary and secondary schools in the Netherlands. The nation-wide challenge for Siceroo was to offer a world-class product within the constraints of an educational budget.

Challenge: The requirement for Siceroo was to provide Windows-based educational software through a modern, well-managed process, and on a low-cost client for primary and secondary schools in the Netherlands

Solution: Win4Lin Terminal Server delivers legacy Windows educational software from Linux servers to Sun's Sun Ray thin-client workstations. This architecture also supports serving multimedia applications over the network to the clients.

Benefits: The environment benefits from the robust, scalable Win4Lin Terminal Server backend, and the state-of-the-art Sun Ray design. Siceroo had the added advantage of having relied on the proven Linux/Unix platform for remote, administration, and unsurpassed reliability. The users (students and teachers) also enjoy a very powerful yet seamless feature-set combining the applications they are already accustomed to, with advanced features such as using smartcard media to save and transfer desktop state.

The Challenge: Siceroo's Thin Client Solution

Siceroo answered this challenge with Zodiac. Zodiac is Siceroo's thin client solution using open standards and best-of-breed technologies. The key for technical implementation is leveraging open source and network computing technologies with ultrathin clients.

This technology is perfectly suited for remote management, avoiding the need for technical knowledge at locations where the workstations are installed. For primary schools this is a great advantage, as system management problems are often an important reason for not integrating ICT into the daily lessons. Siceroo not only presents an integrated package of consulting, implementation, and support services; these parts can also be made available separately. Due to optimal integration of existing high-quality products and their large-scale use in different areas, it is possible to offer the complete package within rigid financial constraints. The technical implementation is very flexible for customizing the functionality and the user interface.

Siceroo's goal was to cost-effectively deliver traditional Windows-based educational software within the Zodiac infrastructure using Sun Ray thin client technology. Students and teachers throughout the Netherlands needed a robust, reliable method of running existing Windows-based educational software. Siceroo's Zodiac has integrated a winning combination with these products.

Ivar Janmaat, CEO of Siceroo, oversees the deployment of these systems in Dutch schools. A typical school's configuration consists of a single Linux server, together with a Sun Ray setup supporting 15–50 concurrent users. Smartcards are used to maintain Win4lin desktop state on the Sun Rays allowing students and teachers to instantly enable sessions on different clients by simply transferring the smartcards. Win4Lin Terminal Server also uses advanced network-based audio to take full advantage of the Sun Rays' multimedia capabilities.

Summary

As with IT organizations, educational institutions throughout the world can significantly reduce costs by choosing Win4Lin Terminal Server as their application platform. Siceroo delivers an exceptional value to Dutch schools, not only with a powerful, reliable, and seamless combination of technology, but also at a far lesser cost, both initial and ongoing, than that of a comparable Windows 2000/Citrix–based solution.

REFERENCES

Case Studies I through IX were provided courtesy of Maria Winslow, author of *The Practical Manager's Guide to Open Source*, ISBN 1-4116-1146-2, *http://www.lulu.com/PracticalGuide*.

Case Studies X through XII where provided by Win4Lin Inc.

Knoppix Quick Start Guide

The following quick-start manual is designed to help the new Knoppix user how to boot their PC using the Knoppix Live CD-ROM. This manual is provided as a compliment to the Knoppix Live Linux CD-ROM and is not intended to replace any documentation that might come with the distribution or associated applications.

Overview: The purpose of this document is to provide the background and understanding needed to use the Knoppix Live CD-ROM and to provide a manual on how to use the core features and applications associated with the Knoppix Bootable CD-ROM.

How To: The quick-start manual will provide tools for you to better understand how to configure and use the Knoppix as a temporary Linux distribution.

License: This work (as defined in section "License") is provided under the terms of the Creative Commons Public License ("CCPL" or License). The work is protected by copyright and/or other applicable law. Any use of the work other than as authorized under the license or copyright law is prohibited. By exercising any rights to the work provided here, you accept and agree to be bound by the terms of the license.

KNOPPIX OVERVIEW

Knoppix is a bootable CD-ROM with the freedom to copy it and give it away to anyone. It contains a collection of GNU/Linux software, automatic hardware detection, and support for many graphics cards, sound cards, SCSI and USB devices and other peripherals. Knoppix can be used as a Linux demo, educational CD-ROM, rescue system, or adapted and used as a platform for commercial software product demos. It is not necessary to install anything.

Minimum System Requirements

The minimum system requirements for Knoppix are very modest and summarized as follows:

- Intel-compatible CPU (i486 or later)
- 16 MB of RAM for text mode, at least 96 MB for graphics mode with KDE (at least 128 MB of RAM is recommended to use the various office products)
- Bootable CD-ROM drive, or a boot floppy and standard CD-ROM (IDE/ATAPI or SCSI)
- Standard SVGA-compatible graphics card
- Serial or PS/2 standard mouse or IMPS/2-compatible USB-mouse.
- The minimum system requirements would allow it to run on a wide variety of PCs even those that are no longer being actively used or without a working hard drive.

Quick Knoppix Facts

Here are some quick facts about the Knoppix Linux distribution.

- The Knoppix home page is *http://www.knoppix.org*.
- Extensive documentation can be found at *http://www.knoppix.net*
- Knoppix is named after Knoppix's inventor, Klaus Knopper.
- Knoppix uses the GNU General Public License if not otherwise specified, the software on the CD-ROM is Free Software falls under the Similar to other Open Source licenses, this means that you can copy, modify, redistribute and even resell the CD-ROM without restrictions, as long as the recipient receives the same license. The source codes of the standard packages on the CD-ROM are available from their respective original providers. Special components such as the Knoppix kernel or the automatic hardware detection source code can be downloaded from The Main Knoppix Site if not already available in the /usr/src directory on the CD-ROM. Individual packages, as specified by the GPL, may fall under another license (for example Netscape). If in doubt, the licenses can be found in the help sections or the DEB-database (dpkg -p package-name) of each software package.
- If you have Microsoft Windows already you can still boot and run Knoppix even if you have windows installed. Knoppix will not interfere with your Windows install, when you are finished with Knoppix you can just remove the CD-ROM and you're back to your original Windows OS.

This is experimental software use at your own risk. The author, developers, or publishers can not be held liable under any circumstance for damage to hardware or software, lost data, or other direct or indirect damage resulting from the use of this software. IF you do not agree to these conditions you are not permitted to use this software.

HOW TO START KNOPPIX

You can run the Knoppix CD-ROM without interfering with your existing operating system on your PC, or you can run it side by side with your existing operating system from an image copied to a storage device like your hard drive or even an attached USB key drive. You can also use Knoppix to install Linux right onto your PC. To start the CD-ROM, set up the BIOS of your computer to boot off the CD-ROM, put the CD-ROM in the drive, and power up the computer. If your computer doesn't support this option, you have to use a boot disk. You can create this disk from the image in Knoppix/boot.img on the CD-ROM.

Booting from a CD-ROM drive

You must boot Knoppix from the CD-ROM drive rather than a hard drive. Knoppix is then expanded on the fly from the CD-ROM and loaded into memory but your installed operating system is left intact.

Setting the Boot order in the BIOS

Look in your computer's BIOS (on many computers you need to push the "delete" or F1 key during the POST) to see whether it is set to boot from CD-ROM. If this is already set, your computer may not be able to read the CD-ROM (some notebooks have problems with black-coated CD-ROMs, for example). Some computers will use the new BIOS settings only after a hard reset.

You may after receive a message after using you have run Knoppix and boot into your other OS that says "File kernel.exe not found or defective" and "reinstall" shortly after boot. Do not be immediately alarmed simply take the Knoppix CD-ROM out of the drive and restart the computer.

Cheatcodes

Cheatcodes are used to pass options to Knoppix to help with getting it working on difficult hardware. You type them into the boot screen and press enter/return. The format is "kernel option option option ...." Usually knoppix is the right selection for the "kernel." You can type more than one cheatcode before pressing enter. Also note that some options can take on values.

RUNNING FROM A HARD DRIVE OR OTHER STORAGE DEVICE

The Knoppix Poor Man's Install

You may have read about how to dual boot Windows and Linux using a boot loader (e.g., GRUB, LILO, loadlin, etc.), and may have even seen people describe these options as "easy." Easy is a relative term, and many of these solutions have merit, but this particular solution is one, which will give you full functionality with the Knoppix live CD-ROM that you already have. There are no strange applications to Google for or download, you do not have to edit any scripts, and you do not have to use the console. Everything described here can be done from the graphical desktop or the boot prompt, just as with Windows. There may be fancier and more elegant ways to accomplish this, but the point here is to be basic. Having said that, don't get the impression that this isn't powerful. It is. You will be able to perform virtually any task that someone with a hard drive installation can perform, but without a lot of the hassle. Moreover, this type of installation is virtually unbreakable, because the whole system is contained in just one read-only file. So, there is no way to ruin the system configuration. Many experienced Linux users use and develop powerful applications with this very setup, not because they don't know how to do it any other way, but because this method provides fewer problems.

If you can load and run the live CD-ROM, and if you have some storage option available to you that is not formatted in NTFS (preferably a hard drive partition, but could be a USB flash drive or some other recognized storage device), you're ready to go. This how-to is for Knoppix 3.4 or later.

Be sure to read and understand the introductory information on the WIKI page Poor Man's Install *http://www.knoppix.net/wiki/Poor_Mans_Install.*

1. Partition as necessary just as you would for a full hard drive install or dual boot. That way, if or when you decide to make the switch to a hard drive install, you're halfway there already. Reserve at least a gig for the image partition but make it more in the range of five to ten gigabytes if you eventually want to make it a root partition for a hard drive install, and if you have

room. As long as you are partitioning anyway, reserve 0.5 GB or more for Linux swap, and create one or more partitions for data and programs, including the persistent home, however big you need or want (we'll call that hdb5 in the example). You may also want a FAT32 partition for sharing data between Linux and Windows. I recommend Qtparted for easy graphical partitioning, which is already on the Knoppix disk. With the more recent versions, you CAN safely repartition an existing NTFS partition. If you want your persistent home (PH) as a partition, the script will format it to ext2 and wipe out everything currently on that partition in the process, so plan for that in advance. You can also save the PH as a file in an existing partition if you prefer. Boot the Knoppix CD-ROM, using the default configuration, or whatever cheatcodes you're accustomed to using. For example, you might use knoppix26 to load the 2.6 kernel. Find the storage device you want to use (not NTFS), and make it writable.

2. Create a persistent home (PH). A persistent home is a location for saving files and programs. Think of it as a combination of "My Documents" and "Program Files" in Windows (in fact, you could create subdirectories with those functions, or even those names, if you want, but let's worry about that later). If you don't want to partition, just save your PH as a file wherever you like. Click the penguin icon on the toolbar, and click Configure. From there, you can see the links to set up a persistent home, and to save your configuration. Do the PH now picking a non-NTFS location if you save it as a file, or picking a partition to be reformatted using ext3 (e.g., I used my whole hdb5 partition, but I could have saved it as a file in that partition if I had existing data, or if I didn't want it reformatted), log off and restart. From now on, you will add a cheatcode to get Knoppix to recognize that home (in my case, home=/dev/hdb5 or home=scan).

3. Boot the CD-ROM with whatever cheatcodes you used before, but include the following cheatcode as well (I'll use hdb1 as the example for where I want the OS folder located): tohd=/dev/hdb1/. So, if you created your persistent home at the hdb5 partition, your boot might look like this: knoppix26 home=/dev/hdb5 tohd=/dev/hdb1, or if you saved your PH as a file and didn't partition, it might be: knoppix26 home=scan tohd=/dev/hdb1. The boot process will copy the image there and continue booting off the CD-ROM. Log off and restart.

4. This time, you want to restart and substitute the cheatcode fromhd=/dev/hdb1 for the tohd location you specified in step 3. For example, knoppix26 home=scan fromhd=/dev/hdb1. The boot process should now be a lot faster, and you can remove the CD-ROM until the next time you boot. If you haven't already saved your configuration, you can do so now. Save it wherever you like (not NTFS)—if you want to use the same location as

your persistent home, go ahead. Following the example above, your cheatcode string might now be: knoppix26 home=/dev/hdb5 myconfig=/dev/hdb5 fromhd=/dev/hdb1, or knoppix26 home=scan myconfig=scan fromhd= /dev/hdb1. Add any other cheatcodes you want or need, as long as each is separated by a space. If you aren't familiar with saving a configuration, basically it allows you to change the default Knoppix configurations that come on the CD-ROM, so you can define your printer file, or change the background on your desktop, or add icons, and Knoppix will remember these customizations with each reboot, provided that you add the myconfig cheatcode when you boot.

5. Now that you're all set up, you can easily find your saved documents in your home directory. You don't have to remember the details—just click the house icon in Konqueror.

6. The easiest way to install programs is by using Klik. Open Konqueror (not Mozilla or any other browser), and type in the following URL: http:// klik.berlios.de/ then follow the instructions to install Klik. You will see a number of programs available to you for automatic installation. If you don't see the one you want listed, you can try the following command (still experimental) klik://softwarename into the address block of Konqueror.

INSTALLING KNOPPIX PERMANENTLY ON YOUR PC

You can install Knoppix to a hard drive, if you wish, though installation is not required for productive use. Knoppix is designed and intended to be used as a GNU/Linux (*http://www.gnu.org/gnu/linux-and-gnu.html*) Live Linux CD-ROM and not a HD installed Linux distro. A HD installed Knoppix will give you a running GNU/Linux system but it is not easy to support or administrate and add/remove of software is complicated and is best left to GNU/Linux experts. Examples of such issues can be found in the Hdd Install / Debian / Apt forum (*http://www.knoppix.net/ forum/viewforum.php?f=5*). If you a new user and not a GNU/Linux expert & want a HD installed system then skip the LiveCDs and go directly to a distro designed to be installed to a

Once Knoppix is installed on a hard drive, it's no longer a Knoppix Live Linux CD-ROM but a Debian based GNU/Linux system. Something to note is that Debian developers/users/mentors do not consider Knoppix installed to a hard drive to truly be Debian. They will not support Knoppix users and will tell them to go to Knoppix.net for support. You can ask about alternatives to a HD install and get advice on other distributions in The Lounge forum—*http://www.knoppix.net/forum/viewforum.php?f=7*. The knoppix-installer was written and maintained by Fabian Franz but now appears to be collaborative effort between Fabian, Klaus Knopper, and Kano of Kanotix. See Knoppix Installer (*http://www.knoppix.net/wiki/Knoppix_Installer*) for more detailed information.

Beginning a Knoppix HD install

Boot off the Knoppix disc. At the KDE desktop, in the konsole command-line window enter the command:

```
sudo knoppix-installer
```

In the knoppix-installer, the arrow keys move focus and space bar selects options. Be sure the root partition is among the first 4 partitions on the drive, formatted with ext2 or ext3, and is set to "active." The swap partition must be formatted with "linux-swap." Installation and subsequent booting will not continue otherwise.

Types of installation

There are three types of installs for Knoppix users that want to install Knoppix directly to the hard drive.

The *Debian install* is an installation that is similar to running Debian from the hard drive. The features of a Debian install are:

- Allows multiple users on the install.
- Bears the closest resemblance to a "normal" Debian installation.

The *Knoppix install* copies the Knoppix Live Linux CD-ROM to hard disk, which provides the following:

- A copy of the Live Linux CD-ROM on the hard disk
- Works exactly as the CD-ROM-based system does except apt-get can be used to add more software and the system is no longer read-only.
- Does not allow multiple users and login is automatic.
- Carries kernel command line to new system (i.e. cheat codes) except for vga, initrd and BOOT_IMAGE.

The *Beginner install* is not likely to be your regular Knoppix installation it is more likely to

- Uses Knoppix Hardware detection
- Carries kernel command line to new system (i.e., Cheat codes) except for vga, initrd and BOOT_IMAGE work as expected.

The general consensus seems to be that most problems and confusion arrive with people using the Knoppix or beginner type of installation. The Debian type install is now the default choice and is preferred over the beginner. More experienced users will probably want stay with the Debian type install. Users not familiar with setting up hardware or maintaining a GNU/Linux system may not want to do a Debian style install, and instead choose the beginner or Knoppix types. If you choose beginner or Knoppix, be aware that you are still using the auto-configuration so you can change your cheatcodes, the flip-side is that changes you may think you are making permanently will be overwritten when you reboot. It is the balance of convenience of hardware setup (especially if you change hardware) versus having a more regular installed Linux (Debian) system.

Installing Gnome

To install Gnome (*http://en.wikipedia.org/wiki/Gnome*), you have to comment all the lines in /etc/apt/sources.list except the unstable ones. Then issue the root command:

```
apt-get update
apt-get install gnome
```

In order to have gnome-session working you must execute the following command and choose metacity and/or gdm:

```
update-alternatives --config x-window-manager
```

OTHER RESOURCES

- Knoppix – *www.knopper.net*
- Free Software – *http://en.wikipedia.org/wiki/Free_software*
- GNU Public License

```
License Copyright (c) 2005 Mark R. Hinkle (mrhinkle@gmail.com).
Permission is granted to copy, distribute and/or modify this document
under the terms of the GNU Free Documentation License, Version 1.2
or any later version published by the Free Software Foundation;
with no Invariant Sections, no Front-Cover Texts, and no Back-Cover
Texts. A copy of the license is included in the section entitled "GNU
Free Documentation License".
```

Index